THE
RANDOM HOUSE TIMETABLES OF HISTORY

**Random House
New York**

Manufactured in the United States of America

1 2 3 4 5 6 7 8 9

Second Edition

New York   Toronto   London
Sydney   Auckland

CONTENTS

THE
RANDOM
HOUSE
TIMETABLES
OF HISTORY

The First Civilizations 4000–2000 BC

Susa ware: Sumerian pottery, *c.* 4000 BC

Bronze bust of Sargon I

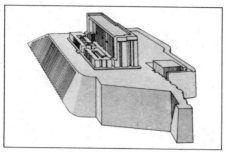

White temple in the Sumerian city of Uruk, *c.* 4000 BC

Sumerian cuneiform
writing on a clay tablet

The Pyramids of Giza
embody the advance of
Egyptian architecture.

Early duck decoy found
in Nevada

The mysterious Stonehenge structure refers to astral
bodies.

The First Civilizations

★ Principal Events

Assisted by the invention of writing and the wheel, the world's first urban civilizations grew up and flourished in Mesopotamia, and later in Egypt, in the fourth millennium BC. Mesopotamian city-states emerged from ancient agricultural and religious settlements, encouraged by the immigration of the Sumerian people into the area, and grew rich from agriculture and long-distance trade. With growth, however, came conflicts between cities, although none achieved permanent supremacy. In Egypt early unification and centralization led to the Pyramid Age with its celebration of the pharaoh's authority. In both areas hereditary monarchies were set up c.3000 BC, with a bureaucracy that placed emphasis on public works, especially canal building. Toward 2000 BC, Sumeria was threatened by barbarian invasions, while Egypt declined from internal stresses, as Minoan civilization emerged.

The Americas

The American continents had been uninhabited until c.40,000 BC, when prehistoric man migrated from Asia across the Bering Strait. Radiocarbon dating of artifacts places man there definitely by 20,000 BC. This early man was a hunter of large animals, using spears with fluted projectile points.

♦ Religion

The development of religious ideas in early history was closely related to the rise of settled agriculture and the emergence of the first states and empires.

The change from a hunting economy to one based on arable agriculture was reflected first of all in the rise of fertility cults in which the central figure was a mother or earth goddess.

With the growth of urban civilizations in the fertile valleys of the Nile and the Euphrates, a priest-dominated society grew up with a system of gods, each related to a particular city or region. As the authority of the state and the priesthood became more centralized this was reflected in the changing importance of particular gods, and in Egypt in the rise of the doctrine of divine kingship and the construction of increasingly elaborate temples and royal tombs culminating in the Age of the Pyramids.

Literature

Writing developed in Mesopotamia as the Sumerians tried to simplify and regularize earlier picture writing and ideograms; a system for depicting sounds rather than ideas was probably invented by temple clerks in response to the need to record tribute payments and wages in the Mesopotamian city temples. With the development of the regular cuneiform style of script, writing became a skill for every aspiring man to acquire.

4

Literature had its origins in oral chronicles such as the Gilgamesh epic in Sumeria and in written prayers in Egypt, where a hieroglyphic script developed after 3400 BC and poetry emerged during the Pyramid Age. By 2000 BC, China was developing independently an elaborate system of word signs.

Art and Architecture

In Egypt and Mesopotamia, the development of pottery and small domestic articles, cosmetic implements, and jewelry occurred in the Neolithic period, but with the growth of states and technological advances sophisticated metal crafts and stone sculpture developed. In the absence of stone, builders in Mesopotamia used as their basic medium the baked mud brick, which they later decorated with ceramics and copper reliefs, while the finest sculpture and much beautiful jewelry was produced in metal. In Egypt, stone was used for a series of monuments, culminating in the pyramids, as well as for a highly sophisticated tradition of sculpture with its own rules of proportion that persisted for over 1,000 years.

Throughout this period in China and after c.3000 BC in the Aegean, the manufacture of fine decorated ceramic ware anticipated the artistic achievements of subsequent centuries.

Music

Music probably originated in man's desire to express himself more richly and formally than he could in speech alone; ritual chants rapidly developed into musical forms with special meanings. Widely separated cultures produced similar kinds of instruments, adapting natural objects: bone flutes and whistles found in Hungary and Russia date from c.25,000 BC.

Science and Technology

The elaborate civilizations of Mesopotamia and Egypt depended for their birth and development on a settled agriculture practiced by Neolithic peoples in these regions since c.8000. Without it they could not have sustained either the increased population or the specialization of urban life. Once secure, these societies spawned a remarkable series of technological advances. The 4th millennium BC saw the invention of the plow, the wheel, the sailing boat, and methods of writing. Stone tools gave way to those of copper and bronze, that came into use c.2500 BC.

Scientific method as we know it—the systematic testing of theories about the material world—did not develop until much later, but the technical knowledge of these early societies was very sophisticated. The pyramids remain one of the finest engineering feats of all time and in west Asia, as later in China and Mesoamerica, the mathematics used by priests provided the basis for the development of other sciences.

4000-3800 BC

Principal Events

Farming settlements found in the lower Mesopotamian plain since 5000 BC probably included the sites of the future royal cities of Endu, Uruk, Nippur, and Girsu by 4000 BC.

The need for irrigation led to a more concentrated population and complex social systems.

The site of Babylon was settled by Sumerians c.4000.

The Nile cultures were based on farming villages c.4000.

The Americas

Remains of corn at Bat Cave in central New Mexico indicate that primitive agriculture was developing as a supplement to hunting and gathering.

Religion and Philosophy

Fertility cults arose with settled farming. Sacramental concepts and techniques centered on fertility of the soil, its products, and seasons. These cults in the Near East were associated with the cycle of death and rebirth and took as the chief divinity a sexual mother goddess or a non-sexual creator—the earth goddess, known as Ninna in Mesopotamia.

Literature

The Sumerian language was in use by 5000 BC, and a pictographic script developed by 4000 BC. Although this communicated ideas by the use of pictures, it gradually began to take on a more formal appearance with agreed symbols standing for ideas. This simplified the task of the Sumerian picture writer.

Art and Architecture

The appearance of painted pottery coincided with the late Neolithic/early Chalcolithic period, a transition period between the late Stone Age and the early uses of copper. Richly decorated pottery dating from c.4000 BC has been found in Anatolia at Hacilar and in Assyria at Arpachiyah.

Music

The harp, in prehistory, probably developed from the archer's bow, played over a covered pit to add resonance. In Mesopotamia musicians played flutes, as well as drums and rattles.

Science and Technology

Neolithic or New Stone Age settlements prospered in Egypt, Mesopotamia between the Tigris and Euphrates rivers, and in other parts of the East, between 8000 and 3500 BC. Stone tools included polished stone axes and a type of flint sickle mounted in an animal's lower jawbone. The flints were mined. Buildings were reed and wattle huts or made of hand-molded clay bricks dried in the sun.

Principal Events

Jewish tradition dates the creation from 3761 BC.

 The Americas

In Chilca, on the Peruvian Pacific coast, approximately 100 families lived in a cluster of conical grass and cane huts, fishing and cultivating beans and gourds.

 Religion and Philosophy

Burial cults had existed since early prehistory. A specific site was often marked by a mound, and sacrifice and ritual eating of the dead were frequently involved. The placing of artifacts in the graves indicated a desire to ensure the continuity of life.

Cave paintings at **Lascaux** and **Trois Frères, France,** indicate that as far back as 20,000 BC Cro-Magnon men had witch doctors. They are pictured along with the animals hunted.

 Literature

The first use of writing is attributed to the Sumerian city of Uruk. Simplification of the characters in earlier pictographic script led them to the idea of using conventional symbols to represent the sound of a word rather than the idea it conveyed. Motifs on painted pottery indicate that a script incorporating phonetic elements was in use in Uruk by 3700 BC.

 Art and Architecture

In Egypt black-topped polished bowls **(Badarian ware)** and terra cotta figurines were produced. Ivory combs and cosmetic articles also date from this period.

 Science and Technology

Clay seals were used *c.*4000 in the Middle East, to place the owner's name on pots.

Land transport vehicles in Sumeria included sledges.

The wheel was invented in Mesopotamia during the period of the establishment of city states. It took two forms: a stone potters' wheel, and a cartwheel, made from a single, solid piece of wood.

3600-3400 BC

★ Principal Events

Uruk (modern Warka), the greatest Sumerian city, already possessed many features of the city-state by 3500 BC. At least twelve autonomous cities, including Ur, Lagash, Umma, and Kish, developed over the next millennium.

The pastoral Sumerians moved into the Mesopotamian plains and encouraged the growth of this civilization, *c.*3500, building a network of canals for irrigation.

The Americas

In Canada's southwest Yukon, the beaver tooth gouge came into use. It became an important tool for woodworking in the subarctic area.

Religion and Philosophy

Before the third millennium BC peoples of Mesopotamia worshiped nature gods in human form, each god being associated with a city temple and the temples themselves occupying a central place in city life. The gods were organized as a democratic council, which reflected the political relations among the various city-states.

Literature

Temple clerks recording wages, tribute, and stores had developed after 3500 BC some 2,000 signs, which were engraved on clay tablets. The linking of these signs with sounds made it easier to write names and abstract ideas as well as lists of objects. As Sumerian words were largely of one syllable, the system is called a *syllabary*.

Art and Architecture

The Sumerians in Susa, capital of Elam (SW Iran), became associated with a variety of remarkably fine pottery vessels, on which sharp geometric devices were brilliantly interwoven with stylized figures of birds, animals, and men.

Egyptian Amratian culture, *c.*3600 BC, showed technical advances on the Badarian period. Decorated ivory and bone combs were found, and figures of animals such as hippopotamuses appear on pottery.

Music

Drum and reed pipe music bloomed in Mesopotamia. Called bull and reed music, it symbolized strength and weakness with the use of drums for a vigorous beat and pipes for the melody.

Science and Technology

Copper, fashioned into beads as early as 6000 BC in northern Europe, was smelted from ores or melted as the native metal over wood fires since 4000 BC in Sumeria.

Kilns were introduced *c.*3400 in Sumeria. Many pots were fired at once, and raised above the fire, thus protecting the painted designs from wood ash. Shadow clocks originated in Sumeria *c.*3500 BC.

Principal Events

The Nile Valley provinces (nomes) had been merged into two separate kingdoms—Upper and Lower Egypt—by 3300 BC.
City-states began to develop in Syria and Palestine c.3300.
The Proto-literate period, when writing was first used in Sumer c.3500–3000 BC, coincides with the semi-legendary rule of the First Dynasty of Kish.
Mesopotamian influence is thought to have stimulated Egyptian cultural development c.3400 BC.

The Americas

In Valdivia, Ecuador, pottery has been found dating from c.3200 BC. It is the earliest known in the Western Hemisphere.

Religion and Philosophy

The religion of Egypt before the foundation of the dynasties was based on totemism, the idea that there is a relation between kinship groups and specific animals and plants. Each independent principality had its own totem. **Horus** the falcon was that of Bedhet in the north, while the god **Seth,** represented by a he-goat, protected Naqadah in the south. Above these local gods was the sun god, Re, the source of all life.

Literature

An Egyptian hieroglyphic script developed after 3400 BC, possibly influenced by trading contacts with Sumeria. A hieroglyph could represent either a sound, an idea, or an identifying mark attached to another sign. The syllabic signs did not indicate differences in vowel sounds, as did the Sumerian script.

Art and Architecture

Undecorated stone vases from Egypt's Gerzean period superseded vessels of the Amratian culture. Spherical and cylindrical jars were light and skillfully hewn out of solid blocks of hard stone by means of flint borers. Votive objects, tomb paintings, and palettes depict battles, ships, animals, and vase bearers.

Music

Religious music was performed by musicians chanting and playing on reed pipes, flutes, drums, and tambourines as part of the liturgy of temple worship in the Sumerian city-states.

Science and Technology

Metal-molding was practiced in Sumeria by 3200 to make copper and bronze axes with molded sockets for holding the shafts. Previous models had weaker sockets of folded metal.
The Egyptian Copper Age began in the Upper and Lower Kingdoms c.3200 and lasted until 2000 BC, after which iron and bronze artifacts were made.

3200-3000 BC

★ Principal Events

The Delta Kingdom of Lower Egypt was conquered c.3100 by Menes (Narmer), who came from the south and unified Egypt into a single monarchy. He is attributed with the founding of the First Dynasty, which he ruled from his new capital at Memphis.

The Phoenicians, a Semitic-speaking people, began to settle the coast of Syria c.3000 BC.

Copper was widely used throughout the Near East c.3000 BC.

The Americas

Pictograph cave in Montana was first used as shelter, c.3000. On its walls are drawings of men and animals in black, white, and red.

Religion and Philosophy

The religion of Mesopotamia reached its classical form with the rise of more centralized political units in the early dynastic period. There were four main gods: **Anu,** god of heaven; **Enlil,** god of the winds; **Ninhursag,** goddess of birth; and **Enki (Ea),** god of water. Hierarchical relationships between the gods reflected the growing separation between the strata of Mesopotamian society. Divination of dreams and interpretation of entrails were practiced.

📖 Literature

A cuneiform script was in use in Sumeria by 3200 BC. It consisted of vertical, horizontal, and oblique strokes made with a sharpened wooden stylus on a wet, hand-sized clay tablet. The name comes from the Latin *cuneus* (wedge) and refers to the wedge-shaped strokes of the stylus.

Art and Architecture

Mesopotamian cylinder seals dating from the **Proto-literate period** were used in the business of temple administration and bear the miniature prototypes of the relief friezes that were to become important in Sumerian art. They reached a high degree of craftsmanship by the Akkadian period.

The Palette of Narmer, c.3100 BC, a carved slate tablet from Hierakonpolis in Egypt, shows the king wearing the crowns of both kingdoms.

Music

Egyptian pottery depicts instruments like those used in Mesopotamia, including harps, drums, sistra (metal rattles on a U-shaped frame), and reed pipes of various lengths.

Science and Technology

Boats, as depicted on Egyptian pottery, had squared sails and many oars. Reed boats navigated the Nile c.3000 BC.

Plows take the form of a forked branch in Mesopotamia and Egypt, the forks being held by the plowman and the sharpened end, or share, being drawn through the soil by oxen. Such plows were shown c.3000 BC in Egyptian picture writing, although used earlier.

Horse-drawn chariots were recorded in Mesopotamia c.3000 BC.

10

Principal Events

Cretan Neolithic culture gave way to bronze-based culture *c.*3000 BC. **Sumerian cities** came to be ruled by hereditary kings from 2900 onward. The Archaic Tablets of Ur came from this Early Dynastic or Classical Sumerian age. **Public works in Egypt**, especially canal construction, led to the growth of the Egyptian bureaucracy in the Early Dynastic period, when a national government first developed.

The Americas

People living at Indian Knoll on Kentucky's Green River depended on a shellfish diet. They buried their dead under mounds of discarded shells.

Religion and Philosophy

The priests at Memphis in Lower Egypt established the Memphite theology after the unification of Upper and Lower Egypt. Their god **Ptah** was believed to have created the world and was known as the patron of craftsmen. The creation myth associated with him is more abstract than those of the pre-dynastic period, and testifies to the sophistication of the Memphite priesthood.

Literature

As cuneiform spread, writing began to serve a wide range of social needs, although there is no indication that it was used for anything but practical purposes.

The Babylonians and Assyrians kept lists and inventories for business and legal purposes. There is an Egyptian record of farming procedures.

Art and Architecture

Complex tombs for Egyptian notables were constructed. These *mastaba* consisted of underground funerary chambers with stone or brick structures above. **In Mesopotamia**, a typical temple of the Ubaid period, 2900–2800 BC, had a facade decorated with niches dedicated to the cult of the god Enki. Sculpture of the period consisted of terra cotta statuettes of both men and women.

Music

Vertical (end-blown) flutes, sistra, and tambourines were played in processional music, suggesting the possible use of music in courtly ritual in Mesopotamia and Egypt *c.*3000 BC.

Science and Technology

Populations in Mesopotamia and Egypt had increased by 2800 BC owing to improved agricultural methods. Despite its primitive appearance and action the fork-branch plow brought greatly increased crop yields. **Cotton** was grown in India *c.*3000 BC.

2800-2600 BC

 Principal Events

Gilgamesh, the legendary king of Uruk, *r.c.*2750 BC.
Records of Sumerian kings began with Mebaragesi of Kish *c.*2700.
The Old Kingdom Of Egypt, a 500-year period of stability and cultural splendor, began *c.*2700 with the reign of Zoser. Egypt also expanded toward Nubia, *c.*2600.
Akkadians came to dominate the northern Mesopotamian plain in the Early Dynastic II period.

 **The Americas**

Copper implements and ornaments were fashioned by the "Old Copper" Culture of Wisconsin from ore found in the area around Lake Superior.

 Religion and Philosophy

In the Egyptian early dynastic period the king became associated with **Horus,** the falcon deity of Hierakonpolis in Bedhet. **Classical Egyptian religion** described an optimistic vision of an ordered cosmos, itself an expression of the predictability of life in Egypt governed by the regular flooding of the Nile River.
The first pyramid tombs were built in Egypt *c.*2700 BC.

 Literature

Literature had yet to emerge, but writing was becoming an important tool of social advancement and literary form was evolving in the oral tradition of the Sumer-ian-Babylonian epic of *Gilgamesh,* mankind's first great poem.

 Art and Architecture

The outstanding advance of Egyptian Old Kingdom architecture was the building, under the direction of royal architect Imhotep, of Zoser's step pyramid at Sakkara *c.*2700. Later the Great Pyramid at Giza and the Great Sphinx of Khafre would be built *c.*2500 BC.
Egyptian royal sculpture concentrated on idealized figures with an emphasis on set proportions.

 Music

A harp from ancient Egypt has been unearthed, dating *c.*2500 BC. It has a lower sound chest to improve its resonance. About the same time, doubled reed flutes were played, probably in unison.

Science and Technology

Mesopotamian metallurgy advanced significantly by 2600, for example in the development of soldering techniques, used to make the ornaments found in the royal tombs at Ur.
The first calendar of 365 days was invented by the Egyptians. The first pyramid, of King Zoser, was built *c.*2700. Its construction involved a practical knowledge of geometry that was not formulated in theory for many centuries.

Principal Events

Conflict between Sumerian cities such as Ur, Kish, and Lagash reached a climax *c*.2500.
A prosperous culture emerged at Yangshao in China *c*.2500.
Royal power reached its zenith in the Egyptian Old Kingdom *c*.2500 under the pharaohs Khufu and Khafre.
A sea-going Minoan Civilization developed in Crete *c*.2500.

 **The Americas**

The first pottery known to be made in North America was found at Stallings Island, Ga. It was made *c*.2400.

 Religion and Philosophy

The concept of divine kingship was well established by 2500, as was the existence of a specialized priesthood. Both contributed to the force of royal authority. The king became identified with the god Horus, who by this time was associated with the whole land of Egypt.

 Literature

Another script was evolving on the Indian continent, not yet settled by Aryans—the Indus (or proto-Indian) script, found on seals dating back to *c*.2500 BC in which each sign seems to have had a single phonetic value.
In Sumeria, the Akkadians produced a simplified version of only 550 symbols, seen in the legal code of Urukapina *c*.2400.

 Art and Architecture

Early Minoan art was characterized by marble statuettes of goddesses (Cycladic idols). *c*.2500 BC and vases made from Cretan and imported stone.
Mesopotamian decorative arts—in particular the use of gold and copper, lapis lazuli, and other fine inlays—achieved a high degree of craftsmanship. In China the painted ceramics of the late Neolithic Yangshao culture, *c*.2500, have geometric patterns painted in black and red pigments.

 Music

Two kinds of harp, dating from *c*.2400 BC, were uncovered during the excavation of the royal tombs at Ur, in Mesopotamia. One had a lower sound chest and the other an upper sound chest.

Science and Technology

Bronze alloys were widely made in Mesopotamia by 2500 BC; they were a mixture of copper and tin ores and were fashioned into ornaments, tools, and weapons. Copper ores were plentiful and widespread in Syria; some Sumerian bronzes are very hard as they accidentally contained silicon.
The Great Pyramid of Khufu was finished *c*.2500. It is 481ft (146.6m) high and covers 5 hectares.
Egyptian wooden boats were shown on tomb walls from 2500.

2400-2200 BC

★ Principal Events

Sargon the Great built Akkad in northern Mesopotamia, conquered Sumer, and created an empire stretching from the Persian Gulf to the Mediterranean c.2350. His soldiers settled at Ashur, the future Assyria.
Urukapina, King of Lagash, introduced reforms but was ousted by Lugalzaggisi of Umma. The Indus Valley civilization around the cities of Harappa and Mohenjo-daro emerged c.2300.
The Gutians destroyed the Akkadian Empire c.2230.

The Americas

On the shores of Lake Lahonton in northwestern Nevada decoys made of reeds and feathers were used to attract ducks.

Religion and Philosophy

With the decline of the Old Kingdom, the idea of survival after death was extended to include people other than royalty for the first time. This may have been a reflection of the growing power of the nobility.

Literature

The first literature dates from c. 2300 BC in the prayers of Egyptian pyramid texts. Also preserved in papyri is the "Pessimistic Literature," which includes the *Prophecy of Neferty* and *Admonitions of an Egyptian Sage*, the *Tale of an Eloquent Peasant*, and *A Dialogue of a Desperate Man with his Soul.*

Art and Architecture

Narrative reliefs and stelae proclaimed the achievements of Mesopotamian culture in the Akkadian period, while **King Sargon's bronze bust** is one of the greatest examples of ancient portrait sculpture.
The earliest Indus Valley cities of Harappa and Mohenjo-daro were constructed of fire-baked bricks and utilized such features as corbeled arches. Among the few known vestiges of Indian art are seals with animal motifs and figurines.

Music

Antiphonal forms, in which two choirs or a priest and choir chant responses, appeared in the ritual music of Sumerian temples under the Akkadian ruler Naram-Sin c.2200 BC.

Science and Technology

Weaving with looms had been practiced well before 3000 BC in west Asia and Egypt. By 2300, horizontal looms, with the warp thread pegged on the ground, were usual in the Near East.
Weight standards and accurate scales were used in Egypt from 2200 BC. For example, the dried fish eaten by miners in Egypt was measured by their masters using stone weights.
Sewage and drainage systems were built in Harappan cities.

14

Principal Events

Gudea of Lagash restored disrupted Sumerian commercial prosperity in southern Mesopotamia.

Ur-Nammu of Ur drove out the Gutians and established a brief Sumerian renaissance. After Egypt had expanded into Nubia and west Asia on a large scale, its Old Kingdom ended in anarchy with the collapse of the central government, 2181.

King Mentuhotep of Thebes reunited Egypt c.2060.

 The Americas

In Middle America the earliest pottery was made near Guerrero, Mexico c.2000 BC.

 Religion and Philosophy

Stonehenge, built c.2000, to serve as some sort of religious facility, testifies to the astronomical knowledge of Wessex.

 Literature

A Chinese script emerged, although it was not standardized and no examples survive. A "concept script" in which each idea had a corresponding sign, it replaced a system of knotted cords and was used to record commands and perhaps chronicles and poetry.

In Babylon, the first known library, composed of clay tablets, existed by 2000 BC.

 Art and Architecture

A group of diorite statues of Gudea, the famous ruler of Lagash, c.2130, represents the finest works of Sumerian artistic revival.

The temple of Ur—a ziggurat dedicated to the moon goddess Nanna—was built by the Sumerian King Ur-Nammu.

Minoan pottery c.2200–2000 BC is represented by ceramics with a creamy white glaze over a dark ground.

 Science and Technology

Ziggurats became most refined c.2000 BC. These Mesopotamian buildings served both as storehouses for grain and as platforms for astrological and astronomical observations.

The Bronze Age reached the Neolithic settlements and nomadic cultures of western Europe c.3000–2000 BC.

Hittites and Assyrians 2000–1200BC

The Minoan palace of Knossos was a center of worship.

Egyptian ship building technology improved *c.* 1300 BC

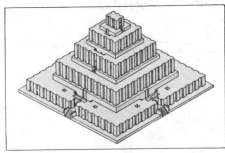

Ziggurat at Elam, used for both grain storage and astronomical observation, 13th c. BC

Shang dynasty bronze-casted ritual vessel

Funerary mask of Egyptian king Tutankhamen

Mycenaean capital, 14th c. BC

Hittites & Assyrians

Principal Events
An influx of Aryan tribes, at the beginning of the second millennium BC, disrupted the civilizations of Sumeria, the Indus, and to a lesser extent Egypt, while adapting well to the existing cultures, especially in Babylon. After 1600 the Egyptians, the Hittites in Anatolia, and the Assyrians all developed large-scale military organizations to sustain their growing imperial ambitions. In the Eastern Mediterranean new civilizations began to emerge in this period.

The Cretan Minoans created a sea-based empire and a flourishing, peaceful civilization based on Knossos, and Mycenae began to establish itself as a power in southern Greece, where olive and wine farming formed the basis of future economic development.

After the fall of the Minoan civilization Mycenae took over much of its maritime power and culture, but with further invasions from the north *c.*1200 BC it too declined.

The Americas
The previous period was characterized by the domestication of wild plants in North and South America. In the years 2000-1200 BC this tradition spread, and agricultural villages grew up. Pottery was made in South, Middle, and North America by 2000 and weaving of cloth was developing.

Religion and Philosophy
The incursions of Aryans and other invading peoples into the main centers of civilization in the Near East disrupted the established religious traditions, dispersed some of their elements, and introduced new ones. The gods of the newcomers reflected their warlike nature, and the worship of their gods evolved into ecstatic sacrificial cults. Their impact upon Egypt, however, was transitory, and the traditional religious system continued and developed, interrupted by a brief but interesting monotheistic interlude under Pharaoh Akhenaton in the early 1300s BC. Once the more turbulent areas of Mesopotamia had settled to orderly lives of commerce and agriculture in city centered communities, the first codes of law and concepts of citizenship were devised. In this period the basis of the Judaic tradition, with its emphasis on ethical monotheism, was laid among the Israelite tribes.

Literature
Cuneiform became more sophisticated after 2000 BC, but a more important development was the emergence of the first consonantal (BCD) script, far simpler to master than earlier syllabic systems of writing, none of which has remained in use. The Syrian Ugaritic script, however, which developed in the mid-2nd millennium BC, also possessed three vowel signs, although the five-vowel alphabet would not be elaborated until

after 1000 BC by the Greeks who would draw on a variety of Semitic scripts.

Literature of the period ranged from narrative and love poetry in Egypt to historical narrative among the Hittites, the religious Vedas in India, and the ethical and divinatory Ching philosophy in China.

Art and Architecture

The brilliant civilization that emerged in Crete reached its peak of cultural achievement between 1900 and 1500 BC with palaces of a highly functional design and decorative arts whose grace and vitality reflected a long period of peaceful development. Minoan fresco painting, sculpture, and painted pottery were characterized by a humane outlook and love of nature and movement. The influence of Minoan art extended to Mycenae.

Temple architecture revived in Egypt with the Middle Kingdom and enjoyed its golden age in the 14th and 13th centuries. The New Kingdom ruler, Akhenaton, who made sun worship the sole cult during his reign, built some of the finest of these and introduced a revolutionary naturalism into royal portrait sculpture.

Chinese bronze workmanship was the most advanced in the world, and calligraphic art was beginning to develop.

Music

The development of a metalworking technology in ancient civilization enabled craftsmen to make metal instruments based on older instruments made from organic materials and stone.

Bells of bronze replaced stone chimes, and bronze, copper, or silver trumpets replaced hollowed horns. A metal tube with a more cylindrical bore than animal horn gave a brilliant tone.

Science and Technology

Trade and warfare were the main stimuli of technological advance in the 2nd millennium BC. Larger sailing ships were used to bring tin from the Mediterranean countries to Mesopotamia and to carry away bronze objects made using the tin; radical improvements took place in chariot design, but the greatest technological event was the mastery of iron by Hittite smiths. Although they lacked heat enough to melt the metal, the Hittites made iron implements by hammering them out of the heated ore. The resultant metal, albeit flawed by slag, could be tougher and harder than bronze. Weapons, sword blades in particular, benefited while metalwork for decorative purposes in iron, bronze, gold, or silver became highly refined, as the objects found in the tomb of Tutankhamen show. Bronze vessels of superlative craftsmanship were made in China too under the Shang dynasty.

2000-1920 BC

★ Principal Events

The brief Sumerian renaissance centered on Ur continued until c.1950 BC when Semitic Amorites overran much of Sumeria This was the beginning of a long period of instability in Mesopotamia.

In Egypt the Middle Kingdom reached its height with the 12th Dynasty, 1991–1785, after Amenemhet I had subdued the nobility and restored prosperity. Building, art, and international commerce flourished.

The Americas

At the site of Boston, fishermen made an elaborate fish weir consisting of 65,000 stakes interwoven with branches to trap their prey in tidal waters.

♦ Religion and Philosophy

Amenemhet I, the founder of the Egyptian 12th Dynasty, claimed descent from **Amun,** a local god of his native Thebes. From this time Amun, a father of the gods, and the Heliopolitan god Re were identified as **Amun-Re,** emphasizing the change in the royal family and confirming the divine right of the king to rule all of Egypt.

📖 Literature

The Egyptian Coffin Texts 2040–1786, found on coffins and papyri, include spells, ritual texts, and mythological stories. Their purpose was to give the dead person power in the after-life, and after 1570 they would evolve into a more unified text, the Egyptian **Book of the Dead.**

Art and Architecture

In Egypt, the establishment of the Middle Kingdom in 1991 BC was marked by an economic and artistic revival. The Great Temple of Karnak, built during the 12th Dynasty, c.1991–1785 showed a high level of craftsmanship in tomb reliefs, gold ornamentation, and paintings. Middle Kingdom sculpture adheres rigidly to rules dictating proportion and posture devised in the Old Kingdom despite a new element of naturalism in royal portraiture.

Music

The yellow bell, or huang chung, was the name given to an absolute (fixed) pitch produced by a bamboo pipe of set length. It is attributed to a mythical Chinese emperor of c.2000 BC.

⚛ Science and Technology

The shaduf, a device for raising water from one level to another with a bucket, appears on Mesopotamian seals c.2000. This is an Egyptian invention still used in the Nile region.

Early Chinese technology is suggested by the finding of jade plaques, which could only have been worked effectively with metal tools.

Iron weapons and ornaments, dating from 2000 BC, have been found in the Near and Middle East.

20

★ Principal Events

Senusret III, 1887–1849 BC, further consolidated royal authority in Egypt by suppressing provincial rulers (nomarchs) and assisted the rise of a bureaucratic and trading middle class.

Unrest in Sumeria centered on conflict between the cities of Isin and Larsa, during which the area broke down once more into independent city-states.

The Semitic language of the Amorites gradually superseded Sumerian in Mesopotamia, between 2000 and 1700 BC.

The Americas

The Red Paint peoples, who lived on the banks of Maine's Penobscot River, spread red ocher over their dead and their grave offerings.

Religion and Philosophy

The Canaanite religion emerged in Palestine with **El** as supreme god, and **Baal,** god of rain, vegetation, and fertility sharing the central position. The Canaanite religion was an important influence, both negatively and positively, on Israelite culture. It is possible that **Yahweh,** the sole god of Israel, was an Israelite name for the Canaanite El.

Art and Architecture

The Bell-Beaker culture in central and western Europe made good-quality red ceramic beakers decorated with horizontal bands of geometric patterns. **In China,** wheel-turned **Lung-shan** black pottery (named after a site in Shantung) replaced the Yangshao type at the end of the Neolithic period. With thin walls and a metallic, burnished finish, it marked a great technical advance and was commonly used for ritual purposes and funerary ware.

Science and Technology

Early iron technology involved repeated hammering of the ore until most of the slag was beaten out. Wood or charcoal fires are not hot enough to melt iron. This can only be accomplished in some kind of blast furnace, which was not developed until the Middle Ages.

★ Principal Events

Hammurabi the Great of Babylon, *c.*1792–1750 BC, an Amorite, subdued the other cities of Mesopotamia and built an empire from the north Euphrates to the Persian Gulf, ruling with a code of laws based on principles absorbed from Sumerian culture.
The Middle Kingdom of Egypt ended *c.*1786 BC, weakened by an influx of the "Hyksos," a Semitic people from Syria.
The Indus civilization, already in decline, was destroyed by invading Aryans *c.*1760 BC.

The Americas

Cotton textiles decorated with designs of bird, animal, and human figures in contrasting colors, were woven in the Huaca Prieta area of northern Peru.

Religion and Philosophy

The migrations of Aryans and other peoples from the Black Sea area helped to disperse religious ideas and practices. The Hurrians who invaded Upper Mesopotamia at this time transmitted elements of Sumerian beliefs northward to Hittite areas.

Literature

The Babylonian ritual poem, the Epic of Creation, first written about 2000 BC, had reached a classic form as part of the ceremonies associated with the new year. It told how the god Marduk slew the sea monster Tiamat, and created men as servants of the gods. Babylonian literature of the period is infused with a sense of metaphysical pessimism.

Art and Architecture

The Minoan palaces at Knossos, Phaestos, and other Cretan sites were rebuilt on a grander scale in the Middle Minoan period, 1900–1600, with more varied architectural features such as light shafts and efficient sanitation. By about 1760 BC, Minoan potters were producing fine Kamares ware pottery in graceful and varied shapes with a profusion of floral and geometric motifs. Craftsmen specialized in small works such as faïence figurines.

Science and Technology

Cosmetics in Egypt, already used in the 4th millennium, included perfumery oils extracted from fruits by pressing them through a cylindrical cloth bag, held upright with sticks. Filter pressing methods of this kind are still used in the food and chemical industries.

★ Principal Events

The Hyksos became firmly established in the Delta region of Egypt and adopted Egyptian culture. By 1700 BC a dynasty of Hyksos pharaohs was established.

The Babylonian Empire slowly crumbled under Hammurabi's son c.1700 while culture and religion flourished.

A natural disaster on Crete caused the Minoan palaces to be rebuilt c.1700 BC.

The Hittites, an Aryan people, grew powerful in Anatolia.

The Americas

At La Florida, on the central coast of Peru, a temple of field stones and mud mortar was built around this time. The buildings included a large pyramid.

♦ Religion and Philosophy

The complex law code devised by Hammurabi the Great of Babylon c.1792– c.1750, was created in response to the needs of increasing trade, usury, and commerce. It sought to end blood feud and personal retribution and replace these with a secular state code based on the idea of citizenship. For example, one of the articles of the code stated that if a man's home fell down and someone was injured, then the owner was to be held responsible.

Literature

The ancient Greek script, Linear B, was deciphered only in 1953 by Michael Ventris (1922– 56). It flourished at Mycenae in the 12th century BC but dates back earlier than this and may derive from Linear A, an undeciphered script used by the Minoan civilization of Crete. Linear A dates from 1700 BC and is a syllabic script.

Art and Architecture

A major revival of Mesopotamian art marked the rule of **Hammurabi,** c.1792– c.1750. Old palaces and buildings were strengthened and new ziggurats constructed. To the north, the city of Mari, partly built under the ruler **Zimrilim,** c.1779– c.1761 BC, is remarkable for its size. Its 200 rooms cover 10 acres (4 hectares), and the fine painted decorations include narrative pictures such as the investiture of Zimrilim.

Science and Technology

Bronze-casting in Mesopotamia followed the *cire perdue* method, a one-off process necessarily reserved for valuable items. Objects were modeled or sculptured in wax, covered with clay, and the wax melted out to make a mold for the molten metal. Hollow objects were made by molding the wax around a clay center

1680-1600 BC

Principal Events

The Minoans established a sea-based empire in the eastern Mediterranean under their semi-legendary King Minos *c.*1650 BC, creating the Minoan golden age centered on Knossos.

The Babylonian Empire was increasingly threatened by the influx of Aryan Kassites from the north *c.*1600 BC.

The Shang dynasty, which introduced writing to China, developed an urban civilization *c.*1600 BC.

The Americas

Bitterroot peoples, who had inhabited the Alpha Rockshelter near the Salmon River in Idaho since *c.*6000 BC, lived by hunting, fishing, and gathering.

Religion and Philosophy

The royal palace at Knossos was a center for the worship of nature gods with human and animal characteristics. These deities included a fertility goddess associated with snake worship and possibly a bull-god. The surviving palace is decorated with a bull's horn motif and is thought to have provided the model for the Labyrinth in the Greek myth of the Minotaur.

Literature

The first known Phoenician inscriptions, found at the city of Byblos, date from *c.*1600 BC. From Byblos, a main trading center for papyrus, the Greeks took their word for books, *biblia.* The Phoenicians developed the simplest of all the consonantal scripts, reducing the number of symbols used to represent sounds to 22.

Art and Architecture

Minoan culture was approaching its golden age. Wheel-thrown pottery decorated with figures, a wide range of gold jewelry, and fine quality seals were made, together with miniature sculptures in bronze, terra cotta figurines, and ivory carvings. Carved vases of stone and marble appeared *c.*1600 BC with relief decoration, some in the shape of bulls' heads, reflecting the Minoan passion for bull sports and the religious significance of this animal.

Science and Technology

Ships underwent improvement in the second millennium BC. A major impetus for sea trade came from the Mesopotamians, who had probably become cut off from their major sources of tin in Syria and so imported the metal to make bronze. Many vessels sailing the eastern Mediterranean were built from planks and could be made up to 40ft (12m) long. Minoan ship design was particularly influential.

Sea battles took place toward the end of this millennium.

★ Principal Events

The Hittites plundered Babylon in c.1550 under King Mursilis I. In their wake the Kassites ruled there for 400 years.

The Hyksos were driven from Egypt in c.1570 BC by the Theban kings Kamose and Amosis, who established the New Kingdom, sparking a growth of nationalist feeling.

Mycenaean civilization was growing on mainland Greece and has left rich "shaft graves."

Minoan civilization reached its height c.1550 BC.

The Americas

In Illinois, Wisconsin, Ohio, Indiana, Michigan, and Ontario, the Glacial Kame peoples used the gravel ridges formed by melting glaciers for burial sites.

♀ Religion and Philosophy

The religion of the Hittites, who overthrew Babylon in the mid-1500s, derived from many sources. Several of their gods were attributed characteristics that varied locally, and they indiscriminately absorbed the gods of other tribes. However, the mother goddess and the weather god were always retained, the dominance of the latter reflecting the importance of rain to fertility.

Literature

Egyptian love songs had evolved into a sophisticated literary form by 1200 BC. Although the surviving songs date from the New Kingdom (c.1570– 1085), many are clearly from older sources. They are vigorous, direct, and lyrical in their appeal to the senses. "When the wind comes it desires the sycamore tree; When you come near to me, you will desire me."

Art and Architecture

Egyptian art experienced its classical flowering under the New Kingdom, c.1570– 1085. A standard temple plan, often on a monumental scale, was established, with floral motifs as characteristic decoration on the columns. A spirit of freedom produced lighter and more elegant sculpture, coupled with precise rendering of detail, but formal rules were preserved. Fine quality work in precious materials reflected the influence of new trade links.

Music

A lutelike instrument with fretted fingerboard appears in a wall painting in an ancient Egyptian tomb dating from about 1520 BC. Earlier types are found in Mesopotamian pottery c.2000.

Science and Technology

Plows were improved c.1600 in Mesopotamia, by the invention of a share and sole that dug deeper furrows.

Glass bottles appeared in Egypt c.1500 BC. Glazed beads and glass imitations of precious stones have been found dating from a thousand years earlier, but this is the first evidence of work with molten glass.

Fine metalwork in iron, copper bronze, gold, and silver, with filigree and inlay work, reached a new peak in Egypt.

1520-1440 BC

★ Principal Events

Mitanni, a kingdom of Aryan Hurrians in northern Mesopotamia, **the Hittites**, and **Assyria** all grew as military powers c.1500 BC.

Thutmose I of Egypt established an empire in the Near East between 1520 and 1510 and began the construction of the valley of the tombs of the kings at Thebes.

Minoan civilization was destroyed c.1450, probably by an earthquake at Thera.

The Americas

Ocós, on the coast of Guatemala, developed into one of the first permanent village sites in Mesoamerica.

Literature

Cuneiform had become entirely syllabic with fewer and more simplified characters, each having a phonetic value. This development culminated in the **Syrian Ugaritic script**, one of the first scripts with vowel signs. The earliest examples of writing in this Semitic language date from 1400 BC and describe Canaanite mythology.

Art and Architecture

Minoan culture was extending its influence to Greece, particularly in Mycenae. The Minoans' love of depicting nature in their art is exemplified in the lively frescoes of the palaces, in works such as the unique painted limestone coffin, c.1450, from Hagia Triada, Crete, and in the richly decorated pottery that flourished c.1500–1450, depicting marine creatures of many varieties.

Music

The oldest known Chinese instruments are suspended stone chimes and globular bone flutes, dating from about 1500 BC. They were played in the early part of the Shang dynasty.

Science and Technology

Chinese bronze urns and vases appeared suddenly c.1500 BC under the Shang dynasty with no previous evidence of a metal technology (except for jade carving). Shang bronzes were molded in sections to extremely complex designs.

Cementation steel was made by the Chalybes, a subject people of the Hittites. This, the earliest form of steel, is made by repeatedly hammering red-hot iron together with charcoal until carbon enters the iron.

Principal Events

After the volcanic eruption at Thera, *c.*1450, Cretan civilization revived and continued to spread to mainland Greece. **Mitanni** conquered Assyria *c.*1440 BC to become a military power equal to Egypt. **Amenhotep III,** 1417–1379 BC, extended the Egyptian Empire and brought peace and prosperity at home, which was threatened by the attempted religious reforms of his successor, Akhenaton, and by internecine murders.

The Americas

At a cemetery near Port au Choix, Newfoundland, treasured and useful articles, as well as carved images of animals and birds, were buried with the dead.

Religion and Philosophy

Egyptian religion went through a short-lived phase in which only one god was worshiped in the reign of Akhenaton, *r.c.*1379–1362. He suppressed the older gods including Amun-Re and instituted **Aton,** represented by the solar disk, as the only god. During his reign the only other god acknowledged was King Akhenaton himself, who was thought to be eternally revitalized by Aton's rays. After Akhenaton's death, however, Egypt reverted to its traditional gods.

Literature

Hittite literature flourished between 1600 and 1200 BC. It was written in cuneiform or, for private communication, in an older pictographic script. There are royal decrees, treaties, a law code, religious instructions, and some Sumerian and Babylonian tales. The literary style is distinguished by laconic vigor and lack of verbosity.

Art and Architecture

A more naturalistic style of Egyptian royal portraiture was encouraged by **Akhenaton,** *r.c.* 1379–1362, who constructed a new palace and temple to the sun god at Tell el Amarna. A head of his consort **Nefertiti** is one of the most beautiful works of this short-lived Amarna style. The temple of Amun and Colossi of Memnon were built under **Amenhotep III,** 1417–1379. Examples from **Ras Shamra** (Ugarit) show a high standard of Phoenician decorative art.

Music

Bamboo culture in Southeast Asia produced an unusual music, mixing the sounds of blown pipes, such as flutes, and struck pipes in the form of bamboo xylophones.

Science and Technology

An Egyptian water clock, *c.*1400 BC, had bucket-shaped vessels from which water drained by way of small holes in the bases. Hours were marked inside the vessels. Mathematics may have developed from linear measurement used in the division of land in Egypt and Mesopotamia. Measurements were often made in units based on parts of the body, such as the Egyptian cubit, from the elbow to the fingertip.

1360-1280 BC

★ Principal Events

Under Ashur-uballit I, Assyria again became a military power.
Tutankhamen ruled as pharaoh in Egypt, c.1348–1340 BC.
Hittites destroyed the empires of Mitanni c.1360 BC, conquered north Syria and Aleppo, and built a major empire in the Near East.
Mycenaean civilization reached its height c.1320 BC.
Rameses I reestablished the Egyptian Empire in the Near East c.1319 BC. Rameses II fought the Hittites at the battle of Kadesh in 1299 BC.

The Americas

The inhabitants of the **Pinto Basin** of southeastern California used pulverized, hard shell seeds, particularly acorns, to form a large part of their diet.

◊ Religion and Philosophy

The **Aryan invaders of India** brought with them a religion which came to be embodied in the **Vedas,** a set of sacred hymns codified by the end of the 2nd millennium BC. The Vedic pantheon of nature gods included **Indra,** the storm god, **Agni,** the fire god, and **Soma,** the intoxicating ritual juice; these and many other gods were involved in a complex mythology and an elaborate system of ritual.

Literature

The origin of the **Greek alphabet** is attributed in mythology to the Phoenician Cadmus (son of Agenor, king of Tyre), who is said to have brought 16 letters to Boeotia c.1313 BC. Evidence from Mycenae indicates that this legend may have some basis in fact. The Phoenician consonant signs certainly provided a model for the Greeks, who later added vowel signs.

Art and Architecture

The **tomb of Tutankhamen** with its rich furnishings included a sarcophagus with a gold and lapis lazuli funerary mask.
Under China's Shang dynasty at An-yang, mastery of bronze casting produced distinctive vessels, drums, and bells, some with calligraphic ornamentation.
Tholoi (beehive tombs), including the Treasury of Atreus, with great vaulted ceilings, were built at Mycenae, in the 14th century.

Music

Copper and silver trumpets found in the tomb of Tutankhamen date from about 1320 BC. The brilliance of their tone contrasted with other instruments in use at the time.

⚛ Science and Technology

Currency, in Egypt, took the form of copper ingots in the shape of a stretched oxhide. These oxhide ingots were often transported by ship, as we know from Egyptian wrecks.
Egyptian chariots were improved by increasing the number of wheel spokes from four to six and the movement of the axle rearward, so that the rider's weight was more evenly distributed. This prevented seesawing movements over rough ground, giving a smoother ride.

Principal Events

A truce was agreed between Egypt and the Hittites *c.*1270 as both came under pressure from migrations of "sea peoples."
The Trojan War reflected stresses in Mycenaean culture from Dorian invasions, *c.*1200.
Shalmaneser I of Assyria, *r.*1274–1245, took Babylon from the Kassites and defeated the Hittites and the Hurrians.
Moses led the Jews from Egypt *c.*1250 BC.

The Americas

The Olmec people, who had settled in Mexico by 1500 BC, were developing an agricultural culture that definitely indicated a civilization of high order.

Religion and Philosophy

The Israelites left Egypt *c.*1250 BC under the leadership of Moses, who instituted worship of a single god, **Yahweh,** to whom the tribes were bound by a covenant promising them possession of Canaan (Palestine). The Israelites quickly conquered much of Canaan, and their monotheistic religion became common to the "twelve tribes" of Israel.

Literature

The Vedas, verse hymns dealing with sacrificial and magical formulae, were written in Sanskrit between 1500 and 1200 BC in India. The foremost is the *Rigveda.* The hymns include incantations and spells for good health and long life. Indian liter-

ature of this period was primarily religious in inspiration.

Art and Architecture

Rameses II, *c.*1304–1237, completed the colonnaded hypostyle hall at Abydos, with fine funerary reliefs. His rock temple at Abu Simbel was one of the most grandiose achievements of Egypt's New Kingdom. Hewn from a pink sandstone cliff with an entrance 105ft (32m) high, it extended 200ft (61m) into the mountain and was flanked by four massive statues of the king. He also added to the Temple of Luxor and erected a colossus of himself in the forecourt.

Music

Vedic chant, a sung form of ancient Hindu scriptures, was established by 1200 BC and is the world's oldest continuous musical tradition. It was based on a three-note scale system.

Science and Technology

Cavalry soon challenged the charioteer in war. Saddles and reins were developed in south Turkey, but stirrups were not used for 1,000 years and did not reach Europe until *c.*700 AD.
Hittite ironsmiths scattered with the destruction of the Hittite Empire, *c.*1200 BC, with far-reaching consequences. The smiths had kept their techniques secret for hundreds of years; but knowledge of them now began to spread, reaching eastern Europe by 1000.

Iron Swords and the Alphabet 1200–700 BC

Phoenician ivory from Nimrud

Bronze axe, *c.*1000 BC

Olmec art in the form of a huge stone head

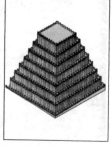

The Ziggurat at Khorsabad

The Black Obelisk depicts the military exploits of
Shalmaneser III.

Chariot from a Greek
Amphora

Assyrian war chariots adorn the gates of
Shalmaneser III

Iron Swords and the Alphabet

★ ### Principal events
Barbarian invasions continued to strike the Near East, obliterating the power of the Hittites and Mycenaeans and limiting Egyptian and Assyrian military ambition. In the same period, however, the smaller trading societies, particularly the Jews and Phoenicians, flourished. The Phoenicians built colonies throughout the Mediterranean, and the Jews established their distinctive identity and claim to the region west of the river Jordan. After 900 the military power of Egypt and Assyria recovered, financed by tribute from their subject peoples, but the focus for cultural development moved to Greece, where the adaptation of the Phoenician alphabet marked the end of the Dorian-imposed dark ages.

In India, the Aryans overran the Ganges area and established a caste system based on the Vedic religion. In China the Shang dynasty fell to their former subjects, the Chou, but this had little cultural effect.

The Americas
Permanent settlements, principally agricultural villages, were being established. The first highly developed civilization - the Olmec - developed in Central America. The Chavin and Paracas cultures of South America produced distinctive art styles. In North America burial mound building began.

Religion and philosophy
Beginning with the period of the Judges, Israelite history shows a continual effort by certain individuals and nomadic groups to defend the purity of the religion of Yahweh against its dilution by the pagan affiliations of the central rulers. This unceasing resistance to the addition of other gods to their faith reinforced the distinctive features of the Judaic tradition.

In China the emergence of a secular philosophy foreshadowed the development of later religious systems, with their characteristic lack of emphasis on the supernatural.

The invasion of Greece by a succession of northern tribes led to a joining of new Olympian gods with older deities. This varied religious atmosphere, contrasting sharply with the rigid, priest-dominated society of Egypt, would play an important part in the emergence of the brilliant culture of 5th-century Greece.

Literature
The Greek alphabet, in which letters were used to represent vowels for the first time, had developed from Phoenician forms by the 8th century BC. It provided the most flexible and economical method of writing yet devised. At about the same time the ballads of the Trojan wars, which had emerged in oral form in the 10th century, were compiled and written down by Homer in the *Iliad* and the *Odyssey*. It is not

entirely clear whether Homer was a single man or the name for a group of poets. But the later Greeks, who drew strongly on Homeric traditions, regarded him as an individual, the father of Greek poetry. Similarly, in Mesopotamia, the Gilgamesh epic neared its final form, and a Chinese poetic tradition grew up.

Art and architecture

The trading societies that emerged during this period helped to spread artistic styles and techniques in the eastern Mediterranean. In Greece foreign influences imported especially by the Phoenicians led to the adoption of complex figurative images in pottery, where previously only geometric patterns had been used. The influence of the Phoenicians was similarly felt in the Hebrew kingdom of King Solomon, who employed their craftsmen to build his Great Temple at Jerusalem.

Monumental architecture ceased to be built in Egypt, but in Assyria the political resurgence of the 9th and 8th centuries led to the restoration of Nimrud and the building of Sargon's palace at Khorsabad.

In Central America the isolated Olmec civilization produced colossal sculpture without the aid of metal tools.

Music

Noticing that there was a mathematical relationship between the length of a pipe or a string and the pitch it produced, musicians in the ancient civilizations linked this relationship with the underlying order of the universe and phenomena of the natural world. This aspect of musical theory would later be expressed in Pythagoras' concept of the harmony of the spheres.

Science and technology

The major technological advance of the 2nd millennium BC—a radical improvement in the quality of wrought iron—was a major factor in the expansion of the later Assyrian Empire. Assyrian ironsmiths were able to make a sharp edge using a process of tempering that involved repeated hammering and quenching in water. For the first time, effective iron swords and axes could be made; these weapons, together with siege towers and the use of cavalry, greatly contributed to the image of Assyrian indomitability. Sharpened iron was first used effectively in agriculture with the introduction of iron plowshares in Mesopotamia. Iron blades withstood wear far better than bronze-shared plows and could cut deeper furrows, which led in turn to greater crop yields.

In South America the Chavin produced beautiful objects in hammered gold, and Chinese bronze and ceramic technology was further refined.

1200-1150 BC

★ Principal Events

The Sea Peoples invaded the eastern Mediterranean from the Caspian Sea area and destroyed the Hittites c.1200 BC. Some settled on the Canaanite coast to become the Philistines.
Rameses III c.1198–1166, repelled their invasion of Egyptian soil c.1190 BC, after which Egypt withdrew into cultural and political isolation.
The Canaanites, a Semitic race, settled in Syria and developed a flourishing culture based on the production of purple cloth.

The Americas

An Olmec ceremonial center at San Lorenzo (in Veracruz), Mexico, located on a manmade plateau, featured colossal stone human heads.

Religion and Philosophy

Successive invasions of Greece culminating in that of the Dorians, c.1200, brought Aryan gods such as Zeus, Apollo, and Hermes, who largely replaced the more nature-oriented gods of the Minoan-influenced Mycenaeans. These gods, who in Greek mythology became associated with Mount Olympus, bore a far more arbitrary relation to human affairs than the original Mycenaean deities.

Literature

Ten thousand Hittite cuneiform tablets constituting the state archives at Bŏgazkŏy, the capital, survived the destruction of the empire c.1200 BC. These represent the main source of information on Hittite history and culture.

Art and Architecture

With the decline of the Egyptian New Kingdom major architectural programs ended, and the sarcophagus of **Ramesses III**, d.1166, is one of the last major works in the classical New Kingdom style.
The earliest form of Greek art was the Proto-Geometric style of pottery decoration painted with zigzags and wavy lines. This pottery probably originated in Athens, the leading city at the end of the Bronze Age.

Music

Secular music was established as an important part of the life of the Assyrian court c.1200. Minstrels were highly regarded and music held a recognized place in court entertainment.

Science and Technology

Phoenician sea trade, by 1200 BC, supplanted that of Minoan Crete and would later focus on the docks of Tyre and Sidon.
Early food technology included the preservation of fish by drying, smoking, and salting, thus allowing it to be stored. Such methods were used widely in the Bronze Age, but in particular by the Greeks and Phoenicians who were great eaters of fish.

1150-1100 BC

Principal Events

Nebuchadrezzar I, *r.*1124–1103, of Babylon restored stability in Mesopotamia, facilitating the recovery of Assyrian trade disturbed by the Hyksos.
The Egyptian monarchy fell under the growing influence of the priesthood of the sun god Re, the Amun, causing political and economic stagnation *c.*1100.
The Shang dynasty in China consisted of 30 kings in fraternal succession but declined through internal unrest *c.*1100 BC.

The Americas

Woodland hunters in eastern North America depended on the canoe in their search for game. River travel gave them access to new forest areas.

Religion and Philosophy

The Israelites began to assimilate Canaanite ideas during the period of the Judges, which ended *c.*1050 BC. The Yahweh of Moses and his nomadic followers absorbed features of the Canaanite deities as Israelite society became more settled and structured. Religious purists such as **Rechabites** and **Nazarites** opposed this degeneration of the monotheistic ideal.

Literature

The collection of myths and folklore that coalesced into the *Gilgamesh* epic in Mesopotamia was now approaching its final form. It combined religious elements with story themes that were to become widely popular throughout the Middle East, including references to a flood, the quest for immortality, and the friendship of two great warriors.

Art and Architecture

San Lorenzo, the earliest Olmec site, was established *c.*1150. The chief Olmec art forms were large stone monuments, including colossal heads, some weighing over 40 tons.

Music

Pentatonic scales became prevalent in the East. The five notes of these scales, still characteristic of Eastern music, were often related to north, south, east, west, and center.

Science and Technology

Vitreous enameling was an achievement of the later Mycenaeans. This process involves fusing glass materials onto a metallic base and first appeared in Cyprus in the form of glass decorated gold rings.

1100-1050 BC

Principal Events

Tiglath-Pileser I of Assyria conquered Mesopotamia and the eastern Mediterranean, defeating Babylon and exacting tribute from the Phoenician city-states. After his death c.1077, **the Aramaeans** took Babylon and destroyed Assyrian power, driving the Canaanites south.
The Philistines, a trading people, conquered **the Jews** who had settled in Palestine after leaving Egypt and were at this time a loose confederation of tribes ruled by the Judges.

The Americas

Inhabitation began at Poverty Point, an alluvial fan formed by the Arkansas River in northern Louisiana, 1050 BC.

Religion and Philosophy

Religion in Iran before Zoroaster (6th century BC) bore similarities to the early Vedic religion of India. Many of the Iranian pantheon of gods coincided with Vedic ones, including **Mithras**, the cult of fire, and **Haoma**, the sacred liquor.

Literature

Traces of the Gilgamesh epic can be found in the Trojan ballads, which culminated in the poetry of Homer, as well as in Hebrew and other classical literature. The adventures of Gilgamesh, king of Uruk, and his friendship with Enkidu, a wild man sent to destroy him, were the center of a pessimistic poetic cycle that combined realism with myth.

Art and Architecture

In China the artistic traditions of the Shang dynasty were perpetuated by the Chou, c.1122– 221. Jade and ritual bronze vessels became increasingly elaborate, palace architecture developed, and roof-tiling and bricks were introduced. Wall painting probably began during this period.

Music

The reed mouth organ or shêng developed in China. It has several bamboo pipes rising from a wind chest into which air is blown though a mouthpiece.

Science and Technology

Iron plowshares were developed in Mesopotamia c.1100 BC. Hard enough to take a sharp cutting edge, they advanced agricultural technology. The Phoenicians are thought to have developed the bireme c.1100.

★ Principal Events

Aramaean rule in Assyria produced little military or cultural activity.

In Greece, monarchical city-states including Athens, Thebes, and Sparta developed c.1000 based on wealth derived from trade and agriculture.

Saul became the first king of the Jews c.1020 BC, with powers limited by religious tradition.

Aryan rule was established in north India by 1000 BC.

The Chou dynasty was set up in China in 1027 BC.

The Americas

The peoples of the **Paracas peninsula** in Peru, beginning c.1000, wrapped their dead in richly embroidered textiles, which distinguished the culture.

Religion and Philosophy

Chinese philosophy emerged during the Chou dynasty, 1027–221 BC, as increasing control over nature and the growth of social stability led to a demystification of thought. Irrigation replaced prayers for rain, and heaven *(T'ien)* was seen as rewarding virtue, thus giving man the power to control his own destiny through being virtuous.

📖 Literature

The Greek alphabet is thought to have begun evolving after 1050 BC as the Greeks modified symbols they had borrowed from the Phoenicians to suit the sounds of their own language. The name alphabet comes from the first two symbols, *alpha* and *beta*. By using signs for vowels as well as for consonants the Greeks made a crucial advance, enabling any word to be written.

Art and Architecture

Egypt's Late Dynastic period was dominated by the high priests of Amun, and primarily religious artifacts were made. Metal was increasingly used to make figurines, and larger statuary was often made in the harder stones such as schist and basalt.

Science and Technology

The mass production of iron tools was a major feature of the Assyrian Empire. The Assyrians themselves were not great innovators, but they made use of iron technology practiced by Hittite and other subject artisans.

Early South American farming settlements appeared on the coast of Ecuador and Peru c.1000 BC. The simple technology of these Neolithic peoples included building in mud, brick, and stone.

1000-950 BC

Principal Events

David, king of the Jews, 1000–961 BC, defeated the Philistines. His successor, Solomon, 961–922, built the temple at Jerusalem and a trading fleet in the Indian Ocean.
Hiram I, king of Byblos, 969–936, consolidated the Sidonian states and assisted Phoenician trade by building a harbor at Tyre, his new capital.
Damascus and Geshu were founded by the Aramaeans.

The Americas

The Woodland tradition of eastern North America began c.1000. This tradition was characterized by burial mounds and elaborate earthworks.

Religion and Philosophy

The foremost Vedic writings were the *Rigveda*, a collection of hymns and sacred formulae of "mantras" that formed the liturgical basis for a priesthood. Cremation of the dead came to replace burial, and there was a differentiation of priestly functions into those relating to actual sacrificial procedures and those relating to the ritual chanting of the sacred hymns.

Literature

Hebrew literature flourished in the 10th century with the composition of the mystical *Song of Songs*, a poetic drama full of lyrical beauty celebrating nature and love. It is attributed in the Bible to Solomon, king of Israel, but its origins may be even older.

Art and Architecture

The Scandinavian Iron Age developed a high level of metal craftsmanship in grave goods. The most outstanding example is the Sun Chariot from Trundholm, Denmark, c.1000. It shows a horse and six-wheeled chariot, with a bronze-gilt solar disk.

Music

Bronze trumpets or lurs date from about 1000 BC. Found in Danish bogs, lurs were made with conical bores ending in flat disks. They are usually found in pairs.

Science and Technology

Assyrian military technology, 1000–700 BC, was stimulated by constant warfare. The Assyrian Ashurnazirpal II was the first to use cavalry units to any extent in addition to infantry and war chariots. The Assyrians also developed siege weapons for attacking the mud walls of enemy cities. Battering rams that rocked to and fro were not very successful, but iron-shod beams, which were raised and allowed to fall, were extremely effective.

Principal Events

Assurdan II, *r.*935–913, briefly restored Assyrian military authority *c.*935 BC. But by 912 Assyria was at its smallest size. **Egypt** re-emerged as a military power, reconquering Palestine in 918, after Shoshenk, *c.*935–914, had reunited Egypt by making his son high priest. **The Jewish kingdom** was divided on Solomon's death into the kingdom of the Israelites in the north and Judah in the south, following opposition to his rule in the north.

The Americas

The monumental stone sculptures at the ceremonial site at San Lorenzo were mutilated and buried by the Olmecs, marking the end of the civilization there.

Religion and Philosophy

Primitive Japanese religion, Shinto, was based on a love of nature. The powers of nature, **Kami**, were seen as beneficent rather than awesome, and pollution was "biological" rather than moral. Pollution from contact with death or menstruation had to be removed by ritual cleansing. They practiced the art of divination by burning bones.

Literature

The Trojan cycle of ballads, which Homer would immortalize in his *Iliad* and *Odyssey*, had probably begun to evolve in the 10th century although they may not have been written down. The cycle told of the 12th-century war between Greece and Troy, the wrath of Achilles, and the wanderings of another Greek hero, Odysseus.

Art and Architecture

The first Temple of Jerusalem was completed *c.*950. Built by Phoenician craftsmen under the direction of King Solomon, it was based on Canaanite and Phoenician models. The main building, decorated with massive carvings in ivory, wood, and gold, was flanked by three-story chambers.

The "Megaron B" temple at Thermon, one of the earliest major examples of Greek architecture, has the characteristic form of later Greek temples.

Music

Psalms were the central feature of the music of the first temple of the Jews. Responses between priests and congregation established the pattern of many later forms of Christian music.

Science and Technology

Chinese chariots had wheels with many more spokes than the chariots of the Middle East, but otherwise differed very little from them. The Chinese, however, who had acquired chariot design from nomads who lived to their west, still placed the axle centrally beneath the platform.

Principal Events

The Phoenician city of Byblos grew up c.900 BC on the Mediterranean coast and became the center of the cult of Baal.

Egypt and Assyria fought in Syria-Palestine 900–830 BC. At the battle of Qarqar, 854, the Aramaeans and Israelites, inspired by Elijah, defeated Shalmaneser III of Assyria.

In Greece there was a gradual shift from monarchies to oligarchies in most of the city-states with the exception of Sparta. The Chavin culture flourished in Peru c.900–c.200 BC.

The Americas

Chavin de Huantar, a town and temple site in northern Peru, emerged as the center of the Chavin culture, known for its unique pottery and sculpture.

Religion and Philosophy

Jezebel, wife of the king of Israel Ahab, r.874–853 BC, built a temple to the Canaanite god Baal. This aroused opposition among the zealous followers of Yahweh, led by Elijah, fl.c.875. Elijah's disciple Elisha inspired the slaying of Jezebel and the complete overthrow of the royal family.

Literature

The Moabite Stone, or Mesha Stele, was erected at Dibon c.850 BC by King Mesha, who composed the inscription on it to commemorate his successful revolt against Israel in the ancient land of the Moabites. It approximates Hebrew, but the script is the Phoenician one from which the Greeks derived the alphabet.

Art and Architecture

Nimrud in Mesopotamia was restored and enlarged by Ashurnazirpal II, 883–859, who built at least two temples and four palaces, decorated with winged human-headed lions in carved stone and reliefs showing the king himself. Ivories from the northwest palace show the widespread assimilation of Phoenician craftsmanship.

Music

Lyres and harps were used to accompany Jewish temple songs. Trumpets and cymbals were played to signal special moments or interludes in the liturgy.

Science and Technology

Iron mines in Italy were worked from c.900 BC, and would later be taken over by the Etruscans. Peruvian gold ornaments of the Chavin culture date from c.900. Goldsmiths used stone hammers to beat gold into stone molds, probably without attempting to melt it.

Principal Events

Shalmaneser III of Assyria, r.858–824, defeated the forces of Damascus and Israel and exacted tribute from the Phoenician cities.

Damascus came to dominate the Aramaean states and subdued the Israelites c.820 BC.

The Medes, an eastern people noted for their horse raising, were first mentioned in Babylonian records c.835 BC.

The Phoenicians colonized the eastern Mediterranean and established Carthage c.814 BC.

The Americas

About 800 BC, at a second Olmec center, La Venta in Tabasco, Mexico, craftsmen produced beautiful jade ornaments and colossal sculpture.

Religion and Philosophy

The orgiastic cult of the nature divinity **Dionysus, or Bacchus,** reached Greece from Thrace and Phrygia. His followers, mostly women known as **Maenads** (mad ones), would take to the hills in ecstasy under the god's inspiration and wander about in *thiasori,* or revel bands. Dionysus was god of fruitfulness and vegetation, and was especially known as the god of wine.

Literature

The Upanishads in India summed up much of the wisdom of earlier Hindu scriptural writing and expressed it in the form of a dialogue between teacher and pupil that would provide the basis for the major philosophical branches of Hinduism. The dialogues bring out the essential unity of Brahman (god) and Atman (soul).

Art and Architecture

The Black Obelisk, known as "Jehu's stele," describes the campaigns of Shalmaneser III, 859–825. The frieze shows King Jehu of Israel making obeisance to him—the earliest representation of a Semite in traditional costume.

Science and Technology

Leather manufacture originated with the animal skins taken by men of the Old Stone Age. Leather technology, however, developed slowly and few of the dates are certain. The Egyptians treated hides with fat, to increase durability, before 1500 BC. Tanning, or soaking the hides in a solution containing vegetable material to make leather, probably evolved much later, as did a method for hardening leather with alum, but all these techniques were in use c.800 BC.

800-750 BC

Principal Events

Assyrian military power declined under a succession of weak monarchs c.800 BC and with it Assyrian wealth.
A Greek renaissance occurred under the stimulus of trading contact with the Phoenicians.
Judah played an important role in a military alliance against the Assyrians c.769 BC.
Jeroboam, 780–740, brought prosperity to the Israelites.
The caste system was now firmly established in India.
Rome was founded in 753 BC.

 The Americas

Cultivation of maize was first undertaken in eastern North America c.800 in the Ohio River Valley.

Religion and Philosophy

The 8th-century prophets of the Old Testament, **Amos, Hosea, and Isaiah,** castigated the moral turpitude of the Israelite rulers and their syncretist tendencies. The prophets rejected contemporary and foreign standards and urged otherworldly ideals, prophesying that the dilution of the old religion would lead to the fall of the kingdom of Israel. This prediction was fulfilled when the Assyrians conquered Israel in 732 BC.

Literature

The Iliad and **Odyssey,** Greek poems of 24 books each, belong in style to the 8th century BC, but little is known of their authorship. They combine ancient legends with a vivid evocation of scene and event and masterly delineation of character. Their literary magic is generally attributed to a single poet, Homer, who may have lived in Asia Minor.

Art and Architecture

Pottery in Greece flourished between c.900 and 750 BC, decorated with a wide range of human and animal figures, which prefigured the classical narrative style. Bronze work, and the small terra cotta figurines made for the new sanctuaries at Delphi and Olympia, herald the emergence of Greek sculpture. New motifs such as floral designs were included in geometric pottery decoration as a result of increased trade with Cyprus and the Near East.

Music

The lyre was popular in Greece. A large form with from three to twelve strings called the kithara was plucked with a plectrum while the player's other hand dampened the strings' vibrations.

Science and Technology

Trade in glassware became widespread, extending as far as the Atlantic coasts. Simple glass technology, such as the manufacture of glass beads, followed this trade and was practiced in Britain c.800 BC.
Crops grown in the Middle East included wheat, barley, flax, and later, cotton.

Principal Events

Tiglath-Pileser III, *r.744– 727*, **Shalmaneser V**, *r.726– 722*, and **Sargon II**, *c.722– 705*, restored Assyrian military power, founding a standing army and often moving subject peoples. Babylon was conquered and Damascus paid tribute to Assyria.
Greek cities founded colonies in Sicily and southern Italy *c.750*.
The Kushite kingdom in Nubia overran Egypt, 725 BC, establishing a Kushite dynasty, 725– 656 BC. A capital, Napata, had been founded *c.800 BC*.

The Americas

The civilization at Poverty Point, La., was at its peak, importing materials from as far away as the Great Lakes and Appalachian Mountains areas.

Religion and Philosophy

The concept of caste that had emerged in India was elaborated by the highest priestly caste, or **Brahmins**. There were four main castes, covering occupations of priests, nobles, merchants, and laborers. Brahmins further developed the earlier Vedic traditions in the *Brahmanas*, prose commentaries on the Vedas. The *Aranyakas* (Books of the Forest) foreshadowed later trends toward a mystical ascetic religious life.

Literature

The first surviving Greek inscription, the Dipylon vase from Athens, is dated *c.710*: "Who now of all dancers performs most gracefully, he shall receive this."
Hesiod, *c.750– 700 BC*, a didactic poet from Boeotia, wrote the *Theogony* and *Works and Days*, providing indispensable information on Greek myths, religion, and agriculture.

Art and Architecture

The art of the late Assyrian Empire flowered under **Tiglath-Pileser III**, *r.744– 727*, and **Sargon II**, *r.722– 705*. Tiglath-Pileser's palace at **Nimrud** was decorated with reliefs in the epic tradition, but freer in style. Sargon's palace at **Khorsabad** was a sophisticated structure covering over 20 acres (9 hectares) with its own drainage system. Man-headed winged bulls guarded the entrance and 7-ft (2-m) reliefs depicted members of the court.

Music

Professional bards in Greece recited or sang epic poems to their own lyre accompaniment, while shepherds played pan-pipes made of reeds of various lengths bound together side by side.

Science and Technology

Siege towers were a later development of Assyrian military inventiveness. These wooden towers on wheels, often armor-plated and fitted with battering-rams, were used to attack the walls of besieged cities. Although clumsy, they were undoubtedly effective; defenders could retaliate only with spears and arrows, grappling at the battering-rams with iron hooks. **Biremes**, ships with double banks of oars, are pictured in Assyrian reliefs of 700 BC.

The Birth
of Philosophy
700–300 BC

Ming portrait of
Confucius, Chinese
teacher of social ethics

Classical Greek
sculpture

Monte Albán, sculpture

Greek black-figure vase
depicting mythological
scene

Scythian gold plaque, 5th c. BC

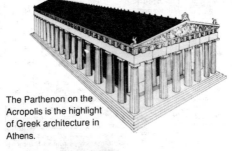
The Parthenon on the Acropolis is the highlight of Greek architecture in Athens.

18th c. portrait of Greek philosopher-educator Aristotle

The Birth of Philosophy

★ Principal Events
Middle Eastern civilization entered a phase of turmoil between the 6th and 4th centuries BC with a series of short-lived empires established by the Babylonians, Persians, and Greeks, while the Magadha Empire grew up in India.

The most striking feature of the period, however, was cultural—a massive shift toward the systematization of thought that took place in literature and the sciences and was manifested above all in the founding of many of the Eastern religions and the principal schools of Western philosophy.

Athens, where culture and democracy flourished in the context of a prosperous city-state, stood at the center of the first brilliant flowering of European urban culture, and although her power even in Greece was limited by Spartan and Macedonian militarism, the conquests of Alexander would carry this culture throughout the Middle East.

The Americas
With the sedentary life firmly rooted in most of North and South America, cultural regionalism developed. While Olmec culture flourished in Mexico, another important civilization was forming in the Mayan highlands. Religion played an increasingly prominent role, with more sophisticated beliefs and practices.

⚛ Religion and Philosophy
Within a remarkably short time, a number of diverse and highly sophisticated religions of world significance arose. Buddhism and Jainism in India marked a break with Brahmanic ritualism. Zoroastrianism in Persia established religious themes that were to spread westward with far-reaching consequences. In China, both Taoism and Confucianism established the doctrine of harmony as their central idea.

The flowering of Greek philosophy is one of the most extraordinary episodes in the history of thought. A questioning of accepted ideas, including the tenets of religion, and an emphasis on rational argument resulted in Greek thinkers from Thales to Aristotle raising most of the issues that have occupied Western philosophy up to the present time. Central concerns were the nature of reality and the basis of virtuous conduct.

📖 Literature
From religious mysteries and epic poems, literature began to develop secular forms of many kinds. The most varied and accomplished emerged in Athens where theater became a medium into which most poetic energy flowed, whether tragic, epic, comic, or lyrical. Poetry flourished, and prose writing developed in the fields of history and philosophy,

although Plato's use of the Socratic dialogue indicated the all-pervading influence of the dramatic form.

Systematization of previous literary developments occurred in all the major cultures of the world. For the first time, the Gilgamesh epic was collected, as were the Indian epics, while in China the teaching of philosophers was written down.

Art and Architecture

Although the Assyrians and Babylonians produced much striking monumental art in the 7th and 6th centuries BC the most significant artistic development of the period was the evolution of Classical Greek art in which a new realism superseded the stylization common to the ancient Near Eastern art.

A narrative style grew up in pottery decoration drawn with a fluid hand in black- and red-figure work. In sculpture the traditional kouros figure gradually took on a more relaxed pose, and a representational style developed—the single most vital step in the emergence of European art.

Greek architects, especially in Athens, designed simple but subtle buildings using austerely ornamented lintels and columns as their basic units and counteracting the effects of foreshortening with the help of mathematics.

Music

Music theories developed in the East and the West, and especially in China, as complex scales were devised, but little is known of the style of music produced at this period. The seven-note scale, later to become the basis of most European music, entered Europe from the Near East through Greece c.550 BC. In India, the basis for the raga was evolving.

Science and Technology

By the 5th century BC the Athenian Greeks had established a rich and complex pattern of manufactures, particularly in pottery and textiles, with trading contacts from the Black Sea to the Rhine. They did not introduce many advances in technology, which they preferred to regard as the preserve of slaves. Their theoretical writings, however, have provided the basis for much Western European science even where, as in the case of Aristotle, this consisted of the systematization of earlier thinking or the elaboration of untested hypotheses.

Greek mathematics began in the 6th century with Pythagoras, but by the 4th century the focus of the science had moved to Alexandria where scientific study flourished.

In China, where military technology may have received a spur from constant attacks by nomadic invaders, the crossbow was invented and a way was found to melt and cast iron.

700-660 BC

⭐ Principal Events

Sennacherib II, 704–681, of Assyria made Nineveh his capital after destroying the rebellious Babylon. Esarhaddon, his successor, c.681–669, rebuilt Babylon and attacked Egypt, captured Memphis, and drove the pharaohs back to Kush in 671.

Tyrants (non-hereditary rulers, mostly of the merchant classes) appeared in many Greek cities and in Athens in 683 BC, assuring growth and prosperity.

Twelve Etruscan cities flourished in central Italy c.675.

The Americas

Cassava was the major food crop cultivated by the Saladero people, early farmers and potters who lived in the valley of the Orinoco River in Venezuela.

📕 Literature

Etruscan inscriptions, mostly liturgical or funerary, dating from c.700 BC, have been found at Magliano, Italy, and elsewhere—indicating the existence of a literature that has been lost. The language is incomprehensible and of unknown origin but the alphabet is Greek-based and led to the development of a Latin alphabet.

🏛 Art and Architecture

Assyrian wall reliefs of the 7th century were incised on stone instead of molded, giving finer detail to scenes of savage conquest of the expanding Assyrian Empire.

Saite artists of the early 7th century attempted to revive the brilliance of the Old Kingdom. Sculpture and bas-relief were elegant, and the new use of hard stone made for a studied and severe style.

🎵 Music

Terpander, the Greek composer, fl. c.675 BC, was a founder of classical Greek music. He is sometimes credited with having completed the octave.

⚛ Science and Technology

Greek silver coins, stamped with an owl design, came into usage in 700 BC. Early coins from Lydia, in Asia Minor, were made of electrum, a gold and silver alloy. Coinage was developed because the barter system was inadequate to deal with the growing trade between the countries of the Middle East and the Mediterranean.

Greek silver mines at Laurion were heavily worked by the Athenians, using prisoner or slave labor.

Principal Events

Sparta became dominant in the Peloponnese after subduing the Messenians in 630 BC. After the reign of **Ashurbanipal,** 668– c.627 BC, a time of military activity in Egypt and artistic splendor, Assyrian fortunes declined suddenly. The **Chaldean Nabopolassar** led a successful revolt in Babylon. **Josiah,** 640– 609, inspired a successful political and religious uprising in Judah, and **Phoenicia** won its independence from Assyria in 627 BC.

The Americas

The Olmec culture, at its height c.1200– 400 BC, was the earliest Mesoamerican civilization to create a primitive state with a political or religious leader.

Religion and Philosophy

Thales of Miletus, c.640– c.546, believed that the essence of all matter was water. His attempt to find simple material causes was seminal to Greek thought.

Literature

A library of 20,000 tablets was established at Nineveh by **King Ashurbanipal,** r.668– c.627, who collected Assyrian, Babylonian, and Sumerian writings, among them the *Gilgamesh* epic and religious and scientific works.

Art and Architecture

Olmec sculptors at La Venta between 800 and 400 BC produced basalt monuments carved in elaborate relief, depicting scenes of historical and contemporary events.

A gold scabbard from Litoi, c.650, showed typical Scythian style of ceremonial weaponry characterized by the designs combining different animals to make a mythical beast.

Music

Scale theory was developed in Babylonia in the Chaldean period (626– 538 BC). Mathematical division of strings produced a four-note scale, which was associated with the four seasons.

Science and Technology

Central European technology thrived at Halstatt, Austria, with the mining, manufacture, and export of iron and salt.

620-580 BC

Principal Events

Nabopolassar of Babylon destroyed Assyria with Median help in 612 and took Nineveh. **Sparta** introduced barrack life and military education c.610.
Nebuchadrezzar II, r.604–562, built a Babylonian empire in Syria-Palestine, taking the Jews to Babylon as prisoners in 586 BC, and ending Pharaoh Neko II's imperial aspirations. **Solon**, who became the archon in Athens in 594, smoothed tensions between aristocrats and merchants.

The Americas

Archeologists estimate that the Zapotec peoples of Mexico began to level off the top of a mountain where they would build the city of Monte Albán.

Religion and Philosophy

Taoism is thought to stem from the work of the Chinese philosopher **Lao Tze**, c.604–c.531, to whom the *Tao-te Ching* anthology is attributed. The Tao is an imperceptible state of void and was exemplified in the childlike innocence in man.
Zoroastrianism, proclaimed in Iran by **Zoroaster**, c.600 proposed a dualistic cosmology of the spirit of good and evil, between which man is free to choose. The Zoroastrian scriptures were the *Avesta*.

Literature

In the Bhagavad Gita, or Song of the Beloved, Hindu sacred literature took the form of poetic dialogues on the soul. In Greece, the period saw the rise of **burlesque plays** with religious themes in which the chorus consisted of satyrs. The **earliest existing Latin inscriptions** — on the Black Stone of the Roman forum and the Manios clasp — date c.600.

Art and Architecture

Babylon was rebuilt by Nebuchadrezzar between 604–562. The decorated glazed bricks of the **Ishtar Gate**, and the famous **Hanging Gardens** were intended to outshine the brilliance of Assyrian palaces.
Etruscan tomb frescoes began in the mid-6th century. Those at Tarquinii depicted scenes from the life of the dead man in a realistic style.

Music

The kettledrum appears as a bowl-shaped drum beaten with sticks in a relief dating from c.600 BC found in Persia.

Science and Technology

Thales, fl.580 BC, "Father of Greek philosophy," made detailed observations on methods of triangulation navigation.
Anaximander, fl.6th century, who believed the Earth to be cylindrical in shape, is thought to have produced the first map of the known world.
The **potter's kick wheel** may have been invented at this time.
Indian mathematical texts of the 6th-3rd centuries BC deal with simple geometric forms, and calculations involving large numbers.

Principal Events

Babylonian power waned after Nebuchadrezzar died in 562.
The Peloponnesian League was founded on Spartan military strength in 560 BC.
Pisistratus, c.600–527, the tyrant, secured Athenian authority in eastern Greece.
Cyrus the Great, d.529, founded the Persian Empire, defeating Media in 549 and Ionia in 547.
The Kushite kingdom reached southward to Khartoum c.550.
The Magadha Empire was established in Bihar c.542.

The Americas

Worship of the jaguar god, revered by the Olmecs and the Chavin cultists, had spread to the San Agustin Culture of Colombia.

Religion and Philosophy

Jainism was developed in India by **Mahavira,** c.560–c.468, a member of the Kshatriya noble caste. It emphasized self-denial and non-violence, and rejected **Vedic** authority in reaction to the dominance of Brahmin ritual. Within the mainstream of Vedism **the first Upanishads** were written epitomizing the doctrines of samsara (rebirth) and karma (inescapable consequences). Unity with the cosmos through contemplation provided the only escape from suffering.

Literature

The poetic style of **Sappho** was echoed in the simpler lyrics of **Anacreon of Teos,** c.570–485, but he had no successors in Greece where literature served a public function linked to religion. **Aesop,** a slave from Thrace who died c.564, wrote popular animal fables to illustrate moral points, some possibly derived from Oriental sources.

Art and Architecture

Attic black-figure pottery achieved technical excellence by the mid-6th century and came to predominate in Greek vase painting. Mythological scenes were depicted in black glaze against a red background. Pottery after 540 was dominated by the red-figure technique.

Music

Pythagoras introduced Chaldean scale theory into Greece c.550 BC. He based a system of tuning on the fact that a string stopped at two-thirds its length sounds a fifth higher than its full length.

Science and Technology

Pythagoras, c.580–500 BC, and his school studied medicine, astronomy, and musical scales and mathematics, particularly the theory of numbers. It is debatable whether Pythagoras invented the theorem that bears his name.
Anacharsis the Scythian and **Theodorus of Samos,** fl.6th century, are thought to have developed the key, a metal anchor with grappling flukes, a lathe, and an improved bellows.

Principal Events

Cyrus took Babylon in 538 BC, thereby assisting the Jews' return to Jerusalem, and Egypt in 525 BC. Darius I, c.558–486, benevolently ruled a centralized empire from the Indus to the Mediterranean, divided into regions (satrapies) for administrative purposes.

Rome expelled her Etruscan kings in 509 BC and became an independent republic.

Cleisthenes reorganized Athenian local government and laid the basis for democracy in 508.

The Americas

Pithouses lined with stone were the Arizona desert dwellings of the Anasazi, forerunners of the Pueblo Indians.

Religion and Philosophy

Confucius, or Kung-Fu-tzu, 551–479, taught social ethics in China. His doctrine was taken up by the rulers and governed the Chinese way of life for over 2,000 years. It embraced elements of traditional Chinese religion and emphasized aristocratic social virtues and conduct harmonious with the heavenly order. It stressed awareness of fate and the decrees of heaven. In Greece **Pythagoras'** theory of numbers and music quickly developed into a mystical cult.

Literature

Classical Greek tragedy began with **Aeschylus**, c.525–456. He developed drama from choral cult songs by introducing dialogue between the actors when tragedy became a regular feature of the spring Dionysiac festivals. **The Boeotian Pindar**, c.522–c.440, wrote patriotic poems often celebrating athletic prowess.

Art and Architecture

Painted grey ware of the urban Ganges cultures, c.500, was a hard wheel-turned pottery decorated with linear and dotted patterns.

Bronze and ceramic vessels and ornamental and ritual jade carvings were the primary Chinese art forms under the Chou dynasty, 1000–200 BC.

Cyrus' funerary monument at Parsagadae, 529 BC, anticipated Achaemenid success with its artistic traditions of Greece and Mesopotamia.

Music

The ancient Greeks developed modes (patterns of sound in descending order, a basis for tunes) with distinct moods, and named them after Greek tribes, such as the Lydian and Phrygian.

Science and Technology

Iron welding, by hammering the red-hot metal, is associated with the name of Glaukos of Chios. Before his time iron sections were joined by elaborate lappings and flanges.

Heraclitus, c.540–c.480, held that fire is the fundamental principle of the universe.

Principal Events

Athens checked Darius' invasion of Greece at Marathon, 490. A second Persian invasion by **Xerxes**, c.519–465, in 480 was stopped by the Spartans at Thermopylae and the Athenians at Salamis.
The Delian League was founded in 478 BC, reflecting Athenian ascendancy in eastern Greece.
Celtic culture spread in Europe c.500 BC.
The Greeks defeated Carthage, 480, and the Etruscans, 474, and thus won control of the sea.

The Americas

By around **500 BC**, the Desert Culture peoples on the New Mexico-Arizona border first grew a drought-resistant strain of maize.

Religion and Philosophy

Buddhism was founded in India when **Siddhartha Gautama,** c.563– c.483 BC, began propagating the insights he achieved through long periods of contemplation. He taught that suffering can be avoided only by following an eight-fold path of moral conduct, non-violence, and meditation, leading to a state of perfect enlightenment, nirvana. **Zeno of Elea,** c.495– c.430, a Greek philosopher, originated the dialectic and supported his argument with paradoxes.

Literature

Sophocles, c.496–406 BC, and Aeschylus continued the tradition of classical tragedy. In his plays like *Oedipus Rex* Sophocles retained a functional chorus but shifted the center of interest to the actors.
During the time of Confucius, 551–479, the five classic *Ching* books reached their final form.

Art and Architecture

Early Celtic bronze wine flagons from the Moselle region. c.460 BC, show how classical and eastern elements were assimilated to produce a new and purely Celtic art form. The human mask is a typical motif.
The Palace of Darius, 522–486, records Persia's victory over the Median kings in the bas-relief friezes on the gigantic columns.

Music

The rise of drama in Greece linked dance, music, and poetry. The chorus performed in an area called the orchestra in front of the stage, after which the modern orchestra is named.

Science and Technology

Athenian culture, reflected in the volume and variety of their trade and industry, was well advanced, producing large quantities of metals, oil, and cloth. Pottery, too, was of the highest quality in design and manufacture and was in great demand abroad.
Anaxagoras, c.500– c.428, who came to Athens from Ionia in c.480, gave the first scientific explanations of celestial events, especially eclipses. He influenced much of Aristotle's scientific work.

460-420 BC

★ Principal Events

Athenian power and culture was at its height under Pericles, c.490–429, who assisted Egypt in an abortive revolt against the declining Persian Empire, 456–454.
Rome expanded into central Italy and the plebeians won new constitutional rights 445 BC.
Buddhism became popular in India, especially among the merchant classes.
The Peloponnesian War between Athens and Sparta began in 431.

The Americas

Mayan civilization was in its formative stages in Central America. Tikal, in Guatemala, later the most important Mayan center, was first inhabited.

◊ Religion and Philosophy

The Greek Sophists, led by Protagoras, c.485–c.410, were agnostic toward the gods. **Socrates**, c.469–399, argued that no one can possibly do that which he knows to be wrong. He followed this principle to the point of political dissent for which he was tried and condemned to death. In China, **Mo Ti**, c.470–391, taught pacifism and universal love; he also established a dialectical method of argument.

Literature

Euripides, c.480–406 BC, last of the great writers of tragedy, dealt with social issues as well as myths, reflecting a growing humanism in Greek drama.

Herodotus, c.485–425, emerged as the first major historian with a lively account of the Persian Wars, while **Thucydides**, 460–400 BC, took a more rigorous approach to the history of the Peloponnesian War.

Art and Architecture

Greek art became increasingly independent of foreign influences and more humanistic in style, reaching its High Classical period between 450 and 400. The "Cretan boy," c.450, from the Acropolis showed a relaxation of the 6th-century kouros pose. Doric architecture became less severe in style. The **Parthenon**, 447–432, built entirely of marble, was the least conventional of this style.

Music

A Chinese text showed how the chromatic scale (of 12 half tones) can be derived from the cycle of fifths, but in practice they used it only to transpose pentatonic scales into "keys."

Science and Technology

Democritus, c.460–370, held the theory that matter was composed of atoms.
Quarries on Mount Pentelicon provided the Athenians with fine milky-white marble, with which they built the Parthenon.
Hippocrates of Cos, c.460–c.377, called the Father of Medicine, explained mind and body conditions in terms of "humors," glandular secretions whose imbalance caused disease. He emphasized dietary and hygienic factors in the maintenance of good health.

★ Principal Events

The Peloponnesian War ended in naval defeat for Athens at Aegospotami in 405 BC.

The Romans captured Veii, an Etruscan city, in 396, but Rome herself was sacked by marauding Celts in 390 BC, who also hastened the Etruscan decline.

Socrates, c.469–399, was put to death in Athens in 399 BC.

The Chou dynasty in China declined in the long "Warring States period," 475–221.

The Americas

Indians in Kentucky were exploring the inner passageways of Mammoth Cave, searching for the gypsum crystals that were plentiful there.

Religion and Philosophy

Plato, fl.4th century BC, founded the Academy in Athens, where philosophy was taught to young members of the Athenian aristocracy, c.387 BC. He advocated subordination of the individual to the all-powerful republic, and also maintained that phenomena perceived by the senses are merely impure copies of the perfect reality of eternal ideas.

Literature

Aristophanes, c.445–388, was the best comic dramatist and topical satirist at the Athenian drama contests. His *Lysistrata,* 411 BC, deals with a strike by women aiming to end war.

The philosopher Socrates, 469–399, invented the cross-questioning (dialogue) teaching method, but his skeptical approach to religion brought him a death sentence.

Art and Architecture

The Greek Late Classical period was between 400 and 323. The more complex Ionic capitals superseded the Doric style, with the richly ornate designs of the **Erectheum** begun c.420. A new naturalism dominated sculpture, as seen with the transformation of the archaic kore in the figure of "Victory" from Olympia c.420.

Music

The Ramayana, a book of Hindu myths, recorded nine basic moods associated with scales in Indian music c.400 BC. Similar to Greek modes, this music anticipated the raga.

Science and Technology

Chinese cast iron appeared c.400 BC. The Chinese, unlike early Western ironsmiths, were able to melt iron to cast it, helped by the high phosphorous content of their iron, which lowered the melting-point; however, it also made the iron brittle. Two centuries passed before the Chinese could produce a satisfactory cast iron.

Principal Events

Athens defeated Sparta in 371 in alliance with Thebes, which became leader of the opposition to Sparta.
Philip of Macedon, *r.*359–336, built up his military strength in northern Greece. Many of the Persian satrapies had become semi-autonomous.
The Persian Artaxerxes III, *r.*359–338, restored royal authority and reestablished Persian rule in Egypt in 343 BC, thus ending the last native pharaoh dynasty.

The Americas

Permanent settlement began at Marksville, on Old River Lake in Louisiana, and continued until the arrival of the white man.

Religion and Philosophy

The Cynics in Greece, such as **Diogenes,** *c.*412–323, believed that happiness needed the repudiation of human values and the adoption of a simple animallike existence. **Aristotle,** 384–322, rejected Plato's idealism, urging a more detailed empirical examination of natural and social phenomena and the doctrine that good consists in individuals achieving the state appropriate to their natures.

Literature

Plato, *c.*427–347, continued the Socratic method in a masterly series of prose dialogues, including the *Republic,* which achieve the quality of a drama of ideas. His pupil **Aristotle,** 384–322 BC, made important contributions to literary criticism, although his books are mainly lecture notes, in *Rhetoric* and *Poetics,* which analyzed classical drama.

Art and Architecture

Idealized grace and beauty were characteristic of Late Classical Greek sculpture. The sensual possibilities of carved marble were explored by **Praxiteles** in "Hermes with young Dionysus," 350, at Olympia. The nude female form was introduced, and Praxiteles' "Aphrodite from Cnidus," 350, initiated a feminine ideal of narrow shoulders and broad hips.

Science and Technology

Aristotle systematized knowledge in the realm of science, logic, politics, and ethics. His scientific thinking, although often merely speculative, was enormously influential. For example, his belief that heavenly bodies move in perfect circles governed Western thinking until the 17th century AD.
Eudoxus, *c.*408–355 BC, studied mathematical proportions and developed a method of successive addition to determine irregular areas; this theory was the forerunner of calculus.

Principal Events

Alexander the Great, having assured his authority in Greece, defeated Darius of Persia, *d.*330, at Issus in 333, and crossed the Indus in 327. He died at Babylon in 323 after turning back to consolidate his authority. His empire had fallen apart by 306.
Chandragupta, *r.c.*321– *c.*297 created the Maurya dynasty at Magadha in India.
Rome had effectively destroyed Etruscan power by 300 BC.

The Americas

The Marpole peoples of the Fraser Delta area in British Columbia were engaged in heavy wood-working, building plank houses and dugout canoes *c.*300.

Religion and Philosophy

Zeno, 334– 262, of Citium, founded Stoicism, claiming virtue to be the only good and wealth, illness, and death of no human concern.
Epicurus, 342– 270, of Samos, believed pleasure to be the essence of a happy life.
Mencius, 372– 289 BC, a Confucian philosopher, saw man as inherently good and urged filial piety.

Literature

The New Comedy flourished in Athens from *c.*330. This was a comedy of manners, using stock characterization and avoiding touchy subjects. **Menander,** *c.*342– 292 BC, was its best exponent but was less popular than **Philemon,** *c.*365– 265 BC. Greek prose style was meanwhile brought to its zenith by the Athenian orator **Demosthenes,** *c.*382– 322 BC.

Art and Architecture

Corinthian columns were first used on the exterior of Greek architecture with the monument at Athens, built *c.*335 to celebrate a victory.
La Tène art from a 4th-century grave at Waldagesheim shows how classical motifs decorating neck torques and bracelets had superseded earlier Celtic styles.
The Appian Way between Rome and Capua was begun *c.*312.

Music

Alexander the Great's invasion of India brought with it new instruments and a developed theory. The introduction of the lute *c.*300 BC and new theories affected Indian music deeply.

Science and Technology

The elements of Aristotle, earth, air, water, and fire, in fact proposed by earlier Greeks, represent an early attempt to systematize nature. These elements could be used to produce each other: for example, smoke (air) and ash (earth) could be made by burning wood (fire).
Epicurus, 342– 270, advanced an atomic theory similar to that of Democritus.

Rome Conquers the West 300 BC –AD 100

Roman civil engineering: the Pont du Gard, Nîmes

The Aphrodite of Melos

Julius Caesar reformed the Roman calendar.

Archimedean screw is still used in Egypt to raise water.

I-shaped Mayan pok-ta-pok court

The Great Stupa of Sanchi, with ornamental gateway

Rome Conquers the West

Principal Events

Despite the constant political unrest that followed Alexander's fall, a cosmopolitan Hellenistic culture spread throughout the Middle East. This was absorbed by Rome, which now emerged as a great power, creating eight provinces by 146 BC, including Macedonia and Spain. Conquest, however, brought with it chronic social conflict in Italy, which finally helped to destroy the Roman Republic and led to the establishment of the empire in 28–27 BC, a constitutional solution that left the problems of expansion untouched.

By AD 100 the empire stretched from Egypt to Britain, bringing to Rome new manpower, art forms, and the many religious cults it incorporated, among them Christianity.

In the East Buddhism and Confucianism grew influential; the former spread by Ashoka in southern India, the latter becoming an integral part of society in China where it would remain so for 2,000 years.

The Americas

Increased population brought urbanization and cultural development in both North and South America. Agriculture increased and became more efficient with the introduction of such methodology as fertilization, irrigation, and terracing. Metallurgy, weaving, and pottery-making advanced.

Religion and Philosophy

Christianity grew from being one of several Jewish nationalist sects into a more universally significant religion, as Paul spread it throughout the Roman Empire and introduced Hellenic ideas. The Christian emphasis on the individual conscience and on love brought persecution in Rome where religion was primarily a public or political concern.

In India a proliferation of Hindu sects provided more popular forms of worship than the traditional Brahminical cult, and important additions to the sacred literature expressed further compromises with the everyday needs of worshipers.

New schools of thought grew up in China, while Confucianism became adopted as the official state religion under the Han dynasty c.140 BC.

Literature

Although Greek literature itself declined, its influence spread first in the wake of Alexander and then through Rome, which built its culture to a large extent on that of Greece.

A Latin literature arose in the third century BC based on Greek models in poetry, drama, and history although under the late republic a number of writers, among them Caesar, Livy, and Vergil, set out to glorify specifically Roman culture and history. The New Testament was written in Greek, still at the end of the first century the lingua franca of the eastern Mediterranean.

The Chinese classical literature flourished, while in India the epics and Buddhist scripture were finalized.

Art and Architecture
Throughout the Hellenistic world private patronage helped artistic production, and collectors' demands were so great that copying and pastiche developed, although many artists explored new ideas. Styles like that of the Pergamon school, marked by a new and masterful handling of emotion, were still for the most part associated with places rather than individuals. The Roman Empire absorbed the art of both the Hellenistic world and Italy. Etruscan iconography was copied, and the basic design for Roman architecture came from Etruscan models. Roman municipal architecture reflected both a strong civic pride and the varied leisure pursuits of Rome's urban elite. Baths, theaters and basilicas, constructed with careful attention to practical requirements, also served to create a dramatic framework for public life. Monuments were erected to commemorate the victories of the late republic and early empire.

Music
Music stagnated in the west under the Roman Empire, but the Jews maintained their vocal tradition from which the Christian Church borrowed heavily later. In the Arab world, music was still a lively art. The progress of music in the East had little influence on Western musicians, but Western incursions affected Eastern music to some degree.

Science and Technology
In the Hellenistic world Alexandria became the focus of scientific work particularly in mapping, astronomy, and mathematics. At the same time Greek technology found its greatest mathematician and experimental physicist in Archimedes.

As Rome expanded it developed the use of concrete and the arch in the building of bridges, roads, and aqueducts, creating a series of civil and military engineering projects that surpassed in scale any since those of the Assyrians and Egyptians. Nevertheless, whether because of the widespread use of slave labor or the stifling effects of a powerful bureaucracy, the Romans, like the Athenians, failed to exploit many inventions of their time.

In China, iron metallurgy improved still further, surpassing any in the West. Chinese astronomy was also active, and the preparation of many useful drugs from plants became a specialty of Chinese medicine.

300-260 BC

★ Principal Events

Alexander's empire had broken into four parts by 297 BC: the Hellenistic kingdoms of Macedonia and Thrace, the Seleucid dynasty in Syria, and the Ptolemaic in Egypt (whose invasion of Palestine in 301 BC revived old tensions with Syria).
Rome gained control of southern Italy and with the defeat of Tarentum in 272 BC came into conflict with Carthage in Sicily.
Ashoka, *c.*274– *c.*236 BC, expanded the Mauryan Empire and promulgated Buddhist principles.

The Americas

The Zapotecs, who were basically peaceful, probably had an army of some kind at Monte Albán, which was strategically located for defense.

Religion and Philosophy

The Yin-Yang school of Chinese philosophy and cosmology, the leading exponent of which was **Tsou Yen,** 340– *c.*260 BC, considered the universe to comprise five elements: metal, wood, water, fire, and earth. The Yin-Yang school thought the universe was governed by the two complementary forces of yin, female and passive, and yang, male and active.

Literature

The last classical writer, Ch'u Yuang, 343– 277, is traditionally described as the author of the celebrated *Ch'u Elegies,* the most famous of which is the *Heavenly Questions.*

Bucolic and pastoral poetry by **Theocritus,** *c.*300– 260, was imitated by his fellow Greeks **Moschus,** *fl.*150, and **Bion.**

Art and Architecture

The Colossus of Rhodes, one of the Seven Wonders of the ancient world, was a huge bronze representation of the sun god Helios, which was built astride the harbor at Rhodes between 292 and 280 BC.

Music

The Indian vina, from which the sitar later developed, was a lute-like plucked instrument thought to have evolved from the instruments carried by Alexander's invading soldiers.

Science and Technology

Euclid wrote his *Elements of Geometry* at Alexandria *c.*300. Alexandria became a center of learning in the century that followed Alexander's death, acquiring a great library and museum. Alexandrian inventions were based on the known principles of the siphon, gear wheel, spring, screw, lever, pulley, cam, and valve. The lighthouse of Pharos, a Greek achievement, stood 250ft (76m) high, with a 35-mile(56-km) beam.

Principal Events

In the first Punic War, 264–241, Rome built her first fleet, took Sicily and the Lipari Islands, and defeated Carthage, which expanded into Spain.
Conflict continued between the flourishing **Hellenistic kingdoms**. **Ptolemy II**, *r.*285–246, extended Alexandria in Egypt.
Bactria left the Seleucid kingdom, and developed a combination of Greek and Buddhist social philosophy, *c.*250.

The Americas

The **Chavin culture**, which had influenced the architecture, ceramics, and textiles of most of Peru since its beginning *c.*900 BC, was disappearing.

Religion and Philosophy

Ashoka, *r. c.*274–*c.*236 BC, made Buddhism the state religion of the Mauryan Empire.
The developing **Shinto religion in Japan** had a hierarchy of deities presided over by the sun goddess **Amaterasu** and her descendants, the imperial family. Past heroes became mythological figures and each clan venerated its own deity.
In China **Hsun Tzu**, 313–238 BC, taught that human nature was fundamentally evil. Goodness required training.

Literature

A **Latin literature** emerged, based largely on Greek poetry, drama, and history. **Naevius**, *c.* 270–*c.*201, was the first Latin epic poet. A freed Greek slave,

Livius Andronicus, *c.*284–*c.*204, wrote plays and translated the *Odyssey*. **Ennius**, 239–169, historian and playwright, was important for his efforts to adapt to Latin the methods of writers such as Euripides.

Art and Architecture

The **Temple of Horus** at Edfu in Egypt, begun by **Ptolemy III** in 237, was planned with one main axis, typical of Egyptian temple architecture. **The Hellenistic period** in Greek art, *c.*323–1st century BC, developed the sensuous possibilities of marble sculpture. The naturalistic poses of the bronze "Eros" from Tunisia and the "Sleeping Hermaphrodite" are typical of three-dimensional realism of 3rd-century Greek sculpture.

Music

The first keyboard instrument was the hydraulis, a water-powered organ. It was built by Ctesibius, who was working in Alexandria from 246–221 BC.

Science and Technology

Aristarchus, 310–230 BC, was the first to maintain that the Earth moved around the Sun.
Archimedes of Syracuse, *c.* 287–212 BC, discovered fundamental laws of floating bodies, made advances in mathematics, and was the greatest of Greek inventors; the "Archimedean" screw is still used in Egypt to raise water.
The crossbow was invented in the 3rd century BC in China. This weapon had a cocking and trigger mechanism similar to that of children's toys today.

220-180 BC

★ Principal Events

In the **second Punic War**, 218–210 BC, **Hannibal**, 247–183, invaded Italy across the Alps in 218 but retreated after Roman aggression in Spain c.206. His alliance with Macedon, 215, involved Rome in eastern Mediterranean politics.

The Roman nobility took control of the wealth from the new provinces while smallholders suffered from military service in the new standing army.

Huang-Ti, r.221–210, completed the Great Wall of China in 214.

The Americas

The Nazca People who inhabited Peru's south coast excelled at pottery, weaving, and the making of textiles.

Religion and Philosophy

Mystery religions and Eastern astrology took hold in Rome in response to the stress of the second Punic War, 218–201 BC. Novel gods, such as the Great Mother of Asia Minor, **Cybele**, and **Dionysus** superseded the traditional deities of Greek origin.

The introduction of the Stoic philosophy to Rome at this time with its emphasis on Fate, encouraged the development of mystical and astrological thought.

Literature

The Chinese Classical period came to a dramatic end with the reign of Ts'in, 221–210. He burned many Confucian texts.

Latin drama emerged with **Plautus**, c.225–184, who used Greek meters and plots from the New Comedy. *Miles Gloriosus*, c. 205, was his best play.

Art and Architecture

Town planning played an important role in Greek architecture. The chaotic market places of Ephesus and Miletus were replaced by public squares.

Music

The Imperial Court of the Han dynasty in China employed more than 800 musicians to impart a rich panoply of sound to the rituals of state occasions.

Science and Technology

A map of the world produced by Eratosthenes, c.276–c.194, a librarian at Alexandria in the 3rd century BC, was a great improvement on its predecessors. He calculated the diameter of the Earth with great accuracy, and did work in number theory.

Glass-blowing spread to Alexandria from Syria via the Romans and for two centuries was the most active of the technologies. Larger vessels and dishes were now made, by blowing the molten glass at the end of an iron blowpipe.

Principal Events

Rome invaded and defeated Macedon, and after further unrest annexed Greece in 147.
Carthage was totally destroyed by a Roman army in the third Punic War, 149–146.
The Arsacid dynasty ruled in Parthia, stretching from the Euphrates to the Indus *c.*150. Under **Menander**, *r.*155–130, the Indo-Greek kingdoms reached over much of northern India.
The Han dynasty in China consolidated imperial authority.

The Americas

Pok-ta-pok, the Mayan game played by heavily padded contestants, featured a rubber ball. Most Mayan cities had the I-shaped courts.

Religion and Philosophy

Within the Vedic tradition yogic thought was codified by **Patanjali,** *c.*150 BC, into the four volumes of the *yoga sutras*, rules dealing with transcendental trance states and mystical liberation. **Bhakti** (popular devotional cults) emerged as well as cults centered on the gods Vishnu, Shiva, and Krishna. The *Bhagavad Gita* was added to the earlier epic poem of the *Mahabharata,* and in it a new emphasis on salvation through the performance of duty emerged.

Literature

The Indian epic Ramayana, with between 20,000 and 40,000 couplets in its various versions, is attributed to the 2nd century BC. It was the forerunner of court poetry and had much influence on literary developments throughout southern Asia. Latin playwright **Terrence,** *c.*190–159, was less popular than Plautus but more influential with works such as *Adelphi.*

Art and Architecture

The "Venus de Milo," *c.*150, was a Pergamene pastiche of preceding sculptural styles. The classical features coldly echoed 5th-century tradition, while the slight twist of the torso accommodated the new taste for multiple view figures. This Hellenistic Aphrodite became the classic source for the Roman models.

Music

A Greek hymn to Apollo composed at Delphi survives from this date.

Science and Technology

A piston bellows with a double action was among Chinese inventions of the 2nd century BC. It provided a regular, steady air draft for the production of higher quality cast iron.

★ Principal Events

Han emperor, Wu Ti, r.140–87, established Confucianism as the basis of Chinese civil administration. 136 BC.

The Gracchus brothers proposed radical land reform to relieve Roman unemployment and poverty. 133 BC. Gaius Gracchus, 157–86, introduced state control of grain imports and allowed landless men into the army in 112. **The Senate** feared the destruction of the constitution and the nobility's power and opposed these measures.

The Americas

The Hopewell culture, which had begun c.300 BC in Illinois, was at its height in Ohio. It featured elaborate earthworks and was an extension of the Adena culture.

🕯 Religion and Philosophy

Tung Chung Su established Confucianism in China as the state cult c.140 BC, combining elements of the Yin-Yang school and Confucianism. He taught that Heaven, Earth, and Man formed a triad that the emperor, ruling by decree of Heaven, must maintain in harmony. This idea was important throughout Chinese imperial history, being associated with the stable order of Chinese society which lasted for 2,000 years.

📖 Literature

Fu poetry, influenced by Chu Yuan, was brought to perfection c.100 BC. Used mainly for description, it combined elements of prose and poetry in a form that was freer than that of the more personal **sao poetry,** which continued to develop. **Ssu-ma Chien,** c.145–86, wrote the first dynastic history of China. His *Historical Record* is notable for its objectivity.

🏛 Art and Architecture

Roman sculpture at first reproduced and imitated the styles of the past. The "Dying Gaul," c.100, was an accurate copy of the Pergamene original. **The steam baths of Stebiae,** c.120, were an early example of domed Roman architecture.

The Great Altar of Zeus at Pergamon was begun c.170. The exterior frieze depicts the battle of gods and giants.

🎵 Music

Music notation had been devised in China, according to Symaa Chian, 163–85 BC, a chronicler who tells of a music master who wrote down a zither tune.

⚛ Science and Technology

Peruvian technology during the last three centuries BC developed the molding of elaborate pottery and metal casting. **Hipparchus,** 190–120 BC, was the greatest Greek astronomer of his time. He estimated the Sun to be millions of miles away, instead of hundreds as previously thought. He also made a catalog of stars.

Principal Events

After Marius' death in 86, Sulla, 138–78, rescinded his reforms. Cicero, 106–43, prosecuted Verres, d.43, for corruption while he was governor of Sicily in 70, and denounced Catiline's attempt to gain a consulship by force in 63 BC, defending the constitutional basis of the republic, which depended upon no one man gaining supreme power. Pompey, 106–48, and Julius Caesar, 100–44, rose to power after Pompey's victories had led to the annexation of Syria.

The Americas

The origin of the culture at Teotihuacán in Mexico has been dated c.100 BC. Teotihuacán grew into the largest ancient city in the Americas.

Religion and Philosophy

The Pharisees in Israel opposed the adoption of Hellenistic culture by their conservative Sadducean rulers and were accused of their emphasis on the regulation of all aspects of life in accordance with Jewish law. However, they enjoyed the allegiance of much of the population because of their personal austerity and asceticism.

Literature

Cicero, 106–43 BC, a politician and philosopher, brought Latin oratory to a peak. His letters are a model of literary style. The Latin poet Lucretius, c.99–55, gave emotional body to Epicurean philosophy in De rerum natura. Catullus, 84–54 BC, showed a mastery of technique and lyrical intensity.

Art and Architecture

Roman arches were used for tenement houses and theaters in the highly populated cities of the 1st century BC.
Silverware brought to Rome following the sack of Corinth began a new taste for luxury articles in Roman circles. "The Old Republican," a portrait bust c.75 BC, captures Roman realism in a grim projection of asceticism and authority.

Music

An Imperial Office of Music was founded in China c.100 BC. The office supervised such activities as standardizing pitch and the building and administration of music archives.

Science and Technology

Only two furnaces, both using charcoal and a draft, could produce iron in a malleable (workable) form in which it could be forged with carbon to produce steel. These were the Catalan iron furnace with two bellows and the two-story shaft furnace. Neither, however, produced sufficient heat to melt the iron completely. Lucretius, c.99–55 BC, a Roman poet, wrote De rerum natura, a scientific treatise praising Epicurus and his ideas.

60-20 BC

★ Principal Events

The Han dynasty in China, 206 BC–AD 220, expanded into central Asia c.60 BC.

Julius Caesar subdued Gaul 58–51 BC, and after defeating Pompey became "dictator" in 45. Civil war followed his assassination in 44 by a pro-senatorial conspiracy. **Octavian (Augustus)**, 63 BC–AD 14, took imperial authority, 27 BC, to centralize power and prevent the unrest from recurring. **Egypt** became a Roman province in 30 BC.

The Americas

An Olmec sculpture from Tres Zapotes, Mexico, bears the bar-and-dot date 31 BC, the earliest recorded in the new world, predating Mayan calculations.

Religion and Philosophy

In Rome **Marcus Cicero**, 106–43 BC, and **Lucius Seneca**, c.55 BC–c.AD 40, developed an **Eclectic philosophy**, drawing on Platonist, Stoic, Epicurean, and Aristotelian sources

Titus Lucretius, c.99–55 BC, composed a long poem, *De rerum natura* (On the nature of things), in which he elaborated the Epicurean theory of physical atomism — a doctrine derived from Democritus that the world is composed entirely of microscopic particles.

Literature

Julius Caesar, c.100–44 BC, wrote his history *Commentaries* on the *Gallic War* in a style of exemplary clarity. **Roman history** was idealized in the *Aeneid*, 70–19 BC, by **Vergil** 70–19 BC, second only to Homer as a model for Western poetry. He also wrote fine pastoral poetry, the *Eclogues* and *Georgics*. **Horace**, 65–8 BC, combined elegance with humanity in his *Odes*.

Art and Architecture

Wall paintings at the Pompeiian **Villa of Mysteries**, c.40 BC, portrayed Dionysiac themes. Roman villas of the 1st century BC increasingly introduced walled gardens and Greek peristyles. The "Augustus" from **Prima Porta**, c.20 BC, displays a naturalistic classicism characteristic of Augustan portrait sculpture.

Music

Panpipes, rattles, and drums were made by the **Hopewell culture** of American Indians, who developed from the fourth century BC in the Ohio Valley.

Science and Technology

The Julian calendar of 45 BC, introduced under Julius Caesar, took a base year of 365.25 days. It was designed by the astronomer Sosigenes of Alexandria, and was inaccurate by a mere 11 minutes per year. This calendar was not supplanted until the 16th century AD, by which time it was inaccurate by ten days. **Water mills** were a feature of Roman technology as early as the 1st century BC, but were only fully described a century later, by Vitruvius.

★ Principal Events

Augustus strengthened the Roman Empire in the north and east and brought peace to Rome. **Tiberius**, *r*.AD 14–37, did the same, although imperial power became increasingly dependent on the approval of the Praetorian Guard (the emperor's bodyguard). **Judea** became a Roman province in AD 6.
The Kushite kingdom in Nubia was in decline *c*.AD 10.
Mexican lake houses were built.

The Americas

A volcano erupted during this period, covering the village of Cuicuilco, on the southwestern edge of the Valley of Mexico.

☿ Religion and Philosophy

Jesus Christ was born in Bethlehem in Judea in 4 BC and crucified in Jerusalem *c*.AD 30.

Literature

Ovid, 43 BC–AD 17, the supreme Roman poet of love, and one of the most influential of classical writers, developed erotic verse into a major form in his long poem *Metamorphoses*. It was completed in AD 8, the year of Ovid's banishment, partly for his witty but irreverent *Art of Love*. His later poetry is skeptical, often elegaic.

Art and Architecture

Roman temples derived their typical high podia and deep porches from Etruscan architecture, while the **Maison Carrée** at Nîmes, *c*.16 BC, has colonnades built in imitation of a Greek façade.
Roman bas-reliefs like that on the **Ara Pacis**, 9 BC, often used a combination of real and mythological figures to evoke contemporary Roman history. **Thermae**, magnificent municipal buildings, were developed at Rome *c*.20 AD.

⚛ Science and Technology

Strabo, *b*.*c*.64 BC, a Greek historian and geographer, wrote on the uses of materials.
A roller bearing for a cart wheel is another example of sophisticated engineering of the 1st century BC; made entirely from wood, it was found in Denmark but probably made in Germany or France.

AD 20-60

Principal Events

Tiberius and Claudius, r.AD 41–54, expanded the empire, instituted social reforms, and consolidated imperial power, although the danger of palace revolutions increased.

Jesus of Nazareth was crucified in Jerusalem c.AD 30. The **Christian cult** was taken to Asia Minor, Greece, and Rome by Paul, fl.1st century AD.

Buddhism was accepted as the official religion of China by **Emperor Ming**, r.AD 58–75.

The Americas

The Izapa, a transitional culture in Guatemala between the Olmec and the Mayan, produced a sculpture at El Bául bearing the bar-and-dot date of AD 36.

Religion and Philosophy

After the Crucifixion, c.AD 30, the early Jewish/Christian sect developed a unique emphasis on the resurrection of a Messiah and the imminent transformation of the world at the dawning of a millennium of universal love.

Paul of Tarsus, fl.1st century AD, who saw the death of Jesus as a universal sign reflecting cosmic forces, spread Christian ideals through the Roman Empire. Contact with Hellenic thought turned Christianity into a world religion.

Literature

Seneca the Younger, 4 BC–AD 65, made nine melodramatic adaptations of such Greek tragedies as *Oedipus*. They influenced Spanish literature and the revenge tragedies of Jacobean England. A noted orator and philosopher, Seneca exercised power in Rome under AD 54–62 but was finally ordered to commit suicide.

Art and Architecture

Roman columns acquired a new function in the support of arches and when used as a free form. The Tuscan and Composite orders developed as more ornate variants of the Doric and Ionic.

Roman villas of the 1st century AD were often decorated with wall paintings which, like that at the **Villa Albani**, made use of idyllic scenes to evoke the peace of the countryside.

Music

Buddhist monks arrived in China c.AD 50 from India, bringing with them chants and decorative melodic features that were incorporated into Chinese music of later periods.

Science and Technology

Metallurgical developments of the Romans include the manufacture of brass and the amalgamation of mercury with gold in the extraction of gold from its ores.

Roman civil engineering left an impressive record, including a 3.5-mile (5.6-km) mountain tunnel, many aqueducts, and 53,000m (85,000km) of roads. The city of imperial Rome received a million cubic meters of water each day through lead piping, which in turn went to cisterns and centrally heated baths.

★ Principal Events

Nero, *r* AD 54–68, rebuilt Rome after a fire in AD 64, which was blamed on the Jews and Christians, who were unpopular because they refused to recognize the emperor's divinity.

Peter and Paul were executed in the ensuing persecution *c.* 64.

Vespasian, *r* AD 69–79, became emperor after a civil war that followed Nero's death.

Jewish religious revolt, 66–70, was defeated by the Romans.

Mongol invaders brought iron and rice to Japan by AD 100.

The Americas

Pit houses, circular mud-covered dwellings partially sunk in the ground, were built by the Mogollón peoples along the New Mexico-Arizona border.

☥ Religion and Philosophy

After the death of Paul, AD 64, and the destruction of Jerusalem in AD 70, the **Pauline version of Christianity,** with its more transcendental significance, became completely dominant. A few Christians who still upheld Jewish law became a small sect without links with either synagogue or Gentile Church. The oral tradition of early Christianity was gradually replaced by composed narratives, the earliest of which was probably the Gospel of St Mark.

Literature

Plutarch, *c.* AD 46–120, the Greek biographer, wrote *Parallel*

Lives of Illustrious Greeks and Romans, a work that approached history from the viewpoint of the characters of the men and women who made it. Shakespeare and many other European writers drew from its vivid portraits of life in Rome and Greece.

Art and Architecture

The Arch of Titus, a triumphal arch of the kind developed in the 2nd century BC, portrayed Roman victories in the Judean War, AD 70.

Stupas, typical Buddhist edifices, derived their dome shape from Vedic tombs. Stupa I at Sanchi, *c.* AD 100, was embellished with a square base, balconies, and ornamental gateways.

Music

Destruction of the Second Temple, AD 70, led to the dispersal of the Jews. To keep their identity, secular music was discouraged and only singing permitted.

Science and Technology

Chinese science was very active under the Han dynasty. Astronomers recorded eclipses and observed planetary motions. Mathematicians constructed "magic squares" of numbers that add up to the same answer in any direction and influenced arithmetic and algebra.

Paper was invented in China *c.* 100 AD.

Chinese inventions of this time include a camera obscura, and convex and concave mirrors.

Early Christianity AD 100–400

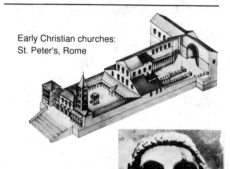

Early Christian churches:
St. Peter's, Rome

Constantine the Great
instituted religious
freedom

Pyramid of the Sun in the Valley of Mexico

Trajan's column depicts Romans vanquishing the Dacians.

Relief at Naqsh-e-Rustan

Wooden planked Roman grain ship

Early Christianity

Principal Events

The Roman Empire reached its greatest extent under Trajan, but further expansion became impossible due largely to pressure from barbarian migrations in the north and east, which brought increased economic and social instability to Rome. Various defensive measures were adopted, such as allying with the barbarians, but Rome remained weak because of the dependence of most emperors on the support of the army. The reign of Theodosius saw the beginning of the close identification of the interests of the Christian Church and the empire in the east.

Cultured and prosperous civilizations arose in India, where the Guptas set up a northern empire and the strong southern Chola kingdom traded with Rome. In Central America the Mayas entered their classic period, while China suffered from instability and lack of central authority.

The Americas

By about the time of Christ, peoples throughout the North and South American continents had arrived at a comfortable plateau of living, although it differed from one area to another. Surplus resources were available for the building of ceremonial centers in Mesoamerica and burial mounds in North America.

Religion and Philosophy

The early church clarified and developed a sophisticated theology in response to attacks from religions whose origins lay outside the Judeo-Christian tradition, including Gnosticism, Manichaeanism, Montanism, and Mithraism. By 395, Theodosius the Great had finally established Christianity as the religion of the empire but with the barbarian invasions began a long struggle against paganism. Missions were sent out to Germanic tribes, and those who were converted largely adopted the Arian form of the Christian faith. Under Pope Damasus the Roman see claimed primacy over the five patriarchates of Rome, Constantinople, Antioch, Jerusalem, and Alexandria, basing its claim on the "Petrine" text.

Buddhism began to influence the development of Hinduism in India and similarly affected religion and society in China.

Literature

With the diffusion of Christianity the scriptures began to spread in translation, notably in Latin, although fragments exist of translations in Gothic (mainly from the New Testament) made by Bishop Wulfila. The influence of the Gospels as well as religious, setting the stage for the Christian allegorical treatment of pagan literature that was to dominate European literature until the 17th century. Homer, Vergil, and Ovid were all interpreted in this way. Classical Latin

74

literature petered out after AD 200.

In China, paper (chih) was invented but took nearly a millennium to reach Europe, where papyrus gradually gave way to stitched parchment or vellum.

Art and Architecture

The Imperial and Hellenistic styles of Rome gradually lost ground, to be replaced in western Europe by the more mysterious and magic art of the Christian period. A recognizable Christian style in art and architecture had developed by the 4th century, by which time the empire was divided into east and west, presaging the lasting division between the Byzantine and Western Christian traditions in art. Into this world of changing imagery the barbarian invaders brought new decorative abilities and tastes, which were also assimilated into the art of Rome.

The Persian culture of the Sassanids and the Indian culture of the Gandhara region were influenced in part by Rome and this influence penetrated China during the late Han period, producing the basis for a recognizable style. Indian art flourished under the Guptas, during whose dynasty the Ajanta cave paintings were done.

Music

Plainsong, a form of religious chant, developed in Europe. St. Augustine, 354–430, warned of the "peril of pleasure" in this music, whose austere unaccompanied line would be the basis of later European developments in polyphony (two or more related melodies played together) and harmony (chord progressions). Eastern music, with its sensuous sonorities, reached its peak.

Science and Technology

In the Greco-Roman world, there was a decline in science and technology, although a brief revival started in the reign of Constantine the Great. The "occult sciences," astrology and alchemy, were held in great esteem, forming the basis for much technological innovation.

Most Western scientists of the 4th century were engaged in translating, collecting, and commenting on the works of earlier thinkers, rather than making observations or doing experiments of their own.

In China, however, in spite of unsettled times, scientific thought progressed as advances were made in mathematics, astronomy, and medicine, while materials technology remained active and productive.

In Central America Mayan culture began its classic period. This would produce remarkable advances in mathematics and astronomy and massive stone buildings constructed without the aid of metalworking.

100-130

Principal Events

Emperor Trajan, r.98–117, expanded into Dacia. His heir **Hadrian**, r.117–38, pursued an essentially defensive policy, suing for peace in order to limit the eastern boundaries of the empire. He established his personal authority in Rome and traveled widely, consolidating Roman power in Britain while building Hadrian's wall.

The Western Satrap dynasty in Malwa, India, made Ujjain a center of Sanskrit learning.

The Americas

The 200-ft (60-m) high, 650-ft (195-m) long Pyramid of the Sun, which would dominate the city of Teotihuacán in the Valley of Mexico, was being built.

Religion and Philosophy

Gnosticism, a diffuse movement based on a variety of religions, some earlier than Christianity, absorbed Christian ideas, giving the Gospels equal weight with Greek and Oriental texts. Many Gnostic sects were proclaimed heretical by the early Church and Gnostic interpretations of the scriptures forced the Church to establish authoritative versions of the Gospels and to consolidate the basis of a universal Church.

Literature

The Latin satirical tradition had begun with **Lucilius**, c.180–102 BC, but culminated with **Juvenal**, c.AD 60–127, whose verse *Satires* on folly and Roman corruption profoundly influenced Western satirists **Tacitus**, c.55–117, like Juvenal, vividly recounted the cruelties of the period up to the death of Domitian in 96, in his *Histories*, 104–09, and *Annals*, 117.

Art and Architecture

The ascending spiral bas-relief narrative on **Trajan's column**, 113, relates and glorifies the emperor's military victories during the Dacian campaign.

The Pantheon, c.118, is an architectural realization of the climax of imperial grandeur.

Monumental stone tomb sculpture appeared in China during the Han dynasty, probably due to foreign influence. The tomb of **Ho Ch'u-ping**, c.117, includes a figure of a horse trampling a barbarian.

Music

The Chinese zither, adopted by Buddhist monks from c.100, brought more instrumental color to their music. Zither players produced sliding runs and delicate harmonic overtones.

Science and Technology

Menelaus, a Greek mathematician, fl.100, wrote the first work on non Euclidean geometry.

Hadrian's Wall was begun in Britain c.122. It was 73.5 miles (18.3km) long, with many forts.

Surgical instruments were well developed in Rome, as described by Celsus in the 1st century, but no pain killing drugs were available to sufferers. There is evidence that the **wheelbarrow** was invented in China at the beginning of the 2nd century.

Principal Events

Emperor Antonius Pius, *r.*138–61, continued Hadrian's peaceful policies and quelled Senate opposition.

The dispersion of the Jews followed the ruthless suppression of a Zealot revolt in Jerusalem in 135.

Migrating Goths settled on the northern Black Sea coast.

Taoism became popular in China, stimulated by military and social instability during the decline of the **Han dynasty** and the introduction of **Buddhism.**

The Americas

The Classic Period of the Mayan civilization began about this time. Ceremonial centers, which would eventually number in the hundreds, were developing.

Religion and Philosophy

The Mahayana school of Buddhism was founded by Nagarjuna, *c.*150–*c.*250, in India. This school, often known as "The Great Vehicle," departed from the traditional Hinayana or Theravada, "Little Vehicle," doctrines in holding that laymen as well as monks could achieve nirvana through the intervention of saints. This development resulted from the impact of the Brahmin religion on Buddhism.

Literature

Asvaghosa, *c.*80–150, was the first known poet and dramatist to write in classical Sanskrit. He was a Brahmin convert to Buddhism who wrote two epic poems, *Saundarananda* and *Buddhacarita* (The Life of Buddha), a philosophical work that became the source for later studies of Buddha's life.

Art and Architecture

The Temple of Mithras, 2nd century, in London, is a typical architectural design of the period with its small size, basilican plan and central apse. Temples were common throughout the periphery of the empire.

Music

Greek modes lived on in the plainsong chants of the Christian Church in an adapted form, ascending rather than descending as the Greek modes did.

Science and Technology

Ptolemy, the Hellenic astronomer and geographer, wrote the *Almagest c.*150. This became the "bible" of astronomers for the next 1,400 years, although it contained few new discoveries. Like Hipparchus and other Greek astronomers, Ptolemy accounted for the erratic paths of planets by suggesting that they moved in epicycles (small circles centered on the rim of a planet's orbit). Ptolemy's *Guide to Geography,* which included Africa and Asia, had great subsequent influence.

★ Principal Events

Plague brought back by troops returning from the wars with Parthia depopulated the Roman Empire in 166–67.

Marcus Aurelius' reign, 161–80, marked the high point of **Stoicism** as the dominant philosophy, with its emphasis on the empire as a "common weal." Marcomanni from Bohemia crossed the Danube, 167, and were settled by the Romans in areas depopulated by the plague. **The persecution of Christians** in Rome increased c.170.

The Americas

Funeral offerings in graves at the Norton Mounds in Michigan were elaborate. Materials imported from great distances indicate vigorous trade.

♦ Religion and Philosophy

Montanus, who appeared in Phrygia c.172, preached that prophecy and revelation had not ended with the death of Jesus. This belief and the expectation of the Second Coming of Christ threatened the stability of the Church, and many Montanists were excommunicated c.177. **Buddhism reached China** in the 1st century AD and began to exert an influence there in the 2nd century, when it received official patronage.

Literature

The prose romance became a popular literary form in both Lat-

in and Greek. *Satiricon,* a romance of Nero's Rome written by Petronius c.60, gained popularity during this time.

Elements of science fiction were introduced into a parody of traveler's tales by a Greek writer. **Lucian,** c.115–200, living in Syria. His *True History* describes a trip to the moon.

🏛 Art and Architecture

One example of **Roman imperial sculpture** is the bronze equestrian portrait of Emperor Marcus Aurelius, c.173, which still dominates the Campidoglio in Rome. **Sculpture from Gandhara** in northwest India of the 2nd to 4th centuries exemplifies the meeting point of Greco-Roman and Buddhist canons of beauty. Delicate reliefs depict the life of the Buddha – the first time he is represented figuratively.

⚛ Science and Technology

Galen, c.130– c.200, a surgeon and philosopher of Alexandria, wrote over 500 works on medical subjects. His experiments on animals led to the science of physiology. Galen's knowledge of the body was influenced by the works of Aristotle and Hippocrates, who believed in vital substances or essences at work in the body. Despite practical knowledge of the circulatory system, he postulated that blood vessels carried the blood to the skin where it was transformed into flesh.

Principal Events

Praetorian scheming prevented the establishment of a strong emperor, 192–93, until **Severus**, r.193–211, reformed the army and reinforced provincial administration.

Caracalla, r.211–17, expelled the Goths and Alemanni and in 212 bestowed citizenship on most free inhabitants of the empire, a token of Rome's reliance on provincial talent.

The Han dynasty in China fell in 220 and was replaced by three separate kingdoms.

The Americas

Although the date of the Great Serpent Mound is unknown, it was probably built before AD 200, when a climate change brought cultural deterioration.

Religion and Philosophy

Origen, 185–254, became head of the Christian Catechetical school at Alexandria c.212. This was the most famous of the Christian schools and offered a wide curriculum including Greek, philosophy, and science. Origen, a Platonist, furthered the synthesis of the Christian Gospels and Greek philosophy, emphasizing the study of the Bible as essential to a proper understanding of Christianity.

Literature

Apuleius, b. c.127, wrote the only Latin prose romance that survives in full. His *Metamor-*

phoses, now known as *The Golden Ass*, relates the hilarious adventures of a man magically transformed into a donkey.

Art and Architecture

Early Christian painting remained stylistically in the tradition of Roman decoration as can be seen in the fresco "The Celestial Refreshment," c.200, in the catacomb of St Calixtus in Rome.

The Synagogue of Dura Europus in northern Mesopotamia is decorated with symbolic frescoes on the subject of Ezekiel in the valley of the bones, typical of the art resulting from the development of mystical religions in the Middle East.

Music

Buddhism became a vital force in China from c.200. Its chants were accompanied by the music of elaborate percussion orchestras of bells, gongs, triangles, drums, and cymbals.

Science and Technology

Alchemists of the first two centuries include Dioscorides of Cilicia, fl.c.60, who described the processes of crystallization, sublimation, and distillation of substances. He also described the use of minerals for medical purposes.

Alchemy, a pseudo-science of obscure origins, sought a philosopher's stone thought capable of changing base metals into gold, and the elixir of life that would preserve youth indefinitely.

The abacus is recorded in use in China c.190.

★ Principal Events

The murder of **Alexander Severus**, r.222–35, instigated a period of military control over the Roman emperor and factional warfare among the troops.
Official persecution of Christians began under **Decius**, r.249–51, as the worship of living rulers became proof of loyalty
The new Sassanid Empire in Persia, founded by **Ardashir I**, r.224–41, took Armenia from Rome in 232. **The first written records** in Japan date from c.230.

The Americas

The Saladero peoples were driven out of coastal Venezuela, migrating to the Caribbean Islands. Their descendants met Columbus.

Religion and Philosophy

Neo-Platonism was founded by **Plotinus**, 205–70; his belief in the superiority of ideas over mundane reality fostered the Christian conception of heaven, widely influencing Christian and Islamic thought. **Mithraism**, a cult based on the recognition of the two powers of good and evil, became popular with Roman legionaries and received official patronage.

Literature

Early Tamil literature, associated with the kingdoms of southern India, dealt with the themes of courtly love and kingship. Its earliest works are the *Eight Anthologies* and possibly the *Ten Songs*, both written c.100–500 by the third of the legendary Sangam literary academies, which are said to have lasted for thousands of years.

Art and Architecture

Realistic portraiture flourished throughout the Roman Empire. Paintings recalled Egyptian mummy portraits in both style and technique. Most exquisite were the delicate miniatures on gold glass medallions, among them the "Family of Vennerius Keramis," c.250.
Sassanid Persia reached its cultural zenith during the reign of **Shapur I**. The rock carvings at Naqsh-e-Rustan, 242–73, record the humiliation of the Roman emperor Valerian.

Music

Heroic poems were sung among the German tribes by bards who accompanied themselves on harps. The songs were narrative lays of couplets set to music.

Science and Technology

In China the use of paper became widespread during the period of the Three Kingdoms, 220–64.
Diophantus of Alexandria, fl.250, wrote the *Arithmetica*, of which six volumes survive in Greek manuscripts. He was the first to introduce symbols into Greek algebra. His numerical equations, together with the Hindu system of numbering, influenced the development of Arabian algebra.

★ Principal Events

The Goths took Dacia in 257. A series of capable emperors from Illyria began with **Claudius II "Gothicus,"** r.268–70, who defeated the Gothic invasion of the Balkans and settled the Goths in the Danubian provinces. In 271, **Aurelian,** r.270–75, drove out the Alemanni who had invaded Italy, but abandoned the Roman province of Dacia. **China** was nominally reunited under the **Western Ch'in dynasty** in 265.

The Americas

The Mochica civilization of Peru was a powerful military society with armies ruled by priest warriors. They created a remarkable art form.

Religion and Philosophy

Manichaeanism, founded by **Mani,** c.216–76, a dualistic religion combining the teachings of Zoroaster, Buddha, Jesus, and Gnosticism became widespread from Europe to China. Mani held that knowledge of oneself and God guaranteed salvation (light) and liberation from one's present fallen condition (darkness). The soul had to be kept pure and in communion with God, both of which could be achieved by an abstemious life.

Literature

Valluvar, c.200–c.300, was the author of the classic Tamil poem the *Tirukkural* (sacred couplets). The work is a collection of aphorisms dealing with government, society, virtue, and love, and has proved almost impossible to translate. The outlook of the poet is so varied that several religious groups in the Tamil region have claimed him as their own.

Art and Architecture

Mochican art flourished on the coast of Peru, c.200–500, and was notable for its naturalistic ceramics, particularly of warrior figures.
Mayan culture grew in Central America from about the first century AD and lasted for the next 900 years. The architectural monuments of this civilization and the cities of Palenque, Copan, Uaxactun, and Yaxchilan were built from the 3rd century onward.

Music

The harp, Europe's main musical instrument, was regarded as a precious possession. Later versions of the instrument became the national emblems of Ireland and Wales.

Science and Technology

In China Huang Fu wrote a treatise on acupuncture, in use since 2500 BC.
Chinese mathematical books describe the Pythagorean theorem; solve problems involving square roots; and give the value of π as 3.1547.
Shafts on chariots and carts first appeared in Europe in the 3rd century although they had been used in China for many hundreds of years.

★ Principal Events

Diocletian, *r.*284–305, divided the empire into eastern and western spheres in 285 with two equal emperors. In 285 the western capital moved to Milan to defend the northern frontiers more easily.
Rome recaptured Armenia and Mesopotamia in 297.
The Mediterranean economy continued to collapse under heavy Roman taxation, *c.*300.
The Franks, Alemanni, and **Burgundians** crossed the Rhine.

The Americas

A Mayan stone slab, or stela, found at Tikal in Guatemala, had an inscription dated at AD 292. It is one of the earliest long-count dated objects known.

Religion and Philosophy

The Desert Fathers in Egypt formed the earliest Christian monastic orders.
St Anthony, 250–355, organized a group of hermits in 305, and **St Pachomius,** *c.*290–346, founded communal monasteries.
Neo-Taoism was created in China. It was influenced by **Kuo Hsing,** *d.*312, and **Wang Pi,** 226–49, who believed in controlling the emotions and in an ultimate all-uniting principle of non-being.

Literature

A more uninhibited and individualistic writing style evolved in China with Taoist and Buddhist thought. The poet **Lu Chi,** *fl.* *c.*300 was the first to express this movement toward original creativity. Simple language styles and folksongs were used by the poet **Ts'ao Chih,** *c.*300.

Art and Architecture

Roman architecture was at its most massive in the early 4th century with the Palace of Diocletian at Split and the Baths of Diocletian and Basilica of Maxentius in Rome.
The fixed hieratic expression on the colossal head of Constantine in the Forum marked a break from Hellenistic realism and heralded the formalized style of Byzantine art.

Science and Technology

Hippology—the science of breeding and managing horses—flourished under the Romans.
Clinker-built boats, made from overlapping wooden planks fastened with iron rivets, were developed in northern Europe in the 3rd century.
By order of Diocletian, Roman emperor from 284 to 305, all books on the working of gold, silver, and copper were burned to prevent counterfeiting. The effect was to increase interest in alchemy and magic as a method of turning base metal into gold.

★ Principal Events

Constantine, c.285–337, became interested in Christianity and granted religious freedom to all religions in 313. He founded Constantinople as his eastern capital in 330 and gave Christian bishops a major administrative role in the empire.

The Gupta dynasty united much of northern India under **Chandra Gupta,** c.320, and introduced a classic period of urban culture in north India.

The Americas

At the Mayan ceremonial center of Uaxactún in El Petéu, Guatemala, a stela dated AD 328 was found. Murals there provide examples of Mayan painting.

♦ Religion and Philosophy

At the Council of Nicaea, in 325, called by Constantine the Great, a group of bishops from all over the Christian world issued a creed stating that God and Christ are of one identical substance. **The Arianist heresy,** stating that only God was divine and that Christ was created as other men, was condemned by the Council. Constantine continued to support Arianism in spite of this.

📖 Literature

Runes were the early Germanic script, used for magical charms and riddles. One of the earliest surviving examples, dating from the 4th century, is the *Mojbro Stone* from Uppland, which says that a man was slain on his horse.

Art and Architecture

The old church of Saint Peter in Rome was built in 330 but destroyed during the Renaissance. The first religious building designed specifically for the needs of Christian worship, its basilican shape determined the layout of the majority of Western churches. **Sta Costanza,** 323–37, also in Rome, is an early example of the alternative centrally planned style of Christian architecture.

Music

Psalms used by the Christian Church in its liturgy were among the first Christian chants. They were sung as responses by two choirs, or a priest and congregation sang alternate verses.

Science and Technology

Mathematics developed by the Central American Mayas was the first to make use of a symbol for zero. Mayan arithmetic was based on the number 20 and is notable for calculations involving very large numbers. One reason for this may have been the smallness and cheapness of the Mayan unit of money, the cocoa bean.

Yu Hsi studied the equinoxes c.330 and was one of the first astronomers to describe the precession of the equinoxes.

Principal Events

Julian, 331–63, tried unsuccessfully to organize a pagan Church and campaigned against the Franks.

The Persians recaptured Mesopotamia in 364.

Samudra Gupta, the Indian emperor, conquered Bengal and Nepal and broke the power of the tribal republics in northwest India. This marked a victory for caste over tribe.

The Pallava dynasty was set up in southern India c.350.

Japan conquered Korea c.360.

The Americas

Arizona's Canyon de Chelly, with its red sandstone walls, was occupied for about 1,000 years, beginning c.350, by Anasazi and later Pueblo Indians.

Religion and Philosophy

The Latin Fathers of the Church, **Jerome**, c.347–420, and **Ambrose**, 340–97, began their life's work of theological writing and furtherance of monasticism in the West. Jerome was baptized in 366, after he had studied Latin literature. His Latin translation of the Bible, the Vulgate, is still important today.

Literature

The golden age of classical Sanskrit began with the rule of the Guptas, 320–535. The poet and dramatist **Kalidasa**, 388–455, excelled in the epic genre of the *kavya* school.

Art and Architecture

Hsieh Ho's *Six Canons of Painting* is the earliest work on the theory of art, written in the mid-4th century. The Taoist **Ku K'ai Chih**, c.344–406, produced masterly landscapes and genre paintings, conforming to Ho's artistic definitions.

Gupta art flowered with some of the great paintings at the Ajanta caves in the north Deccan. Massive Buddhist stupas were built, with a marked stylistic influence from central Asia and China.

Music

Persia under the Sassanid dynasty, 224–642, was rich in musicians and well developed instruments. Azâda's songs were celebrated in poems. Trumpet, lute, and mouth organ flourished.

Science and Technology

Mayan calandars, superior to those of early Christianity, were developed in order to calculate the year more accurately for religious purposes.

Mayan astronomy was in some ways very advanced, owing to the Mayan concern with time. Thus the Mayas calculated the length of a year on Venus and used it partly to work out the dates of religious festivals.

Principal Events

Roman absorption of the Germanic tribes was reaching its limits.
The Visigoths crossed the Danube in 376 and were settled as military allies by **Theodosius the Great**, *r.*379–95.
Stilicho, *c.*368–408, a Vandal Roman commander, defeated a Visigoth invasion under Alaric.
Christianity received official support from the emperor **Theodosius**, *c.*346–95.
Persian power was at its zenith under **Shapur II**, *r.*309–79.

The Americas

The building of Old Stone Fort, a series of walls on a bluff overlooking the Little Duck River in Tennessee, was begun about AD 1 and completed by 400.

Religion and Philosophy

The spread of Buddhism in China was greatly speeded by **Kumarajiva**, 344–413, who translated Mahayana Buddhist texts from Indian into Chinese.
Theodosius the Great, *r.*379–95, extirpated Arianism and linked the Christian Church with the Roman state.

Literature

The childhood and licentious youth of **Saint Augustine**, 354–430, before the time when he became a Christian convert in 387, is described in his *Confessions*, 397–401.

Art and Architecture

Roman art became increasingly stiff and formalized, as with the ivory diptych of **Stilicho** (a Vandal leader in the Roman army) and his wife Serena, *c.*396. The Jonah Sarcophagus in the Lateran in Rome shows the merging of late Roman classical style with Christian motifs.

Music

Chinese music was further enriched by foreign influences. After the conquest of Kutcha in Turkestan, 384, drums, cymbals, and Persian harps with upper sound chests were imported.

Science and Technology

Chinese astronomers of the 4th century believed, fairly correctly, that the blue of the sky was an illusion and that the Sun, Moon, and stars float freely in space.

The New
Barbarian Kingdoms
400–700

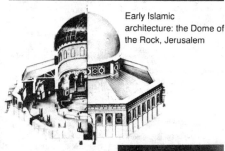

Early Islamic architecture: the Dome of the Rock, Jerusalem

Ceremonial urn from Tiahuanaco, site of a pre-Inca culture

Attila the Hun led an attack on Gaul

Japanese Buddha sculpture, 7th c.

Mosaics from San Apollinare in the Mausoleum of Galla Placidia

Chinese T'ang pottery figure

Merovingian buckle, 6th c.

Early Christian churches: San Stefano Rotundo, Rome

The New Barbarian Kingdoms

Principal Events

After the fall of Rome in 476, the Western Roman Empire divided into a galaxy of unstable "barbarian" kingdoms, which adapted Roman institutions, while the Byzantine Empire became cut off from the west despite Justinian's brief expansion c.550. The growing independence of the papacy and the new monastic movement made Christianity a powerful political weapon among the barbarian kingdoms, so that national conversion and the suppression of heresy had a more than religious significance.

The teachings of Mohammed brought a new unity and aggression to the Arabs, who threatened Constantinople and expanded toward India.

The T'ang dynasty completed the development of the Chinese imperial system, on which Japan modeled its own, while India split into smaller kingdoms with the fall of the Guptas, although the classical era they initiated outlasted them.

The Americas

Mayan architecture flourished, with many of the great ceremonial sites built. Teotihuacán was destroyed at its height, weakening Kaminaljuyú and the civilizations of the Mayan lowlands. Irrigation facilitated farming in southwest North America, while effigy mounds were built in the woodlands.

Religion and Philosophy

With its consolidation and the removal of the threat of alien ideas, the Christian Church turned in upon itself and became engaged in a series of fierce internal doctrinal disputes centering on the many interpretations of the nature of Christ. At the same time Western monasticism emerged with the founding of the Benedictine rule.

Islam arose as a small sect in the early 7th century and quickly became a powerful cohesive movement with an aggressive evangelical mission. By 700 it had spread throughout the Middle East. After the death of the prophet Mohammed, however, it became subject to internal schismatic tendencies deriving from the conflicts between the temporal and spiritual aspects of the Islamic religion.

Buddhism advanced beyond the borders of the Indian subcontinent; by 700 it had become firmly established in both China and Japan.

Literature

The classical tradition of literature largely disappeared with the fall of Rome in 476 but survived in Byzantium and in Christian monasteries where a few late Latin works were influential. Western European literature centered around the heroic myths of the Germanic invaders and the Celts, sung by bardic poets whose verse forms Christian writers later adapted to religious poetry. With the founding of Islam in the Arab world the Koran was collected, but the re-emergence of Arabic poetry would await the prosperous dynasties of the 8th century.

In India and in China under the T'ang dynasty lyric poetry flourished, both religious and secular, while a Japanese writing and literature emerged.

Art and Architecture

The fall of the Western Empire in 476 enabled new art forms combining Celtic, Scandinavian, German, and Roman styles to develop in northern Europe, reaching their high point in the exquisite illuminated manuscripts produced by the Irish and Northumbrian monasteries.

Byzantine art, a sacred and stylized offspring of late Roman art, spread from Greece to Italy, blossoming in the 6th century with the building of Hagia Sophia in Constantinople and S. Vitale at Ravenna—the main cultural center in Italy after the fall of Rome.

Middle Eastern culture, divided until the 7th century between Byzantine and Persian influences, later collapsed before the onslaught of Islam, which absorbed certain elements of church design but forbade the use of representational imagery.

Japanese art during the Asuka period developed a style of its own distinct from that of China and Korea.

Music

In India, ragas were well established by the 5th century, having evolved from traditional melodies and scale theory that utilized many seven-note scales and complex rhythms to evoke various moods. In the West, by 600, Christian monks had developed plainsong to a level of accomplishment, codified by pope Gregory I, that placed it lastingly in the liturgy.

Science and Technology

Chinese science and technology were by far the most active and inventive of this time. Under the T'ang dynasty the sciences and arts were encouraged and science was no longer hampered in any way by religious dogmas or prohibitions. Chinese attitudes to medicine were particularly enlightened: even before the 5th century medical treatment was regarded as a public service and was administered by the state. In astronomy, practical chemistry, and mathematical calculation China also led the world.

By contrast Western science had dwindled to commentaries, and even these often met with discouragement of an extreme kind. Boethius, one of the last important Western commentators of science and philosophy, was executed in 524 by Theodoric the Ostrogoth for advocating a return to political and intellectual liberty. Although overshadowed by China, Indian mathematical, astronomical, and medical sciences also advanced.

Principal Events

The western capital of the Roman Empire retreated to Ravenna in 402.

The Visigoths under **Alaric** sacked Rome, 410, and invaded Spain in 415 under **Ataulf**, displacing the Vandals, who then moved to Africa.

The Franks and Burgundians, who created the first barbarian kingdom inside the empire, occupied Flanders and the Rhineland in 406.

The Americas

Buildings constructed c. 400 at Kaminaljuyú in Guatemala were copied from the architecture of Teotihuacán, probably by invaders from that city.

Religion and Philosophy

Nestorius, consecrated Bishop of Constantinople in 428, maintained that Christ was both divine and human. Three years later **The Council of Ephesus** declared this view heretical. **St Augustine of Hippo,** the greatest theologian of Christian antiquity, combined the New Testament with Platonism. In *The City of God,* c. 410. he described predestination. **The Nestorian Church** developed in Asia Minor.

Literature

Buddhist sacred literature, in its earliest complete forms, appeared in the 5th century Pali texts that collected together the *Jataka Tales* (birth stories). These 547 tales consisted of prose and verse fables about the former births of the Buddha, often in animal forms. Similar tales are found in Aesop and in non-Buddhist Indian literature.

Art and Architecture

The hieratic and stylized form of Roman art can be seen in the ivory carvings "Scenes from the Passion," dating from the early 5th century. Classical ideals of proportion and anatomy were no longer considered important. **Christian architecture** was a blend of Roman and indigenous styles, AD 400– 600. In Egypt monasteries with frescoes were built at Bawit and Sakkara, and the basilica of St Mena was constructed near Alexandria.

Music

The marimba, played today by the Bantu in Africa, developed from a xylophone introduced to Africa by Indonesian immigrants in the 5th century.

Science and Technology

The university of Constantinople was founded in 425 by **Theodosius II,** 401– 50, the Roman emperor of the East, who later (438) produced the **Theodosian Code,** a systematization and simplification of the Roman legal code.

Principal Events

The Huns' attack on Gaul, led by **Attila**, c.406–53, was defeated by a Roman/Visigothic alliance in 452, and their invasion of Italy stopped on Attila's death.

The Vandals attacked Rome in 455 from North Africa and annexed the Mediterranean islands.

After St Patrick's conversion of Ireland the Irish monasteries developed into centers of Christian learning.

The Americas

Although there were many sizes and shapes, bows and arrows were definitely in use in southwest North America by c.450, increasing hunting potential.

Religion and Philosophy

The Council of Chalcedon, 451, in response to the claim of **Pope Leo I** to universal supremacy, declared the Patriarch of Constantinople to be of equal authority. This council also emphasized that Christ had both a human and a divine nature, countering the doctrine of **Monophysitism**, which stated the essential unity of Christ. **St Patrick**, entrusted by Pope Celestine I to convert the Irish people, landed in County Wicklow, Ireland, in 432.

Literature

Japan assimilated Chinese civilization in the first four centuries AD and evolved a writing system of extreme complexity by adapting the script of the monosyllabic Chinese language to convey the phonetics of Japanese. 5th-century songs and myths would not appear in texts until the 8th-century histories *Kojiki* and *Nihon Shoki*.

Art and Architecture

The Mausoleum of Galla Placidia in Ravenna, c.450 shows a Byzantine influence in its plan and its decorations. The mosaics were made over a period of one hundred years and illustrate the shift from the light, decorative qualities of Rome to the somber and awe-inspiring images of a wholly Byzantine style.

Music

Japan adopted music and dance that were to die in their countries of origin. Supple Indian and Chinese forms were considered female, and Korean and Manchurian forms male in character.

Science and Technology

Chinese scientific instruments of the 5th century included water-driven armillary spheres, which revolved in phase with the stars, and a compass, in use since the 2nd century, whose pointer was a metal spoon balanced on its bowl. These spoons would not be replaced by magnetic needles until the 9th century.

Principal Events

The Western Roman Empire ended in 476 when **Odoacer**, *d.493*, set up a barbarian kingdom in Italy. But **Theodoric the Ostrogoth**, *r.471–526*, invaded Italy in his turn in 488.

The Frankish king Clovis I, *r.481–511*, defeated the Roman governor in Gaul in 486 and set up the Merovingian dynasty. **In China** political fragmentation prevented the development of Chinese culture, while Buddhism won many converts.

The Americas

A stela dated 460 was placed at Copán, Honduras, a temple city of the southern Mayan lowlands. Copán was an intellectual center for the Mayans.

Religion and Philosophy

The Shakta and Tantra cults became important in India, emphasizing mystical speculations on divine fertility and energy. These doctrines were regarded as unorthodox by religious teachers. Tantrism was also an important trend in the Buddhist tradition.

Under the Guptas, Vishnaism flourished as a separate cult distinct from **Shivaism**.

The **Yogacara** school of meditative techniques flourished within Buddhism.

Literature

The Jewish Haggadah texts in Palestine and Babylonia used legends, stories, and anecdotes to illustrate ethical and theological matters dealt with in the Talmud. This material, with its lively embellishment of such Old Testament stories as that of Noah, influenced the similar treatment of biblical tales in the miracle plays of medieval Western Europe.

Art and Architecture

The church of St Stefano Rotondo in Rome, 468–83, is exceptional for its entirely circular plan, although the centrally planned style continued a tradition that reached back to the Pantheon.

Chinese art during the Six Dynasties period, 220–589, developed the Han tradition of monumental stone sculpture. In 460 a series of rock-cut shrines were begun in the caves of Yun-kang which contain a 45-ft (13.7-m) figure of a Buddha.

Music

Confucian ceremonies in China closely integrated music, dance, and poetry. Chinese court music and dance expressed the form and calligraphy of poems around which they were created.

Science and Technology

Boethius, 480–524, wrote on the four advanced "arts," geometry, arithmetic, music, and astronomy. Two of these manuscripts survive, *De Institutione Musica*, and *De Institutione Arithmetica*.

Principal Events

Odoacer surrendered in 493 to Theodoric, who set up an Ostrogothic kingdom that was initially recognized by Byzantium, 497. He built his capital at Ravenna. **Clovis** was baptized in 497, becoming the first non-heretical barbarian king and thus winning the support of the papacy and the emperor against the heretical Germanic tribes. In 507 he drove the Visigoths into Spain.

The Americas

The Anasazi, whose descendants were the Pueblos, farmed near Mesa Verde, Colorado. They first built pit houses, but later they moved to cliff dwellings there.

Religion and Philosophy

Buddhism grew in China at the expense of the more elite cult of **Confucianism**. There were two schools of Buddhism, the **T'ien-T'ai sect**, rationalists who sought to integrate Hinayana and Mahayana Buddhism, and the **Mahayana Amitabha sect**, who believed that salvation required reflection on the **Amitabha Buddha** as well as general meditation.

Literature

An oral literature of heroic verse known as **Heldenlieder** developed among the tribes of western Germany. From these songs and from pagan hymns and laments emerged later epic narratives, notably the story of Siegfried and Brunhild, which

was incorporated into Germanic epics like the 13th-century *Song of the Nibelungs* and into the heroic sagas of Iceland.

Art and Architecture

Manuscript illumination was an important art form of the early Christian period. Only four religious texts survive, including the *Vienna Genesis*, a luxurious work on purple ground, and the *Rossano Gospels*, the earliest illustrated version of the New Testament. Both texts date from the early 6th century.

Music

Irish song, carried through Europe by minstrels and monks, revitalized musical composition. It was classical verse, which might be sung to a melody repeated as often as required.

Science and Technology

Indian astronomical literature shows an upsurge that lasted a century, beginning with the publication in the late 5th century of the work of the astronomer **Aryabhata**, 476–550. This mentions rotation of the Earth and the epicyclic movements of planets. He also obtained an extremely accurate calculation for π. **Metal stirrups**, invented in 5th-century Korea and used by the Avars on their incursions from Asia, were first seen in southern Europe c.500.

Principal Events

The Byzantine emperor **Justinian the Great**, r.527–65, temporarily reconquered North Africa in 534 and Italy in 554, and codified Roman law. His alliance with the papacy led to the suppression of heresy in the empire. **Khosru I**, r.531–79, brought Persia to its greatest strength in a protracted war with Byzantium. **The Gupta dynasty** in north India fell in 550.

The Americas

Tiahuanaco was the site of a pre Inca culture near Lake Titicaca on the Peru-Bolivia border, forming in time a widespread cultural "empire."

Religion and Philosophy

St Benedict, c.480–547, founded the first Benedictine monastery c.529. He laid down a complete set of rules for monastic life, including a period of probation before full membership in the monastic community, prohibition of ownership, and most important of all, rules for obedience, celibacy, and humility. His monastic ideal was of a self-contained and self-sufficient community.

Literature

Aristotelean logic was translated into Latin by **Boethius**, c. 480–524, the last great Roman writer. A Christian who served as a minister under Theodoric the Ostrogoth, he was condemned to death and in prison wrote *De consolatione philosophiae*, 523, a treatise in verse and prose on free will, good, and evil that helped spread Greek thought in the Germanic world.

Art and Architecture

The age of **Justinian** saw the flowering of Byzantine architecture. The architecture and mosaics of **S. Vitale**, Ravenna, 526–48, were the splendor of Italy. The great cathedral of **Hagia Sophia** in Constantinople, 532–37, was an architectural and engineering triumph.

King Theodoric's mausoleum in Ravenna, c. 530, is surmounted by a colossal domed monolith, a fitting tribute to the half-barbarian, half-civilized king.

Music

Musical letter notation was introduced by **Boethius**, c.475–525, in *De Institutione musica*, his treatise that was the authoritative work on music until about 1500.

Science and Technology

Justinian, Byzantine emperor, r.527–65, closed the Athenian university because the teachers were not Christians. **John Philoponus**, fl.c.530, speculated that a projectile would gain momentum from the mechanism which fired it, thus arriving at a crude idea of inertia. **Paleontology** was furthered in China in 527 with a book by **Li Tao Yuan** in which he described animal fossils. **Indian decimal notation** began in the 6th century; on later inscriptions a dot signified zero.

Principal Events

Byzantium had reconquered most of the Mediterranean seaboard by 560, but by 571 the Lombards had taken Italy and settled in the North.

The Frankish kingdom stayed divided because of the Merovingian custom of equal division of inheritance between the king's sons.

Persia took southern Arabia from the Abyssinians in 576.

The introduction of Buddhism to Japan in 552 marked the start of a period of Chinese influence.

The Americas

In the Upper Mississippi and Great Lakes area, Woodland peoples constructed their burial mounds in the shapes of birds or animals.

Religion and Philosophy

Buddhism, supported by the Soga clan, was officially introduced into Japan in 552. **Mazdakism,** founded by **Mazdak,** *fl.* 560, in Iran was an offshoot of **Manichaeanism.** Mazdak held that good (light) and evil (darkness) acted by free will and evil (darkness) by chance. Light could only be released into the world by asceticism, vegetarianism, and non-violence.

The prophet Mohammed, was born *c.*570 in Mecca.

Literature

Alliterative bardic verse romanticizing the heroism of Celtic warriors had become an established literary form by the middle of the 6th century. Odes and lays in praise of **King Urien,** *fl.*547–59, were attributed to a Welsh bard Taliesen (by Nennius, *c.*800) who may have been a mythical figure. These would later be collected in the 14th century *Book of Taliesen.*

Art and Architecture

The distinctive Japanese art style of the Asuka period, 552–645, culminated with the temple complex of Horyu-ji Nara. The courtyard with its Pagoda, Konda (Golden Hall) and Kodo (for meetings) was based on the traditional Chinese and Korean layout.

The solid ivory throne of Maximian, archbishop of Ravenna, was carved in Constantinople and was a gift from Emperor Justinian *c.*550.

Music

Harps of six to twelve strings were played by European musicians. The instrument became a symbol of their calling.

Science and Technology

The Ma'daba mosaic, the oldest known map of the Holy Land, shows the area from ancient Byblos to Thebes and has a street plan of Jerusalem. It was made in Palestine *c.* 550.

Silk production was attempted at Byzantium in the 6th century after silkworm eggs had been smuggled out of China and taken there, reputedly by Nestorian monks.

Abacus calculators are described in a mathematical work thought to have been written by **Chen Luan** *c.*570.

Principal Events

Pope Gregory I, *r*.590–604, assisted papal authority by defending Rome against the Lombards.
Persia and Byzantium were at war in Syria–Palestine, 602–28.
The Sui dynasty reunified China in 589 by conquering the southern Chen dynasty.
In Japan, the Soga clan rose to power in 587, introducing a paternalist, Chinese-style constitution.
Irish missionaries worked in Scotland and Germany *c*.600.

The Americas

A Mayan ball court marker, dated 590, in glyph numbers instead of the bar-and-dot system, is carved with the figure of a ball player.

Religion and Philosophy

Mohammed, founder of Islam, received his first prophetic call in 610. Thereafter he began to proclaim his message publicly. His revelation was of a majestic being, the one God, Allah, whose command was that Mohammed was to be his prophet. This and subsequent revelations form the content of the *Koran*, which emphasizes generosity, the goodness and power of God, and retribution on the Day of Judgment.

Literature

An Irish bard, Dallan Forgaill, *d*.597, is credited with the *Eulogy of St Columba*. Its vigorous alliterative style is also found in Irish sagas about the hero **Cú Chulainn**, possibly 7th century, known as the Ulaid cycle. Ireland had a class of professional poets, the filiad. **A Welsh poet**, Aneirin, *c*.600, celebrated northern British heroes in *Y Gododdin*.

Art and Architecture

The Basilica at Turmanin in Syria is a typical eastern variation of Roman Christian architecture, which was common throughout Syria and Palestine before the rise of Islam.
The art of Sassanid Persia of the 5th and 6th centuries shows a combination of Byzantine and Irano-Buddhist styles. Metalwork was highly developed and decorated with complex motifs and intricate filigree work.

Music

Pope Gregory I supervised the compiling and codifying of plain-song *c*.600, giving his name to Gregorian chant, an unaccompanied and unharmonized style that is still used today.

Science and Technology

The diagnosis of disease in China in the 7th century was documented by **Chao Yuan Fang**, *c*.610, who wrote a treatise listing 1,720 diseases classified into 67 groups.

Principal Events

The Muslim era began with the flight of Mohammed, *c.*579-632, from Mecca to Medina in 622. His ideas brought a new unity, sense of responsibility, and aggression to the diverse Arab traders and tribesmen. After Mohammed's death **Caliph Omar**, 581-644 (the head of Islam), expanded the Islamic realm in the Near East.

The T'ang dynasty was founded in China in 618, ruling with a large and powerful imperial bureaucracy.

The Americas

Teotihuacán, at its zenith *c.*500, with a population greater than that of Rome, was conquered and burned. A general decline would begin about 700.

Religion and Philosophy

In **622 Mohammed** and a small following emigrated to Medina after opposition and harassment in their native Mecca. The **Ummah**, or Muslim community, claimed supremacy over tribal or familial loyalties, regarding all Muslims as brothers. In so doing it helped to make Arab society more cohesive. The crucial concept of **jihad** (holy war) was instituted at this time by Mohammed and led to the conquest of Mecca in 630. Mohammed died in 632.

Literature

In **India**, classical Sanskrit literature, which had thrived under the rule of the Guptas, 320-550, reached its late flowering in the poetry of **Bhartrhari**, *c* 570-651, a philosopher who wrote three collections of verses, the *Sataka*, on the sensual pleasures of love, the nature of justice, and the means of liberation from earthly existence.

Art and Architecture

The Great Chalice of Antioch is typical of Christian metalwork from the Roman provinces. It probably dates from the early 7th century, when there was an enormous output of silverware and fine gold jewelry.

The Ashburnham Pentateuch is a masterpiece of vivid narrative illumination dating from the late 6th or early 7th century It is not known where it was made, nor whether by a Jewish or Christian illuminator.

Music

Under the T'ang dynasty, 618-907, orchestral suites and programmatic works, some describing battles, were composed in China. Music-dramas incorporating folk-song developed.

Science and Technology

Chinese surgical treatment in the 7th century included the removal of cataracts.

Windmills, probably invented in Persia in the 7th century, may have had their origin in wind-driven prayer wheels. Another theory, unproven, is that they were inspired by ships' sails. The axis of a wheel, driven by some 6 to 12 sails, was mounted on the first story of a Persian windmill. Stone wheels used for grinding grain were located on the story above.

Principal Events

Disputes about the authority and succession of the caliphate under **Othman**, *d*.656, and **Ali**, *d*.661, led to civil war, which destroyed the unity of the Ummah and led to the establishment of the **Umayyad dynasty** at Jerusalem in 638. The Muslims then took Iran and Egypt. 642, Armenia, 653, and Afghanistan, 664, ruling as an autocratic but tolerant minority.

Japan entered a period of reform in 646, imitating Chinese society.

The Americas

The Mayans' most impressive architectural expression, Palenque in the Chiapas area of Mexico, was being built in a rain forest.

Religion and Philosophy

Following the death of Mohammed, 632, there was a period of conflict in the Ummah over the succession. The supporters of his son-in-law **Ali** were the forerunners of the major **Shi'ite** division of Islam. The puritanical **Kharijites** who opposed Ali withdrew from the main body of the Ummah. The Shi'ites stressed leadership, the Kharijites community and permanent religious aggression.

Literature

The Koran reached its final form 651–52. Written partly in rhymed prose reflecting the mood of Mohammed during his life as a solitary visionary preacher, it was regarded by Muslims as the perfect word of God. Its style and thought permeated the literature of Islam, an expansionist force that took many Persian stories to Europe.

Art and Architecture

The Sutton Hoo treasure comes from the grave of an East Anglian king who died in 654. It includes superb examples of Anglo-Saxon decorative metalwork. **Christian scholars and artists** who took refuge in Ireland during the period of the Anglo-Saxon invasions produced an abstract and extremely ornate style of illumination, the 7th-century *Book of Durrow* being one of the best surviving examples.

Music

Classical Arab music evolved richly under the Umayyad caliphs, 661–750, in Damascus. **Ibn Misjah**, *d. c.*715, codified its theory, embracing eight modes for lute music.

Science and Technology

Greek fire, used in the defense of the Byzantine Empire in the 7th century, was a highly inflammable substance of uncertain composition. Probably a mixture of pitch, naphtha, and potash, it could be discharged from tubes in the prows of ships.

Fine metalwork including cloisonné, enamel, and lathe-turned jewelry was found at the Sutton Hoo ship burial dating *c.*650, showing that metallurgy in the Dark Ages was not only used to make swords.

Principal Events

The Islamic world was divided by disputes, which led to the emergence of the Sunni, Shi'ite, and Khawarij sects, reflecting the problems of succession and the growing discontent at the prosperity of the Meccans, which was increasing at the expense of other Muslims.
A 30-year truce was concluded between the Byzantine and Muslim empires after the failure of the Muslim blockade of Constantinople in 673–78.

The Americas

The sculptured portal, Gateway of the Sun, at Tiahuanaco, Peru, was carved c.700 with 48 relief figures and a central gateway god.

Religion and Philosophy

The Monothelites were condemned as heretics at the ecumenical council at Constantinople in 681. The heresy concerned the divinity and humanity of Christ. The Monothelites, following the decision reached at Chalcedon, claimed that although Christ had two natures he had a single will. The Council insisted on Christ's duality by asserting that both a divine and a human will were in Christ's person.

Literature

The first named English poet, Caedmon, fl.670, used the meter and diction of Old English pagan verse to compose poems on biblical and religious themes at the monastery of Whitby. A nine-line "Hymn on the Creation" is the most generally accepted of several works attributed to him in a 10th-century MS. He was an untutored herdsman, according to the Venerable Bede.

Art and Architecture

The Dome of the Rock in Jerusalem is the first great Islamic architectural monument. Construction began in 688 in the reign of Abd al-Malik, but the design was a creative adaptation of Christian church buildings.
Book illumination reached great heights in Northumberland. The *Lindisfarne Gospels*, c.700, combine the Roman narrative tradition with the decorative skill of the Celts.

Music

Arab modes were nearly identical to Greek modes, but were performed with rich embellishments characteristic of the sinuous ornamentation of much Arab visual art and architecture.

Science and Technology

Swords were the most advanced product of Burgundian and Frankish metallurgy in the 7th and 8th centuries. Their blades were expertly forged, with strips of decorative metal running along the whole length. Handles and scabbards were inset with jewels and welded decorations. **In northern England** the tides and moon were studied by the **Venerable Bede,** c.673–735, who also wrote a treatise on finger reckoning.

Islam Reaches India and Spain 700–1000

The Stupa of Borobudur, Java, 8th c.–9th c.

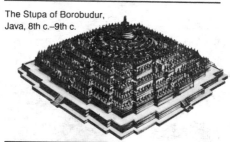

Mayan Puuc architecture: the Nunnery at Uxmal

The Vikings invaded Europe by ship.

Arab manuscript showing preparation of perfumes

Carolingian church, *c.* 800

Islamic architecture: Mosque at Córdoba (interior), built by the Moors

Islam Reaches India and Spain

Principal Events

Invasions from the Muslims in Spain, Vikings in the north, and Magyars in the east destroyed much of Europe's culture and economic strength, although Charlemagne's conquests east of the Rhine brought Germany within the European orbit.

The Muslim world reached from Spain to Afghanistan by 736, and the papacy, although relatively isolated by Muslim control of the Mediterranean, used its new states for political ends, reviving the Roman ideal by crowning its main supporters Holy Roman Emperor. Royal authority in Europe at this time was often precarious, based only on the personal allegiance of a provincial nobility whose power was strengthened by the need to defend the kingdom's frontiers.

In China constant warfare weakened the T'ang armies and the Sung dynasty gained control, while in Japan the Heian period marked a moment of transition to a society run on feudal lines.

The Americas

The year 900 marked the change from the Classic to the Post-Classic period of Mayan civilization in Mesoamerica. In North America, the Mississippian tradition developed in the eastern woodlands and the Pueblo civilization in the southwest. The Tiahuanco-Huari culture dominated in South America.

Religion and philosophy

The Christian Church continued the struggle to assert its authority over the secular powers of the Holy Roman and Byzantine empires while the assertion of the primacy of the Roman popes over the Eastern Church led to an increasing separation of Eastern and Western forms of Christianity. In the West, papal sanction of Charlemagne's empire brought the Church additional prestige. The practices of the clergy, however, were becoming increasingly lax and would eventually prompt the Cluniac reform movement.

In the Islamic world, the Sufi movement was founded and grew, emphasizing an austere mysticism in response to the rational ideal and the reason of orthodox Islam.

The spread of Buddhism within Japan continued and won official support.

Mayan religion reached its elaborate hierarchical form at the height of the empire's power in Central America.

Literature

Chinese literature of the T'ang dynasty reached its finest form in the evocative poetry of Li Po, Tu Fu, and Wang Wei in the 8th century. With the later decline of the dynasty, social criticism and an elegiac mood appeared. Chinese influence on Japanese literature gave way to new vernacular forms of Japanese verse and prose.

The spread of Islam led to more sophisticated themes in Arabic poetry and to an extension of Arabic influence into Persian literature.

The epic saga took shape in Norway and Iceland. In England scholastic Latin developed and the growing power of Anglo-Saxon vernacular literature showed itself in the saga of *Beowulf*, in religious poetry, and in the *Anglo-Saxon Chronicle*.

Art and architecture

After the period of confusion that followed the decline of the Roman Empire, European art again flourished. A Germanic decorative style subordinating realistic representation to stylized patterns is found in jewelry, Viking carving, and Celtic manuscripts. In architecture, elements of the Romanesque developed, based on a combination of Roman, Byzantine, and Carolingian art, replacing the Italian basilicas of the early northern churches with more complex structures using a system of bays often with vaulted roofs.

Islamic art entered its classical age in the 9th century, the religious ban on figurative art producing a wealth of geometric designs in architectural detail, while Islamic and Christian styles mingled in Spain.

Buddhist art flourished throughout the East, contributing to a mingling of cultural styles as Chinese influence reached Japan, while China itself felt the impact of Indian ideas.

Music

The establishment of the Divine Office and Mass by the 9th century encouraged the development of chants more complex than Gregorian chant. At the same time, the Muslim invasion of Western Europe brought schools of singing, lute playing, and musical theory, which would have a lasting influence on European music over the next five hundred years.

Science and technology

The rise of Islam transformed the course of European science and philosophy. The Arabs were heirs to the Hellenic Greeks and acknowledged their role as custodians of that culture. Following the Athenian tradition they founded a number of schools for wide-ranging, unprejudiced, and objective study, most important of which was the Academy of Science at Baghdad. A great respect for Greek learning, and particularly for Aristotle, may have held them back from even greater discoveries, but some Arab scientists rejected Aristotle, arguing for a more experimental approach to science. With the spread of the Arab Empire, Arabic became the language of science outside the Far East, absorbing elements of Indian astronomy while benefiting to a lesser extent from achievements in China. Many Arabic texts on astronomy, chemistry, and mathematics retained their influence until modern science began in Europe with the work of Galileo and Newton.

Principal Events

Pope Gregory II, r.715–31, appointed St Boniface, c.672–754, to convert Germany
The Umayyad Arabs took Spain in 715.
Leo III, r.717–41, defeated the second Arab siege of Constantinople, 717–18, and began the iconoclastic controversy in 726, asserting the religious authority of the emperor and limiting the spread of monasticism.
The Nara period in Japan began with the establishment of a capital at Heijō in 710.

The Americas

In the transition period the Pueblo Indians of the North American Southwest gave up their pithouses and began building aboveground communal dwellings.

Religion and Philosophy

Iconoclasm as a movement began, 726, when the Byzantine emperor **Leo II** prohibited the use of icons as idolatrous, claiming the emperor was God's "vice-regent" on earth.
A period of severe repression and conflict between Church and state followed in which sacred images of Christ, the Virgin Mary, and various saints were destroyed.
The Islamic religion reached India in 712 and Spain in 715.

Literature

The Venerable Bede, 673–735, wrote his *History of the English Church and People,* a major source of information on England between 597 and 731. He drew on wide sources in creating a work of literary and historical value.
In India, the Sanskrit dramatist Bhavabhutti, fl.730, wrote three outstanding plays, two of which tell the story of **Rama.**

Art and Architecture

Byzantine icons have survived from Sinai, Constantinople, and Rome. The early beginnings of defined painting schools can be seen in the life-size "Enthroned Virgin and Child," c.705, commissioned by Pope John VII.
Chinese Buddhist sculpture combined the traditional linear delicacy with the Indian sense of form, resulting in such superb statues as the seated stone Buddha, 711.

Music

The first composition by known European composers took the form of tropes, melodic passages added to the liturgy either as new music or as variations on the preceding plainsong melody.

Science and Technology

Mayan science, with its detailed astronomical observations and advanced use of mathematics, reached its peak.

Principal Events

Charles Martel, *c.*688– 741, stopped the Muslim invasion of Europe at Poitiers, 732, and assisted Boniface in Germany. His son **Pepin**, *r.*747– 68, campaigning in Italy, established papal temporal power by a donation of land to the papacy, 756.

Al Mansur, *r.*754– 75, founded the **Abbasid Caliphate**, defeating the Umayyads in North Africa and the Near East, 750.

The Gurjara-Pratihara dynasty defended India against the Muslims after 740.

The Americas

In 756 the **Hieroglyphic Stairway** at Copán, Honduras, was dedicated. Copán hosted, *c.*765, an assembly to correct the Mayan calendar.

Religion and Philosophy

The Classical period in Mayan culture in Central America reached its height. Mayan cosmology saw the earth as a crocodile, and the Mayans placated their gods with sacrifices.

Buddhism in Japan became the state cult in the reign of **Shomu**, who built a magnificent Buddha (**Daibutsu**) and a temple (**Todaiji**) in Nara, in 743– 52.

Literature

Nearly **49,000 poems** survive from China's golden age of poetry, the **T'ang dynasty**. **Tu Fu**, 712– 70, showed his mastery of imagery in such lines as "Blue is the smoke of war, white the bones of men." Equally famous is **Li Po**, 701– 62 who wrote of wine and companionship. **Wang Wei**, 699– 759, was a painter and poet of nature. The strict 8-line *shih* form predominated.

Art and Architecture

The Iconoclastic age lasted in the Byzantine Empire from 726–843. In order to stop the cult of images and discourage monasticism, all figurative representations, except of the Cross, were either defaced or destroyed.

The earliest Orissan-style temples were built at Bhuvanesvar in east India, 700– 800. A hollow terraced pyramid supported a conical beehive-shaped spire.

Music

The Arabs in conquering Spain brought with them **the lute** (the first fretted instrument to arrive in Europe), **the rebec** (an ancestor of the violin), and the violin type of bow.

Science and Technology

Jabir, or **Gebir**, *c.*721– 815, the "father of Arabic chemistry," left evidence of a systematic approach to this science, relatively uncluttered by alchemical superstitions. For example, Jabir described the manufacture of nitric acid and how it may be used in extracting silver and gold from their ores or salts.

Gunpowder, probably invented in China in the 8th century, was used initially to make fireworks and only much later in weaponry.

Principal Events

Charlemagne, r.768–814, united France and conquered Italy in 774, northern Spain in 777, Saxony in 785, and Bavaria in 788. **Baghdad** became the Abbasid capital in 762.
An Umayyad dynasty emerged at Córdoba in Spain, 756, tolerating Jews and Christians. **Scandinavian trade** with Byzantium began c.770.
Turkish and Tibetan tribesmen threatened western China c.763.

The Americas

An influential civilization, the Mississippian Culture, flourished in the central and lower Mississippi River valleys after 700.

Religion and Philosophy

The new Anglo-Saxon humanism was introduced in France by the Northumbrian monk **Alcuin**, c.732–804, who met **Emperor Charlemagne**, 781, and became an important figure in the **Carolingian Renaissance**. Alcuin encouraged the study of the liberal arts. His revision of the liturgy of the Frankish Church was carried throughout Charlemagne's empire and he created a new edition of the Vulgate.

Literature

Beowulf, the greatest surviving Anglo-Saxon epic poem, dates between 700 and 1000. A vivid narrative of a warrior's struggles against dragons and sea monsters, it is based on north European heroic legend, with elements of moral and religious significance probably added by later Christian writers. Chinese poet **Po Chü-i**, 772–846, wrote didactic verse.

Art and Architecture

The Great Mosque at Córdoba was built by Spain's Arab conquerors, 785–990. The naves use elegant star vaulting and the whole was intricately decorated with colored marbles and precious stones.
The Book of Kells was produced in Ireland at the end of the 8th century. It is the finest and most elaborate of early Western illuminated manuscripts.

Music

"Ut Queant Laxis" — written c.770 — was an early medieval hymn tune in the then unusual form of six separate phrases, each starting a step or half step higher than the previous one.

Science and Technology

Printing with blocks from which the letters stand out in relief was invented in Japan in or prior to the 8th century.
Bells and organ pipes, made at this time from bronze, indicate an advance in European metalworking.

★ Principal Events

Charlemagne was crowned Holy Roman Emperor, 800, reviving the idea of a Western Roman Empire. Byzantium recognized the title in 812.

The Bulgar kingdom reached its peak under **Krum**, r.808–14.

Ghana was an important trading kingdom, bringing gold from southern Africa to the Sahara.

Emperor Kammu, r.781–806, instituted the Heian period in Japan, 794–1185, in which indigenous feudalism superseded the Chinese-based social order.

The Americas

The Frescoes at Bonampak in the Mexican jungle were painted c.800. A splendid example of Mayan art, they illustrate the Mayan lifestyle.

Religion and Philosophy

The Tendai and Shingon sects were founded in Japan c.805 by Buddhist monks returning from a visit to China.

Sankara, 780–820, the most important member of the new **Vedanta school of philosophy** in India, affirmed the one true reality (**Brahma**) as the source of all things. He also wrote commentaries on the *Upanishads* and *Brahma Sutra*.

Literature

A rebirth of European learning took place under **Charlemagne**, 768–814, who encouraged the copying of old manuscripts. His biography was written by the German monk **Einhard**, 770–840, in personal and political terms. Charlemagne's court at Aachen attracted scholars such as **Alcuin**, c.732–804, an Anglo-Latin writer and cleric with a humanistic outlook.

Art and Architecture

A Viking earth barrow, c.800, contained the Oseberg ship, as well as a cart, several sledges, and numerous small decorated objects. The delicate interwoven wood carvings of figures and abstract motifs are typical of northern art.

Charlemagne's Palace Chapel at Aachen in Germany was consecrated in 805. Local Roman remains and the church of S. Vitale in Ravenna were used as models in an assertion of the continuity of the empire.

Music

Arab music entered its golden age under **Harun al-Rashid**, c.764–809, whose musical tastes are revealed in *The Arabian Nights*. A style of romantic song flourished in the period.

Science and Technology

Arab paper was made in Baghdad for the first time, 793, following the capture of Chinese papermakers during the battle for the city of Samarkand in 751.

Viking ships of the 9th century were clinker-built (using overlapping planks) with square sails, a single steering oar aft, and many rowing oars. Their narrow hull shape made them faster than Mediterranean ships.

The Baghdad Academy of Science replaced Jundishapur, Persia, as the center of scientific learning c.800.

820-850

Principal Events

The Carolingian Empire was divided into three parts at the Treaty of Verdun in 843. **Scandinavians**, having founded Kiev and Novgorod, absorbed Byzantine culture and religion through trading contacts. *c.*850. **Al-Mamun the Great**, *r.*813–33, set up a House of Knowledge in Baghdad and encouraged the most glorious epoch of the Abbasid dynasty.
The Abbasid capital moved to Samarra in 836.

The Americas

The civilizations of Tiahuanaco and Huari merged and began to spread their influence and cultural style over most of Peru.

Religion and Philosophy

Ahmad Ibn Hanbal, 780–855, within the **Sunni branch of Islam**, founded the most orthodox of the four schools of Islamic law, which holds that the *Koran* as interpreted by the Islamic community contains the answers to all moral questions. In 833 **Hanbal** was imprisoned for refusing to accept **Mutazili** rationalist doctrines. **The Ch'an school**, the precursor of Japanese **Zen** Buddhism, developed in China.

Literature

Arabic literature had a strong tradition of lyrical desert poetry, which re-emerged at the peak of the **Abbasid Empire**, 786–861. The lyrics of **Abu Nuwas**, *c.*762– 815, reflected the town life of the caliphates, while Islam influenced the religious poetry of **Abu al-Atahiya**, 748–826. Another poet, **Abu Tamman**, *c.*807–50, edited the fine Hamasu anthology.

Art and Architecture

The constructional and geometric skills of Islam are seen in the spiral ramped minaret of the **Malwiyya Mosque**, begun at Samarra in 848.

Music

Plainsong notation, which originated in Europe in the 9th century, first consisted of marks like accents over syllables to denote a rise and fall in pitch; they did not indicate by how much.

Science and Technology

Spanish metal mines were taken over *c.*850 by the Moors, who also prepared pure copper by reacting its salts with iron – a primitive forerunner of modern electroplating methods.
Al-Farghani, or Alfraganus, *d.*850, wrote the *Elements*, a summary of Ptolemaic astronomy studied in Europe until 1600. **Algebra**, as a word, first figures as al-jabr, meaning transposition in a treatise by the Arab mathematician **Al-Khwarizmi**, *d. c.*850. The Arabs based their algebra on both Greek and Indian maths.

Principal Events

Frequent invasions and the weakness of the monarchy gave new power to the provincial nobility in the Carolingian states and in Italy caused a decline in papal authority.
Roman and Byzantine Christianity officially split in 867.
Basil I of Byzantium, *r*.867–86, attacked the Muslims in Mesopotamia and stimulated a revival of Byzantine civilization.
The Bulgarians were converted to Christianity in 865.

 **The Americas**

The Mayans completed two waves of migration that took them out of the Mexican lowlands and into the Yucatán Peninsula.

 Religion and Philosophy

The Fourth Council of Constantinople was called in 867–70 by **Basil I**. It deposed Photius, patriarch of Constantinople, who had challenged the pope's authority in the East, and reinstated Ignatius, *c*.800–877, thus ending the schism with Rome.

 Literature

Vernacular literature in both prose and verse was created in Germany and Britain, best shown in the plain narrative style of the *Anglo-Saxon Chronicle*, a history begun during the reign of **Alfred the Great** *c*.870–99. The heroic **Edda** lays began to develop in Iceland after 860.

 Art and Architecture

The Middle Byzantine age, 867–1025, saw a second flowering of Byzantine art with the energetic redecoration of pre-Iconoclast churches. The mosaic of the "Madonna and Child" in the church of Hagia Sophia dates from 867. Figurative representation became increasingly stylized with the characteristic Byzantine distortion of a face—a small mouth, a long nose, and huge, wide open eyes.
The early German abbey of Corvei was begun in 873.

 Music

Organum, the practice of singing extra lines of music at intervals of a fourth or a fifth above or below plainsong, appeared in the 9th century. This was primitive polyphony.

 Science and Technology

Al-Rhazi, a physician and encyclopedist, *c*.920, and **Al-Khindi,** a scientist and philosopher, *c*.873, were exceptional in objecting to alchemical and Aristotelian dogmas. They sought new concepts of the nature of motion and heat and encouraged the use of experiments to solve scientific problems.
Bardas reorganized the University of Constantinople in 863 for the teaching of science. Soon afterward the teaching was again suppressed by **Basil II,** *r*.963–1025.

★ Principal Events

Urban development in northern Europe, stimulated by long-distance overland trade, was disrupted by Norse raiders c.900.

The Bulgarians warred constantly with Byzantium under **Symeon I**, r.893–927.

The Chola dynasty displaced the Pallavas in India in 888.

The T'ang dynasty in China fell in 907 and was followed by a period of weak imperial authority and constant barbarian invasions.

The Americas

Monks Mound, or Cahokia, which was under construction c.900 and took over two centuries to complete, extends over 18 acres in Illinois.

Religion and Philosophy

The Abbey of Cluny in France was founded, 910, marking a revival of the monastic movement. It was here that the **Cluniac reform movement** began, which introduced the notion that the Church hierarchy has a responsibility for clerical discipline and formed the basis of a widespread attack on abuses and corruption in the Church.

Literature

Classical Japanese literature emerged in the **Heian period**, 794–1192. The *Kokinshu*, 905, was an anthology of short poems with themes of love and nostalgia, showing the flexibility made possible by the phonetic *kana* script. The Welsh monk **Asser**, d.909, wrote a biography of Alfred the Great, 893.

Art and Architecture

Phnom Bakheng became the new administrative and religious center of Cambodia during the Angkor period, 889–1434. The "mountain temple" design has a single base supporting six tower-like structures.

Music

Pitch notation was required to communicate to singers the relationship of two parts in an organum. A Flemish monk called **Hucbald**, 840–930, first used letters to denote pitch.

Science and Technology

Cotton and silk manufacture was introduced into Spain and Sicily by the Moors in the 9th and 10th centuries.

Lateen sails, triangular fore-and-aft sails, which may have appeared in the eastern Mediterranean in the 2nd century, were brought to the West in the 9th century by the Arabs.

★ Principal Events

Rollo, *c.*860– 932, founded an independent dukedom of Normandy in 911 and was baptized in 912.

Henry I, *r.*919– 36, became the first Saxon king to rule a unified Germany, whereas the French monarchy was weak.

Umayyad culture reached its zenith in Spain under **Abd ar-Rahman III,** *r.*912– 61.

The rise of a military class in Japan resulted in civil strife in the provinces, 935– 41.

The Americas

A struggle for control of the Oaxaca Valley of Mexico had begun *c.*900 when the Mixtecs invaded the Zapotec stronghold.

◊ Religion and Philosophy

Sufism, a mystical literary and philosophical movement within Islam, stressed divine love through the immediate personal union of the soul with God. It developed as a reaction against more orthodox interpretations of the *Koran,* and **Al Halláj,** who was crucified in 922 for his teachings, became revered as a Sufi martyr.

Literature

Lyric and elegiac Anglo-Saxon poetry survives in a manuscript known as the *Exeter Book.* This included individualistic poems such as "The Seafarer" as well as work by an earlier poet, **Cynewulf,** *fl.*850. "The Dream of the Rood" was a notable poem on the Crucifixion.

▥ Art and Architecture

During the Chola period, 907– 1053, in India, improved metal-casting techniques enabled notable achievements in figurative images, especially in portraying the complex and balanced poses of the dancing Shiva.

♪ Music

Organs were installed in abbeys and cathedrals of Europe by the 10th century. They were played to support parts of the organum sung by the choir, and followed the sung lines.

⚛ Science and Technology

Córdoba, in Spain, reached its height as a center of Islamic science in the 10th century under **Abd-ar-Rahman III,** 912– 61. **Optical lenses** of four kinds were described by **Than Chhiao** in China *c.*940.

★ Principal Events

Otto I, *r.*936–73, ended the recurrent Magyar invasions at the battle of Lechfeld in 955 and became the first Saxon Holy Roman Emperor in 962.
The Northern Sung dynasty, founded in 960, brought a more modern humanism to Chinese government, social organization, and thought.
A Muslim **Ghaznavid** dynasty grew up in Afghanistan in 962.

The Americas

The Nunnery at Uxmal in Mexico was the highest achievement of a very late Mayan architectural style called Puuc. It was completed in the 10th century.

Religion and Philosophy

Sa'adia ben Joseph, head of the **Jewish academy in Babylon,** is known as the father of Jewish philosophy. He defended orthodox Judaism by reaffirming a belief in one God against gnostic dualism. He also repudiated the earlier **Koraite** rejection of the Talmud (the oral tradition of law) in favor of the Torah (the original scriptures that were given to Moses).

Literature

In China, with the continuing decline of the T'ang dynasty and the unrest of the 10th century, nostalgia suffused the **tzu poetry** of **Li Yu,** 937–78. The *tzu* poets adapted the irregular structure and colloquial language of Chinese folk verse, usually sung to a tune.

Art and Architecture

An Imperial Academy of painting was founded in western China during the Ten Kingdoms period, 907–80. **Ching Hao,** 900–60, wrote an essay on landscape painting that stressed the metaphysical implications of the art.

Music

The tambura, a 4-stringed lute-shaped instrument, developed in India in the 10th century as a drone accompaniment to melodic instruments.

Science and Technology

The alembic, an apparatus for distilling chemicals and perfumes, was illustrated in Arabic books of this time. The alembic played an important part in Arab chemistry and strongly influenced its development.

Principal Events

Hugh Capet, r.987–96, became king of France and reasserted royal authority over the nobility, pope, and emperor.
Venice was given trading privileges in the Byzantine Empire in 992.
Viking invasions of Europe reached their peak c.1000, threatening southern France and Italy.
Basil II of Byzantium, r.963–1025, took Greece from the Bulgarians in 996.

The Americas

Quetzalcóatl, priest-ruler of the military aristocracy of the Toltec people in central Mexico, abdicated in 987.

Religion and Philosophy

The Vikings, whose incursions into the Christian world reached a peak c.1000, worshiped gods similar to those of the Germans. There were two tribes of gods, one of them (**the Aesir**) led by Odin, who lived in the castle Valhalla where he was joined by heroes killed in battle and assisted by them in a perpetual fight against wolves.

Literature

A revival of Persian poetry using the Arabic alphabet produced the national epic *Shah-Nama* (Book of Kings) by **Firdausi**, 935–1020, who used legend and history in verse that became a model for Arab epics.

An **Anglo-Saxon historical poem** with a central theme of feudal loyalty was *The Battle of Maldon*, c.995.

Art and Architecture

Romanesque architecture after 950 possessed a grandiose quality that derived partly from the use of stone vaults below the roofs and partly from a more unified concept of the church, which developed in response to the needs of the clergy, monks, and pilgrims who used them. Two main plans were influential—that of an ambulatory with radiating chapels as at St Martin at Tours, and the chapels on either side of the main apse at Cluny Abbey.

Music

Chinese temple music under the Northern Sung dynasty, 960–1279, involved huge choruses with orchestras of zithers and mouth organs in an organum style of complex sonority.

Science and Technology

The windmill reached Muslim Spain from Persia in the 10th century.
Mining in Christian Europe centered on the Harz Mountains in the 10th century, where the Saxons mined copper and iron.
Gerbert, a French mathematician, 940–1003, who became Pope Sylvester II, is thought to have introduced the astrolabe and Arabic (Indian) numerals into Europe from Córdoba. He has also been credited with the invention of a mechanical clock c.996.

The Crusades
1000–1250

Bayeux tapestry: William the Conqueror and companions

Chichén Itzá architecture, Mexico

European pedal-powered treadle loom

Classical Khmer architecture: temple complex at Angkor Wat

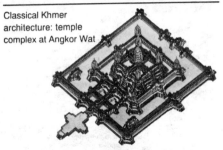

Crusading Knights: Hospitaller, Teutonic, Templar

Genghis Kahn: Mongol leader

Early Gothic: León Cathedral

The Crusades

⭐ Principal Events

Europe now began to take the offensive, expanding geographically and economically, her population rising. A new spirit of confidence, epitomized by the cosmopolitanism of Norman culture, brought a series of attacks on the Muslims in Spain and in Syria, where the Crusades provided an aggressive outlet for the military nobility of the flourishing feudal system. The papacy reached the height of its power during the reign of Innocent III, 1198-1216, in spite of continuing opposition to the gradual concentration of its power both from within the Church and from secular rulers.

In the 13th century Genghis Khan set up a Mongol Empire in China, swept across Asia and threatened Europe and North Africa, creating the largest empire ever known and bringing a new peace and unity to Asia in his wake. He did not, however, conquer India, where the various Muslim rulers built up their authority in the north.

The Americas

The first white men to explore the Americas came from Scandinavia, but their visit had little impact.

The Inca Empire was beginning in the Cuzco Valley in Peru, while in another valley in Mexico the Aztecs appeared. The Pueblo tradition flourished in the southwest United States.

⚱ Religion and Philosophy

In the emerging struggle for power between the Church and the rulers of the new European states, the papacy succeeded in asserting its right to judge the morality of secular political actions at the same time as it took the lead in the reform movements within the church.

In both the Muslim and Christian worlds, there was a revival of philosophy and a return to the Greeks, especially Aristotle. This was essential to the rise of scholasticism, an important philosophical movement within the Catholic tradition, based on the notion that dialectical reasoning as well as faith and revelation could illuminate the mysteries of Christian belief.

The Mahayana form of Buddhism, which allowed lay salvation, spread from China to Japan. There it evolved into a popular devotional cult centered on ritual chanting, in sharp contrast to the elitist monasticism of Zen, which was also emerging within Japanese Buddhism at this time.

✍ Literature

Of the European literatures, French was the most influential in the development of new literary forms in the 11th and 12th centuries, producing the chanson de geste in written form, the Arthurian romance tradition, and the lyrical vernacular poetry of the troubadours, all of which soon became international. The common heritage of warfare against the Muslims in Spain was the subject of the French *Chanson de*

Roland and also of the great Spanish epic *El Cid*.

In the Near East the solitary genius of Omar Khayyám flourished, while in Japan the late Heian period saw the emergence of underivative Japanese styles including the literary diary of which *The Tale of Genji*, written by a lady at court, is the best known example.

Art and Architecture

The transition from Romanesque to Gothic architecture involved a structural and visual change in the aisled church, beginning in France and England. Separate inventions—stronger pointed arches at Cluny and rib vaults at Lessay—were then combined as in the vaults of Durham, which were supported by buttresses beneath the gallery roofs. External flying buttresses, first used at Notre Dame, allowed Gothic architecture to develop. With these the building became an independent frame in which larger windows were inserted. Bar tracery produced the lovely patterns of French 13th century architecture, which spread swiftly across Europe, reaching Cologne in 1248 and England with the additions to Westminster Abbey in 1245.

Castles developed from the primitive motte-and-bailey to the sophisticated designs of the Crusaders' permanent garrisons, such as the Krak des Chevaliers (first fortified 1110) in Syria.

Music

Polyphony developed further in both the religious and secular music of Europe in the Middle Ages, having long existed in folk music, particularly in Britain. At the same time set musical forms, like the ballade, virelai, and rondeau, evolved from songs and dances. Both developments reflected the medieval delight in uniting contrasting elements in a consistent whole.

Science and Technology

Arabic science and philosophy reached its height in the 11th century with the work of such major figures as Avicenna, al-Biruni, and Alhazen in the Middle East and Averroes in Spain, but soon afterward it declined. It was at this time, in the early 12th century, that the influence of Arab science began to show itself in Europe with the introduction of Arabic numerals. These were used in the already powerful business world of Italy which, unlike China and the Arab lands, was to develop an economy based on money. Other signs of the power Europe was to achieve were rapid growth in the silk and glass industries in the south and the use of coal and the beginnings of cast iron manufacture in the north. This technology owed a heavy debt to Chinese expertise, brought to Europe at this stage via the Arab world but later derived directly from China, which would trade extensively with Italy after the visits of Marco Polo.

★ Principal Events

Basil II, 958–1025, briefly restored Byzantine authority in Syria, Crete, and south Italy and destroyed the Bulgarian army. **Canute**, 994–1035, built a unified Danish Empire comprising England, Norway, and Denmark. **Mahmud**, the brilliant Muslim ruler of the Ghaznavid Empire in Afghanistan, 997–1030, plundered and annexed the Punjab. **The Chola dynasty** of Tamil kings unified southern India and took Ceylon and Bengal, 1001–24.

The Americas

Leif Ericson visited North America c.1000, calling the area Vinland. A Norse colony was established at L'Anse aux Meadows in Newfoundland.

Religion and Philosophy

Saint Symeon (Simon), c.949–1022, "The New Theologian," developed the orthodoxy within the Greek Church on meditation and revelation in a mystical direction.
Pope Benedict VIII, r.1012–24, promulgated a decree against clerical marriage and concubinage at the Council of Pavia in 1022.

Literature

The greatest of all Japanese novels, The Tale of Genji, was written by the court lady **Murasaki Shikibu**, 978–c.1031; it is an elaborate, realistic tale of court life. Japanese ladies of the Heian court wrote witty prose, notably the *Pillow Book of Sei Shonagon*, c.1000.

Art and Architecture

Ottonian architecture in Germany took its cue from **St Michael's Hildesheim** (designed apparently by Bishop Bernward) with its unvaulted double choirs and arcades of square piers alternating with round, short columns. **Dravidian architecture** reached a peak of sophistication under the Chola period in India. The great **Temple of Shiva** at Tanjore with its pyramid and dome-shaped finial profoundly influenced Southeast Asian architecture.

Music

A cantus firmus was used as a fixed melody about which a line of embellishment could be worked. In this could be seen the origins of counterpoint.

Science and Technology

Avicenna (Ibn Sina), 980–1037, and **Al-Biruni**, 943–1048, were two of the greatest Arab encyclopedists of science. **Avicenna** wrote on astronomy, physics, and medicine, which he also practiced, and his theory and methods were taught in Europe for the next 700 years. **Al-Biruni** wrote on mathematics, astronomy and astrology, geography, and history, and was the first botanist to analyze the structure of flowers by methods important to plant classification.

Principal Events

William I, a vassal of the French king, became Duke of Normandy in 1035, organizing Normandy on full feudal and military lines.
The Umayyad dynasty in Spain fell as a result of racial and religious pressures in 1031. The support of **Pope Leo IX**, r.1049–54, for monastic reform stimulated the concept of papal supremacy over secular rulers.
Yaroslav, r.1019–54, brought Kievan Russia to its peak (promoting education and building).

The Americas

The architecture of **Chichén Itzá**, in the central Yucatán, Mexico, began to show strong Toltec influences after 1000, particularly the feathered-serpent motif.

Religion and Philosophy

Avicenna, 980–1037, also known as Ibn Sina, was an eclectic Muslim thinker and physician. He wrote *The Book of Healing*, a monumental encyclopedia elaborating mainly Aristotelian theories of philosophy and medicine.
Buddhism became firmly established in Tibet in 1038.
Pope Leo IX, r.1049–54, issued stern decrees against simony (the purchase of ecclesiastical office), thereby identifying the papacy with Cluniac reform.

Literature

The **Sung period**, 960–1279, in China was mostly an age of prose. Its great writers were Ou-

Yang Hsiu, 1007–72, and **Sung Chi**, 998–1061, who collaborated on a Confucian history. **Su Shih**, 1037–1101, widened the subject matter of tzu (song form) poetry and introduced vernacular words, thus contributing to Yan "drama" which resembled opera.

Art and Architecture

The Muslims raided west India between 1000 and 1026, defacing many of the temples. This led to the building of the most important **Gujarat temples** with characteristic colonnaded halls and "pyramids" of massed cupolas. **Wulfic's Rotunda of St Augustine's Abbey**, Canterbury, 1049, marked the end of English architectural isolation; both this and the later **Westminster Abbey**, 1055–65, of Edward the Confessor, used Continental models.

Music

Guido d'Arezzo, c.997–c.1050, advocated the use of the staff (a grid of horizontal lines) in notation and made simple rules for defining relative pitch of notes, later revived as the tonic solfa.

Science and Technology

Illustrated botanical texts were published in China in the 11th century. These had medical as well as botanical importance since the pharmacology of drugs obtained from plants was a highly advanced science in China. **Alhazen**, or Ibn al-Haitam, c.965–1038, wrote *Optical Thesaurus*, the first important work on dioptrics (the optics of the eye), which influenced the work of **Roger Bacon**, the 13th-century English scholar.

★ Principal Events

Ferdinand of Castile, r.1035–65, recovered Portugal from the Muslims in 1055.

William of Normandy, introducing a fully feudal society, conquered England in 1066, while another Norman kingdom was established in southern Italy in 1068, finally ousting the Byzantines.

The Berber dynasty of Almoravids built a kingdom in Algeria and Morocco, 1054.

The Ottoman Empire began with the capture of Anatolia in 1071.

The Americas

An elaborate underground water system was begun c.1050 to irrigate crops and supply the city of Casas Grandes in northern Chihuahua, Mexico.

Religion and Philosophy

The schism between the papacy and the Greek Christian Church was fixed in 1054, when **Pope Leo IX** closed Greek churches in southern Italy for unorthodox practices, such as the use of leavened bread in the Mass.

Berengar of Tours, 999–1088, argued that reason could justify the contravention of authority. He denied the doctrine later known as transubstantiation, but was finally forced to recant, 1059.

Literature

In **Persia** the scientist, mathematician, and poet **Omar Khayyám**, c.1048–1122, wrote *The Ru-*

baiyat (quatrains), which express es a rational, pessimistic, and hedonistic philosophy – ideas then unacceptable to orthodox Islam. It is not certain how many of the almost 500 quatrains were written by him.

Art and Architecture

The Byodo-in Temple, 1053, in Japan has the brilliance and delicacy of ornament typical of the **Fujiwara** culture. The Phoenix Hall houses a wooden Amida Buddha by the contemporary sculptor **Yocho**.

Science and Technology

Mold boards, curved boards on plows which overturn the plowed earth and thereby improve soil structure and aeration, came to be used in Europe from the 11th century onward, although they had been known in China for 1,000 years.

Omar Khayyám, c.1048–c.1122, a Persian poet and mathematician, solved cubic equations by geometric methods c.1075, and worked at the sultan's court in Merv, reforming the Muslim calendar.

Principal Events

Pope Gregory VII, *r.*1073–85, and Emperor Henry IV, *r.*1050–1106, clashed on the investiture issue, over the respective rights of the Holy Roman Emperor and the papacy in appointing bishops. **The Almoravids** annexed Moorish Spain, 1086, but **Alfonso VI**, *r.*1072–1109, retook Toledo. The First Crusade, 1096–99, captured Jerusalem and set up Frankish kingdoms in the Near East. **Alexius I**, Byzantine emperor, *r.*1081–1118, recovered some territory.

The Americas

According to Inca legend, Manco Copac led his followers to the Cuzco Valley in Peru. There the Inca Empire was founded with Cuzco its capital.

Religion and Philosophy

The Dictatus Papae of 1075 by **Pope Gregory VII** (Hildebrand), *r.*1073–85, decreed that popes were able to depose emperors. **Roscellinus**, *c.*1050–1120, was an early proponent of the scholastic tenet of nominalism, holding that the qualities we ascribe to objects, like color, do not exist in reality but are just the product of thought or language. He denied the unity of the Trinity, but he was forced to recant by the Synod of Soissons in 1092.

Literature

The chansons de geste, epic poems consisting of a series of stanzas using a single rhyme and celebrating the history of the Age of Charlemagne, were sung by traveling musicians. The earliest written example, *The Song of Roland*, dates from *c.*1100.

Art and Architecture

Durham Cathedral, unlike all previous church architecture, was vaulted throughout. It used a new and more stable combination of round and pointed arches and had buttressed arches beneath the gallery roof.
The Bayeux tapestry, *c.*1080, whose continuous narrative describes the Norman victory over the English and the events preceding it, was sewn to adorn Bayeux Cathedral, though it was probably made in Canterbury.

Music

Troubadours appeared in Provence late in the 11th century, singing to their own harp accompaniment. They set stanzas of poems to music, producing complete compositions in new forms.

Science and Technology

Chinese medical texts written in the 11th century include one of a qualifying examination for doctors and enlarged editions of medical pharmacopoeias.
Indian commentators on science in the 11th and 12th centuries described the medical uses of yoga meditational techniques.

★ Principal Events

The Seljuk Empire gradually split into separate regencies.
The Concordat of Worms, 1122, brought a compromise to the investiture controversy.
Louis VI of France, r.1108-37, granted urban charters to many French Towns. In **Manchuria** the Jurchen tribes overthrew the Khitai with Chinese assistance, 1116, and destroyed the Chinese Sung dynasty, 1136.
The Khmer Empire in Cambodia reached its peak, c.1100.

The Americas

A **Mogollon-Anasazi pueblo** at Kinishba, Ariz., was inhabited c.1100-1350. It is one of the largest ruin sites in the Southwest.

Religion and Philosophy

St. Anselm, Archbishop of Canterbury 1093-1109, one of the first scholastic philosophers, sought to establish the existance of God by reason, arguing that God must necessarily exist since He is perfect and it is more perfect to exist than not.
Peter Abelard, 1079-1142, French theologian and philosopher, advocated reason as a source of truth. His nominalist ideas led to his condemnation at the Council of Soissons in 1121 for his views on the Trinity.

📖 Literature

A **miracle play** was performed at Dunstable c.1100. In such Latin plays, performed in churches and drawing on both the scriptures and the lives of saints, lie the roots of the medieval drama as later practiced.

Art and Architecture

Chinese landscape painting reached its zenith under the patronage of **Hui Tsung**, r.1101-25. Great care was lavished on tiny details in an attempt to reveal the inner life of the objects shown. Li Chieh's treatise on **Sung architecture** is a blend of learning and practical instruction on survey geometry, uses of building materials, and decorations, and includes recipes for colored glazes for floor and roof tiles.

Music

Three- and four-part polyphony was composed round a cantus firmus, but early in the 12th century two parts were more usual. The harmony often used sounds dissonant to modern ears.

Science and Technology

Silk manufacture began in south Italy in the 12th century as a result of Arab influence and by the 13th century water-powered silk mills were in operation.
Stained-glass windows of the early 12th century demonstrate the high-level glass technology found in Europe. Glass was colored by the addition of particular metal salts; those of copper for green, copper or gold chloride for red, iron or silver for yellow, and cobalt for blue.

★ Principal Events

Alfonso VII, r.1126–57, resumed the conquest of Spain while the Muslim dynasties of Spain and North Africa fought each other. After the fall of the **Frankish kingdom of Edessa** to the Seljuk Turks, 1144, the disorganized Second Crusade failed to halt the Turkish advance, 1147–49. **The communal movement** of the north European towns claiming independence from royal authority reached Rouen, 1145. **Kiev** declined after the death of **Vladimir Monomach**, 1125.

The Americas

The Chibcha culture of Colombia had a highly organized political organization that involved five states, each with a chief. The major one was near Bogotá.

☿ Religion and Philosophy

St. Bernard, 1090–1153, Cistercian abbot of Clairvaux in France, strongly encouraged mysticism and contemplation in opposition to the scholastic rationalism prevalent in Western Christendom. **Honen**, 1133–1212, founder of the Pure Land Sect in Japan, joined the **Tendai Sect** in 1148. **Gratian**, a Benedictine monk, compiled the *Decretum Gratiani*, a collection of canon law, c.1140.

Literature

The first bardic period of Hindi literature began in India. Among the important early epics is the *Prithvi Rah Raso*.

Art and Architecture

At Autun Cathedral in France Gislebertus sculpted all the nave capitals, c.1125–35, the west door tympanum depicting the Apocalypse.
Abbot Suger rebuilt the choir and westwork of **St Denis**, near Paris, c.1140–44. The first example of mature Gothic, its slender pillars and pointed arches allowed big lancet windows with stained glass in the apse chapels; statues adorned the porch.

Music

Trouvères in northern France developed on similar lines to the troubadours, producing *formes fixes* (set structures of contrasting phrases), among them the ballade, virelai, and rondeau.

Science and Technology

Coal was used at Liège for iron-smelting beginning about 1150. **Alcohol** was probably first distilled from wine at Salerno in the 12th century. Although fully able to do so, the Arabs had not made alcohol because it was prohibited by the Koran.

★ Principal Events

Henry II of England, r.1154–89, added Aquitaine and Gascony to the Angevin Empire in France, and heightened the conflict of secular and papal authority by having **Becket**, Archbishop of Canterbury, murdered in 1170.
Saladin, r.1169–93, united the disparate Muslim tribes in Egypt and Syria under the Egyptian **Ayyubid dynasty. Civil War in Japan** among the local clans, 1156–81, accelerated the decline of imperial authority over the feudal magnates.

The Americas

The Aztec Ruins pueblo in New Mexico was abandoned c.1150 soon after it was completed, probably due to climate change. The inhabitants returned c.1225.

☥ Religion and Philosophy

Averroes, 1126–98, the Islamic scholar, began writing his influential commentaries on Aristotle in 1169. He also argued that reason could serve to establish religious truths.
The Waldenses, founded by **Peter Waldo** in 1173 in southern France, rejected the license of the official Church and adopted a simple way of life, electing their own priests.

Literature

The lyrical poetry of the troubadours grew up in 12th-century France. Written in a Provencal dialect and sung to music, it lauded a concept of love as a knightly duty then fashionable in the southern French courts.
Mystère d'Adam c.1175, marks a major development toward popular drama; it is in French, not Latin, uses the vernacular, and was later played outdoors.

Art and Architecture

A change in the design of Cistercian monasteries followed the death of **St Bernard of Clairvaux** in 1153. After the harsh simplicity of **Fontenay**, built in 1139, **Clairvaux III**, 1153, and **Pontigny** apse, c.1185, are richer and more imposing.
External flying buttresses, first used at Notre Dame, Paris, c.1163, enabled clerestory as well as ground floor windows to be treated as a frame, with a thin web of stone and glass between.

Music

The conductus developed as processional music in a chordal style late in the 12th century. Composed for voices or instruments, it was based on original themes rather than plainsong.

Science and Technology

Maimonides, 1135–1204, the great Jewish thinker, worked at the court of Saladin and wrote on medicine, theology, and philosophy. He described diseases and cures in a way that we now recognize as that of psychosomatic medicine.
Averroes, or Ibn Rushd, 1126–98, the leader of Arabic science and the major encyclopedist of his day, worked in Córdoba. His scientific writings led to the Averroist school of scientific thought in Europe.

Principal Events

The Seljuks took Anatolia, 1176, and Saladin took Jerusalem, 1187. The third Crusade, 1189–91, rewon the city.
Muhammad of Ghur, *r.*1176–1206, took Delhi and Bihar in India. A Muslim kingdom was set up at Delhi on his death.
Yoritomo's defeat of the Taira clan, 1185, in Japan inaugurated the Kamakura period.
Emperor Frederick I (Barbarossa), *r.*1152–90, was defeated by the league of Lombard towns in his invasion of Italy, 1176.

The Americas

The Toltec cities of Tula and Chichén Itzá, in Mexico, declined. Tula was burned by Chichimecs, and Chichén Itzá was defeated and then abandoned.

Religion and Philosophy

Zen Buddhism was introduced into Japan in 1191 by the monk **Eisai,** 1141–1215. Zen stressed personal instruction by a master, rather than the study of scriptures, as the way to enlightenment. His techniques included sudden physical shocks and meditation on paradoxical statements. **Neo-Confucianism** emerged in the 12th century in China. **Chu-Hsi,** 1130–1200, one of its most influential exponents, completed his commentaries, *The Four Books*, in 1189.

Literature

The long Middle High German epic **Nibelungenlied**, which has survived in 13th century manuscripts, was written by an unknown Austrian, its hero is Siegfried, it has connections with Scandinavian legends and has influenced many writers and composers, notably Wagner. **Chretien de Troyes,** *fl.*1165–80, developed the prose romance in *Conte del Graal*.

Art and Architecture

In the second Angkor period the Cambodian capital of **Angkor Thom** was rebuilt, 1181–95, followed by temples in **Angkor Wat.** The ashlar façades were deeply carved to resemble gigantic faces.
High Gothic architects used the new construction techniques to varied aesthetic ends and made structure itself ornamental. Most important were **Chartres** and **Bourgues,** 1195, **Canterbury,** 1174, and **Lincoln,** 1192.

Music

The minnesinger created a tradition of German song inspired by the art of the troubadours. Notre Dame choir school in Paris flourished under the great masters Léonin and Pérotin.

Science and Technology

Old London Bridge and the Avignon bridge were built *c.*1175.
Cast iron, made by melting and molding the metal, was first produced in Europe. It was made possible by higher furnace temperatures.
Leonardo Fibonacci, *c.*1170–*c.*1240, the greatest medieval mathematician, wrote the first Western textbook on algebra about 1200.

Principal Events

Venice persuaded the **Fourth Crusade**, 1202–04, to take Constantinople, setting up the Latin Empire of the East 1204–61.
King John of England, r.1199–1216, was forced to sign the Magna Carta, 1215, subjecting the monarchy to the rule of law.
Alfonso VIII, r.1170–1214, defeated the Almohades, 1212.
The Mongols, under **Genghis Khan**, r.1206–27, had invaded China, Persia, and southern Russia by 1225.

The Americas

The nomadic **Mexica** Indians migrated south into the Valley of Mexico, bringing religious practices that included human sacrifice. They became the Aztecs.

Religion and Philosophy

Islam became firmly entrenched in India with the establishment of the Delhi kingdom in 1206.
The True Pure Land Sect (Jodo Shin) was founded in Japan in 1224 by **Shinran**, 1173–1262. For him, salvation came only through faith and the Buddha's grace. Because it rejected monasticism and ascetic practices, this became, and still is, the largest Buddhist sect in Japan.

Literature

The German minnesinger tradition, parallel to the Provençal courtly poetry, is exemplified in the songs of **Walther von der Vogelweide**, c.1170–1230, a wanderer and a beggar. He discarded the older strict form, as did his contemporary. **Wolfram von Eschenbach**, fl.1200–20, author of the great German romance, the grail-story *Parzival*, c.1210.

Art and Architecture

The Peruvian Chimú capital of Chanchan had adobe buildings with trapezoidal doors and intricate geometrical surface designs. Pottery played an important part in decoration. **An International style** known as **Rayonnant Gothic** was born in 1220 at Amiens Cathedral.
The massive "Black Pagoda," a Jain temple of the sun, was begun at Kanarak in Orissa c.1200. Only the base, carved with erotic reliefs, survives.

Music

Muslim rule in northern India after 1206 strengthened secular music and featured the use of the **sitar**. Southern Indian music remained restrained and classical, favoring the **vina**.

Science and Technology

Stückofen, the precursors of blast furnaces, operated in Styria, central Europe, as early as the 13th century. These furnaces burned charcoal.
Universities founded in Europe in the early 13th century included those of Paris and Oxford.
Roger Bacon, c.1214–c.94, was one of the few important experimenters in medieval English science. He had an extensive knowledge of astronomy and medicine and employed lenses to correct defective vision.

Principal Events

Assimilation of native ideas by the ruling minority created a fusion of Muslim and Hindu cultures in northern India by 1230.
The Mongols annexed the Chin Empire in China, 1234, overran eastern Europe, and set up the Tatar state of the Golden Horde on the lower Volga in 1242.
Alexander Nevsky, r.1236–63, prince of Novgorod, defeated the Teutonic Knights, 1242.
Jerusalem was lost to the Turks in 1244 and the Seventh Crusade, 1248–50, achieved little.

The Americas

The people who lived at Moundsville, Ala., were skilled architects who built remarkable mound enclaves and created a unique art form.

Religion and Philosophy

The Franciscan and Dominican orders of friars, devoted to the care of the poor and the sick, spread quickly, 1225–30.
Nicherin, 1222–82, a Japanese Buddhist monk, added a highly nationalist element to Japanese Buddhism. By 1250 he had proclaimed the *Lotus Sutra*, the central writing of the Mahayana tradition, as the supreme Buddhist scripture. He desired to end Buddhist sectarianism in order to regenerate and unify Japan against China.

Literature

The Icelandic Classical period culminated in the work of **Snorri Sturluson**, 1179–1241, who wrote the *Edda*, a handbook that set out the Icelandic myths and the types of poetic diction used in old Norse poetry.
Literature in Japan declined with the Kamakura period, 1192–1333, but war tales, especially the *Heike monogatari*, c.1215–50, became an established form.

Art and Architecture

The Sainte Chapelle, Paris, was built, 1240–48, as St Louis' palace chapel and to house the Crown of Thorns relic. The walls are like continuous sheets of glass and made the design a symbol of prestige.

Music

"Sumer is icumen in," an English song of astonishing form, written c.1240, was the first recorded canon. It is a four-part round over a two-part repeated pattern in the bass parts.

Science and Technology

Frederick II, Holy Roman emperor, r.1220–50, a serious student of natural science, wrote a treatise on falconry that is a model of natural history for its combined learning and observation.
Stern-mounted rudders were first fitted to European ships at this time, although the Chinese had invented them centuries earlier.
Navigational charts came to be first used by Western sailors in the 13th century.

The Mongols Unify Asia 1250–1400

The harbor of Venice's waterways, late 12th c.

Kublai Khan was the grandson of Genghis Khan.

Chimú portrait jar

The Black Death: Flagellants whipped themselves as public penance.

St. Thomas Aquinas: Italian religious philosopher

Ming vase: Potters used Persian cobalt for underglaze painting.

God spede ye ploug̅ i sende us korne i nou

Frontispiece to *Piers Plowman*, a Christian allegorical poem

The Mongols Unify Asia

Principal Events

In Europe the crusading mentality gave way to a more flexible, commercial society, epitomized by the rise of the Italian city-states, the Hanseatic League of trading towns in the north, and merchant and trade guilds. Kings came to depend more closely on popular support and called parliaments in which they consulted a wider section of the population, including townsmen. After 1300, the growth of European population and prosperity gave way to famine and plague, which reduced many towns and introduced a period of retrenchment. The population decline, however, increased the bargaining power of the laborers, later enabling the peasantry to escape serfdom.

The Mongols brought prosperity and trade to much of Asia, but their empire was fragmented by religious conflict. Their benevolent rule in China was replaced by the native Ming dynasty in 1368.

The Americas

The first known white colony (established c.1014) continued in Newfoundland. The prehistoric Pueblo culture reached its peak c.1300 and began to decline. Prehistoric Mayan civilization was in its last centuries, while the Aztec Empire emerged. The Chimú and Inca empires were expanding by conquest.

Religion and Philosophy

The scholastic tradition in European philosophy, which sought to strengthen religious faith with the help of reason, culminated in the work of Thomas Aquinas, Duns Scotus, and William of Ockham, all of whom looked to the work of Plato and Aristotle. Ockham, however, was also an empiricist, disputing the self-evidence of the principles of Aristotelian logic, like the final cause, and of Christian teachings, like the existence of God.

The reign of Pope Boniface VIII marked the summit of papal power. Following the move to Avignon, 1305, the power of the papacy declined.

The vernacular writings of Langland and Wycliffe, both Englishmen, foreshadowed the Reformation in condemning priestly corruption while advocating spiritual as well as social equality.

The Islamic world produced its most original thinker, the scholar Ibn Khaldun.

Literature

Italian writers of the early Renaissance, particularly Dante, Petrarch, and Boccaccio, drew on the passion-ate and poetical faith of St. Francis, the philosophical theology of Aquinas, and the new lyricism of the French troubadours to forge a brilliant literature. Honored by the princes of the Italian states, they explored in allegories, love poems, and philosophical writings the contradictions between classical humanism and Christian ideals. Italian vernacular poetry and prose was the latest to emerge among the Romance languages, but the work of writers such as Boccaccio opened the way to the vivid portrayal of contemporary life that marked the work of Chaucer in England and became characteristic of Renaissance literature.

Art and Architecture

Art and architecture in Europe between 1250 and 1400 show their initial indebtedness to France, a nation that had achieved success both politically and artistically. German patrons sent for architects to build "in the French manner," while Italian masons grafted details from Rayonnant Gothic architecture onto buildings that were essentially the piled masses of Italian Romanesque. Everywhere much time, skill, and money were lavished to make buildings bigger and more ornate and objects more intricate and naturalistic, both in religious and secular spheres. The period saw the "birth" of Italian painting in the works of Cimabue, Giotto, and Duccio and the beginnings of modern sculpture with Nicola Pisano and his son, Giovanni.

Cultures in Southeast Asia became more distinct, yet borrowed freely from each other. Comparatively little survives from India at this time.

Music

Late medieval European music was increasingly complex and brilliant, requiring more exact systems of notation. The beginning of the Renaissance produced an easing of the Church's nearly exclusive hold on serious composition and, as patrons began to sponsor secular music, compositions began to show signs of greater individuality and independence.

Science and Technology

European trade and industry, although violently arrested in the mid-14th century by the Black Death, expanded rapidly in the first century of this period. Italian galleys carried cargoes of glass, silk, and finished metal goods to northern Europe and elsewhere, returning laden with textiles from the Hanseatic cloth towns and metals from the mines of central Europe.

Intellectual life, including that of the newly founded universities of Oxford and Paris, was also vigorous. Although in science Scholasticism was still the rule, signs of a breakthrough to a more experimental approach began with the works of Oresme and Buridan in Paris and William of Ockham in England, whose ideas conflicted with those of the scholastic's ultimate scientific authority, Aristotle.

By the end of this period Arab science was limited to the teachings of a few wandering scholars, and China, the home of accurate scientific reasoning and technology, had declined due to an unwieldy bureaucracy.

1250-1265

★ Principal Events

Gold currencies were introduced in Florence and Genoa, 1252, and bankers, such as the Bardi in Florence, flourished.

Chinese silk became available in Europe in 1257 along the silk route opened up as a result of Mongol expansion.

Kublai Khan, r.1260–94, set up the Yüan dynasty in China.

In England, de Montfort's Parliaments, 1264–65, reflected the improved status of townsmen and lesser knights.

The Americas

The Mayans, who were excellent navigators, were engaged in extensive trading by sea-going canoe. They ranged as far south as Panama and Nicaragua.

Religion and Philosophy

St Thomas Aquinas, c.1225–74, the greatest scholastic philosopher, stated his belief in the power of reason in *Summa Contra Gentiles*, 1264, in which he presented arguments designed to convince the non-believer of the power and truth displayed in Christianity. This work, together with his *Summa Theologica*, 1266–73, was influential in giving a strong Aristotelian basis to Catholic philosophy.

Literature

Laudi (praises to God) became a common form of religious song in Italy during the period following the death of **St Francis**, 1226. The Franciscan friar **Jacopone da Todi**, c.1230–1306,

was the greatest poet of this style. Written in an Umbrian dialect, his ardent mystical laudi counterposed a love of God with a harsh awareness of the secular world.

Art and Architecture

The French Rayonnant Gothic style, characterized by circular windows with wheel tracery, was exemplified on the western facade of **Rheims Cathedral**, begun in 1255, and also in Spain at **Leon Cathedral**, 1255–1303. The choir of **Old St Paul's**, London, begun in 1256, also incorporated French features. **Nicola Pisano**, c.1225–c.84, the greatest sculptor of his generation, completed a pulpit for the baptistery at Pisa, 1260.

Music

The motet, a polyphonic form with different words sung simultaneously in the various parts, in which the *cantus firmus* was reduced to a repeated rhythmic phrase, developed after c.1250.

Science and Technology

Gold florins were first struck in Florence in 1252.

The first cannons, employed by the Moors perhaps as early as 1250, were simply iron buckets charged with gunpowder and filled with stones. They were ignited by means of a touch hole near the bottom of the bucket.

Vincent of Beauvais, d.1264, was a major encyclopedist. His *Speculum Majus*, unequaled in length until the 18th century, summarized the scientific and philosophical views of the major scholastic writers.

Principal Events

Louis IX of France, r.1226–70, the most powerful and respected monarch in Europe, died in Tunis on the ninth and last Crusade.
Mongol peaceful rule in Asia inspired a Venetian trader, **Marco Polo**, 1254–1324, to visit China in 1271–95.
Rudolf of Hapsburg, from an old Swabian family, was elected King of Germany in 1273 and thus became founder of the Hapsburg dynasty.

The Americas

A severe drought in the Southwest, which was to persist for 23 years, began in 1276 in the area of Mesa Verde; the culture there was in its classic stage.

Religion and Philosophy

Roger Bacon, c.1214–c.94, a Franciscan philosopher interested in science, magic, and mathematics, in 1272 wrote *Compendium Studii Philosophiae*, attacking clerical influence. He was unusual in valuing experiment as a worthwhile and useful source of knowledge.
Madhava, 1197–1276, an Indian thinker whose life was remarkably similar to that of Christ, denied the Sankara doctrine of the illusory nature of the world.

Literature

The ghazal – a 7th-century form of Arabic love poetry celebrating mystical and worldly love in mono-rhymed verses without logical sequence – was developed by Persian Sufi mystics, notably

Rumi, 1207–73, in "Divan."
Roman de la Rose, a French poem of 22,000 lines in 8-syllable couplets, completed by 1280, included an elaborate allegory on the psychology of love.

Art and Architecture

The influence of the Four Great Masters on landscape painting of the Mongol **Yüan dynasty** in China, 1264–1368, brought a greater robustness and broader color spectrum to this important art form.
The Benin (Nigeria) bronze-casters' "lost wax" technique was developed in the late 13th century, introduced by tradition from Ife.

Music

Notation was developed for shorter time values as intricate parts were introduced to overlie lines of long notes. The new notation clarified the time relationship between the parts.

Science and Technology

Commercial fishing, encouraged by the many meatless fastdays of the Christian calendar, grew rapidly during the Middle Ages in Europe. The Hanseatic League fishery, in the Baltic, reached its peak, 1275–1350, with catches of 13,000 tons of herring a year.
The spinning wheel may have been invented by 1280 but was not commonly introduced into Europe until the 14th century when it would replace the distaff and loose spindle.

1280-1295

Principal Events

The defeat of the Mongol invasions of Japan in 1274 and 1281 strengthened the Japanese military clans.

The Danish Magna Carta, 1282, united royal power.

Tripoli and Acre fell to the Mamelukes, 1289-91.

The Yüan dynasty in China restored canals and built roads.

Osman, 1259-1326, founded the Turkish Ottoman principality in Bithynia in 1290.

The western Mongols rejected the khan's authority in 1295.

The Americas

Mayapán, the capital of the Itzá, who were the last strong Mayan tribe, c.1283 was the last site of prehistoric Mayan civilization which disappeared by 1450.

Religion and Philosophy

Duns Scotus, c.1265-1308, an English scholastic philosopher and a Franciscan monk, drew on the work of Plato. He was a realist, denying the nominalist view that the qualities we perceive, such as the color green, are merely products of thought and do not exist in the real world. He rejected the idea of predestination and inclined to the Pelagian view that man can alter his fate by his conduct.

Literature

One of the major figures in Catalan literature, **Raymond Lully,** 1232-1315, was a poet, mystic, philosopher, and theologian who produced 243 works. *Blanquerna,* 1289, is notable as a philosophical study of Utopia and the forerunner of the novel.

The exploits of the 13th-century Tannhäuser, a knight and poet of the **Minnesinger** school, were described in legend and ballad.

Art and Architecture

Cimabue, c.1240-1302, one of the first great Italian painters, worked toward the realistic depiction of physical form and human emotion, as in his "Sta Croce crucifix," 1283.

In England one of the earliest lierne vaults, characterized by small ribs running from one major rib to another, was built at **Pershore Abbey,** 1288. Lierne vaults became a purely decorative, typically English device.

Music

In China, during the Yüan dynasty, 1264-1368, music was encouraged. Opera developed in the theater with recitative (musically declaimed words), arias, and melodies for set moods.

Science and Technology

Spectacles, with convex lenses, were first recorded by an Englishman, Roger Bacon, 1286. By the early 14th century they were factory-made in Venice.

Albertus Magnus, c.1200-80, a German encyclopedist, classified plants by their structures.

Principal Events

Venice was governed by a narrow oligarchy of merchants who consolidated their power by crushing the popular and patrician revolts of 1300 and 1310.
A conflict over papal authority led **Philip IV**, *r.*1285–1314, of France to call one of the first Estates-General in 1302 to appeal for national support.
Military anarchy in Italy drove the papacy to Avignon in 1309.
The African Empire of Mali, based in Sudan, flourished.

The Americas

Emerald Mound, which extends over eight acres near Natchez, Miss., was built *c.*1300 as a ceremonial center for the Natchez Culture peoples.

Religion and Philosophy

Pope Boniface VIII instituted the Jubilee year of 1300, when plenary indulgence was granted to those visiting Rome.
The papacy moved to Avignon in 1309, under Clement V, where it remained for nearly 70 years. The French influence over the papacy in this period marked the beginning of the decline in its temporal power.

Literature

Marco Polo recorded in a Genoese prison, *c.*1298, the story of his travels in China and Asia. His account was the basis of Western knowledge of China.
Heinrich von Meissen, *c.*1250–1318, was a representative of the school of middle-class poets who succeeded the knightly Minnesingers adapting Minnesinger traditions to poems dealing with theology and philosophy.

Art and Architecture

The frescoes by Giotto, 1266–1337, in the Arena (Scrovegni) chapel in Padua, painted *c.*1305, show solidity, naturalistic detail, and perspective, and represent the turning point in Italian painting. By contrast **Duccio di Buoninsegna**, *c.*1260–1315, the first great Sienese painter, summed up the mastery of the Byzantine tradition in his "Maesta" for Siena Cathedral, commissioned in 1308.

Music

The madrigal emerged in Italy. Usually set for two or more voices, it was in a strict poetic structure corresponding to the *formes fixes* of France.

Science and Technology

Stanches, or navigation weirs, which maintain a depth of water for ships, were built in European rivers and canals and include one built on the Thames in 1306.
Gunpowder for artillery appeared in Europe *c.*1300.
Watermarks were first used in papermaking in Italy in the late 13th century.

Principal Events

Bad harvests in 1315 brought famine to much of Europe, slowing population growth.

In north India, where Muslim dynasties ruled from Delhi since 1206, a Turkish Tughluk dynasty was founded in 1320.

In Mexico the Aztecs founded the capital Tenochtitlán in 1325 and began to colonize Central America.

Uzbeg, r.1312–41, converted the Mongol Golden Horde to Islam and brought Mongol prosperity to its height.

The Americas

The Pueblo Culture's golden age ended, and a regressive period, marked by abandonment of the great cities and migration south and east, began.

Religion and Philosophy

Giovanni Monte Corvino, 1247–1328, established the first Christian missions in China and baptized **Khaistan Kuluk,** r.1307–11, the third great Khan of the Chinese Yüan dynasty.
Marsilius of Padua, c.1275–1342, wrote *Defensor Pacis,* 1324, a famous treatise espousing the supremacy of lay power over the Church, and claimed that all power derives from the people, for whom the ruler is a delegate.

Literature

The theme of spiritual love developed by such Tuscan poets as **Guido Cavalcanti,** c. 1260–1300,

was given expression by **Dante Alighieri,** 1265–1321. In his *Divina Commedia,* begun c. 1307, he describes his journey through *Inferno, Purgatorio,* and *Paradiso,* giving insight on medieval views and religious beliefs. It made Tuscan Italy's literary medium.

Art and Architecture

The Paris school of manuscript illumination flowed in the work of **Master Honoré,** d.1318.
Second generation "decorated" Gothic architecture in England developed with the building of Ely Cathedral Lady Chapel, 1321–48, whose undulating blind arcading and curvilinear tracery derived from geometrical forms.
Giovanni Pisano, c.1245–1314, completed the pulpit in Pisa Cathedral, 1310, synthesizing Gothic and classical elements.

Science and Technology

Drainage mills, windmills that operate drainage scoops, were invented in the 14th century. (In the 16th century the Dutch used such mills for recovering land for agriculture.)
Chaulmoogra oil, for the treatment of leprosy, was first seen in 14th-century China. It was the only effective treatment for leprosy until the 20th century.
Linen clothes were widely worn in the 14th century for the first time. This led to an improvement in personal cleanliness and decline in diseases.

★ Principal Events

The Ottoman Empire expanded into Thrace, 1326–61. **Edward II** of England, r.1307–27, was deposed and killed, 1327.
The Hundred Years War of England and France broke out in 1337 as a result of the rival claims to the French throne of **Edward III**, r.1327–77, and **Philip of Valois**, r.1328–50.
The Hanseatic League grew politically powerful c.1340. Alfonso XI of Castile, r.1312–50, ended the African threat to Spain in 1340.

The Americas

The Aztecs settled on an island in Lake Texcoco with their capital, Tenochtitlán, which would flourish until the Spanish conquest.

⚥ Religion and Philosophy

William of Ockham, c.1300–c.49, an Englishman, was the last of the great scholastic Franciscan philosophers. He broke with the Aristotelian realism of **Aquinas** and took a nominalist position. His importance lies in his development of a sophisticated logic and epistemology of more than a purely theological significance, which was to have a great effect on later secular philosophy.

📖 Literature

Petrarch (Francesco Petrarca), 1304–74, gave passionate form to Italian love poetry in his "Canzoniere," sonnets and madrigals inspired by his unrequited love for Laura. An admirer of Roman and Greek ideals, his humanistic outlook influenced other writers.
The Persian mystic poet Hafiz, 1320–88, used complex lyrical imagery in ghazal form.

🏛 Art and Architecture

In the Muromachi (Ashikaga) period in Japan, 1392–1573, painters followed previous traditions such as continuous narrative scrolls. Renewal of contact with China and Korea introduced new techniques such as the art of painting.
The Perpendicular style of architecture in England first appeared in Gloucester Cathedral cloister, where the ribs of the vault spread out into fan-vaulting.

🎵 Music

Ars nova was a term coined by **Phillipe de Vitry,** 1291–1361, to describe new and freer forms of music. The earlier forms became known as *ars antiqua.*

⚛ Science and Technology

Salt-glazing of pottery was practiced in the Rhineland from the 14th century. The potter threw salt over wares in the final stages of firing in the kiln, this produced a fine glaze that sealed off the wares.
The cross staff, a primitive form of sextant, was popularized for use in navigation by **Levi ben Gerson** of Provence, 1288–1344. **The spinning wheel** was pictured in the Luttrell Psalter of 1338.

Principal Events

Italian economic decline followed the fall of the Bardi bankers after the English monarchy repudiated its debts.

Cola di Rienzo, 1313–54, was murdered after his attempt to set up a Roman republic independent of the papacy.

The Black Death destroyed up to half Europe's population between 1348 and 1350, totally disrupting commerce.

During the Hundred Years War England profited from pillage and the ransom of captives.

The Americas

The sixth Inca ruler, Inca Roca, expanded the city of Cuzco, as well as building a bridge across the Apurimac River.

Religion and Philosophy

The Flagellant movement arose in response to fear of the Black Death, but was condemned by **Pope Clement VI**, 1349. The Flagellants sought to avoid divine wrath by whipping themselves thrice daily. They began in Italy and spread to Germany and the Low Countries, where they toured the countryside proclaiming flagellation as the way to salvation.

Literature

The Italian novella was developed by **Giovanni Boccaccio**, 1313–75, in the *Decameron*, 1353, a collection of 100 witty and bawdy tales set in the time of the Black Death. Their human-

ism and breadth of social and psychological observation had an enormous influence on Renaissance literature everywhere. Boccaccio was influenced by Greco-Roman styles.

Art and Architecture

Italian painting followed the Sienese tradition in the works of **Simone Martini**, *c*.1284–1344, and of **Pietro and Ambrogio Lorenzetti**, both active in the first half of the 14th century. Papal patronage in the palace of Avignon brought numerous Italian artists to France. Giotto's earlier detailed studies of nature influenced the decoration of the **Tour des Anges**, *c*.1340, by **Matteo Giovanetti**.

Music

Religious music still favored triple time as symbolic of the Trinity, but growing acceptance of **duple** (beats in groups of two) time advocated in *ars nova* showed growth of secular music.

Science and Technology

The Black Death of 1348–51 caused a severe decline in European trade and power, badly affecting labor intensive industries such as agriculture, mining, and fishing, which did not recover for over a century.

Double-entry bookkeeping methods are known to have been used by the Massari family of Genoa *c*.1340, although they were probably used before that by the Hanseatic League, the Medicis, and the Fuggers.

Principal Events

The Holy Roman Empire was changed by papal decree, the **Golden Bull**, from a monarchy to an aristocratic federation.
The ransom of John II of France by England provoked the **Jacquerie**, a peasant revolt against war taxes, which was violently suppressed in 1358.
The Ming dynasty in China was created after a popular revolt against the Mongols, 1368.

The Americas

The Norse colony in Newfoundland was less closely tied to Europe after 1367, when the last royal ship made the voyage to North America.

Religion and Philosophy

The Sufi branch of Islam spread into India, Malaya, and Africa south of the Sahara. "**Piers Plowman,**" a vernacular poem probably by the English parson **Langland** begun c.1362, attacked corruption in the state and Church. The poem is an appeal on behalf of the poor and a plea for spiritual equality.

Literature

A great Christian allegorical poem, "Piers Plowman," attributed to **William Langland,** c.1332–1400, brought to Middle English the alliterative tradition of Anglo-Saxon verse in a series of 11 dream visions.
A more mysterious allegory was the anonymous *Sir Gawain and the Green Knight,* c.1370, an Ar-

thurian romance. *Pearl* was found in the same manuscript.

Art and Architecture

Potters of the Ming dynasty in China, 1368–1644, discovered underglaze painting using imported Persian cobalt. Their harmonious blue designs on white ground balanced their favorite opulent shapes and sinuous line.
Italian architecture's continuity with Romanesque was shown in the new design for the east end of Florence Cathedral by **Francesco Talenti.** Only external details such as windows are borrowed Gothic.

Music

Guillaume de Machaut, c.1300–77, was the chief figure of *ars nova.* The complex forms he used involved modulation, intricate cross-rhythms, and great independence of line.

Science and Technology

Oresme, c.1325–82, and **Buridan,** 1300–58, in Paris, criticized Aristotle's doctrine of motion. They were influenced by the idea of *impetus,* conceived by **Philoponos,** c.530, and later developed into a theory of motion by Galileo.
Iron cannons were used by the Germans from 1350 onward.

★ Principal Events

The Ottomans took Adrianople.
Rival popes were created in
Rome and Avignon, 1378, after
the breakdown of negotiations
over plans to reform the papacy.
Popular revolts in Florence in
1378 and England in 1381 were
suppressed.
Constitutional reform in Florence
marked the beginning of Florentine power in 1382.
Moscow emerged as the focus
of Russian opposition to the
Mongols after the defeat of the
Tatars at Kulikovo in 1380.

The Americas

Ñancen Pinco, ruler of the Chimú
Empire c.1370, began his con-
quests along the Peruvian coast.
The empire was overcome by the
Inca c.1465.

Religion and Philosophy

John Wycliffe, c.1320–84,
and his followers the Lollards,
a religious group with noble
supporters in England, spread
ideas that were unacceptable
until the Reformation. In *On
Civil Dominion*, 1376, Wycliffe
proposed a propertyless church
and argued for direct access to
God for individuals.
In the Netherlands disciples
of Gerard Groote, 1340–84, who
espoused a nonritualized, humane Christianity, formed the
Brothers of the Common Life.

Literature

The No play emerged in Japan in
a classic form established by
Kanami Motokiyo, 1333–84, and
his son **Zeami Motokiyo,**
1363–1443, who wrote most of
the 100 plays that survive from
this period. No drama is formal
in style, incorporates music and
dancing, and is performed without scenery by males who wear
masks to portray women, old
men, or supernatural beings.

Art and Architecture

**English Perpendicular architec-
ture** matured. Canterbury Cathedral nave had smoothly shafted
columns rising to the lierne
vaults.
The Hindu Vijanagar dynasty of
the Deccan, India, 1336–
c.1614, favored an almost
baroque style. Groups of small
buildings were characteristic,
and columns were often sculptured with groups of figures and
animals.

Music

Meistersinger in Germany took
over the lyric art of the aristocratic Minnesinger. Meistersinger were traders and craftsmen
who founded guilds to set and
keep up standards for their art.

Science and Technology

Lock gates on Dutch canals date
from at least 1373. By 1400,
locks were an integral part of
navigation and drainage systems
of Italy and Germany.
Geoffrey Chaucer, an English
writer, c.1345–1400, described
what may be the first scientific
work in English, *The Equatorial
Planetarie*, which deals with a
device for predicting the paths
and positions of planets.

Principal Events

Portugal assured its independence by defeating Castile at Aljubarota in 1385.
Tamerlane, r.1369–1405, conquered Central Asia, defeated the Golden Horde, 1391, and destroyed the kingdom of Delhi in 1398, delaying the Ottoman advance westward into Europe.
The Ming dynasty began to develop a naval empire c.1400.
In England, Richard II's absolutist reign, 1377–99, was ended by the nobles; Henry IV took the throne, 1399.

The Americas

The Southern Death cult was part of the Mississippian culture from c.1400–1700. Human sacrifice was depicted on artifacts in this period.

Religion and Philosophy

Ibn Khaldun, 1332–1406, the Islamic scholar, was unique in the medieval era. The greatest social thinker until modern times, he based a theory of society on social cohesion and cyclical patterns of growth and decay. In his masterwork, the *Muquaddimah*, he outlined a philosophy of history and laid the foundations for what he called "a science of culture."

Literature

The first truly native English poetry was created by Geoffrey Chaucer, c.1345–1400, influenced by French and Italian styles. His best works include

Troilus and Cressida, c.1387, and *Canterbury Tales,* c.1395.
Confessio Amantis, c.1390, by English poet **John Gower,** 1325–1408, told moralistic stories of courtly love.

Art and Architecture

The rebuilding of Milan Cathedral, 1387, in the northern Late Gothic style showed the influence of and enthusiasm for French ideas. Building continued throughout the Renaissance.
Tamerlane's mausolea at Samarkand were built in the decade after Baghdad's capture, 1393. Their tall domes on high drums and colorful glazed relief-tile decoration would be the inspiration for Timurid architects 1405–1500.

Music

Dissonances and great embellishment in music were part of the general concern with richness and diversity seen in European art of the time. Paris produced the best examples.

Science and Technology

Forged iron guns weighing 600lb (272kg) were used by Richard II, r.1377–99, to defend the Tower of London.
Mechanically wound steel crossbows were developed.
Weight-driven clocks, often employing elaborate striking mechanisms, appeared in Europe at this time. The earliest surviving clock in England is in Salisbury Cathedral, installed in 1386.
Observatories were among the last achievements of Arab science.

Printing and Discovery 1400–1500

Johann Gutenberg's moveable-type printing press

Spanish explorer Christopher Columbus died in poverty.

Savonarola was burned for criticizing corruption in Florence.

The conquest of Constantinople by the Ottoman Turks

Facade, San Maria
Novella

Jain manuscript, 14th c.–
15th c.

"Venus" by Sandro
Botticelli

Printing and Discovery

Principal Events

In spite of a generally static economic climate the move toward national sovereignty increased at the expense of papal authority. The process of the consolidation of the European states continued, and the power of the monarchs over the nobility grew gradually with the help of ostentatious artistic patronage and ambitious foreign wars. In Spain, united under Ferdinand and Isabella, the Moors were finally expelled, and Ivan I established the power of Moscow by bargaining with the Tatars.

Byzantium fell to the Ottoman Turks in 1453, closing the eastern Mediterranean to Christian traffic, but European expansion began to the west as the Spanish and Portuguese thrones sponsored the exploration of alternative routes to India around the coast of Africa.

In China, the Ming dynasty made contact by sea with India and Africa and fought to protect its weak northern frontiers.

The Americas

The century ended with the exploration and discovery of America at Cuba and the Bahamas by Christopher Columbus. It was to be the last period in which the civilizations of North and South America would be untouched by European influence. The empires of the Incas and the Aztecs expanded.

Religion and Philosophy

The relationship of Church and state was a major subject of controversy in 15th-century Europe, while the corrupt practices and moral laxity of the established religious orders came under attack. Reformers and critics of religious authority spelled out many of the themes that would be elaborated in the Protestant Reformation of the next century. Savonarola, an Italian monk, denounced corruption in Florence and the abuse of political power, calling for a regeneration of spiritual values and a steadfast devotion to asceticism.

In Bohemia the Hussites identified religious reforms with Bohemian nationalism while humanist writers in Italy, England, and Holland argued for the separation of religious and secular law and the freedom of conscience of the individual. In another sense the power of the universal Church was challenged in Spain where the crown set up the Spanish Inquisition.

Literature

Compared with the vitality and initiative of Boccaccio and Chaucer, European writers of the early 15th century produced less distinctive work. Learning rather than literature held sway and the revival of interest in classical studies led by the Humanist scholars in Italy had its main impact only after 1454, when the development of printing by Gutenberg in

Germany produced a rapidly increasing flow of books. Two outstanding writers who drew on medieval traditions were Villon, France's first great lyrical poet, and Malory, who dominated English prose with an adaptation of Arthurian legend. Lively vernacular poetry emerged in Scotland with Henryson and Dunbar and also in Florence and Naples late in the century.

Art and Architecture

Fifteenth-century European art was profoundly affected by the artistic Renaissance that emerged in Italy—a stylistic revolution characterized by a revival of interest in Greek and Roman antiquities that brought with it a new interest in the anatomy of the human form, in proportion, and in perspective, combined with a new sense of human dignity and confidence. Beginning in Florence, and fostered by widespread court patronage both ecclesiastical and secular, it spread rapidly to other parts of Italy and culminated at the end of the century in the masterpieces of Mantegna, Botticelli, Bellini, Leonardo, Michelangelo, and Bramante.

The Gothic style in architecture still flourished even in Italy and took new forms with the Perpendicular style in England, while International Gothic brought a new realism to European painting and sculpture.

Music

European music was dominated by the brilliance of the Franco-Flemish composers, the first great musical school. The church favored an international style of music and would admit no other styles, but national composers successfully challenged the Franco-Flemish school in the quality of their work, especially in the field of polyphonic songs.

Science

Important changes occurred in the economic and industrial organization of Europe. The Hundred Years War ended and with the Renaissance feudal methods of exchange gave way to more dynamic systems of trade. Technological change—in agriculture, mining, textiles, and glassmaking—continued, bringing a steady expansion of industry. The breakthrough of the century was the creation of Gutenberg's bookprinting industry at Nuremberg.

Ships and navigational instruments had been undergoing steady improvement and by the end of the century provided explorers with the means to sail to all parts of the globe. Maritime successes stimulated the founding of schools of navigation, which produced men trained in mathematics and curious about science but relatively untrammeled by the religious ideas that had ruled the minds of educated people of earlier medieval times.

Principal Events

Tamerlane's victory at Angora in 1402 brought temporary disorder to the Ottoman Empire.

Chinese naval expeditions to India and Africa for commercial and military prestige began in 1403.

Burgundian ambitions led to a French civil war with the Armagnacs in 1404.

Venice seized Vicenza, Padua, and Verona to become the dominant power in northern Italy.

Florence won access to the sea by buying Pisa in 1405.

The Americas

In Kentucky, near a saltwater spring that had been visited by animals and hunters for centuries, peoples of the Fort Ancient culture settled permanently.

Religion and Philosophy

The Chinese emperor Ch'eng Tsu, *r.*1403–24, sponsored the publication of an 11,095-volume encyclopedia in 1403.

The Council of Pisa, 1409, attempted to resolve the Great Schism in the papacy. This had arisen in 1378, with Urban VI in Rome and Clement VII in Avignon as rival claimants, backed by the empire and France.

John XXII, the compromise candidate, satisfied no one, however, and the schism continued until 1417.

Literature

The Mabinogion collection of Celtic tales and heroic legends was preserved in the Welsh *Red Book of Hergest*, c.1375–1425.

These anonymous stories contained a wealth of ancient mythology. They fused narrative with dialogue, conveying the vitality of the oral tradition from which these tales emerged, probably during the 11th century.

Art and Architecture

The International Gothic Style introduced a new realism into the painting of landscape, costume, and animals, exemplified in the wings of the altarpiece at Dijon, by **Melchior Broederlam**, *d.c.* 1410.

Gothic and Renaissance styles were linked in the bronze doors of the Florence Baptistery, sculptured by **Lorenzo Ghiberti**, 1378–1455, from 1403–52.

Burgundian sculpture was characterized by the "Well of Moses," 1401, by **Claus Sluter**.

Music

Under the Ming dynasty, 1368–1644, music declined in China. Long pieces, interspersing new material with a refrain, were played on the zither and tunes modulated for special effect.

Science and Technology

Technical treatises on military engineering and ballistics abounded in the early 15th century, especially in Germany and Italy. Among the most famous was the *Bellifortis* of 1405 by **Conrad Kyeser**, a German.

Archimedean screws, used for lifting water in Dutch polder dams, are known from 1408.

Perspective, used first in painting but later in scientific and architectural drawings, was discovered in the early 15th century by **Filippo Brunelleschi**, 1377–1446.

Principal Events

Mehmet I, r.1413–21, reunited the Ottoman Empire and consolidated power in the Balkans.
Henry V of England, r.1413–22, captured Normandy, 1417–19, after his victory at Agincourt in 1415.
The papal schism was ended at the Council of Constance, 1414–17, where **Huss,** 1369–1415, the Bohemian religious reformer, was burned for heresy.
Henry the Navigator, 1394–1460, began his systematic exploration of the African Coast.

The Americas

A 12-year period of drought began in 1413 in the southwestern part of New Mexico. Salado peoples moved into the valley of the Gila River about this time.

Religion and Philosophy

Pope Martin V, r.1417–31, whose election ended the Great Schism, moved the papacy permanently to Rome in 1420 and consolidated Church unity.
John Huss, c.1369–1415, a Bohemian follower of Wycliffe, criticized the papacy for the sale of indulgences (absolutions from sin) and urged a literal interpretation of the Bible. He denied the infallibility of an immoral pope and claimed the supremacy of the state over the Church.

Literature

Miracle plays based on biblical themes or the lives of saints were enacted in popular style in England and Europe. **John Lydgate,** c.1370–1451, English imitator of Chaucer and Boccaccio, produced the *Troy Book* and *Siege of Thames, c.*1420. **Perez de Guzman,** c.1370–c.1460, Spanish historian and poet, examined the theory of history and role of the historian.

Art and Architecture

The Duc de Berry commissioned the "Tres Riches Heures," c.1415, from the Limbourg brothers. His extensive patronage included the less-known "Très Belles Heures," and he built twelve elegant castles.
The design for Innocenti (Foundling) Hospital in Florence, 1419, by **Filippo Brunelleschi,** 1377–1446, began the architectural Renaissance in Italy and established Brunelleschi's reputation as one of the finest Renaissance architects.

Music

Composers set parts to imitate each other. Polyphony related melodies to the *cantus firmus*, and counterpoint used rhythmically related tunes.

Science and Technology

Drift nets up to 360ft (140m) long, towed behind fishing boats, were introduced by the Dutch fishing industry in 1416. These nets greatly improved the size of herring catches. The fish were preserved by a salting process improved by the Dutch.
Navigation was studied by experts from many nations at the court of **Henry the Navigator,** of Portugal 1394–1460.
Observatories were among the last achievements of Arab science. **Ulugh-Beg,** 1394–1449, made astronomical tables.

1420-1430

⭐ Principal Events

The Bohemian Hussites under **John Zizka**, *c.*1370–1424, were defeated in a series of imperial crusades, 1420–33.
Henry V of England was recognized as heir to the French throne, 1420. **Joan of Arc**, *c.*1412–31, then inspired a new French national unity in support of **Charles VII**, *r.*1422–61.
Peking became the Ming capital in 1421.
Murad II, *r.*1421–51, led an Ottoman attack on Constantinople in 1422.

The Americas

Itzcoatl, *r.*1428–40, led the Aztecs in a series of wars of conquest that would result in the emergence of a large and powerful empire in Mexico and Guatemala.

🕯 Religion and Philosophy

The Hussites were Bohemian followers of John Huss. They believed that the laity should receive both the wine and bread in communion instead of bread alone. **Thomas à Kempis**, *c.*1379–1471, wrote the *Imitation of Christ c.*1425. This simple book, emphasizing the need for a moderate asceticism, was considered at the time to be the most influential Christian work since the Bible.

Literature

Alain Chartier, *c.*1390–1440, wrote the allegorical poem "La Belle Dame Sans Merci" in 1424. An attack on courtly love,

it reflected political unrest in France after the defeat at Agincourt. In *Le Quadrilogue invectif*, 1422, a political pamphlet, he called for French solidarity to combat the turmoil of the Hundred Years War, using prose form to convey his plea.

🍷 Art and Architecture

Masaccio, *c.*1401–28, the first of the great *quattrocento* painters, used simplicity, naturalism, and light in a new way in his Brancacci Chapel frescoes, Florence, 1425–28.
One of the masterpieces of the International Gothic style in Italy was the "Adoration of the Magi," 1423, by **Gentile de Fabriano**, *c.*1370–1427.

🎵 Music

Choral polyphony using four independent parts now grew up. The voices (parts) were finely blended and the harmony euphonious, avoiding the dissonances common in earlier music.

⚛ Science and Technology

Nicholas of Cusa, 1401–64, wrote that the Earth, and not the heavens, revolved daily, a refutation of the accepted Ptolemaic astronomical system. Nicholas's idea was based upon philosophic notions and not on observable scientific data.
Hollow-post mills, invented *c.*1430 in Holland, were an improved form of windmill in which the size of the rotating sail arms was reduced and a shaft was passed from them through a hollow post to drive machinery in a building below.

Principal Events

Alfonso V of Aragon, *r.*1416–58, campaigned in Italy and took Naples in 1435.

The banking and wool merchant Medici family controlled Florence, 1434–94.

Hapsburg control of the Holy Roman Empire became virtually hereditary with **Albert II**, *r.*1438–39.

John VIII, *r.*1425–48, of Byzantium, inspired serious opposition by accepting the primacy of the pope in 1439.

The Americas

A very well fortified settlement was under construction at Angel Mound on the Ohio River in Indiana. A clay-and-mud wall surrounded a village with 11 mounds.

Religion and Philosophy

Nicholas of Cusa, 1401–64, in his *De Concordantia Catholica*, 1433, argued for the General Council's authority over the pope. However, the council's lack of power led him to reverse his position by 1437. Cusa also contributed to the sciences and philosophy. He wrote *Of Learned Ignorance*, in 1440, arguing against the possibility of ever attaining eternal truths.

Literature

The Italian Leon Battista Alberti, 1404–72, a brilliant Renaissance figure who was an architect, sculptor, and musician, wrote *Della Famiglia*, 1434, containing a theoretical treatise

within a discussion of household affairs. Styled on Latin models, it displayed a pessimistic view of contemporary life. He also published works on ethics, jurisprudence, and architecture.

Art and Architecture

Donatello, 1386–1466, an Italian and one of the greatest figures of 15th-century art, executed his classic bronze masterpiece "David" *c.*1435.

Flemish painting was revolutionized by **Jan van Eyck**, *d.*1441, who not only perfected an oil painting technique using brilliant color and subtle light effects but also brought an everyday realism to such works as "The Adoration of the Lamb," 1432.

Music

Secular polyphony developed as part-songs were combined with the four-part texture of "learned" music. This is a style that still lives on in barbershop quartet singing in the United States.

Science and Technology

Textile industries in the 15th century used **alum** to fix vegetable dyes, such as indigo, madder, and saffron, to cloth. Black dyes were made at this time by mixing green vitriol (iron sulfate) with oak galls to make the intensely black iron stannate. In textile finishing, **gigmills** (as first drawn by Leonardo da Vinci) were being used to raise the nap of cloth into a woolly texture.

★ Principal Events

After losing Serbia, the Ottoman Turks defeated a Hungarian crusade against them in 1444.
Charles VII created a French standing army free from feudal obligations.
Wars in Italy caused a rise in diplomatic activity, and artistic patronage became a major factor in a ruler's prestige c.1440.
Japan, under Ashikaga rule since 1336, underwent a period of cultural refinement c.1440.

The Americas

The Xius, one of the Mayan tribes, revolted in 1441 against the rival tribe, Cocoms. Mayapan disintegrated.

Religion and Philosophy

In 1440, **Lorenzo Valla**, 1407–57, attacked papal political claims by asserting that the *Donations of Constantine*, an anonymous document that supposedly granted universal temporal power to the papacy, was a forgery. As a humanist of the Italian Renaissance, Valla accused the medieval philosophers of deliberately misunderstanding and poorly interpreting the works of Plato and Aristotle.

Literature

Bengali literature, which had existed in India since the 10th century, was enriched by the rhymed version of *Ramayana*, made c.1440 by Kirttivasa, b.1385, and by the lyrical *Song of Krishna* by Chandidas, 1417–77. In Spain, the Marquis of Santillana, 1398–1458, wrote Italian-style sonnets that enriched the poetic tradition.

Art and Architecture

In Italy Domenico Veneziano, d.1461, represented the most advanced stage of mid-century Florentine painting in his "St Lucy" altarpiece, 1445.
Rogier van der Weyden, 1400–64, a major mid-15th century Flemish artist, produced a more emotional style than van Eyck. His great "Deposition" was painted c.1435.
Fra Angelico, c.1387–1455, and **Fra Filippo Lippi**, c.1406–69, both linked Gothic and Renaissance styles.

Music

The use of the interval of a third (long established in England) standardized harmony in polyphony but the increasing preoccupation with harmony itself led to dull and static rhythms.

Science and Technology

Johann Gutenberg, c.1400–68, of Strasbourg, began printing with movable metal type, a process invented in Korea in the 15th century. Gutenberg's books were the first to be printed in this way in the West, yet no printed work bearing his name exists. Letters were cast in type metal, composed into sentences on a type stick, and set up as pages of type before being inked for the press. It is possible that Gutenberg designed his press along the lines of wine and linen presses.

Principal Events

The alliance of Florence, Naples, and Milan, 1450, inspired by Medici diplomacy, ensured the balance of power among the Italian states.

The fall of Constantinople in 1453 to the Ottoman ruler **Mehmet II,** *r.*1451–81, ended 1,000 years of Byzantine rule.

George Podiebrad, 1420–71, ended the Bohemian religious wars with conciliatory policies.

The Wars of the Roses between the houses of Lancaster and York began in England, 1455.

The Americas

Among the Aztec artisans were the feather workers who mounted feathers on cloth. The feathers were part of tribute paid to **Montezuma I,** *r.*1444–59.

Religion and Philosophy

The Indian mystic Kabir, 1440–1518, attempted to merge some aspects of the Hindu creed with Sufist Muslim ideas. Kabir, originally a weaver from Benares, rejected Hindu beliefs in idols and castes but accepted the institutions of reincarnation and eventual release. His followers were known as **Kabirpanthis.** This movement was a forerunner of the movement of Sikhism.

The first printed Bible was produced in Mainz in 1456.

Literature

Medieval French verse forms were infused with vigor and blunt realism in the lyrical poetry of **François Villon,** 1430–*c.*63, in which he recalls his wasted life. He was awaiting execution when he wrote *Ballad of a Hanged Man.*

Diego de San Pedro, *fl.*1450, was best known for his sentimental novels that influenced the Spanish novel.

Art and Architecture

The study of perspective absorbed **Paolo Uccello,** *c.*1397–1475, whose famous "Battles," 1454–57, also possess an eerie, dreamlike atmosphere.

The frescoes of S. Francesco, Arezzo, 1452, by **Piero della Francesca,** *c.*1420–92, were outside the mainstream of Italian painting and closer to the diffused naturalism of Flemish art with their mathematical precision and use of light and shade.

Music

National forms evolved in polyphonic song, with the *frottola* in Italy and the *lied* in Germany matching the richness of the established *chanson* in France.

Science and Technology

Instrument-making in Europe became centered on Nuremberg *c.*1450, and Augsburg *c.*1475.

Calendar reform was undertaken *c.*1450 under the direction of the astronomer **Puerbach,** 1423–61 The Julian calendar, commissioned by Julius Caesar and accurate to 1 day in 128 years, was wrong by 10 days in 1450. However, revision was not finished until 1582.

Quadrants, for determining latitude at sea, were used by European seafarers *c.*1456.

Principal Events

Venice fought the Turks for control of the Mediterranean, 1463–79.
Louis XI, r.1461–83, aided French unification by ending provincial and urban privileges.
The Onin War, 1467–77, resulted from a succession dispute among the Ashikaga in Japan. This was a prelude to a century of war.
The kingdom of Songhay, based on the Middle Niger region, reached its zenith under **Sonni Ali,** r.1464–92.

The Americas

By c.1466, ruler Pachacuti Inca Yupanqui, r.1438–71, had completed his subjugation of the Chimú Empire, extending Inca control over all of Peru.

Religion and Philosophy

The Unitas Fratrum (Bohemian Brethren), founded by Peter of Chelchich, d.1460, broke with the Utraquists in 1467. They were a militantly democratic sect who, like the Taborites, rejected subordination to Rome.

Literature

Scottish poetry flourished with "The Testament of Cresseid" by **Robert Henryson,** c.1425–1508, a tragic and powerful sequel to Chaucer's poem. **William Dunbar,** c.1460–1520, was less earnest but more versatile. His "Dance of the Seven Deadly Sins" is similar to Villon in its macabre vigor.

The Scottish poets combined romance and satire with idiomatic language.

Art and Architecture

Leon Battista Alberti, 1404–72, writer, musician, painter, and architect, crystallized Renaissance ideas on architectural proportions and harmonious design. His use of classical elements for the church of San Sebastiano, Mantua, 1470, deprived it of an "ecclesiastical" flavor.
Hans Memling, c.1440–94, a German who settled in Bruges, became a successful Flemish painter and influenced later Italian art.

Music

The Franco-Flemish school included Guillaume Dufay, c.1400–74, Johannes Ockegham, c.1430–95, and Josquin des Prés, c.1450–1521, who used popular tunes in his work.

Science and Technology

Carracks, the earliest form of modern sailing ships, are illustrated on a French seal of 1466. These ships had three or four masts, raised decks fore and aft, and a stern rudder and tiller for steering; by 1500 they weighed as much as 600 tons. They supplanted the trading galleys for ocean voyages, and a military version followed—the galleon.
Tables for navigation were revised by the German astronomer **Johann Müller,** 1436–76.

Principal Events

Ivan the Great, *r*.1462–1505, adopted the title of tsar in 1472 and subjected Novgorod to Muscovite rule in 1478.
Burgundy was reunited with France, 1477. In spite of the Pazzi plot to assassinate him, **Lorenzo de' Medici**, 1449–92, ruled in Florence and exhausted the stagnant economy with his flamboyant foreign policy.
The marriage of Ferdinand and Isabella, 1469, would unite Aragon and Castile in 1479.

The Americas

The year 1476 marked the completion of the Inca Empire's conquest. Topa Inca Yupanqui, *r*.1471–93, took control of parts of Bolivia, Argentina, and Chile.

Religion and Philosophy

Sir John Fortescue, *c*.1394–*c*.1479, in *De Laudibus Legum Angliae*, *c*.1470, praised English over Roman law and introduced the principle of "innocent until proven guilty."
Set up in 1478 by Ferdinand and Isabella with the reluctant permission of the pope, who regarded it as a breach of Church privilege, **the Spanish Inquisition** persecuted converted Jews and Muslims as well as Catholic intellectuals, among them Ignatius Loyola.

Literature

Arthurian legend was unified in the epic prose romance *Morte d'Arthur*, 1469–70, by **Sir Thomas Malory**, *d*.1471. Its admirably plain style and its creative adaptation of medievalism to modern thought deeply influenced later writers. It was published in 1485 by **William Caxton**, a key figure in the development of English printing, which he began in 1476.

Art and Architecture

The equestrian monument to Bartolomeo Colleone, in Venice, commissioned in 1479 and executed by **Andrea del Verrochio**, *c*.1434–88, showed a masterly rendering of movement and a use of light and shade that anticipated Michelangelo.
In Mantua Andrea Mantegna, 1431–1506, painted his fresco "Camera degli Sposi" at the Gonzaga Palace, 1474, and in Florence **Sandro Botticelli**, 1444–1510, produced his "Primavera" *c*.1478.

Music

The mass attained a great variety of structure, although the use of the *cantus firmus* throughout, in many ingenious modifications, brought unity to the form.

Science and Technology

Rifles were first made *c*.1475, according to armory records in Turin and Nuremberg. These were muzzle loaders, in which the lead bullet was made slightly larger than the bore so that it had to be forced into the barrel, giving a tight fit.

1480-1490

Principal Events

Ivan the Great ended the Tatar threat to Moscow, 1480, and annexed Tver in 1485.
The Spanish Church and the **Inquisition** came under royal control after a concordat with the pope in 1482.
The Portuguese Bartolomeu Diaz, 1450–1500, rounded the Cape of Good Hope, 1487–88.
The Wars of the Roses ended with the dominance of **Henry VII** (Tudor), r.1485–1509, who established royal independence from baronial support.

The Americas

The magnificently carved 20-ton Aztec Calendar Stone, also known as the Sun Stone for the image of the Sun God it bears, was completed about this time.

Religion and Philosophy

Rodolphus Agricola, c.1443–85, was an early Dutch humanist who influenced Erasmus. In his lectures at Heidelberg, given from 1484, he expounded a philosophy emphasizing the freedom of the individual and the intellectual and physical development of the self.
The existence of witchcraft was admitted by the Church in 1484 and its practices condemned. *Malleus Maleficarum*, 1487, described witchcraft and encouraged its suppression.

Literature

Humanist poetry emerged in Italy where **Luigi Pulci**, 1432–84, treated the heroic Charlemagne theme irreverently in *Morgante Maggiore*, c.1483. Another Florentine poet, **Angelo Poliziano**, 1454–94, wrote the first secular play, "Orfeo," 1480.
Matteo Maria Boiardo, c.1441–94, wrote Latin eulogies and lyric love poems including his epic *Orlando Innamorato*.

Art and Architecture

English Perpendicular Gothic style with its extremely intricate vaulting is seen in the **Divinity School** at Oxford University, completed 1480.
The rebirth of Venetian painting began with **Giovanni Bellini**, c.1430–1516, whose "Madonna and Saints," 1488, has resonant colors and novel lighting.
Medici patronage in Florence produced the first great Renaissance villa. **Poggio a Caiano**, begun c.1482 by **Giuliano da Sangallo**, 1445–1516.

Music

Keyboard instruments improved in Europe. A Flemish painting of 1484 depicts an organ with a chromatic keyboard. The clavichord had a range of up to four octaves.

Science and Technology

Leonardo da Vinci, 1452–1519, painter, sculptor, architect, engineer, and scientist, began service as a military engineer with Cesare Borgia, 1476–1507, in 1502. Working mainly in Milan and Florence, he made scientific drawings of animals, human, and plant anatomy, rocks, and optical systems. He also conceived and drew a helicopter, a mobile canal cutter, and several kinds of pumps. However, most of his designs were never built, as mechanics lagged behind his inventiveness.

Principal Events

Spain captured Granada, the last Moorish outpost, and expelled 200,000 Jews, 1492.
Christopher Columbus, 1451–1506, discovered the New World, 1492, on his search for a western route to India.
Vasco da Gama reached India around Africa, 1497–98.
Charles VIII of France, r.1483–98, invaded Italy, 1495, but was expelled by an alliance including the empire, the papacy, and Venice, formed to protect Italy from foreign domination.

The Americas

For the English, **John Cabot**, 1450–98, explored North America. **Treaty of Tordesillas**, 1494, divided the colonial world between Spain and Portugal.

Religion and Philosophy

The French statesman **Philippe de Comines**, c.1447–c.1511, argued that taxes needed sanction of the Estates General, the representative body of nobles, gentry and clergy.
With the defeat of the Medicis in Florence, **Savonarola**, 1452–98, established city rule free from corruption and along democratic lines. His sermons criticizing aristocratic and papal corruption led to his death at the stake in 1498.

Literature

German satirical writing reached the common man in the popular and influential *Ship of Fools*, 1494, by **Sebastian Brant**, c.1458–1521, which mocked vice in rhyming couplets.

In Persia, the death of the poet and mystic **Jami**, 1414–92, ended the classical period of Persian Sufi poetry. He was notable for such romantic verse as "Salaman u Absal."

Art and Architecture

The two giants of the Italian **Renaissance** emerged. **Leonardo da Vinci**, 1452–1519, painted his "Last Supper" in the refectory of Sta Maria delle Grazie, Milan, in 1495–98. His rival **Michelangelo**, 1475–1564, sculpted the St Peter's "Pietà" in 1499 when 24 years old.
Donato Bramante, 1444–1514, one of the greatest architects of the High Renaissance, designed the spacious gallery of **Sta Maria delle Grazie**, Milan, dating from 1492.

Music

Music printing began in Germany but was developed fully in Venice by **Ottaviano dei Petrucci**, who patented his process in 1498. His technique led to the birth of music publishing.

Science and Technology

The voyages of Diaz, Vasco da Gama, Columbus, and Magellan, in the late 15th and 16th centuries, encouraged the founding of navigation schools in Portugal and Spain. These schools produced a new group of expertly trained mathematical and nautical technicians, which greatly influenced the standing of science in Europe.
Dissection of human cadavers had been practiced for a century in Europe but systematic dissections, in medical schools of Padua, began c.1500.

The Reformation 1500–1600

Martin Luther founded Protestantism.

Benin bronze figures from West Africa

Church of a diocesan bishop, Mexico City

Tempietto of San Pietro, Rome

Sistine Chapel frescoes: "Birth of Adam" by Michelangelo

Selim the Grim, Ottoman sultan

Caravaggio introduced simple realism in painting.

German peasant revolts, Swabia

The Reformation

Principal Events

The Reformation brought a new dimension to Europe's dynastic wars and social conflicts. As the Italian states declined, Spain, invigorated by wealth from the New World, led the Catholic offensive against England, the Netherlands, and the Protestant German princes. Royal authority increased with the decline of papal authority, but the religious and political debates, and the new wealth from confiscation of church lands, enabled an eloquent and powerful middle class to challenge royal power.

European expansion continued. Much of the American coastline and the Far East was reached by all the major powers, although only the American civilizations succumbed to the explorers. Japan experienced vigorous expansion, and the Moguls brought a stable and flourishing culture to India with the establishment of an extensive empire under Babur and Akbar.

The Americas

European settlement in the Americas began on Santo Domingo, 1494. There was exploration and colonization by England, Spain, Portugal, the Netherlands, and France. The civilizations of Mexico and Peru flourished. Explorers sought glory and wealth, the extension of Christianity, and new trade routes.

Religion and Philosophy

The Protestant Reformation took place in western Europe, arising from objections to many of the doctrines and practices of the medieval Church. Reformers attacked the worldliness of clergy, the stifling of intellectual progress, and the inability of the Church to provide spiritual leadership. Luther stated that faith alone was the basis of salvation, believing that no intermediary between man and God could alter his salvation. Calvin in Geneva also rejected the power of his church to alter who was saved and who damned by God. The general questioning of religious authority gave a new dimension to the already critical question of the relation of church and state, leading for example in England to rapid changes in official religion. By 1600 the Reformation had spread to almost all of northwest Europe, and there were also large numbers of Protestants in France, Poland, and Hungary.

Literature

With the spread of the Renaissance the 16th century brought moments of great brilliance to national literatures, particularly those of England, France, Italy, Spain, and Portugal. In England, the work of Wyatt and the Elizabethan poets and dramatists culminated in the genius of Shakespeare, who created a body of lyric poetry and drama of unmatched scope and power. Rabelais and Montaigne dominated French

158

writing, and poets such as Ronsard began the move toward classical themes in French literature. Pastoral idealism found expression in the Iberian Peninsula and Italy, and epic poetry flourished.

In China the novel form emerged, and in both India and Turkey, Islamic influence revitalized literary traditions.

Art and Architecture

With the work of Michelangelo, Leonardo, Raphael, and Bramante at the beginning of the 16th century, Italian Renaissance art reached a climax in the development of perspective, the analysis of the human form, and the celebration of classical models. By 1520, however, this peak was past. Mannerism followed with its lack of harmony, distorted forms, and search for novelty. Later in the century, the naturalistic experiments of Caravaggio, and Carracci's reassertion of classical canons in new dramatic compositions, pointed toward a new style—Baroque. Italy remained the official arbiter of taste in Europe, but the styles were more readily absorbed by the still solidly Catholic France and Spain. In the Protestant north the Reformation replaced church patronage with that of merchants, encouraging the growth of secular art forms. Exploration in the New World carried European art abroad.

Music

The growing Protestant church in Europe redefined the liturgy for its own use, and sacred music began to be performed by lay people in church and their homes, widening the basis of religious music. City councils and individual patrons established their own groups of musicians, raising instrumental music to the same status as choral music.

Science

A scientific revolution began in Europe in the 16th century and with it a long-held conception of the nature of the universe died. The century began with the later work of Leonardo da Vinci—a series of brilliant inventions that came to little because the scientific principles needed to realize them were hardly known—and culminated in Kepler's exact scientific calculations, based on Copernicus' idea of a Sun-centered universe and the precise astronomical observations of Tycho Brahe. This work finally destroyed the Aristotelian picture of the universe as a group of perfect crystal spheres centering on, and revolving about, the Earth, and opened the way for Galileo.

Advances were also made in medical science, particularly in anatomy, chemistry, larger-scale iron production, and mining technology. Despite opposition from the Church, by 1600 science was firmly based on the experimental method and had turned its back on theology.

1500-1510

Principal Events

The Italian wars provided an opportunity for conflict between the Hapsburgs and the Valois (French kings) until 1559. This caused a decline in the prosperity and autonomy of the Italian cities.

The Portuguese claimed Brazil and established regular trade with India, 1500. The Spanish introduced African slaves to the West Indies, 1501.

Ashikaga prestige in Japan was in decline.

The Americas

Amerigo Vespucci, 1454–1512, in 1501 led a Portuguese voyage to explore South America, which he called a "New World." In 1507 it was named America.

Religion and Philosophy

Erasmus, c.1466–1536, a humanist scholar, wrote *Praise of Folly*, 1509, which satirized church corruption and scholastic philosophy.

Literature

Commedia dell'arte developed from earlier peasant traditions in Italy. Actors improvised farce from a set scenario using stock characters such as Pedrillo, who became the French Pierrot, and the stupid but agile Harlequin. This boisterous form of theater had little literary merit but influenced later drama, especially the comedies of **Molière** in France.

Art and Architecture

The Renaissance reached its height in Florence and Rome *c.* 1500–20. **Leonardo da Vinci,** 1452–1519, painted the "Mona Lisa," 1503–06, achieving a more naturalistic effect by leaving outlines blurred. **Michelangelo,** 1475–1564, also in Florence at this time, completed the statue of "David," 1504. **Donato Bramante,** 1444–1514, built the Tempietto of S. Pietro, Rome, 1502, and was invited by Pope Julius II to design the new St Peter's, 1506.

Music

The single or solo line drew the interest of composers of the early 1500s, reacting to the increasing complexity of polyphony. Their interest is seen in their airs and lute songs.

Science and Technology

T. B. von Hohenheim Paracelsus c.1493–1541, professor of medicine at Basel, made advances in chemistry although his system of iatrochemistry (chemical doctoring) was a mixture of observed fact and superstition.

The coach was invented in Hungary, probably in the early 16th century, but would not appear in England until the 1580s. It differed from covered wagons in having a strap suspension and a pivoted front axle. Queen Elizabeth I owned an early coach.

Principal Events

Russia took Smolensk from Po
land in 1514.
Charles V, 1500–58, created the
Hapsburg Empire, inheriting the
Spanish crown, 1516, and being
proclaimed Holy Roman emperor
in 1519.
Ferdinand Magellan, c.1480–
1521, sailed through the
Pacific Ocean, 1519–21, and
Hernando Cortés, 1485–1547,
conquered the Aztecs in Mexico,
1519–21. **Portugal** controlled
the import of spices from the
East Indies c.1520.

The Americas

Juan Ponce de Léon, 1460–
1521, explored Florida, 1513.
Vasco Núñez de Balboa, 1475–
1519, crossed the Isthmus of
Panama to the Pacific, 1513.

Religion and Philosophy

The **Utopia**, 1516, of **Thomas
More**, c.1478–1535, depicted an
imaginary island lacking the
evils of Europe.
Machiavelli, 1469–1527, wrote
The Prince, 1513, a ruthlessly
pragmatic analysis of politics.
Martin Luther, 1483–1546, af
fixed his 95 Theses to the door
of Wittenberg Castle Church in
1517.
Sikhism, a combination of
Hinduism and Islam, was found
ed c.1519 by **Nanak**, 1469–1539.

Literature

The Portuguese dramatist **Gil
Vicente**, 1470–1536, wrote nat
uralistic plays, full of intrigue
and psychological insight. The
innovative English poet and hu
manist **John Skelton**, 1460–
1529, wrote scathing attacks
on the court and clergy. His
German contemporary **Ulrich
von Hutten**, 1488–1523, used
dialogues to champion the cause
of the Reformation.

Art and Architecture

Michelangelo in Rome com
pleted the Sistine Chapel fres
coes, 1512, and **Raphael**,
1483–1520, the Stanza fres
coes in 1514, with their dazzling
use of perspective.
Leonardo left for Amboise,
France, 1516.
English Gothic art in its final
stage was seen in Henry VII's
Westminster Chapel, 1503–19.
His tomb in the chapel by **Torri
giano**, 1472–1528, was the first
use of Italian Renaissance mo
tifs in England.

Music

The fantasia, toccata and varia
tions, and the ricercar
(forerunner of the fugue) were
new instrumental forms devised
to exploit the individual qualities
of musical instruments.

Science and Technology

Coins containing copper mixed
with gold or silver came into use
in Europe in the early 16th cen
tury as a result of the great in
crease in prices caused in part
by large imports of Spanish sil
ver from Peru. **Henry VIII of Eng
land**, r.1509–47, in particular,
debased the currency in this
way. Although later recoinage
partly improved the real value of
money, alloying became the rule.
A mass production technique for
casting small brass objects was
practiced in Italy at this time.

1520-1530

Principal Events

Portuguese traders reached China, 1520–21.
Frederick III of Saxony, r.1486–1525, led the princely support for Luther, 1483–1546.
Peasant revolts in Swabia, inspired by Luther's example and by discontent with feudal obligations, were ruthlessly suppressed in 1525.
Babur, 1483–1530, founded the brilliant Mogul Empire in north India in 1526.
The Medici were driven out of Florence in 1527.

The Americas

Spaniard Hernando Cortés, 1485–1547, subjugated central America in 1519. **Montezuma**, r.1502–20, was killed, and the Aztec Empire ended, 1521.

Religion and Philosophy

Luther was excommunicated in 1520. At the Diet of Worms, 1521, he argued for "justification by faith alone," the doctrine that no intermediary priest can aid salvation. Luther's attacks on the Catholic Church led to a rejection of papal authority and marked the start of the Protestant Reformation. This doctrine was adopted by many princes for its political implications. Luther translated the Bible into the vernacular c.1525.

Literature

Italian court life and etiquette were vividly portrayed in the *Libro del Cortegiano*, 1528, by **Baldassare Castiglione**, 1478–1529.

Portuguese poetry reached its peak with the epic *The Lusiads*, 1572, by **Luís Camões**, c. 1524–80.

Art and Architecture

German painting showed two trends. **Grunewald**, 1480–1528, painted the Isenheim altarpiece, c. 1512–16, in the late Gothic style but **Dürer**, 1471–1528, who had visited Italy, made use of Renaissance ideals in his "Four Apostles," 1526.
Venetian painting broke from the Renaissance emphasis on drawing and perfect form. The Pesaro altarpiece, 1519–26, by **Titian**, c.1487–1576, used a dramatic juxtaposition of contrasting colors and diagonals.

Music

German hymns or chorales were composed in the 1520s and were firmly established by the end of the century. Set in four or five parts, they were often written to existing popular tunes.

Science and Technology

Blast furnaces, able to produce large quantities of cast iron, gradually evolved from earlier Stückofen. Cast iron so made was mostly used in weaponry, an industry in which England led Europe, selling to any customer who could pay the price, whether friend or enemy.
Coal became a major fuel in mid-16th century industrial Europe as the price of wood soared and forests disappeared. Coal mines opened in Liège and Newcastle.

Principal Events

Protestantism spread throughout northern Europe. **Henry VIII** of England, *r.*1509–47, dissolved the monasteries, 1536–39.
Francisco Pizarro, *c.*1471–1541, a Spaniard, conquered Peru for booty, from 1531.
The Afghan Sher Khan, *r.*1539–45, expelled the Mogul emperor Humayan and reformed the administration.
Suleiman the Magnificent, *r.*1520–66, brought Ottoman power to its zenith.

 The Americas

Francisco Pizarro, leaving Panama, 1531, captured (and later executed) Inca ruler **Atahualpa**. Pizarro's men fought over Inca wealth.

 Religion and Philosophy

The Anabaptists, who prophesied the imminent end of the world, gained control of Munster in Germany in 1534.
The Mennonites, a Dutch sect, shared the Anabaptists' belief in pacifism and pastoralism.
In 1534, Henry VIII of England assumed full authority over the English Church.
Ignatius de Loyola, 1491–1556, formed the Catholic Jesuit order in 1540.

 Literature

Meistersang, a form of poetic song based on minstrel tradition, was popular in Germany. It was enlivened by the work of the devout Lutheran poet **Hans Sachs**, 1494–1576, a cobbler with a talent for comic verse.

Ludovico Ariosto, 1474–1533, poet, dramatist and satirist, published *Orlando Furioso*, 1532, the greatest Italian epic of romantic chivalry.

 Art and Architecture

The Reformation had interrupted patronage in Basel and forced **Hans Holbein**, 1497–1543, to seek work in England, where he arrived in 1526 with a letter of introduction from Erasmus to Sir Thomas More. After 1532 he settled there and painted court portraits. **The Wu school** in China, including **Wen Chengming**, 1470–1559, and **T'ang Yin**, 1470–1523, worked away from the Imperial Academy, painting rich landscapes with genre scenes.

 Music

Consorts of instruments (viols or recorders) were cultural perquisites found in many wealthy homes. Families of instruments were usually played separately to give euphonious sonorities.

 Science and Technology

Telesio, an Italian who lived 1509–88, proposed the first system of physics to rival Aristotle's. His theory argued that heat and cold were the motive powers of the universe, an idea that would later influence the work of the English philosopher **Francis Bacon**, 1561–1626. **Andreas Vesalius**, 1514–64, accepted the chair of anatomy in Padua, 1537, and shocked the Church by dissecting corpses. His book *De Humani Corporis Fabrica* (1543) would advance knowledge of internal anatomy.

Principal Events

John Calvin, 1509–64, established a puritan theocracy at Geneva in 1541.
The Catholic Counter Reformation inspired Charles V to conduct the Schmalkaldic War, 1546–47, against the Protestant princes.
Brittany was united with France in 1547.
The Portuguese were the first Europeans in Japan, 1542, where the Jesuit **Francis Xavier**, 1506–52, founded a mission in 1549.

The Americas

France's **Jacques Cartier**, 1491–1557, attempted to colonize Quebec in 1541. **Hernando De Soto**, c.1500–42, discovered the Mississippi River, 1541.

Religion and Philosophy

John Calvin 1506–64, promoted the Reformation in Geneva, 1541. He espoused the doctrine of predestination – that God had already elected those to be saved – but it was believed that exemplary conduct signified election. **Decrees issued by the Council of Trent** on Church reform in 1545–47 initiated the Catholic, or Counter, Reformation.
Thomas Cranmer, 1489–1556, issued the Church of England's *Book of Common Prayer*, 1549.

Literature

La Pléiade, a group of seven French poets, of whom the greatest was **Pierre de Ronsard**, 1524–85, established the Alexandrine meter of a 12-syllable line and emphasized the dignity of the French language while turning to classical themes. Their manifesto was written by **Joachim du Bellay**, 1522–60, in *Defense et Illustration de la Langue Française*, 1549.

Art and Architecture

French Renaissance art copied Italian models as the painters **Rosso**, 1494–1540, and **Primaticcio**, 1504–c.70, and the architects **Vignola**, 1507–73, and **Serlio**, 1475–1554, came to France to work on the Palace of Fontainebleau, 1528–60. **Mannerist painting** in Italy, like the "Madonna with the Long Neck," 1534–36, by **Girolamo Parmigianino**, 1503–40, shows an elongation of figures, a lack of harmony, and a search for the new and unusual.

Music

The lute became popular as an accompanying instrument. It could be used to accompany the new contrapuntal madrigal style that grew up in Italy after 1530. Later the English adopted it.

Science and Technology

A Sun-centered universe was proposed in the book *On the Revolutions of the Celestial Orbs* by **Nicolas Copernicus**, 1473–1543, published in the year of his death. In this revolutionary work, the Earth, Moon, and planets, and outside them the stars, orbited around the Sun in circles. This theory is the basis of modern cosmology. Zoological and botanical works were published in the mid-16th century by the French biologists **Gesner**, 1516–65, **Belon**, 1517–64, and **Rondelet**, 1507–66.

Principal Events

The Peace of Augsburg, 1555, permitted each German prince to decide the religion of his subjects. After Charles V's retirement and later abdication **Philip II of Spain,** r.1556–98, took over the Catholic offensive, while **Elizabeth I,** r.1558–1603, confirmed England's Protestantism.

The influx of American silver to Spain accelerated inflation and caused hardship to the poor, but encouraged the rise of a European middle class.

The Americas

The Indian population of Spanish America, about 7,000,000 in 1550, declined as Indians died of European diseases. By 1600 they numbered about 1,000,000.

Religion and Philosophy

Many English Protestant bishops, including Cranmer, were burned at the stake in the reign of Queen Mary. Elizabeth, her successor, reestablished the Protestant Church but continued to burn heretics.

The Holy Roman Empire acknowledged Lutheranism in the Peace of Augsburg, 1555.

Protestantism in Scotland was united by the Calvinist **John Knox,** 1513–72, and became the national faith by Act of Parliament in 1560.

Literature

Among the great comic prose works of world literature, *Gargantua* and *Pantagruel* were completed in 1552 by **François Rabelais,** c.1494–c.1553. This bawdy, satirical tale of two grotesque giants was an erudite allegory vigorously attacking established institutions and conventional wisdom, mocking superstitious fears and defending free will.

Art and Architecture

The historian and painter **Vasari,** 1511–74, published the *Lives of the most excellent Painters, Sculptors, and Architects* in 1550.

Palladio, 1508–80, designed the Villa Rotunda, Vicenza, c.1550, beginning work c.1566. With its four porticos and symmetrical plan, it is an example of his search for classical and harmonious proportions. **Benin bronze figures** of West Africa adopted freer poses as a result of contact with Portuguese culture.

Music

Sacred polyphony declined in influence after the Council of Trent, 1545–63, regularized the musical forms suitable for the mass of the Roman Catholic Church.

Science and Technology

Georg Bauer (Agricola), 1494–1555, a German doctor, gave a full description of mining, smelting, and chemistry in *De Re Metallica,* published at Basel in 1556. Agricola's book is still the major source on technology in the later Middle Ages.

Discoveries of metals in the 16th century included that of mercury, c.1550, in Peru. Mercury was later used to extract silver from its ores by amalgamation. Zinc, bismuth, cobalt, and nickel were other metals used in alloys or mixtures.

Principal Events

The French wars of religion began, 1562, between the Catholics and the Protestant Huguenots (mostly nobles and townsmen in west and south France). **The Calvinist** and predominantly mercantile Dutch provinces began a long war of independence from Spain, 1568. **Nobunaga**, 1534–82, introduced a dynamic period of Japanese centralization and expansion. **Akbar**, r. 1556–1605, expanded the Mogul Empire and created a tolerant cosmopolitan culture.

The Americas

Britain's **John Hawkins**, 1532–95, transported black slaves from West Africa to the Spanish West Indies, 1562–67. **St. Augustine, Fla.**, was founded, 1565.

Religion and Philosophy

The adoption of the 39 Articles in 1563, combining Protestant doctrine with Catholic church organization, finally established the Church of England. There were many dissenting groups, among them the Puritans, who opposed church ritual, the Separatists, who rejected Anglicanism entirely, the Presbyterians, who had synods instead of bishops, and the Brownists, a communistic sect. All but the Brownists and Catholics were tolerated.

Literature

The English poets **Thomas Wyatt**, 1503–42, and the **Earl of Surrey**, c.1517–47, wrote in sonnets and blank verse – forms perfected by the Elizabethan poets **Shakespeare**, **Walter Raleigh**, 1552–1618, and **Edmund Spenser**, 1552–99.

Art and Architecture

Flemish painting saw the emergence of the individualist **Pieter Bruegel the Elder**, c.1525–69, one of the greatest landscape painters and a remarkable satirist, whose series "The Months" dates from 1565. **Indian Mogul art** assimilated the Persian tradition of miniature painting, which emphasized sumptuous decoration and lively color patterns. This was combined with indigenous styles in the illustrations of Akbar's life in the *Akbar-nama*.

Music

Japanese music began to win its individual character with the popularization of national forms of vertical bamboo pipe *(shakuhachi)*, three-stringed guitar *(samisen)*, and zither *(koto)*.

Science and Technology

Letter symbols for algebra and trigonometry were pioneered by **Vieta**, a French mathematician, 1540–1603. Words had previously been used for variables, the substitution of letters such as x and y greatly speeded up calculations and also removed many previous ambiguities. **Gerhard Kremer Mercator**, 1512–94, published a map, 1568, using a projection that has since borne his name. **The potato** was introduced to Europe from South America by the Spaniards c.1570.

★ Principal Events

A European alliance defeated the Ottoman fleet at **Lepanto** in 1571, but Venice failed to use the opportunity to regain control of the eastern Mediterranean.
The Portuguese began their settlement of Angola, 1574.
The Dutch provinces, with increasing involvement in trade outside Europe, united in opposition to Spain, 1579.
England's Sir Francis Drake, *c.*1540–96, circumnavigated the world, 1577–80.

The Americas

British navigator Sir Francis Drake, *c.*1540–96, on a voyage around the world in the *Golden Hind*, claimed California for **Queen Elizabeth I**, in 1579.

Religion and Philosophy

Jean Bodin, 1530–96, a major French political theorist, published his *Six Books of the Commonwealth* in 1576, arguing that the basis of any society was the family. His most important contribution was an analysis of sovereignty. He argued that in any state sovereignty was necessary to prevent anarchy and that the exercise of monarchical power in conformity with the natural law was unquestionable, as it had divine authorization.

Literature

Michel de Montaigne, 1533–92, began his *Essays* in 1580.
In China the realistic, erotic novel the *The Golden Lotus* was published *c.*1575.

John Lyly, *c.*1554–1606, wrote *Euphues*, 1578–80, an early novel of manners.
Torquato Tasso, 1544–95, published *Jerusalem Liberated* in 1575 and the pastoral romance *Aminta* in 1573.

Art and Architecture

The brilliant Monoyama period in Japan, 1573–1615, is seen in the castle at Azuchi, built for **Nobunaga**, 1576–79, which contained large rooms decorated with murals. Screens painted with strong colors on gold ground came into fashion.
Spanish colonial architecture in the late 16th century, like Mexico Cathedral, 1563–1667, was based on contemporary Spanish mannerist styles but derived a pre-Columbian flavor from the native Indian labor.

Music

Javanese fleeing the spread of Islam reached Bali and kept early traditions of Indonesian music in the works for the gamelan orchestra (mostly tuned percussion instruments).

Science and Technology

Sir Thomas Gresham, 1519–79, established by will the first British institute for teaching science, which later housed the Royal Society.
Decimals were introduced to mathematical calculations in physics by **Simon Stevin**, 1585.

Principal Events

Portugal and Spain were united under **Philip II** of Spain, 1580. **England** assisted the Dutch revolt in 1585, executed the Catholic **Mary, Queen of Scots** in 1587, and defeated the **Spanish Armada** in 1588.
Pope Sixtus V, r.1585–90, a supporter of the Counter Reformation, began the internal reform of the papacy.
Hidayoshi, r.1584–98, expelled the Portuguese missionaries from Japan in 1587.

The Americas

The first British child in America, **Virginia Dare,** was born, 1587, on Roanoke Island. The colonists had mysteriously disappeared by 1591.

 Religion and Philosophy

Akbar, the greatest Mogul emperor of India, r.1556–1605, attempted to establish "**Din Illahl**" as a universal religion acceptable to his many Hindu subjects. Vegetarianism and other Hindu practices were supported by Akbar. Although the Din Illahl movement was influential for some time after Akbar's death, it would be discouraged by **Emperor Aurungzebe,** r.1658–1707, and would eventually collapse under the 18th-century Muslim revival.

Literature

English drama entered its great period. **Christopher Marlowe,** 1564–93, in his *Dr. Faustus, c.* 1588, perfected the blank verse

of *The Spanish Tragedy* by **Thomas Kyd,** 1558–94. **Sir Philip Sidney,** 1554–86, in his verse-prose *Arcadia*, 1590, drew on a tradition of pastoral romance established in Spain by **Jorge de Montemayor,** c.1520–61, in his *Diana.*

Art and Architecture

English court portraiture and domestic architecture were given impetus by the Reformation. **Longleat,** 1567–80, was a house built in the rectangular style with large expanses of windows by **Smython,** c.1536–1614.
The Mannerist style emphasizing the bizarre and the tortuous spread through Europe, to Spain with **El Greco,** 1541–1614, to Germany in the works of artists like **Spranger,** 1546–1611, and to France with the second **Fontainebleau School.**

Music

Equal temperament (based on equal half-tone divisions) was proposed by Prince Tsai-Yu in his *Handbook of Music.* It predated the West's recognition of its importance to harmony.

Science and Technology

Tycho Brahe, 1546–1601, and his assistant **Johannes Kepler,** 1571–1630, extended Copernican theory. Brahe made accurate observations of planetary movements. Using these results, Kepler calculated the actual orbits of the planets, which he found to be ellipses and not perfect circles. Kepler's results established astronomy as an observational science, free from any religious considerations.

Principal Events

Henry IV, *r.*1589- 1610, ended the French wars of religion and granted equal rights to Catholics and Huguenots in the **Edict of Nantes**, 1598.
The Dutch took over much of Portugal's former trade with the East Indies, 1595.
Japan invaded Korea, 1592- 93 and 1597- 98, but was expelled by the Chinese.
Spanish power gradually declined owing to the stagnation of her internal economy and the lack of a middle class.

The Americas

The conquest and colonization of New Mexico by Spanish explorer **Juan de Oñate**, 1549?- 1624?, began in 1598. The settlement of **San Juan** was established.

Religion and Philosophy

A Protestant movement, opposed to Calvinism, grew up in the United Provinces, denying the doctrine of predestination and arguing for religious tolerance. The movement came to be called **Arminianism**, after **Jacobus Arminius**, 1560- 1609, who defended the Arminians in a controversy with his colleague **Gomarus. The Edict of Nantes**, 1598, granted liberty of worship to the Huguenots, the French Protestant sect.

Literature

William Shakespeare, 1564- 1616, consummate master of the English language, began *c.*1591 to produce a stream of comedies, tragedies, and historical dramas revealing a remarkable range of human experience and thought. By 1600 he had written some 20 plays, including the comedy *As You Like It* and the romantic tragedy *Romeo and Juliet*.

Art and Architecture

The precursors of Italian baroque painting were radically opposed to each other. "The Loves of the Gods," 1597, in the Palazzo Farnese by **Annibale Carracci**, 1540- 1609, returned to the classical ideals, but with an emotional, anecdotal appeal and complex composition. "Doubting Thomas," *c.*1600, by **Caravaggio**, 1571- 1610, introduced a vivid realism and simplicity seen in the portrayal of Christ and the Apostles as ordinary men.

Music

Sonata Pian'e Forte, 1597, by Giovanni Gabrieli , 1557- 1612, was composed for two consorts, the first ensemble piece in which instrumentation was specified.

Science and Technology

Chinese pharmacology was summed up by Li Shi-Chen in his *Great Pharmacopoeia*, 1578. Chinese medicine was completely conservative and few new treatments were reported. **Galileo**, 1564- 1642, wrote in 1597 stating his agreement with the Copernican system. Three years later, **Giordano Bruno** was burned by the Inquisition as a heretic for propagating the same idea.

Galileo and the New Science 1600–1660

Modern science and the Aristotelian world view squared off at the trial of Galileo.

Defenestration of Prague

Oliver Cromwell's death plunged England into anarchy.

The renowned Taj Mahal was built as a mausoleum.

"Apollo and Daphne"

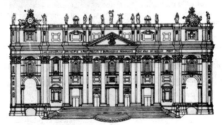

Facade of St. Peter's Rome by Maderna exemplifies Baroque architecture's emphasis on unified composition.

Galileo and the New Science

Principal Events

The political and religious tensions generated by the Reformation in the previous century were brought to a head in the Thirty Years War, which involved most of the European powers and left the Holy Roman Empire in particular devastated from constant military activity. Although England remained out of the war, the same conflicts over religion and constitutional authority led to the execution of Charles I in 1649, but the establishment of the Commonwealth proved no solution.

Colonial trade expanded throughout the world bringing skirmishes and trade wars in India, America, and Europe as the European powers jostled for supremacy, regarding control of trade as a tangible form of political power.

In China the Manchu dynasty brought strength and prosperity, while Japan withdrew into isolation after experiencing the disruptive impact of Christianity and European trade.

National Events

The 17th century saw the colonization of the New World. The religious situation in Europe influenced colonial development, as Protestant and Catholic nations competed for wealth and power. Dissidents escaping persecution were among those who sought refuge in the colonies. Others sought opportunity.

Religion and Philosophy

As the basic assumptions and methodology of the natural sciences underwent a dramatic change with Galileo's suggestion that the workings of natural phenomena could be described exactly, philosophical and religious thought was also transformed. Theories of society based on the natural condition of man were common and resulted in the concept of the social contract, which could be renounced if the ruler rejected his duties to his subjects. Such ideas were used to justify widespread religious revolts.

Descartes and Hobbes laid the foundations of modern philosophy by attempting to return to first principles, using only scientific or mathematical tools, and the same reliance on reason brought the beginnings of Deism, which would become popular in the 18th century.

In England in the Civil War, utopian ideas linking political and religious aims abounded.

Literature

The Elizabethan age in English literature culminated in the later work of William Shakespeare whose plays and sonnets epitomize the innovative power and humanism of the Renaissance, while in Spain Cervantes produced his picaresque *Don Quixote*. As the century wore on the religious and political conflicts between Royalists and Puritans were reflected in English literature with the poetry of Marvell and Milton.

In France an attempt to systematize the rules of language and literature was made by the newly founded Académie Française, which would stand until the 19th century, and an interest in classical models produced the dramas of Corneille and the verse of Malherbe.

Art and Architecture

Baroque art emerged in Italy in the 1600s and reached its peak in the mid-17th century in the works of Bernini, Pietro da Cortona, and Borromini. Its stylistic emphasis was on unity of composition, so that the parts were subordinate to the whole, an effect most expertly achieved in sculpture and architecture. Throughout the 17th century, Baroque spread from its basically Roman origins to Catholic Europe but had least influence in northern Protestant countries in spite of the achievement of Rubens and Vandyke.

Bourgeois Dutch art flourished during the long war of independence from Spain, while native English painting was relatively unaffected by European developments, although Charles I patronized many continental artists. In France the tradition of rationalism produced the restrained classicism of Poussin and Claude.

Indian art flourished at the height of Mogul power.

Music

Many of the forms of music current today had their beginnings in 17th-century Europe. The suite was developing to provide the basis of the later sonata, and opera and ballet were evolving from court entertainments. Italy was the center of the stage, and interest in the solo line pressed forward the development of a new style of madrigal and fine singing styles.

Science and Technology

Religious dissent marked this period in Europe, and from it rose the beginnings of modern science. The century was only a few weeks old when the Italian Giordano Bruno was burned at the stake for heresy. He had conceived of the universe as infinite in time and space and filled with a multitude of suns each bearing planets, everything being in constant motion. His views were a major threat to orthodox theology at a time when the Catholic Church was threatened by the Reformation. Bruno's death probably persuaded Galileo, another Italian, to retract his belief that the Earth moves, and helped to shift the scene of progress toward the Protestant countries of Northern Europe.

The concept of scientific method was established and practical endeavor stimulated invention and inquiry. For example, the pumps required to clear water from mines prompted the investigation of air pressure and facilitated an understanding of the heart's action.

★ Principal Events

Power struggles in Japan resulted in the Tokugawa (Edo) period, 1603, which advanced education and economic growth.
Charles IX, r.1604–11, a Protestant, succeeded to the Swedish throne after the deposition of his Catholic predecessor.
The anarchy in Russia resulting from rivalry among the boyars (nobility) began under **Boris Godunov**, r.1598–1605, who was opposed by a pretender, the false **Dmitri**.

The Americas

The Gulf of St Lawrence and the St Lawrence River were explored for France by **Samuel de Champlain**, c.1567–1635, during voyages beginning in 1603.

⚲ Religion and Philosophy

Faustus Socinus, 1539–1604, in Poland, argued that Christ, although sinless, was not divine. He inspired the Polish Unitarian movement, which denied the existence of the Holy Trinity.
Johannes Althusius, 1557–1638, a Dutch Calvinist, said in 1603 that voluntary agreement should be the basis of political association. He advocated republican government.
The Tung-lin Academy, founded in China, 1604, revived Confucianism and attacked graft.

📖 Literature

Miguel de Cervantes, 1547–1616, blended and transcended the realistic and idealistic veins of Spanish prose writing in *Don Quixote*, published in

two parts in 1605 and 1615. Its satirical theme of an amiable landowner who fancies himself an adventurous knight had a universality and a delicate juxtaposition of humor and sadness that influenced many later novelists.

🏛 Art and Architecture

Parisian town planning, like the Place Royale, 1605, with its smaller terraced houses, was the result of Henry IV's policy to support the new merchant classes and improve traffic circulation.
Painting in China within the traditional schools was dominated by literati and theorists, like **Tung Ch'i-ch'ang**, 1555–1636, who, in his "Dwelling in the Ch'ing-pien Mountains," emphasized the spiritual message of landscape.

🎵 Music

Dances for lutes and consorts became popular, providing musical forms such as the *pavane, galliard, allemande,* and *gavotte,* which were later gathered into composite pieces called suites.

⚛ Science and Technology

De Magnete, a study of magnetism and electricity, was published in 1600 by an Englishman, **William Gilbert**, c.1540–1603. He suggested that the Earth was a giant magnet with its own magnetic field.
Galileo Galilei, 1564–1642, studied the motions of falling bodies and discovered that they accelerated constantly toward the Earth. Galileo, the father of experimental science, drew conclusions from observation and experiment only, without theological speculations.

Principal Events

In Japan the Tokugawa introduced **Confucianism** as the official religion, 1608, and Dutch traders arrived, 1609, rivaling the Spanish and Portuguese in the Far East.

The settlement of the French wars of religion was threatened by the murder of Henry IV, *r.*1589–1610.

The Americas

The first permanent English colony was founded at Jamestown, Va., in 1607. In 1609 Champlain fired on the Iroquois, setting a pattern of Indian relationships.

Religion and Philosophy

John Dee, 1527–1608, Elizabeth of England's astrologer, helped to revive mystical interest in mathematics in England. As a magician and scientist he was a leading representative of the Hermetic tradition of alchemical study. This tradition, which sought to establish mystical connection among empirical phenomena with the help of experimentation, influenced the Cambridge Platonists and the development of Newtonian science.

Literature

Ben Jonson, *c.*1572–1637, poet, critic, and playwright, wrote *Volpone,* 1607, *The Alchemist,* 1610, and other comedies notable for their honesty. Other English dramatists were **John Webster,** 1580–1625, with *The White Devil,* 1608, **Thomas Middleton,** 1570–1627, **Thomas**

Dekker, 1570–1641, and the prolific **Francis Beaumont** and **John Fletcher,** *fl.*1606–16.

Art and Architecture

Art and architecture in Mogul India reached its greatest achievement during the reigns of **Jahangir,** *r.*1605–27, and **Shah Jehan,** *r.*1628–58. Painting was characterized by the realism and vigor of Jahangir's picture albums, which were primarily portraits and depictions of the hunt. Later, Shah Jehan would build the Taj Mahal, 1632–43, the most renowned structure in India, as a mausoleum for his dead wife.

Music

Orfeo, 1607, by Claudio Monteverdi, 1567–1643, is the earliest European opera extant. The form arose from a search for a new way to express the ideals of classical drama.

Science and Technology

The telescope was invented by the Dutchman Hans Lippershey, *c.*1570–1619, in 1608.

Astronomia Nova, published in 1609 by Johannes Kepler, 1571–1630, argued that the planets moved around the Sun in ellipses and at varying speeds.

The moons of Jupiter and phases of Venus were discovered by Galileo in 1610.

1612-1618

★ Principal Events

The influence of the English East India Company extended to India, ousting the Portuguese as a rival to the Dutch.

Persecution of Christianity began in Japan, 1612, although trade with Europe increased.

The accession of Mikháil Romanov, r 1613–45, in Russia established royal authority by ending local autonomy and strengthening serfdom.

A group of Tungus tribes in Manchuria grew powerful under **Nurháchi,** 1615–16.

The Americas

French Roman Catholic missionaries arrived in Canada, 1615. In Virginia, 1612, **John Rolfe,** 1585–1622, began the cultivation of tobacco.

Religion and Philosophy

Francisco Suarez, 1548–1617, a Spanish Jesuit, argued in *On Laws,* 1612, that a contract between ruler and subject was the basis of sovereignty. He hoped to refute James I of England's claim to rule by divine right.

The Dutch rejected Arminianism at the Synod of Dort, 1618. But after the publication of Arminius' works in 1629, they would be granted freedom of worship in the United Provinces.

Literature

Shakespeare's profound tragedies including *Hamlet, Lear,* and *Othello,* dealt with heroes trapped as much by the human condition as by their individual flaws of character. After 1608 he began writing his last, enigmatic plays, in which a spirit of reconciliation appears, among them *The Tempest, c.*1612. He retired to Stratford in 1613.

Art and Architecture

Italian baroque painting was dominated by the influence of the Carracci and Caravaggio. **Guido Reni,** 1575–1642, painted "Aurora," 1613, in the Carracci style. In Flanders, **Peter Paul Rubens,** 1577–1640, shows the influence of Caravaggio in his work "Descent from the Cross," 1611–14.

Palladian architecture was introduced to England by **Inigo Jones,** 1573–1652, whose Queen's House, Greenwich, 1616, is thoroughly classical.

Music

The violin made its orchestral appearance in the *Vingt quatre violons du roi,* set up by Louis XIII, r 1610–43, as a court band. Later, bands of several consorts had up to 35 players.

Science and Technology

The Art of Glass Making, 1612, by the Italian Antonio Neri, was one of many handbooks that helped the spread of technology. **John Napier,** 1550–1617, introduced logarithms in 1614. Logarithmic tables prepared by **Henry Briggs,** 1561–1631, greatly facilitated their use.

Sanctorius, 1561–1636, founded the study of metabolism with his *De Medicina Statica,* 1614. He weighed himself over thirty years, recording changes in weight, pulse, and temperature.

Principal Events

The Thirty Years War began in 1618 after a nationalist and Protestant revolt in Bohemia. By 1619, **Emperor Ferdinand**, r.1619–37, had restored Catholicism in Bohemia.
Spanish troops invaded the Protestant Palatinate to ensure a route to the Netherlands.
The Pilgrim Fathers landed in North America in 1620.
Batavia was established by the Dutch as the center of their Eastern spice trade, 1619.

The Americas

In 1620, the Mayflower arrived at Cape Cod, Mass., bearing the Pilgrims. In Virginia, 1619, the first black slaves arrived.

Religion and Philosophy

Francis Bacon, 1561–1626, elaborated a sophisticated method of establishing scientific truths, using observation and experiment to test hypotheses, in *Novum Organum*, 1620. He argued for the usefulness of scientific knowledge in giving man mastery over nature and conceived a scientific Utopia in *The New Atlantis*, 1627, which foreshadowed later developments in mid-17th century scientific thought.

Literature

The English metaphysical poets, who included **George Herbert**, 1593–1633, explored the unity of flesh and spirit in a style that influenced modern poetry. Erudition, wit, reason, and passion were best combined in the devotional and love poems of **John Donne**, 1572–1631, *(Anniversaries)*, who as dean of St Paul's from 1621 preached a series of fine sermons.

Art and Architecture

The baroque style was epitomized in the magnificent sculptures of **Gianlorenzo Bernini**, 1598–1680, whose "Apollo and Daphne," 1622–25, established him as the greatest sculptor since Michelangelo.
Reality, allegory, and myth are combined in one of **Rubens'** masterpieces, the gigantic Medici cycle painted for the Luxembourg Palace, Paris, 1622–25.

Music

Figured bass developed in Italian lute songs. Beneath the melody was written a base line with figures and signs to indicate the harmony of the inner parts without writing chords in full.

Science and Technology

Harmonice Mundi, 1619, by Kepler, returned to the ancient concept of the harmony of the spheres in trying to find a relationship between music and astronomy. This work nevertheless contained a third law of planetary motion.
Francis Bacon published *Novum Organum*, 1620, in which theories are drawn from hypotheses and tested by observation and experiment.

1624-1630

Principal Events

England, the United Provinces, Denmark, and France allied against the Hapsburgs, 1625.
In France, Richelieu, 1585-1642, rebuilt royal power, attacking the Huguenots, 1628.
French settlements in the West Indies began in 1625, exporting sugar and tobacco, and emigration to Canada was encouraged among traders and fishermen.
The Tungus Manchus overran Korea, ousting the Ming dynasty from the Liao Basin, 1627.

The Americas

Virginia became a royal colony, 1624. In 1626, **Peter Minuit,** c.1580-1638, governor of New Netherlands, bought Manhattan which became New Amsterdam.

Religion and Philosophy

Herbert of Cherbury, 1583-1648, attempted to establish a belief in God based on rational inquiry rather than faith in *On Truth,* 1624. His belief that the basic tenets of religion were reasonable and universal was central to the growth of Deism.
Hugo Grotius, 1583-1645, a Dutchman, developed the theory of international law in *On Law,* 1625. He aimed to make war more humane, arguing that nations, like individuals, are bound by natural law.

Literature

Spanish drama was dominated by the popular and prolific **Lope de Vega,** 1562-1635, whose ingeniously plotted verse plays mixed comedy and tragedy.

Pedro Calderón de la Barca, 1600-81, added deeper characterization in plays that reflected the richly ornate **culteranismo** style of the poet and satirist Luis de Góngora, 1561-1627.

Art and Architecture

Classicism in French painting was developed by **Nicolas Poussin,** c.1594-1665, whose "Triumph of David," 1626, shows an abstraction and modeling based on antique ideals.
Realism and the skillful use of color and light began to appear in Spanish painting in such works as the "Scenes from the life of St Bonaventura," 1629-30, by **José Ribera,** 1591-1652, and in the works of **Francisco de Zurbarán,** 1598-1664.

Music

Fugue developed, principally in Germany, as a contrapuntal treatment of one main theme. It remained the dominant form for solo organ until the 1700s but also had wider applications.

Science and Technology

Johann Glauber, c.1603-68, discovered many chemical compounds, including benzene, acetone, and hydrochloric acid.
William Harvey, 1578-1657, discovered the circulation of the blood in 1628, but this was not confirmed until later improvements in the microscope took place. By studying valves Harvey realized that blood must flow in one direction only. His mechanistic view of man perfectly complemented Galileo's mechanistic universe.

-Principal Events

The Dutch East India Company seized part of Brazil for its sugar and silver, 1630.

Gustavus Adolphus, *r.*1611–32, of Sweden invaded the Holy Roman Empire, 1630, to protect the Protestant cause against ruthless Catholic suppression.

Magdeburg was sacked in 1631 by the Catholic general Tilly, 1559–1632.

The war in Europe dislocated previous patterns of trade and industry and the search for colonial wealth increased.

 The Americas

In 1630, the Puritan ''Great Migration'' brought more than 1,000 settlers to Massachusetts. **Roger Williams**, *c.*1603–83, founded Providence, 1636.

 Religion and Philosophy

Galileo Galilei, 1564–1642, an Italian, began modern science by uniting mathematics with physics. He distinguished real or ''primary'' qualities such as mass, from subjective ''secondary'' qualities such as color. The religious opposition to his work highlighted the challenge of experimental science to the Aristotelian world view, both philosophically and politically.

 Literature

The Passion Play at Öberammergau, Bavaria, the most famous survivor of its genre, was inaugurated in 1634. It has been performed every ten years except for three wartime interruptions.

 Art and Architecture

Roman high baroque painting was represented in the works of Pietro da Cortona, 1596–1669, whose masterpiece, the ceiling of the Gran Salone, Palazzo Barberini, painted in 1633–39, was a skillful illusion, its center seemingly open to the sky. **Anthony Van Dyck,** 1599–1641, working at the English court, brought sophistication and elegance to English portraiture in the ''Equestrian portrait of Charles I,'' 1633.

 Music

Bel canto, a lyrical style of singing, developed in Italy. *Castrati,* men who had been castrated before puberty, were renowned for their high, sweet, powerful voices, often used in opera.

 Science and Technology

In Dialogues Concerning Two World Systems, published in 1632, Galileo presented the evidence for a heliocentric solar system in which the Earth moves. In 1633, Galileo was forced to retract his views.

Fen drainage in England since the 1620s had increased farm land. Fertilizer experiments also aided agriculture. English trade and industry prospered, especially coal production, iron mining, and metallurgy.

The slide rule was invented in 1632 by Oughtred, 1575–1660.

1636-1642

★ Principal Events

After the Shimabara revolt of the Christian peasantry, 1637, Japan cut her foreign trade and cultural contacts.
France first entered the Thirty Years War in 1639.
Spain was weakened by the establishment of Portuguese independence and a Catalan nationalist revolt in 1640.
England was close to civil war in 1641 after constitutional opposition to royal absolutism.

The Americas

Anne Hutchinson c.1591–1643, banished from Massachusetts, joined **Roger Williams**. In the **Pequot War**, 1636–37, in New England over 600 whites died.

Religion and Philosophy

Cornelis Jansen, 1585–1638, a Frenchman, attacked the Jesuits and proclaimed strict predestinarianism, while staying within the Catholic Church, in the *Augustinus*, 1642. **Blaise Pascal**, 1623–62, supported the Jansenist movement in France, where it appealed to the nationalist opposition to papal power. The Jesuits rejected these views because they implied the denial both of free will and the universality of redemption.

Literature

French writers applied strict classical rules under the influence of **François de Malherbe**, 1555–1628. **Pierre Corneille**, 1606–84, successfully adapted these in a series of tragedies in Alexandrine couplets, starting with *Le Cid*, 1637. His artificial but powerful plays based on Spanish and Roman heroes made drama the chief form of French classical literature.

Art and Architecture

Dutch art found its greatest painter in Rembrandt van Rijn, 1606–69, whose psychological insight and technical virtuosity produced "The Night Watch," 1642. **Jan Vermeer**, 1632–75, painted domestic interiors and **Frans Hals**, c.1580–1666, lively portraits.
The greatest of the baroque architects, **Francesco Borromini**, 1599–1667, produced his masterpiece of spatial ingenuity, **S. Carlo alle Quattro Fontane**, 1634–44.

Music

Dynamic markings, such as *p* (piano) and *f* (forte), were used for the first time in 1638 by **Domenico Mazzochi**, 1592–1665, in Italy. He was quickly followed by other composers.

Science and Technology

Le Discours de la Méthode, 1637, by René Descartes, 1596–1650, established the deductive method, by which theories are deduced from observations and experimentally tested for validity. He also invented coordinate geometry, in which position can be described mathematically, an advance vital to the growth of engineering and the calculus.
Two New Sciences, published by Galileo, 1638, dealt with dynamics and helped to establish experimental science.

Principal Events

The New England Confederation was founded in 1643 for defense against the Indians.
The Manchus set up the **Ta Ch'ing** dynasty at Mukden, 1644, replacing the Ming dynasty.
The English Civil War, 1642–46, resulted in military victory for Parliament and the Puritans after the reorganization of their army, in 1645. Attempts to find a constitutional settlement failed.
France confirmed its new military superiority by defeating Spain at Rocroi, 1647.

The Americas

Massachusetts, Plymouth, Connecticut, and New Haven formed the New England Confederation, 1643, for defense.

Religion and Philosophy

René Descartes, 1596–1650, who founded modern philosophy, attempted to establish a philosophical system from first principles alone, relying on mathematical logic and using systematic doubt as his method. He espoused a total dualism between mind and matter, arguing that the physical world was governed by deterministic laws, while the clarity and distinctness of ideas established their truth independently of any experience.

Literature

English prose had acquired a new eloquence in *Anatomy of Melancholy* by **Robert Burton** 1577–1640. This tradition was extended by **Sir Thomas Browne**, 1605–82, whose *Religio Medici*, 1643, was a reflective study of a doctor's spiritual life. An equally individualistic writer, **Izaak Walton**, 1593–1683, began to write *The Compleat Angler*.

Art and Architecture

French landscape painting as developed by **Claude Lorrain**, 1600–82, involved the formal arrangement of trees and a panoramic background as the setting for diminutive foreground figures, as in "Hagar and the Angel," 1646.
Individualist schools in China broke away from traditional painting. **Kung Hsien**, c.1620–89, painted vast landscapes of great originality, such as his "A Thousand Peaks and a Myriad Rivers."

Music

Ballet developed at the French court in the reign of Louis XIV, r.1643–1715, who first danced it in 1651. Brought from Italy, ballet had been known at the French court since c.1581.

Science and Technology

Blaise Pascal, 1623–62, invented an adding machine in 1642. He also deduced the principles of hydraulics and investigated the theory of probability, showing that chance can be assessed mathematically.
Evangelista Torricelli, 1608–47, demonstrated in 1643 that air pressure is sufficient to hold up a column of mercury about 76 cm high, thus producing the first barometer. This discovery laid down the fundamental principles of hydromechanics.

1648-1654

⭐ Principal Events

The Peace of Westphalia ended the Thirty Years War in 1648 with every participant exhausted. **The Fronde,** a series of noble and peasant uprisings in France, tried to substitute government by law for royal power and voiced economic grievances but was crushed, 1648–53. **Charles I,** r.1625–49, of England was executed and a Commonwealth set up under **Oliver Cromwell,** 1599–1658. His Navigation Act, 1651, led to war with the Dutch, 1652.

The Americas

Maryland, 1649, granted rights to all Christians who asserted belief in the Trinity. Parliament, 1651, passed the first **Navigation Act** for colonial administration.

🔥 Religion and Philosophy

Utopian social and religious ideas flourished in England after the Civil War. **George Fox,** 1624–91, founded the pacifist and egalitarian Friends, or **Quakers,** in 1652, while the **Diggers,** an agrarian communistic group, believed that religious ideas had diverted man from asserting his political rights in this world. **The Levelers,** another Puritan group, led by John Liburne, 1614–57, demanded an egalitarian and republican society.

📖 Literature

English poetry reflected the political conflict of Puritans and Royalists. The Cavalier lyricists included **Sir John Suckling,** 1609–42, **Robert Herrick,** 1591–1674, and **Richard Lovelace,** 1618–57, whose best work was collected in *Lucasta,* 1649. On the Puritan side, **Andrew Marvell,** 1621–78, wrote poems on nature during the 1650s.

Art and Architecture

French classical architecture was initially developed by **François Mansart,** 1598–1666, whose Château de Maisons Laffitte, with its elegance, clarity, and cool restraint, epitomized his subtly proportioned style. **Classical compositions** and the use of indirect lighting are combined in the highly personal style of **Georges de la Tour,** 1593–1652, whose "St Sebastian," c.1650, suggests the influence of Caravaggio.

🎵 Music

The koto became the national instrument of Japan. Its strings and movable bridge produced various five-note scales. Its solo music was often composed in the form of variations.

⚛ Science and Technology

The air pump, developed c.1650 by Otto von Guericke, 1602–86, was used to show that sound cannot cross a vacuum. In 1654 Guericke conducted a famous experiment in which two teams of horses tried and failed to separate two evacuated hemispheres, thus demonstrating the power of air pressure, later to be harnessed in the first steam engines.

★ Principal Events

The rise of Brandenburg and Russia as military powers brought a new conflict in the Baltic and Poland, 1655–60.
The Venetians drove the Turks from the Dardanelles, 1656, following a period of anarchy among the Ottomans.
Anarchy after Cromwell's death led to the restoration of the English monarchy, 1660.
The war between France and Spain ended, 1659, emphasizing the Spanish decline and the rise of French power.

The Americas

The Navigation Act of 1660 restricted colonial trade. Peter Stuyvesant, 1592–1672, was the New Netherlands' harsh governor, 1646–64.

☦ Religion and Philosophy

In *De Corpore*, 1655, Thomas Hobbes, 1588–1679, following Descartes' mathematical method, suggested that the universe comprises material particles moving in a void. This atomism had also been stated in his political tract, *Leviathan*, 1651, in which he argued that in a state of nature men would fight because of their natural selfishness; they could only escape by means of a contract whereby they renounced their freedom to a supreme ruler.

📖 Literature

The greatest Dutch poet, Joost van den Vondel, 1587–1679, turned from satire to write his religious drama *Lucifer*, 1654.
In Germany, literature revived after the Thirty Years War, 1618–48. Poetry was much influenced by Lutheranism, and the poet and mystic **Paul Gerhardt**, 1607–76, wrote outstanding hymns, including "O sacred head sore wounded."

Art and Architecture

Realism and a superlative handling of color distinguish the works of the Spanish court painter **Diego de Vélazquez** 1599–1660. His "Las Meninas," 1656, an informal royal group, represents the culmination of his remarkable style.
Bernini's genius as an architect was affirmed in his Piazza of St Peter's, begun in 1656, which was both simple and original in design and reflected the dignity and grandeur of Mother Church.

Music

The violin was perfected in Italy by the Amati, Stradivari, and Guarneri families from 1650 to 1740. The great brilliance of violin tone soon overwhelmed the softer viols, which died out.

⚛ Science and Technology

Christiaan Huygens, 1629–95, a Dutchman, invented the pendulum clock from 1656.
Accademia del Cimento, the first scientific research institute, was founded in Florence, 1657.

The Age of
Louis XIV
1660–1720

King Louis XIV of France

Chinese emperor K'ang-hsi's reign was one of peace.

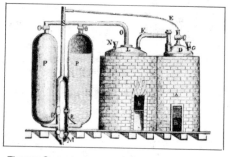

Thomas Savery's steam engine had a substantial design flaw.

In Salem, women were persecuted in the name of religious superstition.

Johann Sebastian Bach, German composer

St. Paul's Cathedral

French comedic playwright, Molière

Reflecting telescope invented by Issac Newton

The Age of Louis XIV

★ Principal Events

Louis XIV's schemes for the expansion of France brought him into conflict with the major European powers. The spectacle of his rule as an absolute monarch dominated 17th-century European politics, arousing the envy of lesser rulers including James II of England who was expelled in 1688 for trying to emulate him. This second English Revolution finally confirmed the victory of Protestantism and the rule of Parliament, which would serve to inspire the Enlightenment thinkers of the following century, particularly in France itself.

Outside Europe the major powers fought for colonies—valued for their dual role as sources of raw materials and luxury goods like tobacco, sugar, and spices and as markets for the home country.

The Mogul Empire in India declined after Aurungzebe had made the dynasty unpopular with his policy of intolerance toward Hinduism.

National Events

A rivalry for dominance in the New World between the French and the English was underway. European conflicts brought war to the colonies. The English colonial population was larger, but the French had alliances with numerous Indian tribes. By 1713, with the Treaty of Utrecht, Britain had gained the advantage.

♦ Religion and Philosophy

European theories of knowledge and politics underwent important changes in the latter half of the 17th century, at a time when Newton's revolutionary ideas on the workings of the universe were transforming Western science. In Britain Newton himself, Locke, and Berkeley took the empiricist position that knowledge was obtained by experience alone, in direct contrast to the rationalist views of thinkers like Spinoza and Leibniz, who argued that knowledge of the world could be obtained by deductions from certain key principles like the nature of substance. Empiricism would dominate British philosophy thereafter and was to have a major influence on the thinkers of the French Enlightenment. Among political theorists, Locke and Pufendorf argued that political authority depended upon consent and took the form of a contract between the people and the king.

Literature

Neoclassical drama, based on logic and Greco-Roman stylistic rules, reached a peak in France in the tragedies of Racine and comedies of Molière. After the comic license of early Restoration drama, English writers such as Dryden also turned to classical models, laying the ground for the Age of Reason. English journalism began with Addison and Defoe, and satire developed with Alexander Pope.

The period also saw the publication of the chief work of the two greatest English Puritan writers, Milton and Bunyan, as well as developments in baroque poetry and picaresque prose in Germany and the emergence of new prose and verse forms in France with La Fontaine.

In Japan, Basho emerged as the supreme haiku poet.

Art and Architecture

France replaced Italy as the center of the arts in Europe. They were dominated by the royal patronage of Louis XIV, who rebuilt Versailles using the talents of Lebrun, Le Vau, Hardouin-Mansart, and Le Nôtre. Baroque architecture was at its purest in Italy, at its most restrained in England, and at its most extravagant in Spain and Portugal. Painting during the latter half of the 17th century produced few masterpieces although the works of Murillo in Spain, Pozzo in Italy, Claude Lorrain in France, and the landscapists in Holland were exceptional. In American colonies architecture and painting adapted European styles to their own conditions.

The Rococo style emerged in France in the late 17th century, bringing to interior decoration the use of swirls, scrolls, and conchs in design, and finding a stylistic parallel in the elegant paintings of Watteau, dealing with life at court.

Music

Baroque music grew up in Europe in the second half of the 17th century in the princely states of northern Italy and Germany. The freewheeling melodic lines and firm harmonic structure in the works of such composers as Diderik Buxtehude, 1637–1707, and Johann Sebastian Bach, 1685–1750, paralleled the ornamented but firm qualities of Baroque architecture.

Science and Technology

Isaac Newton's account of the workings of the universe surpassed Galileo's and provided a new framework for scientific thought. His exceptional insight into nature found definitions for concepts such as inertia and gravity that cannot easily be sensed. Newton's view of the universe, as one obeying set laws, accorded with the spirit of Protestant inquiry into the purpose of creation, in complete opposition to the Catholic world of personal salvation and divine intervention. Scientific advance in England and Holland was also stimulated by wealth from their growing trade.

Scientific communities grew up and provided scientists with the means to pool their researches, facilitating the spread of information and ideas internationally, while increasing the scientist's stature by granting him royal patronage. However, the growth of these communities contributed to the new division in men's minds between the impersonal sciences and the humanities.

187

1660-1666

★ Principal Events

Louix XIV began his personal rule in 1661 marked by a suppression of noble authority and the creation of a bureaucracy for local government.

K'ang Hsi, r.1662–1722, introduced a period of Chinese cultural splendor.

The English acquired Bombay in 1661 and took New Amsterdam from the Dutch in 1664.

The Spanish colonies became a prize sought after by the major naval powers in the reign of **Charles II**, 1665–1700.

The Americas

The British defeated the Dutch in New Amsterdam, 1664, renaming it New York. The French crown took control of Canada, 1663, from a private company.

☿ Religion and Philosophy

Mercantilists, such as **Thomas Mun**, 1571–1641, in England and **Jean-Baptiste Colbert**, 1619–83, in France held that governmental regulation of the economy was necessary to increase the power of the state, since a nation's economic power depended on the bullion at its disposal. A key factor was the monopolization of colonial trade by the mother country.

The Royal Society was founded in England in 1662.

Literature

German baroque literature was dominated by the influence of **Andreas Gryphius**, 1616–64, whose comedies and religious poems were collected in 1663.

Another baroque writer was **Hans Grimmelshausen**, c.1621–76, whose *Simplicissimus*, a graphic account of the experiences of the peasantry in the Thirty Years War, is regarded as the start of the German novel.

Art and Architecture

Spanish painting was represented by the works of **Bartolomé Esteban Murillo**, 1617–82, who founded the Seville Academy and became its first president, 1660. Eight of his 11 paintings for the almshouse of San Jorge, 1661–74, are regarded as his masterpieces.

The greatest exponent of Baroque, Gianlorenzo Bernini, 1598–1680, went to Paris to redesign the Louvre, 1665. His plans were rejected, but he made a superb bust of Louix XIV.

Music

The Restoration in England brought the first public concerts in the modern sense. But music there would decline for two centuries after the death of **Henry Purcell**, 1659–95.

Science and Technology

The Royal Society was founded in London, 1660, and the French **Académie Royale des Sciences**, in 1666.

Marcello Malpighi, 1628–94, used a microscope to discover capillary blood vessels in 1661, thereby confirming Harvey's theory of blood circulation.

Robert Boyle, 1627–91, a British physicist, found that gas pressure varies inversely with volume (Boyle's law, 1662). His book *The Sceptical Chymist*, 1661, defined the concepts of element, alkali, and acid.

Principal Events

Louis XIV invaded the Spanish Netherlands but was opposed by the United Provinces, 1667–68.
The English and Dutch fought an indecisive trade war, 1665–67.
Russia defeated Poland for the Ukraine, 1654–67.
The Mogul Emperor Aurungzebe revoked Hindu toleration in 1669, causing unrest in India.
The English founded the Hudson Bay Company for the exploration of North America.

The Americas

The Massachusetts Bay Colony had taken over the government of Maine by 1669. **Carolina's** Fundamental Constitutions, 1669, drew on **John Locke**.

Religion and Philosophy

The German Pufendorf, 1632–94, based his concept of natural law on "socialitas," the essentially social nature of man. He believed that agreement was the basis of political relationships and that human dignity implied the equality of all men.
The Old Believers broke with the Russian Church in 1667 to counteract the reforms of the patriarch **Nikon,** 1605–81, who introduced Greek practices and reformed the parish clergy.

Literature

The Greek "unities" of action, time, and space were given dramatic form in the French classical drama of **Jean Racine,** 1639–99, and **Molière,** 1622–73. Racine's *Andromaque,* 1667, blended poetic style with tragic passion. In comedies such as *Le Misanthrope* and *Tartuffe,* Molière exposed upper- and middle-class hypocrisies, mastering both plot and dialogue.

Art and Architecture

Dutch landscape painting was exemplified in "The Avenue of Middlemarnis," 1669, by **Meindert Hobbema,** 1638–1709, and in "Windmill at Wijk," c.1670, by **Jacob van Ruisdael,** c.1628–82, a great Dutch landscapist.
The palace of Versailles in France was first remodeled in 1669 by **Louis Le Vau,** 1612–70, France's leading baroque architect. The park and gardens at Versailles were designed by **André Le Nôtre,** 1613–1700, from 1662.

Music

The trio sonata was developed by Germans and Italians, using a quick forte movement adapting *aabb* dance form with sections in contrasting moods and keys, and a slow second movement.

Science and Technology

Isaac Newton, 1642–1727, conceived of gravity, 1664–66, correctly concluding that it obeys an inverse square law. He discovered the spectrum, 1666, and invented the reflecting telescope, 1668.
Francesco Redi, c.1626–97, disproved previous theories of the spontaneous generation of lower animals by showing in 1668 that flies are needed to produce the eggs of maggots.
A calculating machine that could multiply and divide was made by Leibniz, 1646–1716, in 1671.

1672-1678

Principal Events

The French again attacked the Dutch in 1672, backed by riches gained through the mercantilist economic policy of **Jean-Baptiste Colbert**, 1619–83. They were opposed by Spain and the empire, who feared French strength in the north.

A two-party system emerged in England in the 1670s.

The Americas

Jacques Marquette, 1637–75, and **Louis Joliet**, 1648–1700, explored the Mississippi River, 1673. **King Philip's War**, 1675–76, ravaged New England.

Religion and Philosophy

Spinoza, 1632–77, a Dutch philosopher, attempted to find a rational explanation of the universe and argued that since God cannot be other than He is then the world, His creation, cannot be other than it is. In his *Ethics*, 1675, he held that free will was an illusion, which would be dispelled by man's recognition that the world was completely determined. He supported democracy as the most natural form of government, and rejected Descartes' dualism of mind and body.

Literature

John Milton, 1608–74, an English poet who was politically prominent on the Puritan side, published in 1674 his final version of *Paradise Lost*, written, 1658–63, in strong blank verse, showing man as obsessed by sin. In Mexico, a Spanish nun, **Juana Inez de la Cruz**, published *A Nosegay of Poetic Flowers.* Her works are among Latin America's best.

Art and Architecture

The classical landscape tradition of Poussin in France continued with **Claude Lorrain**, 1600–82, whose "Evening," 1672, expresses a questioning melancholy. **Jules Hardouin-Mansart**, 1646–1708, officially supervised building at Versailles after 1678. **Christopher Wren**, 1632–1723, the greatest English architect, began work on St Paul's Cathedral, 1675. It is a classical work with baroque overtones.

Music

The chorale prelude, a free composition based on a hymn tune, exploited the varied capabilities of the organ. **Buxtehude's** chorale preludes influenced young composers such as **Bach**.

Science and Technology

Greenwich Observatory, founded in 1675 principally to improve navigation, marks the standard meridian of longitude.

The speed of light was calculated for the first time in 1675 by **Olaus Roemer**, 1644–1720, and shown to be finite.

A single-lens microscope was made by **Anton van Leeuwenhoek**, 1632–1723, a Dutch biologist who discovered protozoa, 1677, and bacteria, 1683.

The calculus was independently developed by Leibniz and Newton.

Principal Events

Brandenburg sent an expedition to West Africa in 1680.
Louis XIV moved his court to Versailles to consolidate his independence from the nobility and the Parisians, 1682.
K'ang Hsi took Formosa, 1683, which had been wrested from the Dutch by a Chinese pirate in 1661.
The Turks besieged Vienna, 1683, but later were defeated at **Mohacs**, 1687.
Robert de la Salle explored the Mississippi for France.

The Americas

In **1682**, **William Penn**, 1644–1718, arrived in Pennsylvania. The colony's **Frame of Government** granted religious toleration and an elected assembly.

Religion and Philosophy

Ralph Cudworth, 1617–88, an Englishman, published his *True Intellectual System*, 1678, admitting mental as well as material forces to science. He belonged to the **Cambridge Platonist** group of Christian humanists associated with the religiously tolerant "Latitudinarian" followers of Arminius.
Jacques Bossuet, 1627–1704, upheld Louis XIV's absolute monarchy against Protestantism, arguing that any legally formed government is sacred.

Literature

A forerunner of the English novel, *Pilgrim's Progress*, 1678, was an allegorical journey through life, told in plain prose with a wealth of narrative detail that overrode the narrow puritanism of its author, **John Bunyan**, 1628–88.
Madame de Lafayette, 1634–93, wrote *La Princess de Clèves*, the first French court romance of psychological depth.

Art and Architecture

The Poussinistes/Rubensistes controversy was sparked off by the French Academy's publication of rules for painting, 1680. **André Félibien**, 1619–95, defended the orthodox view, which valued drawing, idealism, formalized rules, and the work of Poussin. **Roger de Piles**, 1635–1709, led the revolutionaries and argued the importance of color, imagination, and the works of Rubens. The Academy was officially associated with the ideas of Poussinistes.

Music

Continuo was played on a keyboard instrument—often a harpsichord—filling in the harmony between treble and bass lines, as in the cantatas of **Alessandro Scarlatti**, 1660–1725.

Science and Technology

The pressure cooker was invented, 1679, by **Denis Papin**, 1647–1712. Papin also experimented on steam engines, using both the vacuum made by condensing cylinders and the power produced by the expansion of steam as water boils.
John Ray, 1627–1705, laid the groundwork for modern plant classification in his *Historia Generalis plantarum*.

★ Principal Events

The Edict of Nantes, granting freedom of worship to Huguenots in France, was revoked by Louis XIV in 1685. Many Huguenots emigrated.

Russian eastward expansion led to conflict with China, 1683–89. **James II of England,** r.1685–88, was expelled for trying to restore Catholicism. **The Bill of Rights,** 1689, confirmed a constitutional monarchy.

In Japan, the Genroku year period, 1688–1704, saw the rise of a merchant culture.

The Americas

In North America the English and French vied for control. **King William's War,** 1689–97 was inconclusive. **The Dominion of New England** was established, 1686.

Religion and Philosophy

Isaac Newton, 1642–1727, published the *Principia* in 1687. He defended the idea of a gravitational force by arguing that science should merely establish observed regularities, without speculating about underlying mechanisms. His view that the same set of laws, comprehensible with the aid of the physical sciences, apply throughout the universe was fundamental to the development of the mechanistic and optimistic philosophy of the 18th century.

Literature

The French poet Jean de la Fontaine, 1621–95, read his *Discours en Vers* to the Academy in 1684. His verse *Fables*, begun in

1668, conveyed human insights through the old tradition of animal stories.

In Japan, the succinct three-line poetic form called **haiku** reached a peak in the poetry of **Matsuo Basho,** 1644–94.

Art and Architecture

The arts in France under Louis XIV were dominated by **Charles Le Brun,** 1619–90, who was director from 1663 of the French Academy and was also responsible for the Versailles Galerie des Glaces, completed 1684, and the Salons de la Guerre and de la Paix, 1686.

Venetian architecture was represented by the Sta Maria della Salute, c.1631–87, by **Baldassare Longhena,** 1598–1682. It was classical in conception but had baroque overtones.

Music

Baroque composers' awareness of modulation through a cycle of fifths brought more harmonic interest to their music, but tuning problems grew when harmony wandered from the home key.

Science and Technology

Newton's *Principia*, probably the most important book in science, was published in 1687. The first section deals with the behavior of moving bodies and enunciates Newton's three laws of motion, as well as the principles of gravitation. The second deals with the motion of bodies in fluids, and also wave motion. The third utilizes the principles expounded in the earlier sections to explain the motion of bodies on the Earth and in the universe. It was a revolutionary conception.

Principal Events

William of Orange, r.1688–1702, who reigned jointly with his wife, James II's daughter **Mary**, brought England into the war against France.

Peter the Great, r.1689–1725, began his policy of Russian expansion toward Azov for an outlet to the Black Sea and visited western Europe.

English trade in India grew and a factory was set up in Calcutta in 1690.

European sugar traders competed in the West Indies.

The Americas

The settlement of Salem, Mass., was the site, 1692–93, of a series of witchcraft trials. Nineteen people were convicted and executed.

Religion and Philosophy

John Locke, 1632–1704, produced the first thorough empiricist study in *An Essay Concerning Human Understanding*, 1690. He denied the existence of innate knowledge, arguing that the mind was a "tabula rasa" (a blank slate) that was only filled in by sensory experience. His *Two Treatises on Government*, 1690, which justified the English Revolution of 1688, claimed that rulers' legitimacy depended on their protecting the citizens' rights.

Literature

Restoration English drama, which had been dominated since 1660 by the influence of the poet, critic, satirist, and playwright **John Dryden**, 1631–1700, culminated in *Love for Love*, 1695, by **William Congreve**, 1670–1729. This was an improvement on the comedies of **William Wycherley**, 1640–1716, including the bawdy play *The Country Wife*, c.1674.

Art and Architecture

Spanish Baroque style in architecture was derived from the works of **José Churriguera**, 1665–1725, whose east end of San Esteban, Salamanca, 1693, shows the extravagant surface decoration and richly gilded ornament called Churriguesque.

The leading exponent of the Baroque style of illusionist decoration in Italy was **Andrea dal Pozzo**, 1642–1709, whose ceiling of S. Ignazio, Rome, 1691–94, was a masterpiece of perspective and trompe l'oeil.

Music

The concerto was developed by **Arcangelo Corelli**, 1653–1713, and others as a concerto grosso for a group of instruments and orchestra or for a virtuoso solo performer with orchestra.

Science and Technology

Christiaan Huygens, 1629–95, a Dutch physicist, put forward a wave theory of light, 1690. Newton at this time proposed a particle theory. Later science would prove them both right.

1696-1702

Principal Events

Charles II of Spain died in 1700 leaving **Philip, duke of Anjou** and grandson of Louis XIV, as heir to his lands. This led to the **War of the Spanish Succession,** 1702–13.
Hungary was recaptured from the Turks and by 1699 was restored to Austrian control.
Frederick III, the elector of Brandenburg, assumed the title King of Prussia with the consent of the emperor and became **Frederick I of Prussia,** *r.*1701–13.

The Americas

Biloxi, Miss., was founded, 1699, by **Pierre le Moyne,** 1661–1706. Detroit, Mich., was founded, 1701, by **Antoine de la Mothe Cadillac,** 1658–1730.

Religion and Philosophy

Govind Singh, 1666–1708, the tenth guru of the Sikh religion, began a strategy of armed resistance to Mogul persecution and in 1699 gave the common surname Singh (meaning "lion") to the Sikhs. He also introduced the strict practices of the Sikhs, who were pledged to wear a turban, to carry a knife, and never to cut their hair. The Sikhs eventually dominated the Punjab.

Literature

John Dryden ended a fruitful career with *Fables Ancient and Modern,* 1699. He also wrote a significant political satire on Monmouth and Shaftesbury in

Absalom and Achitophel. His clear, elegant verse and prose had influenced many, including **Samuel Butler,** 1612–80. *All for Love* was Dryden's best play.

Art and Architecture

Baroque architecture in England was exemplified in Castle Howard, designed by **John Vanbrugh,** 1664–1726, from 1696. He worked with **Nicholas Hawksmoor,** 1661–1736, on this and other buildings.
The beginnings of the **Rococo** style were seen in the "arabesques" and "grotesques" designed by **Jean Bérain,** 1640–1711, and **Claude Audran,** 1658–1734.

Music

Fugues in organ music were often paired with a free composition for contrast, giving the prelude and fugue or toccata and fugue found in many works by Buxtehude and Bach.

Science and Technology

The first practical steam engine was invented, 1696, by **Thomas Savery,** 1650–1715, a British engineer. **Thomas Newcomen,** 1663–1729, another British engineer, invented the atmospheric steam engine, used until 1934 to pump water from mines. Both engines had a great drawback: the cylinder had to be cooled at each stroke, wasting 99% of the heat from the fuel. **Agriculture** was improved by sowing seeds in rows with a drill invented in 1701 by **Jethro Tull,** 1674–1741, in England.

Principal Events

The French won control of the *asiento* contract in 1702, which allowed them to transport black slaves to the Spanish colonies. **Portugal** joined the alliance against France, acting as a base for operations in Spain, 1703. **The duke of Marlborough,** 1650–1722, defeated the French at **Blenheim**, 1704. After **Aurungzebe's death** in 1707, the Mogul Empire disintegrated as local princes asserted their autonomy, seeking assistance from European traders.

The Americas

The War of the Spanish Succession erupted in the colonies as **Queen Anne's War**, 1702–13. It ended with France losing territory in Canada to Britain.

Religion and Philosophy

In **The Grumbling Hive,** 1705, **Bernard de Mandeville,** 1670–1733, argued that all individual actions are motivated by self-interest, but the net effect of many such actions is the general good. This idea influenced later *laissez-faire* economists. **The Earl of Shaftesbury's** *Letter concerning Enthusiasm,* 1708, helped to popularize **Deism,** or Natural Religion. Deists criticized formal religions, intolerance, and extremism.

Literature

English journalism arose to satisfy the new middle-class market. **Daniel Defoe,** 1660–1731, journalist, novelist, merchant, and spy, issued the *Review,* 1704, later followed by **Richard Steele's** *Tatler,* 1709, and **Joseph Addison's** *Spectator,* 1711. Addison and Steele were informed and sensible essayists on literary, political, and social issues.

Art and Architecture

The grandeur and formal design of Versailles were emulated throughout Europe in the 18th century with the founding of St Petersburg, Russia, 1703, and in England with Blenheim Palace, 1705, built for the duke of Marlborough by **Vanbrugh.**

Music

German suites by Bach and others mixed free forms such as prelude and toccata with dance forms such as *allemande, sarabande, minuet, gavotte,* and *gigue.*

Science and Technology

Opticks, published by Newton in 1704, encapsulated his work on light. His particle theory of light held great sway for a century before Huygens' wave theory was revived. **Edmond Halley,** 1656–1742, British astronomer royal, proposed the idea that comets orbit the Sun and, using Newton's principles, correctly predicted in 1705 the return of the comet that now bears his name.

Principal Events

The Sikhs became militant and made the Punjab virtually independent of Mogul rule, 1708.
A mass emigration of Germans to America began in 1709.
War between the native Brazilians and the Portuguese erupted after France attacked Rio de Janeiro in the course of the Spanish War of Succession.
The Treaty of Utrecht, 1713, confirmed that France and Spain should not be united and left Britain in control of the *asiento* slave trade.

The Americas

The Parliamentary Act of 1709 offered immigrants who swore allegiance and took the Sacrament the privileges of British citizens.

Religion and Philosophy

In **The Principles of Human Knowledge,** 1710, Bishop Berkeley, 1685–1753, starting from the belief that all knowledge must come from perception, went beyond Locke and argued for an extreme idealism. He claimed that all we perceive is in the mind alone. As a result, to exist is merely to be perceived, and thus the continuing existence of the external world depends on God's external perception of it. Berkeley thus hoped to refute atheism definitively.

Literature

English Classicism found its wittiest poet in **Alexander Pope,** 1688–1744, whose *Rape of The*

Lock was published in its full form in 1714. The main defenders of classicism in France were **Nicolas Boileau,** 1636–1711, **Jean de la Bruyère,** 1645–96, and **Jacques Bossuet,** 1627–1711.

Art and Architecture

European artists, like **Gustavus Hesselius,** 1682–1755, from Sweden, settled in Philadelphia in 1711 and executed realistic portraits and history paintings.
A triumph for Rubensistes was evident in the vast ceiling of the Chapel at Versailles, 1708, by **Antoine Coypel,** 1661–1722, which is in the manner of Roman baroque illusionism.

Music

The pianoforte was invented. It is usually attributed to the Italian **Bartolomeo Cristofori,** 1655–1731, who in 1709 substituted hammer action for the harpsichord's plucking action.

Science and Technology

Jesuit missionaries made an accurate map of China, 1708.
High quality iron was produced in 1711 by **Abraham Darby,** 1677–1717, a British iron worker. The iron was smelted with coke and molded in sand for cheap production, making the cast iron steam engine an economical proposition.
Francis Hawksbee, an Englishman, made the first accurate observations of capillary action in glass tubes in 1709.
Prussian blue, a colored dye, was produced from 1710.

Principal Events

The English East India Company won trading concessions over rival companies from the Mogul emperor in 1717.
Frederick William of Prussia, r.1713–40, laid the foundations of Prussian military power by setting up a standing army.
Louis XIV died in 1715, with France's economy exhausted.
Manchu rule in Tibet was assured by 1720.
The South Sea Company, set up in 1710 to increase British South American trade, collapsed, 1720.

The Americas

Many Scotch-Irish immigrants arrived in the New World, most of them settling in Pennsylvania. New Orleans was founded in 1718.

Religion and Philosophy

The metaphysical views of Gottfried Leibniz, 1646–1716, were summed up in the *Monadologie,* 1714. He saw the universe as comprising an infinity of "monads," dimensionless entities endowed with souls, in pre-established harmony with each other. Leibniz held that God had chosen this as the best of all possible worlds and that the evil in it was necessary. He also worked influentially in symbolic logic.

Literature

The tradition of the picaresque novel (recounting exploits of an adventurer), which derived from Spain, was used by **Alain Le Sage,** 1668–1747, in his *Gil Blas,* 1715–35.
The romantic Japanese dramatist Chikamatsu Monzaemon, 1652–1725, wrote *Love Suicides,* the last of many successful plays both in **Kabuki** (song-dance) and **jojuri** (puppet) forms.

Art and Architecture

The "fête galante," a new genre of painting characterized by exquisite scenes of pleasure and dalliance, was introduced by **Antoine Watteau,** 1684–1721, in the "Departure for the Island of Cythera," 1717.
The first phase of the Rococo in France, 1700–20, largely in sculpture and interior design, was exemplified in the fountains of **Gilles Marie Oppenordt,** 1672–1742, designed about 1715 and showing twisting figures, shells, and scrolls.

Music

Italian became the usual operatic language in Europe although France still kept its own opera.
George Frederick Handel, 1685–1759, composed Italian opera in England after 1719.

Science and Technology

The mercury thermometer was invented in 1714 by **Gabriel Fahrenheit,** a German physicist, 1686–1736.
Jethro Tull brought the horse-hoe to England from France.
Thomas Lombe, 1658–1739, an Englishman, patented a machine to make thrown silk in 1718.

Reason and
the Enlightenment
1720–1760

Marble bust of Voltaire, who influenced the French Enlightenment

Jean-Jacques Rousseau introduced the "noble savage."

Gulliver's Travels by Jonathan Swift

House of Menander, Pompeii

Frederick II reformed the Prussian army

Dutch East Indiaman trading ship

Robert Bakewell's selectively bred sheep

Reason and the Enlightenment

★ Principal Events

A series of dynastic and trade wars overtook Europe, contributing to the growing conflict between centralized monarchical authority, the nobility, and the newly strong mercantile class. In France the supremacy of the monarch over the nobles broke down, producing a political stalemate. In Prussia, Russia, and Portugal, however, the liberal ideas of the Enlightenment were harnessed to the growth of royal absolutism and industrial reform.

The English moved inland in India into the vacuum of the collapsing Mogul Empire, prized both for the value of its produce and the quality of its culture. Here they competed successfully with the French despite the unwillingness of the English government to take on imperial responsibility. At the same time the American colonies, whose economies were beginning to grow, were becoming impatient with Britain's rigid mercantilist policies.

National Events

The American colonies continued to develop, each in its own way, but with a common English identity. As English power in America grew, colonists began to chafe under British economic policies. Colonial assemblies were unable to exercise independent action. Settlers began to move westward increasingly.

Religion and Philosophy

The influence of English empiricist ideas on the philosophical tradition stemming from Descartes led to the great intellectual development known as the French Enlightenment. Montesquieu, Voltaire, Rousseau, and other "philosophes" who contributed to the French Encyclopedia believed in the power of reason and knowledge to liberate man from restrictive political and religious systems.

On religious questions these thinkers tended toward deism or even atheism, and accepted a materialist conception of the universe. In politics they were liberals. Montesquieu sought to classify social systems and analyze their function. The Physiocrats laid the foundation of scientific economics. Others such as Condillac elaborated the basic ideas of materialist philosophy.

In Britain David Hume showed how empiricism could lead to an extreme skepticism.

Literature

European literature was dominated by the critical spirit of the Age of Reason expressed in the work of essayists and satirists such as Pope and Swift in Britain or Voltaire and Montesquieu in France, where polemical writing was in the ascendant. The same desire to grasp social reality found expression in the English novel, whether in the vein of a new realism, with Defoe or Fielding, in the psychological studies of Laurence Sterne, or the picaresque novels of Smollett. In Italy, Goldoni's comedies began a parallel move in the theater away from stock characterization and toward a greater realism.

The basis of modern Russian poetry was established by Lomonosov.

Art and Architecture

Late manifestations of the more emotional baroque and rococo forms were seen in Austria and Germany as well as in European colonial architecture in the mid-18th century. But as concepts of "good taste" emerged during the Enlightenment, combined with a more exact and careful study of the aesthetics of classical art, the exuberance of the early 18th century became restrained within realist, or neoclassical modes. Interest in fantasy shifted from the Baroque to chinoiserie or rococo "Gothick," in the search for new stylistic forms.

Native Indian art was in decline, and European styles were introduced to India by the advancing colonialists. The impact of European expansion in the cultural sphere was also found in China.

In Japan color printing techniques were developed, and the art reached a new peak in the work of Utamaro.

Music

Italian influence on European music waned, except in opera and song. The French evolved instruments and musical theory, but the Germans and Austrians, patronized by their princes, made the most use of these developments and ushered in the classical age of music. In the work of Joseph Haydn, 1732–1809, the symphony found a champion to establish its form.

Science and Technology

Great technological innovations were created, and were stimulated by, the Industrial Revolution. In England the textile industry, with its need for large-scale bleaching and dyeing processes, gave a boost to practical chemistry and to machine technology. The flying shuttle produced the large quantities of cloth that demanded bleaching, and modern methods were invented to provide the great amounts of acid employed in the process. Similarly, the need to transport more raw materials and finished products by sea than ever before encouraged navigational innovation. An early form of the sextant and the first accurate chronometer were invented. Meanwhile pure scientific research continued in the form of discoveries, particularly in plant physiology and growth. Early work on electricity was performed at Leyden University and in America, providing the basis of later experiments into the nature of electric currents and their potential.

1720-1724

Principal Events

The English South Sea Company and the French Mississippi scheme, which had both aimed to restore royal finances, collapsed in 1720.

The Pragmatic Sanction, 1713, establishing the indivisibility of Austria-Hungary, was accepted in 1720.

In North America, Spain occupied Texas 1720– 22, to prevent a French invasion, and the Piedmont region was colonized by Swiss, Germans, and Scots.

The Americas

French forts along the Mississippi River spread northward from New Orleans. The first smallpox inoculations were given, 1721.

Religion and Philosophy

Christian von Wolff, 1679– 1754, a follower of Leibniz, made rationalist antitraditional philosophy popular in Germany. Puritan Pietists engineered his expulsion from the University of Halle in 1723, but he later became its chancellor.

Ba'al Shem Tov, c.1700– 60, founded **Hasidism** in Poland. This vibrant orthodox movement within Judaism stressed the joy of religious practice and expression, and rejected academic formalism and elitism.

Literature

Daniel Defoe, 1660– 1731, a prolific writer and one of the founders of modern journalism, turned to fiction (disguised as fact) and revealed a powerful imagination. His novels, including *Robinson Crusoe,* 1719– 20, and *Moll Flanders,* 1722, are noted for their highly realistic descriptions.

Art and Architecture

Easter Island was discovered by the Dutch, 1722. Archeologists have since been baffled by the significance of, and building methods used to erect, the megalithic statues found there.

Austrian art reached its peak in the architecture of palaces, churches, and monasteries, especially those of **Lukas von Hildebrandt,** 1688– 1745. Known as "Austrian Baroque," this style with its florid shapes and lavish decoration paved the way for late German Baroque.

Music

Traité de l'harmonie, 1722, by **Jean Philipe Rameau,** 1683– 1764, provided the foundation of harmonic thought for two centuries, with its clear statement of the function of tonality.

Science and Technology

Smallpox inoculations were first administered in the New World during an epidemic in 1721, when **Zabdiel Boylston,** 1679– 1766, inoculated 240 persons, of whom all but six survived.

Principal Events

Peter the Great of Russia died, 1725, having encouraged industrial growth, centralized the administration, and subdued the nobility.

The ministry of Fleury, 1653–1743, in France began, 1726, introducing a period of peace and economic growth that led to a strengthening of the middle classes.

The Russian border with China was fixed in 1727.

The Americas

The Great Awakening, a spiritual revival in the colonies, began in 1726. Prominent figures were **Jonathan Edwards**, 1703–58, and **George Whitefield**, 1715–70.

Religion and Philosophy

Giovanni Battista Vico, 1668–1744, an important forerunner of the modern social scientists, outlined his ideas in *Universal Law*, 1720–21, and elaborated them later in his masterpiece, *The New Science*, 1725. Vico held that societies pass from a bestial stage through a patrician stage ruled by a hereditary elite, to a stage where men are equal. He warned that man was never wholly rid of his bestial aspect and might always regress into barbarism.

Literature

Jonathan Swift, 1667–1745, poet, polemicist, and churchman, published *Gulliver's Travels*, 1726, a highly imaginative satire on mankind. Swift wrote brilliantly abusive essays.

The Beggar's Opera by John Gay, 1685–1732, was first played in 1728. It uses elements of Italian opera and traditional songs to create a new style of political satire.

Art and Architecture

Indian art was in decline with the collapse of the Mogul Empire, and European architectural styles began to be introduced in colonial towns, including Bombay where **St Thomas Cathedral** was built.

Catholic Bavaria accepted Italian baroque forms, which in the later work of **Balthasar Neumann**, 1687–1753, took on an almost rococo lightness. His church at Vierzehnheiligen, 1743–72, is richly painted in pink, gold, and white.

Music

Light opera emerged in Germany, where **Reinhard Keiser**, 1674–1739, wrote operas with catchy tunes. He wrote a comic opera in 1726 that used spoken dialogue rather than recitative.

Science and Technology

The chronometer was developed from 1726 by John Harrison, 1693–1776, an Englishman, to aid navigation, as longitude could be determined only by time. He invented the compensating pendulum, so that his chronometers would keep perfect time in any climate.

Plant physiology was founded by the publication of *Vegetable Statics*, in 1727, by **Stephen Hales**, 1677–1761. Measuring plant growth and sap production, Hales realized that air is necessary for plants to grow.

Principal Events

The **Anglo-Spanish War**, 1727–28, forced Spain to end her siege and confirm England's possession of Gibraltar, 1729. **Anna**, *r*.1730–40, empress of Russia, founded the Corps of Cadets to encourage the nobles' participation in administration. By the **Treaty of Vienna**, 1731, the Holy Roman Empire dissolved the Ostend East India Company, England's colonial trading rival in cotton, spices, and saltpeter.

The Americas

North Carolina became a royal colony, 1729, as had South Carolina in 1721. Georgia, planned as a refuge for prisoners, was chartered, 1732.

Religion and Philosophy

Voltaire, 1694–1778, returned to France in 1729 after over two years in England. His *Lettres philosophiques*, 1734, advocating the empiricism of **Isaac Newton** and **John Locke** and the merits of the English political system, had a great influence on the French Enlightenment. Voltaire was a deist and an active liberal fighting for the exercise of tolerance in both religion and politics.

Literature

German ideas of the **Aufklärung** (Enlightenment) were summed up in *Critische Dichtkunst*, 1730, a critical work by the playwright **J. C. Gottsched**, 1700–66. He argued that literature must imitate classical models and be didactic.

Romanticism was foreshadowed in France by the **Abbé Prévost**, 1697–1763, the prolific author of *Manon Lescaut*, 1731.

Art and Architecture

Palladianism, a revival of interest in the restrained classicism of Vitruvius, Palladio, and his English follower Inigo Jones, marked an English reaction against Baroque. It was pioneered by **Colin Campbell**, *d*.1729, and taken up by **Lord Burlington**, 1694–1753, who encouraged **William Kent**, *d*.1748, and **Isaac Ware**, *d*.1766. **Giuseppe Castiglione** 1698–1768, settled in China *c*.1730, and was the first Western painter to be appreciated there.

Music

Virtuoso players such as **Antonio Vivaldi**, *c*.1675–1741, advanced the techniques of their instruments and led to a distinction between music for professional and amateur players.

Science and Technology

Stellar aberration, a change in the position of stars caused by the Earth's motion, was detected in 1729 by an Englishman, **James Bradley**, 1693–1762. This was the first absolute confirmation of Copernicus' theory that the Earth moves around the Sun.

Cobalt was discovered in 1730 by George Brandt, 1694–1768, a Swedish chemist.

The **reflecting quadrant**, a forerunner of the sextant, aided navigation. It was invented in 1730 by John Hadley, 1682–1744.

Principal Events

England prohibited trade between her American and West Indian colonies by the Molasses Act of 1733.
War over the succession, 1733–35, weakened Poland.
The French Compagnie des Indes was firmly established in India by 1735.
Class distinctions between the merchant and military groups in Japan became blurred during a long period of economic decline.

The Americas

Independence Hall in Philadelphia was begun in 1732. **Benjamin Franklin**, 1706–90, began publication of *Poor Richard's Almanack*.

Religion and Philosophy

In his Treatise on Human Nature, written from 1734 to 1737, **David Hume**, 1711–76, argued from empiricist presuppositions that knowledge was unattainable. He said that since connections were unobservable our belief in them was irrational. Hume held that the basis of moral judgment was man's subjective reaction of approval or disapproval of the effects actions have on himself and others.

Literature

The Italian **Scipione Maffei**, 1675–1755, published his erudite study of the history of Verona, *Verona Illustrata*, in 1732. **Montesquieu**, 1689–1755, a leading French thinker and satirist, wrote his *Considerations of the Causes of the Grandeur of the Romans and their Decadence*, 1734, an outstanding piece of sociopolitical analysis.

Art and Architecture

Venice took the lead in Italian art with the painting of **Giovanni Tiepolo**, 1696–1770, and **Antonio Canaletto**, 1697–1768. **Servandoni**, 1695–1766, began work on the facade of Ste Sulpice in Paris, 1732. It relied on antique architecture and heralded a reaction against Rococo.

Music

Religious cantata and oratorio were developed on a grand scale by **Bach** and **George Frederick Handel**, 1685–1759, to embrace all musical techniques but without the use of operatic staging.

Science and Technology

Systema Naturae was published by **Carl Linnaeus**, 1707–78, a Swedish botanist, in 1735. He defined the differences between species and formed the idea of classifying plants and animals into species and genera, classes, and orders.
The flying shuttle was invented in England in 1733 by John Kay, 1704–64.
Rubber was found in South America by Charles Marie de la Condamine, 1701–74, while on an expedition to measure the curvature of the Earth, 1735.

★ Principal Events

Russia and Austria clashed with the Turks over their Polish policy. The Russians captured Azov but by the Treaty of Belgrade, 1739, were prevented from keeping a fortified Black Sea base there.

Commercial rivalry in America between England and Spain brought an end to a period of peace for England, with the war of Jenkins' Ear, 1739–48. The war resulted from a dispute over trading rights in the Spanish colonies.

The Americas

John Peter Zenger, 1697–1746, appointed public printer for New Jersey and New York, 1737. Zenger had been acquitted in 1735 of libel.

Religion and Philosophy

John Wesley, 1703–91, an Anglican minister, founded the Methodist movement in England. After a spiritual experience in 1738, Wesley began evangelical open air preaching and drew up a set of "Rules" for his followers, who formed "bands"—small groups for mutual encouragement and for teaching and prayer. They believed in a personal relationship with God and were noted for their good works. The Methodists finally broke with the Church of England in 1795.

Literature

Voltaire (F. M. Arouet), 1694–1778, wit, poet, dramatist, and epitome of the Enlightenment in his scorn for prejudice and distrust of accepted ideas, wrote the philosophical poems *Le Mondain*, 1736, and *Discours sur l'Homme*, 1738. Stressing the value of experience, he later satirized ideas of human perfectibility in *Candide*, 1759, a tale of innocence abused.

Art and Architecture

French art was divided between the officially accepted art in the rococo vein, like the frivolous, mildly erotic work of **François Boucher,** 1703–70, who had adopted much of Tiepolo's technique, and the more solid realistic genre scenes of **Jean Chardin,** 1699–1779, which reflected a contemporary taste for northern painting, especially 17th-century Dutch masters. **Herculaneum** was discovered in 1738.

Music

Contrapuntal writing reached a masterful zenith under Bach, with music of great power and intricacy, as in the "Kyrie" from his *Mass in B minor*, 1738.

Science and Technology

Daniel Bernoulli, 1700–82, a Frenchman, related fluid flow to pressure in 1738.

Principal Events

Frederick II the Great of Prussia, r.1740–86, introduced religious toleration and agricultural reform, consolidated royal authority, and reformed the army. In 1740 he occupied Silesia, thus striking the first blow in the War of the Austrian Succession, 1740–48.

Elizabeth of Russia, r.1741–62, gave new authority to the Senate.

The Marathas took Bengal, 1742–44, and disturbed English trade in Bombay.

The Americas

Alaska was discovered, 1741, by **Vitus Bering**, 1680–1741, sailing from Russia to see if North America and Asia were connected by land.

Religion and Philosophy

The puritanical Wahhabi movement within Islam was founded by **Muhammed ibn Abd al-Wahhab**, 1703–92. He advocated a return to the original principles of Islam and condemned as polytheistic the decoration of mosques and the cult of saints, which he saw as intervening in the personal and direct relationship between the faithful and God. In 1744 the powerful Saudi family in central Arabia adopted the principles of the Wahhabi sect.

Literature

The crowning achievement of Augustan poetry is seen in **The Dunciad** of **Alexander Pope**, appeared in its final version, 1743.

This was a mock heroic attacking the betrayal of literature by hack writers, using elements of Homer, Vergil, Dante, and Milton and defending a role for the poet as a conserver of the values of society.

Art and Architecture

Color printing was developed in Japan, c.1742 with outstanding results by **Kitagawa Utamaro**, 1753–1806, who was one of the greatest exponents of the ukiyo-e school of painting. This "floating world" art form was famous for its depiction of sensuous women. In England, **William Hogarth**, 1697–1764, attacked the social abuses of his time. He often followed a narrative of events in a series of paintings as in "Marriage à la Mode."

Music

Equal temperament was worked out in Germany. It made modulation to distant keys possible, as in the **Well-tempered Klavier**, 1722–44, by **J. S. Bach**, 1685–1750.

Science and Technology

Anders Celsius, 1701–44, a Swede, devised the Celsius scale of temperature, c.1744, with 0° the freezing point of water and 100° the boiling point.

The crucible method of making steel by heating scrap iron was found in England, 1740, by Benjamin Huntsman, 1704–76.

Mikhail Lomonosov, 1711–65, rejected the phlogiston theory and suggested the law of the conservation of mass.

Traité de Dynamique, 1743, by Jean d'Alembert, 1717–83, solved problems in mechanics.

Principal Events

Frederick II began the Second Silesian War, 1744–45. France and Prussia defeated the Austrians and their allies at the battle of Fontenoy, 1745.
In North America, English forces took Louisbourg, 1745, and made new conquests from the French in the West Indies.
In India, the Frenchman **Joseph Dupleix,** 1696–1763, took Madras, 1746. However, all these conquests were restored by the **Treaty of Aix-la-Chapelle,** 1748.

The Americas

The Presbyterian College of New Jersey, renamed Princeton University in 1896, was chartered, 1746, to educate clergy.

Religion and Philosophy

In **The Spirit of Laws,** published 1748, the French social theorist **Charles Montesquieu,** 1689–1755, examined the relationships between a society's laws and its other characteristics such as religion and economic organization, drawing on an immense range of information about other cultures. He elaborated a study of types of governmental systems and analyzed the prerequisites of their proper functioning.

Literature

Italy's greatest comic dramatist, Carlo Goldoni, 1707–93, wrote *The Servant of Two Masters,* 1745. A skillful and prolific craftsman, he substituted a script and more realistic treatment of character and situation for commedia dell'arte, the traditional Italian comic form in which actors playing stock roles improvised upon an outline scenario.

Art and Architecture

Chinoiserie, a taste for Chinese art and design, became popular in Europe in the 1740s.
Spanish colonial architecture was executed in a baroque style, especially in Mexico. The collision with existing cultures introduced new motifs like the Puebla tiles on the Church of San Francisco, Acatepec.

Music

The symphony orchestra gained the basis of its present form at Mannheim court under **Johann Stamitz,** 1717–57, who trained his players to produce controlled extremes of loud and soft.

Science and Technology

The Leyden jar, developed at the University of Leyden, 1745, was able to store a large charge of static electricity. It was used in the first investigations into the nature of electricity.
John Roebuck, 1718–94, a British inventor, developed a process for manufacturing sulfuric acid, used to bleach textiles, on a large scale in 1746.

Principal Events

Louis XV, r.1715–74, met united opposition from the nobility and clergy in France when he tried to introduce new taxes on their wealth to pay for his war expenses, 1751.
Robert Clive, 1725–74, seized Arcot, 1751, in search of personal power and booty, and thus established English authority over southern India, ousting the French opposition.
The Chinese invaded Tibet, 1751, following a growth in Chinese population and wealth.

The Americas

In **1749**, Britain granted 200,000 acres of land on the upper Ohio to a group of Virginians who formed a land company.

Religion and Philosophy

The first volume of the French Encyclopédie appeared, 1751. Edited by **Denis Diderot**, 1713–84, and completed in 1772, this is a monument to the "philosophes" of the French Enlightenment and aimed to advance reason, knowledge, and liberty. The contributors, who included **Etienne Condillac**, 1715–80, the Lockean philosopher, were deists or atheists who held liberal political views and a materialist conception of the universe.

Literature

The English novel, which had been pioneered by **Samuel Richardson**, 1689–1761, in *Pamela*, 1740–41, flowered in the masterpiece *Tom Jones*, 1749, by **Henry Fielding**, 1707–54.

Laurence Sterne, 1713–68, mastered a vein of black humor in *Tristram Shandy*, and **Tobias Smollett**, 1721–71, the picaresque tradition in *Roderick Random*, 1748.

Art and Architecture

The "Gothick rococo" became a fashion in England with the remodeling of Strawberry Hill House, 1749, by **Horace Walpole**, 1717–97. The library fireplace combined motifs from medieval tombs in Westminster and Canterbury Cathedrals.
British and French artists such as **Joshua Reynolds**, 1723–92, and **Jacques-Germain Soufflot**, 1713–80, would revolutionize art and architecture after studying art in Rome c.1750.
Pompeii was found in 1748.

Music

American settlers began making a distinctive music with easily carried instruments. Barn dances were held as buildings were completed, and hymn-singing meetings were held in homes

Science and Technology

Benjamin Franklin, 1706–90, working in America, flew a kite in a thunderstorm, 1752, to prove that lightning is electrical, and from his results developed a lightning conductor.
Selective breeding, pioneered by **Robert Bakewell**, 1725–95, in England, improved livestock. The experimental farming of **Viscount Townshend**, 1674–1738, improved crop rotation.
Georges Buffon, 1707–88, published the first volume of his massive *Histoire Naturelle*, 1749–88.

Principal Events

Sébastião Pombal, 1699–1782, introduced Enlightenment ideas to Portugal, 1751–77, ruthlessly attacking clerical and noble privileges and stimulating industrial growth.
Dupleix was recalled to France in 1754, leaving India to the British. Delhi was sacked by Afghan invaders, 1756–57.
Moscow University was founded in 1755 to promote education among the Russian nobility.
Lisbon was destroyed by an earthquake in 1755.

The Americas

George Washington's troops at Fort Duquesne, 1754, opened the French and Indian War.
Franklin proposed Plan of Union at the Albany Congress, 1754.

Religion and Philosophy

Jean-Jacques Rousseau, 1712–78, published his *Discourse on Inequality* in 1755. In this work, and in *The Social Contract*, 1762, he argued that in a natural state men were equal and that it was only society that creates inequality and misery. He argued that the injustices of society could be minimized if citizens resigned their rights to a government that acted on the "general will."

Literature

The father of modern Russian literature, Mikhail Lomonosov, 1711–65, published his *Grammar*, 1755. Poet and linguist, he set up verse rules and three styles of literary diction that opened up new possibilities in Russian literature.
The lyrical poetry of the German F. G. Klopstock, 1724–1803, who took Greek verse as his model, anticipated Romanticism.

Art and Architecture

A torrent of publications heralded a change in taste in European art, foreshadowing **Neoclassicism**, which would be based on a detailed study of ancient Greek and Roman art. The archeological discoveries engraved by **Piranesi**, 1720–78, in *Antichita Romana*, 1757, and such dissertations on taste as *Dialogue on Taste*, 1754, by **Allan Ramsay**, 1713–84, resulted in an ability to distinguish different phases in antiquity.

Music

The symphony in the hands of Haydn developed greatly from 1750 to 1760, advancing its instrumentation and the form of its contrasting movements, usually four in number.

Science and Technology

Immanuel Kant, 1724–1804, in Germany, published his views on the formation of the solar system in 1755, anticipating the work of Laplace. He also suggested that galaxies of stars exist and that the tides slow the rotation of the Earth. Both of these ideas were verified much later.
René Réaumur, 1683–1757, proved that digestion is a chemical process and invented an 80 degree thermometer scale.

1756-1760

Principal Events

In the **Seven Years War**, 1756–63, Austria was at first defeated by Frederick II.
Clive won control of Bengal at Plassey, 1757.
The Marathas occupied the Punjab in 1758.
Pombal expelled the Jesuits from Portugal in 1759.
Most of **Canada** came under British control after the surrender of **Montreal**, 1760. This ended the need for British garrisons to defend the American colonies.

The Americas

French General Montcalm, 1712–59, and **British Brig. Gen. James Wolfe**, 1727–59, died on the Plains of Abraham. France ceded Canada to England, 1763.

Religion and Philosophy

The Physiocrats of the 18th century were the first scientific school of economics. They regarded agriculture rather than manufacturing as the source of wealth, and advocated the doctrine of *laissez-faire,* or free trade, against the complex trade regulations then in force. The most important Physiocrat was **François Quesnay**, 1694–1774, whose *Tableau economique*, 1758, was the first work to attempt an analysis of the workings of an entire economy.

Literature

Realism in Chinese fiction, exemplified in the satirical novel *Unofficial History of Scholars* by **Wu Ching-tse**, 1701–54, was further developed by **Tsao Chan**, c.1719–63, in *The Dream of a Red Chamber*. In this novel, the grandeur and decline of a Chinese family was described with convincing detail and a new sense of humanity.

Art and Architecture

Russian architecture was based largely on French developments, the combination of baroque forms with rococo decoration producing the extravagant splendor of the Winter Palace, 1754–62, in St Petersburg by **Bartolomeo Rastrelli**, 1700–71. A positive reaction against Rococo in France was seen in the fleeting fashion of "Le Gout Grec" and also in a more significant dependence on antique precedents in the design of the Pantheon by **Soufflot** in Paris.

Music

Sonata form was advanced by **C. P. E. Bach**, 1714–88, who made imaginative use of key relationships and conflicts in the development sections of first movements of his symphonies.

Science and Technology

Carbon dioxide was discovered in 1756 by Joseph Black, 1728–99, a British chemist.
Lomonosov was the first man to observe atmosphere on the planet of Venus, 1761.
The sextant of John Bird (1758) made navigational observations far more accurate.
John Dollond, 1706–61, produced the first achromatic lenses in 1757 in England.

211

Revolution in America and France 1760–1800

Neoclassical painting,
"The Oath of the Horatii"
by David

Iron bridge at
Coalbrookdale

The American
Revolution was a war for
independence.

French Revolution: the separation of Louis XVI from his own head

Samuel Crompton's mechanized spinning mule

Industrial Revolution: James Watt's rotary steam engine

Revolution in America and France

Principal Events

The old order in Europe was fundamentally shaken by three major revolutions—in America, France, and England—which dramatically changed the political and economic basis of Western society and would ultimately transform the world. The American Revolution represented the overthrow of the old colonial and trading system and installed the ideas of liberty and democracy as the ideals of the United States. The French Revolution of 1789 swept away the privileges of the outdated ancien régime and established a new idea of popular right, which would be carried by Napoleon's conquests to stir the rest of Europe to revolt.

In England the Industrial Revolution began in earnest in the 1780s, providing the basis for a fundamental transformation of Western and ultimately global society by accelerating urbanization and creating new sources of wealth, new social classes, and democratic demands.

National Events

The American colonists had become so "English" in their political beliefs that they could not tolerate the inferior status of colonials. Resentment of British rule, particularly taxation without representation, led to a war to ensure that Englishmen in America would enjoy all the rights of Englishmen in England.

Religion and Philosophy

The question of the existence of God became subordinate for many European thinkers to questions of social organization.

In America the revolution was associated with ideas of democracy, liberty, and equality, which in turn inspired the French Revolution.

In Britain new economic thinking reflected the emergence of the industrial system. Adam Smith laid the foundation of modern economics, fostering the liberal doctrine of the free market and the absence of state encroachment on individual freedom. Bentham argued that desire and pursuit of pleasure motivated human behavior. The Scottish Enlightenment advanced social thought with Ferguson's and Monboddo's work on social development and man's origins.

Kant, however, laid the basis for German idealism with his opposition to pure empiricism, claiming that such concepts as time were innate.

Literature

Forerunners of Romanticism emerged in Germany, France, and Britain. The emphasis on unity and order in literary style and the skeptical and rational attitudes of mind that marked the Enlightenment were beginning to give way to increasing respect for human instincts and emotions, sincerity of feeling, and freedom and naturalism of style. This transition, initiated by Rousseau in France, was carried on in Germany by the Sturm und Drang movement whose greatest voice, Goethe, combined passion with discipline. The work of the British poets Gray, Cowper, Burns, and Blake exemplified the transition from classicism to romanticism in English poetic style. Samuel Johnson's work advanced literary criticism.

Art and Architecture

The arts in Europe, and particularly in France, reflected the critical spirit of the Enlightenment by returning to an austere style based on moral and aesthetic theories. Antiquarian and archeological investigation had transformed ideas on cultural development so that the various styles of Greek and Roman antiquity, the Middle Ages, and the Renaissance could now be distinguished. Neoclassicism, which developed toward the end of the 18th century, incorporated this knowledge, adopting Greek and Roman ideals of beauty and ethics derived from antique sculpture, architecture, painting, and literature. This historical concern was also to lead to acceptance of eclecticism and the concept of a modern style.

The European colonial presence in Asia tended to paralyze the development of indigenous artistic styles, but native traditions survived in areas remote from foreign influence.

Music

The classical age of European music was dominated by Joseph Haydn, 1732–1809, and Wolfgang Mozart, 1756–91. Composers pursued variety within movements, building bigger structures by manipulating musical themes and utilizing key relationships and contrasts of instrumental sound, appealing equally to the heads and hearts of their educated audiences.

Science and Technology

In Britain the Industrial Revolution began to transform the face of the nation. James Watt produced the first rotary engine, which could be used to power factories anywhere in the country, while the spinning jenny and the water frame furthered mechanization of the textile industry. Agricultural improvements, including more efficient crop rotation and selective breeding, increased the amount of food produced and provided a surplus for the towns. Developments in hygiene and medicine, such as the water closet, vaccination, and the widespread use of soap, would form the basis for substantial improvements in urban living conditions, many of which, however, were not realized until the 19th century.

Science was linked with liberty in revolutionary France as many academies of science were founded in 1789, while American technology worked against freedom—the success of the cotton gin helping to prolong slavery in the south.

1760-1764

Principal Events

Prussia increased its military power after 1760 and an inconclusive settlement to the Seven Years War followed.

The Treaty of Paris, 1763, confirmed English supremacy in Canada and India.

The War left French government finances in a precarious state despite expanding trade.

Pontiac's Rebellion, an American Indian revolt, was suppressed by the English in Canada, 1763–66.

The Americas

Ottawa chief Pontiac, c.1720–69, led an Indian uprising, 1763, but the British defeated the Indians. The Sugar Act was passed, 1764.

Religion and Philosophy

The Scottish School of Common Sense Philosophy was begun by **Thomas Reid,** 1710–96, who argued in *An Inquiry into the Human Mind on the Principles of Common Sense,* 1764, that Hume's skepticism about attaining true knowledge was against common sense. **Dugald Stewart,** 1753–1828, sought rejection of fruitless metaphysical speculation and the creation of scientific philosophy.

Literature

Jean-Jacques Rousseau, 1712–78, whose concept of the "noble savage" deeply influenced romanticism, published *La Nouvelle Héloïse,* 1761, a novel advocating simple relationships in a natural setting. *The Encyclo-pedie,* edited 1751–72, by **Denis Diderot,** 1713–84, and **Jean Le Rond d'Alembert,** 1717–83, expressed the skepticism of the Enlightenment.

Art and Architecture

Robert Adam with his brother James introduced a new eclectic style of architecture to town and country houses in Britain, like **Syon House,** 1762–69, in which they combined elements of English Palladianism with details of Roman architecture and Renaissance palaces.

Neoclassical painting was developed in Rome, under the impetus of the German archeologist **Johann Joachim Wickelmann,** 1717–68, by his follower **Anton Raffael Mengs,** 1728–79.

Music

The symphony and sonata grew in complexity under the hand of Haydn from c.1760. The first movement had contrasting themes worked over in a development section.

Science and Technology

Joseph Black, 1728–99, a Scottish chemist, defined the difference between heat and temperature, and discovered specific and latent heat, 1760–63. His basic work on heat enabled his friend **James Watt** to build a steam engine.

The spinning "jenny" was invented in England, 1764, by **James Hargreaves.** It could spin several threads at once.

Principal Events

The Sugar Act and Stamp Act
1764–65, by which Britain aimed to recover revenue from the American colonies, aroused local opposition.
England ruled Bengal and Bihar by 1765, maintaining a puppet Mogul emperor.
Ali Bey *r.*1768–73, declared Egyptian independence from Turkish rule, 1766.
Catherine II of Russia, *r.*1762–96, consulted a convention of all social classes to reform Russian law, 1767.

The Americas

The Stamp Act, 1765, increased discontent. A Stamp Act Congress met, 1765, to protest the act, which was repealed, 1766.

Religion and Philosophy

Adam Ferguson, 1723–1816, an early British sociologist, put forward the theory that man's unceasing desire to control nature was the cause of social development in his *Essay on the History of Civil Society*, 1766.
The Judaic religion was interpreted by **Moses Mendelssohn**, 1729–86, in terms of the metaphysics of Leibniz, paving the way for a synthesis of Judaism and modern philosophical and scientific thought, later to develop into Reform Judaism.

Literature

Gothic themes involving the supernatural and the crime of passion appeared in the ultra-romantic novel *The Castle of Otranto*, 1764, by **Horace Walpole**, 1717–97.
Thomas Percy, 1729–1811, published *Reliques of Ancient English Poetry*, 1765.
Karl Bellman, 1740–95, a Swedish poet, began his *82 Epistles* in 1765.

Art and Architecture

Soufflot's church of Ste Geneviève in Paris progressed. The design combined Greek post and lintel systems and attempted to achieve the lightness of Gothic architecture.
The Royal Academy of Art, London, was founded in 1768 under royal patronage. The first President, **Joshua Reynolds**, 1723–92, in "13 Discourses," promoted the "Grand Manner" in English painting.

Music

Christoph Gluck, 1714–87, reformed opera in Paris, stressing the balance between the musical and the dramatic elements. He expressed his ideals in a preface to *Alceste*, 1767.

Science and Technology

The Lunar Society, an informal society of technologists, was founded *c.*1765.
Neurology was established with the work of Swiss physiologist **Albrecht von Haller**, 1708–77. Haller located nerves and showed that nerve impulses stimulate muscles.
Henry Cavendish, 1731–1810, a British scientist, discovered hydrogen in 1766. He also made fundamental, unpublished discoveries in electricity. In 1798 he would calculate the Earth's mass.

1768-1772

★ Principal Events

The American colonies began their westward expansion, settling Tennessee in 1769.
French trade with India increased after the French East India Company lost its monopoly, 1769. Opposition to absolutism in France increased among intellectuals.
James Cook, 1728–79, began the exploration of Australia in the *Endeavour*, 1768–71.

The Americas

British troops in Boston fired on civilians, and five died in the Boston Massacre, March 5, 1770.

♀ Religion and Philosophy

Johann Herder, 1744–1803, German poet and philosopher, was among the first modern thinkers to question the limits of reason. He emphasized the immediacy and therefore the power of feeling—ideas that were later to become the essence of the Romantic movement.
Paul d'Holbach, 1723–1803, the most ardent materialist of the French Encyclopedists, wrote in his *System of Nature*, 1770, that man's life is determined from birth.

Literature

Thomas Gray's *Poems by Mr Gray*, 1768, included the "Elegy Written in a Country Churchyard." Gray, 1716–71, treated themes of history and death in a sensitive, meditative manner.
Gotthold Lessing, 1729–81, a German dramatist, wrote *Emilia Galotti*, 1772.

Art and Architecture

An empirical, scientific attitude to art in England was shown by **George Stubbs,** 1724–1806, in the *Anatomy of the Horse*, published 1766, and in *The Experiment with the Air Pump*, 1768, by **Joseph Wright** of Derby, 1734–97.
French Neoclassic architecture was governed by the severe unadorned classicism seen in the works of **Jacques Gondouin** 1737–1818, of which the **Ecole de Médecine**, Paris, 1769, is a fine example.

Music

Counterpoint declined in importance and the continuo disappeared. Contrapuntal forms such as fugue continued to be used but usually as part of a movement in a larger work.

Science and Technology

The water frame was invented in 1768 by **Richard Arkwright,** 1732–92. Powered by water, it spun cotton into a strong thread.
James Watt, 1736–1819, patented his steam engine in 1769. This engine used a separate cylinder for condensing steam and worked quickly and efficiently. Watt's engine was the first to produce rotary motion.
Luigi Galvani, 1737–98, an Italian, found in 1771 that two metals in contact with a frog's leg cause it to twitch. He had produced current electricity.

★ Principal Events

After Pugachev's revolt, a large peasant and Cossack uprising, 1773–75, Catherine II reformed Russian provincial administration.

The Regulating Act established an English governor general in India, 1773. **Warren Hastings,** 1732–1818, reformed the Bengal administration. Demands by the American colonists that they be represented in the English Parliament led to the **American Revolution,** 1775–83.

The Americas

The Boston Tea Party protested the Tea Act, 1773. The First Continental Congress met, 1774. Lexington and Concord, 1775, opened the Revolution.

Religion and Philosophy

Lord Monboddo, 1714–99, a British anthropologist, believed man's present social state evolved from a previous animal one. This conflicted with the view then current that man was unique. He began publication of his work on language in 1773. **The "Shakers,"** a group of puritanical nonconformists led by **Ann Lee,** 1736–84, began their first colony in America in 1774. They believed total sexual abstinence was the basis of man's spiritual salvation.

Literature

Sturm und Drang (Storm and Stress), a German literary movement expressing subjectivity and contemporary unease, found a genius in **Johann Wolfgang von Goethe,** 1749–1832. His novel *The Sufferings of Young Werther,* 1774, began a cult of the hero ruled by the heart rather than the head. Romantic pessimism was exemplified in the poems of **Novalis,** 1772–1801.

Art and Architecture

Reynolds' supremacy in English portraiture was challenged in 1774 when **Thomas Gainsborough,** 1727–88, moved to London. His "William Henry, Duke of Gloucester," *c.*1775, was deliberately glamorous and richly colored. His later paintings introduced a more lyrical note to English portraiture.

Indian artists in the late 18th and early 19th centuries were dominated by European techniques. The Patua paintings of east India were exceptions.

Music

String quartets were written in large numbers. They were an ideal vehicle for the development of classical designs and allowed the composer to hear his work immediately.

Science and Technology

Oxygen was discovered, 1772, by the Swede **Carl Scheele,** 1742–86. He withheld his findings until after the independent discovery by **Joseph Priestley,** 1733–1804, in 1774. Scheele was also involved in the discovery of chlorine, 1774, tungsten, 1781, and other elements. **Daniel Rutherford,** 1749–1819, discovered **nitrogen** in 1772.

1776-1780

★ Principal Events

The American colonies declared their independence, 1776, and allied with France, 1778, and Spain, 1779. The English overran the southern states, 1778, but were weakened by a French blockade of shipping.
The French government was ruined by the war in spite of the continued financial reforms of **Jacques Necker**, 1732–1804.
Pombal, 1699–1782, completed the reorganization of the administration in Portuguese Brazil, 1777.

The Americas

In 1776, *Common Sense* by **Thomas Paine**, 1737–1809, appeared. The Declaration of Independence, was signed July 4, 1776.

Religion and Philosophy

Adam Smith, 1723–90, founder of modern economics, argued that although manufacturers do not intend to satisfy the general good, they are led to do so by the "invisible hand" of the competitive market. When a producer satisfied his self-interest by selling goods for which there is a demand, he also satisfied a general social need. Smith's *Wealth of Nations* was published in 1776.

Literature

Comedy of manners, revived in England by **Oliver Goldsmith**, *c.* 1730–74, in *She Stoops to Conquer*, 1773, reached a peak in *The School for Scandal*, 1777,

by the Irish wit **R. B. Sheridan**, 1751–1816.
Italian patriotism was stirred by **Vittorio Alfieri**, 1749–1803, whose 19 verse tragedies in the classical mode opposed tyranny.

Art and Architecture

Classicism in Russia under Catherine the Great was led by foreign artists such as the French sculptor **Etienne-Maurice Falconet**, 1716–91, who had executed the equestrian statue of Peter the Great, 1769, and Scottish architect **Charles Cameron**, *c.*1740–1812, who went to Russia in 1779. Cameron decorated several apartments in the palace of Tsarkoe Selo (now Pushkin) near Leningrad for Catherine.

Music

African music as described by Western observers probably resembled music heard today, in which groups of instruments, such as marimbas and drums, freely explore areas of sonority.

Science and Technology

A practical water closet was patented in 1778 in England by **Joseph Bramah**, 1748–1814. Bramah's many inventions introduced practical techniques that founded the engineering industry.
The spinning mule was invented in England in 1779 by **Samuel Crompton**, 1753–1827. It was able to spin high quality thread on many spindles at once.
Cheap soap resulted from the work *c.*1780 of **Nicholas Leblanc**, 1742–1806, in France. He patented his process of producing soda from salt in 1791.

★ Principal Events

American independence was assured by the British surrender at Yorktown, 1781, and formally recognized at the 1783 **Treaty of Paris.**

A sudden growth in the English cotton industry after 1780 marked the beginning of the English **Industrial Revolution.**

Russia occupied the Crimea in 1783.

Hastings made an effective peace with the Marathas, 1784.

The Americas

Gen. George Washington led the Colonial army against the British, who surrendered at Yorktown, 1781; the Treaty of Paris was signed in 1783.

Religion and Philosophy

Immanuel Kant, 1724–1804, in his *Critique of Pure Reason,* 1781, wrote that although knowledge cannot transcend experience, the concepts that organize perception are innate to the human mind and prior to experience. In *Metaphysics and Morals,* 1785, he argued that man's idea of morality is *a priori* and that people act morally when the maxim on which they act is one that they can desire all men to follow.

Literature

The influential French novel *Les Liaisons Dangereuses,* 1782, by **P. A. F. Choderlos de Laclos,** 1741–1803, had a savage tone in contrast to the vogue for high moral sentiment established by Rousseau. The privileges of the upper class were satirized by **Pierre de Beaumarchais,** 1732–99, in *The Barber of Seville,* 1784, and *The Marriage of Figaro.*

Art and Architecture

Neoclassical painting was firmly established in France with "Oath of the Horatii," 1784, by Jacques Louis David, 1748–1825, in which the subordination of color to drawing enforces the theme of heroic self-sacrifice as exemplified by ancient Rome.

The Nightmare by Henry Fuseli, 1741–1825, and the works of **William Blake,** 1757–1827, reveal an emphasis on the bizarre and supernatural in contrast with Academic aims.

Music

Ludwig van Beethoven, 1770–1827, son of a court musician at Bonn, was acknowledged a child prodigy in 1783, the year he published his first composition.

Science and Technology

Uranus was discovered by **William Herschel,** 1738–1822, in 1781. It was the first planet to be discovered that was not known to ancient civilizations.

The first manned flight took place in 1783 in a hot air balloon made and flown by the French **Montgolfier** brothers Joseph, 1740–1810, and Jacques, 1745–99.

James Watt invented the double acting engine in 1784.

Principal Events

The United States began trading with China, 1784, but suffered postwar depression through loss of contact with the West Indies 1784–87.

The American Constitution was signed in Philadelphia, 1787.

The aristocratic parliaments in France blocked proposals for financial reform, 1787.

The founding of The Times newspaper in England, 1788, accompanied the growth of an informed middle class in Europe

The Americas

By the **Articles of Confederation**, ratified 1781, Congress controlled the western lands. The **Northwest Ordinance**, 1787, provided a plan of government.

Religion and Philosophy

Liberalism, the belief that the state should not encroach on individual freedom, was proposed by **Jeremy Bentham**, 1748–1832, in *A Fragment on Government*, 1776. He argued in his *Principles*, 1789, for utilitarianism, the theory that the happiness of the majority of individuals was the greatest good. This was to be achieved by allowing each individual the freedom to maximize his useful achievement by avoiding pain and pursuing pleasure.

Literature

Scottish folk traditions found a passionate and lyrical voice in the poems of **Robert Burns**, 1759–96, whose *Kilmarnock Edition*, 1786, established him

as a skilled writer of songs, satires, and narratives. A deep love of nature, a major theme in romanticism, is found in the blank verse of "The Task," 1785, by the English poet **William Cowper**, 1731–1800.

Art and Architecture

The Academy of Fine Arts in Mexico City, founded in 1785, was staffed primarily by Spanish trained artists who were largely instrumental in introducing Neoclassicism to Mexico.

English caricature was developed by **James Gillray**, 1757–1815, in "A New Way to Pay the National Debt," 1786, and by **Thomas Rowlandson**, 1756–1827, who illustrated Smollett, Goldsmith, Sterne, and Swift, and produced "Imitations of Modern Drawings," 1784–88.

Music

Mozart, 1756–91, was one of the first great composers who tried to live independently without the support of a patron, but he died a pauper.

Science and Technology

Chlorine was first used for bleaching cloth in 1785 by **Claude Berthollet**, 1748–1822.

The threshing machine was patented, 1788, by a Scotsman, **Andrew Meikle**, 1719–1811.

Jacques Charles, 1746–1823, a French physicist, formulated **Charles's law** $c.1787$, that at constant pressure the volume of a gas is related to its absolute temperature.

The power loom, invented in 1785 by **Edmund Cartwright**, 1743–1823, mechanized weaving.

Principal Events

England established convict settlements in Australia, 1788.
Louis XVI, *r.*1774–92, was forced to summon the estates-general in 1789 because of the financial crisis.
The French Revolution began when a group of middle-class radicals took over the administration with the help of the Paris mob and tried to set up a constitutional monarchy, 1789.
George Washington, 1732–99, became the first president of the United States, 1789.

 **The Americas**

The Constitution of the United States was ratified in 1788. The Bill of Rights, ten amendments to the Constitution, was adopted in 1789.

 Religion and Philosophy

In France, 1789–90. Church lands were nationalized and religious orders suppressed.
Edmund Burke, 1729–97, in *Reflections on the French Revolution,* 1790, argued that the replacement of practical politics by utopianism had led to extremism. **Tom Paine,** 1737–1809, in America, wrote *The Rights of Man,* 1791, to oppose Burke's *Reflections.* Paine believed revolution could be avoided only if the causes of the discontent were eradicated.

 Literature

A new tradition of candid biography was begun by **James Boswell,** 1740–95, in his *Life of Johnson,* 1791, bringing to life

his friend **Samuel Johnson,** 1709–84. Johnson, a brilliant conversationalist, editor, poet, and critic, had dominated English literature after 1750 with his *Dictionary,* 1755, the Gothic novel *Rasselas,* 1759, and *Lives of the Poets,* 1779–81.

 Art and Architecture

The "Style Troubadour" originated in France when anecdotal scenes from the lives of wise kings of early French history were used by antiroyalists to accentuate the incompetence of Louis XVI.
Classicism in English architecture was exemplified in the work of **John Soane,** 1753–1837, whose austere and original manipulation of the antique was seen in his **Bank of England Stock Office,** 1792, with its top-lit vaulted hall.

 Music

Domenico Cimarosa, 1749–1801, "the Italian Mozart," composed his most celebrated opera, *Il Matrimonio Segreto,* in Vienna in 1792.

 Science and Technology

Traité Elèmentaire de Chimie, by **Antoine Lavoisier,** 1743–94, written in 1789, founded modern chemistry with its insistence on measurement and standard nomenclature. Lavoisier stated the law of the conservation of mass; he also defined chemical reaction.
Coal gas was first produced in 1792 by **William Murdock,** 1754–1839, a British inventor. In 1790, Watt applied his fly-ball governor to control the speed of a steam engine.

1792-1796

★ Principal Events

France was declared a republic, 1792. Louis was executed, 1793, and during the ensuing terror, 1793–94, many of the nobility were also guillotined as a result of the fear of a counter-revolution backed by Austrian forces.

The French overran Holland and established the Batavian Republic in 1795.

Revolutionary ideas led to the freeing of slaves in the French West Indies, arousing hostility among the European powers.

The Americas

Federal troops ended the Whiskey Rebellion in Pennsylvania, 1794. **John Jay,** 1745–1829, negotiated Jay's Treaty to settle Anglo-American grievances.

Religion and Philosophy

Equal opportunities for women to develop their talents were demanded by **Mary Wollstonecraft,** 1759–97, in her *Vindication of the Rights of Women,* 1792. Her husband, **William Godwin,** 1756–1836, published *Enquiry Concerning Political Justice,* 1793. A radical, he argued that government powers over citizens inevitably bred corruption.

The Cult of Reason and later the **Cult of the Supreme Being** were substituted for Christianity in France, 1793–94.

📖 Literature

William Blake, 1757–1827, one of the most powerful, imaginative artists in English literature,

published the lyrical *Songs of Experience,* 1794, complementing *Songs of Innocence,* 1789. Poet, painter, engraver, and above all, visionary, he issued prophetic warnings of the danger of industrialization and materialism in *The Marriage of Heaven and Hell.*

Art and Architecture

Painting in Revolutionary France was used as a political weapon. David's "Death of Marat," 1793, combines classicism with an element of realism to deify a revolutionary hero and muster republican support.

John Flaxman, 1755–1826, published his illustrations to Homer's *Iliad* and *Odyssey* in 1793. With their simple outline figures they immediately became a major model for Neoclassical painters and influenced later generations.

Music

Niccolò Paganini, the Italian virtuoso violinist, 1782–1840, made his debut in Genoa in 1793, playing his own variations on "La Carmagnole."

Science and Technology

Theory of the Earth, 1795, by **James Hutton,** 1726–97, began modern geology by viewing all geological change as continuous.

The cotton gin, a device used to strip seeds from bolls, was invented, 1793, by **Eli Whitney,** 1765–1825, revitalizing cotton growing in the United States.

The metric system was adopted in France in 1795.

Scientific institutes abounded in revolutionary France, including the Jardin des Plantes and the Ecole Polytechnique.

Principal Events

By the **Treaty of Campo Formio**, 1797, Austria ceded Belgium to France.

Napoleon, 1769–1821, defeated Austria, 1796, but his plans to invade England, 1798, failed and he was prevented by **Horatio Nelson**, 1758–1805, from cutting England off from India at the Battle of the Nile, 1798. In 1799 he overthrew the moderate **Directory** and established a dictatorship, 1799–1804.

The Americas

An undeclared naval conflict over French interference with American shipping was precipitated by the XYZ affair, 1797. The Convention of 1800 ended the war.

Religion and Philosophy

The English Evangelical Movement had emerged within the Church of England, influenced by Methodism. Its followers believed in the certainty of salvation, emphasizing evangelism and social welfare.

Reverend Thomas Malthus, 1766–1834, published his *Essay on the Principle of Population*, 1798, rejecting the possibility of infinite improvements in human conditions on the grounds that population expands more rapidly than the available food supply.

Literature

The Romantic movement in England began with *Lyrical Ballads*, 1798, by **William Wordsworth**, 1770–1850, and **Samuel Taylor Coleridge**, 1772–1834.

The novels of Jean Paul, 1763–1825, included *Hesperus*, 1795, and *Siebenkäs*, 1796–97, which contained both idealism and sentimentalism.

Art and Architecture

The success of Napoleon's Italian campaign, 1796–97, galvanized French art with the public display in the Louvre of looted art treasures. This enhanced the image of Napoleon as a national hero.

The Capitol, Richmond, Va., 1785–98, built by Thomas Jefferson, 1743–1826, was based on the Maison Carrée, Nîmes, and brought Neoclassical architecture to the United States.

Music

The violin was taken to India by British rulers. Indian musicians absorbed it into their music, utilizing its subtleties of intonation and tone color.

Science and Technology

Vaccination, discovered in 1796 by Edward Jenner, 1749–1823, led to the eradication of smallpox.

The nature of heat, or kinetic energy, was discovered in 1798 by the American **Count Rumford**, who noticed that the boring of cannons produced heat and reasoned that heat is a form of motion and not a fluid.

The battery was invented by Count Volta, 1745–1827, in 1800. He developed Galvani's observations into a practical idea for an electricity supply.

The Rise of Industrial Power 1800–1825

Lewis and Clark completed their expedition to the Pacific in 1806.

Robert Trevithick built the first railroad locomotive in 1804.

Lord Byron epitomized the Romantic movement.

Napoleon at Eylau, 1807

Goya's "The 3rd of May" depicts the nationalist revolt in Spain.

Early multi-cultural architecture: "The Brighton Pavilion" by Nash

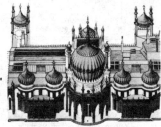

Eleven demonstrators were killed in England's Peterloo Massacre in 1819.

The Rise of Industrial Power

⭐ Principal Events

Inspired by a vision of himself as head of a European empire, Napoleon Bonaparte overran most of Europe but was unable to maintain his conquests. With his final defeat at Waterloo in 1815, the ancien régime was restored to France. His conquests, however, sparked off a multitude of constitutional and nationalist demands throughout Europe, while his occupation of Spain encouraged the Latin American countries to grasp their independence. They remained, however, unable to reorganize themselves economically or to free themselves politically from European influence.

In England, the Industrial Revolution caused the emergence of a new wealthy class and social tensions gave a greater urgency to demands for parliamentary reform, while British naval strength and leadership of the final coalition against Napoleon left Britain the dominant trading power in the world.

National Events

The American nation was developing a spirit of nationalism, of identification not as a colony or state, but with the United States. Land purchases provided room for expansion of a growing population. National authority was expressed in the readiness of Americans to defend US interests.

🜍 Religion and Philosophy

Classical economic theory was developed and systematized in the work of Say in France and Ricardo in England, the latter influencing both sides of the debate about laissez-faire doctrines, which dominated social thought in the early 19th century. At the same time reaction to the social evils of industrial capitalism ranged form Sismondi's warning of class antagonisms to the social experiments of Robert Owen and the Utopianism of Charles Fourier.

The major philosophical school of the period, German idealism, emerged in a country as yet relatively sheltered from the major social upheavals of the time. In particular, Hegel, who would greatly influence the young Karl Marx, argued that historical progress was identical with the advancement of human consciousness, while Schopenhauer and Schelling emphasized man's darker, irrational impulses and prepared the way for Freud and existentialism.

📖 Literature

English Romanticism reached its peak with the work of the poets Wordsworth and Byron, who explored the individual quest for harmony with nature and stressed the independence of the genius from social convention. The historical novel developed by Scott linked an interest in the past with an implicit concern for national identity—a trend echoed in the German concentration on folk-tales and mythology. In other respects, however, German Romanticism, as displayed by Goethe and Schiller, involved a less violent break with 18th-century humanism.

Chateaubriand and Madame de Staël tried to introduce the ideas of the movement to France, but met little success, as classicism still reigned until the work of the poets in the 1820s.

Art and Architecture

European art in the early 19th century saw a reaction to Neoclassicism and the beginnings of Romanticism, involving a shift from formal rules to an emphasis on the subjective—feelings, impressions, imagination—and a preference for fantasy, excess, and the poetic. The influence of Romanticism also inspired an interest in historical and foreign styles of architecture, while in painting it produced the freer technique and the more expressive use of color found in the work of Delacroix. The choice of subject matter also changed to include contemporary and historical scenes, which reflected the nationalist ideas of the time—a tendency heightened in France by the exotic career and lavish commissions of Napoleon. While Neoclassicism came to be rejected by artists in Western Europe, its influence spread elsewhere into Russia and the New World, where it dominated architecture.

Music

Romanticism in European music began to replace classicism as personal expression in the arts took precedence over ideals of formal balance. But the first romantic composers, such as Ludwig van Beethoven, 1770–1827, and Carl von Weber, 1786–1826, were trained in classical techniques and brought restraint to bear on the new sensuous style of music.

Science and Technology

Progress in technology and science in Europe divided between Britain and France. France became the center of pure science, while Britain forged ahead in industrial science. Although automation was invented in France, its potential was not fully exploited. Similarly, atomic theory was first proposed in England but was refined in Europe.

The most important technological innovation was that of powered transport in England and the US, which opened new areas of industrial expansion; in the same period gas lighting transformed city life. Many scientific discoveries, too, would have subsequent importance. Electrical science developed with the discovery of electromagnetism and would stimulate inquiry into the nature of matter as well as producing new sources of energy, while modern chemistry developed under the influence of Gay-Lussac and Avogadro. The study of fossils raised new questions about the age and origins of life.

229

1800-1802

Principal Events

Napoleon established the prefecture as the main instrument of local government subject to central control. He improved education and made a compromise with the Church, 1800–01. His aggressive nationalist campaigns led to victory over Austria, conquest in Italy, 1800, and temporary peace with England in 1802. With the murder of Paul I, **Alexander I**, 1801–25, became tsar of Russia.

The Americas

In 1801 war began with the North African Barbary states. Barbary pirates had interfered with American shipping and demanded tribute. Peace came in 1805.

Religion and Philosophy

Friedrich Schelling, 1775–1854, published his *Transcendental Idealism*, 1800, in Germany, grounding his idealism on external nature. His philosophy of man stressed the force of irrationalism, which, as the source of all evil, could dominate the intellect, wherein lay the power for good.
William Paley, 1743–1805, an Anglican, advanced the idea in *Natural Theology*, 1802, that the design evident in the world implied the work of a creator.

Literature

A more subjective emphasis developed in German literature with the two unfinished novels of **Novalis**, 1772–1801, published in 1798–1801. Both were *Bildungsroman*–novels on the education of the hero and the development of character and temperament, like Goethe's *Wilhelm Meisters Lehrjahre*.

Art and Architecture

The term "picturesque" was introduced in England at the end of the 18th century as an aesthetic category. Characterized by irregularity, variety, and roughness of texture, it had a decisive effect on landscape painting and architecture.
British industrial architecture had developed over the 18th century to include iron frame constructions, which were fireproof and functional.

Music

The piano repertory was rapidly extended by **Muzio Clementi**, 1752–1832, and Beethoven, as the instrument gained a greater range of notes and sound quality.

Science and Technology

The interference of light was shown, in 1801, by **Thomas Young**, 1773–1829, restoring the wave theory first put forward by Christiaan Huygens. Young also studied elasticity, giving his name to the tensile modulus, or scale of elasticity.
Automation using punched cards to control the production of silk fabric was invented in France, 1801, by **Joseph Marie Jacquard**, 1752–1834.
Ultraviolet light in the Sun's spectrum was discovered, 1801, by **Johann Ritter**, 1776–1810.

Principal Events

Nationalist feeling brought a Serbian uprising against the Ottoman rule in 1804. **Napoleon** assumed the title of emperor in 1804. **Britain** resumed the war against him in 1803 and was joined by **Russia, Austria,** and **Sweden** in 1805. Russia was defeated at **Austerlitz,** 1805, but Britain's naval victory at **Trafalgar,** 1805, resulted in a crippling blockade of French shipping.

Napoleon proclaimed himself **King of Italy,** 1805.

The Americas

The territory between the Rocky Mountains and the Mississippi River was bought from France for $15,000,000 and was called the Louisiana Purchase.

Religion and Philosophy

Jean Baptiste Say published his **Traité d'économie politique** in 1803, putting forward his "law of markets," which states that supply creates its own demand with the consequence that depression is the result of overproduction in some markets and underproduction in others, an imbalance that would automatically correct itself.

The Code Napoléon of 1804 nationalized French law and established the principle of equal citizenship.

Literature

Le Génie du Christianisme, 1802, by François René de Chateaubriand, 1768–1848, introduced to French literature a mystical Christianity, which had a great influence on the French romantic writers.

The need for political freedom in Germany was the subject of the play **William Tell,** 1804, by the poet and dramatist **Johann Schiller,** 1759–1805.

Art and Architecture

The Greek revival in European architecture, *c.*1760–1830, was now at its height. Its essence was the exact reproduction of Greek models, which were admired for their simplicity and associated with the beginnings of civilization. It was predominantly used for public buildings. **In the United States,** classic revival architecture was popularized by **Benjamin Latrobe,** 1764–1820.

Music

Short forms for the piano were being composed by **John Field,** 1782–1837, who wrote nocturnes, which would later be popularized by **Frédéric Chopin,** 1810–49.

Science and Technology

Jean de Lamarck, 1744–1829, a French naturalist, coined the term "biology" in 1802. **The first railroad locomotive** was built in England by **Richard Trevithick,** 1771–1833, and first ran in 1804.

Screw-cutting machines and lathes were developed at the engineering works of the Englishman **Henry Maudslay,** 1771–1831, who invented the screw micrometer and schooled many fine engineers.

231

1805-1807

Principal Events

After defeating Prussia, 1806, Napoleon allied with Russia, 1807, and set up the **Continental System** (which Russia was forced to leave for economic reasons in 1810) to exclude British trade from Europe.
The Holy Roman Empire came to an end when **Francis II**, *r.*1792– 1835, who was also emperor of Austria, renounced the title, 1806.
The slave trade was abolished in the British Empire, 1807, although slavery continued in the colonies.

The Americas

Meriwether Lewis, 1774– 1809, and **William Clark**, 1770– 1838, returned in 1806 from their expedition to the Pacific Ocean.

Religion and Philosophy

G. W. F. Hegel, 1770– 1831, the German idealist philosopher, published his first great work, *Phenomenology of Mind*, in 1807. In this and later works Hegel expressed the view that reality is essentially a whole (which he called the Absolute) comprising both mind (subject) and matter (object). The physical world would cease to be alien and objective when, with the attainment of total comprehension, object and subject merged into the Absolute.

Literature

The German romantic poets Brentano, 1778– 1842, and von

Arnim, 1781– 1831, collected folk poems in *Des Knaben Wunderhorn*, 1805– 08.
The lyric dramatic poetry of **Adam Oehlenschlager**, 1779– 1850, was popular in Denmark.

Art and Architecture

Napoleon commissioned portraits and commemorative scenes to enhance his imperial image. Canvases presented an aura of magnificence with allusions to the Roman Empire as in "Napoleon as Emperor," 1806, by **Jean August Dominique Ingres**, 1780– 1867, and *The Battle of Eylau*, 1808, by **Antoine Gros**, 1771– 1835. Napoleonic architecture like the Paris Bourse, 1807, by **A. T. Brongriart**, 1739– 1813, was similarly inspired.

Music

Beethoven straddled the classical and romantic eras, extending the range of sonata form and composing works such as the *Coriolanus Overture*, 1807, directly inspired by literary ideas.

Science and Technology

Gas lighting was introduced in European cities *c.* 1806.
The Clermont, built by **Robert Fulton**, 1765– 1815, an American engineer, inaugurated the first regular steamboat service along the Hudson River in 1807, although a short-lived service had been run *c.* 1790.
The Geological Society of London was founded in 1807.

★ Principal Events

A nationalist revolt broke out in Spain when Joseph Bonaparte, 1768–1844, assumed the throne, 1808. Britain exploited this to attack Napoleon in the Peninsular War, 1808–14. **Austria and Prussia** reformed their army and taxation systems to improve military capacity. **Archduke Charles of Austria** appealed to the Germans to oppose Napoleon but was defeated at **Wagram**, 1809. **France** assumed control of Swedish foreign affairs.

The Americas

In **1808** federal law forbade importation of slaves into the United States. The Embargo Act, 1807, aimed at keeping US ships out of European conflicts.

Religion and Philosophy

Charles Fourier, 1772–1837, writing in France (*The Social Destiny of Man*, 1808) and later **Robert Owen** in England (*A New View of Society*, 1813) advocated social reconstruction on the basis of workers' cooperatives. Owen organized mills at New Lanark, 1800–29, on principles of welfare and justice, but his American experimental community at New Harmony, 1825, was short-lived, as were the communes based on the even more Utopian ideas of Fourier.

Literature

The poetry of the Italian Ugo Foscolo, 1778–1827, extolled the past and the value of art as a permanent shrine to virtue.

The humanism of Johann Goethe, 1749–1832, was expressed in his play *Faust, Part 1,* 1808.

Heinrich Kleist, 1777–1811, published *Penthesilea,* 1808.

Art and Architecture

Davidian ideals were questioned in France by his pupils. Some, **Les Primitifs,** took inspiration from the Bible, Homer, and the Gaelic tales of Ossian. Others like **Anne-Louis Girodet,** 1767–1824, in his "Entombment of Atala," 1808, used unusual mystical subjects.

The investigation of the symbolic, mystical, and religious aspects of landscape took place primarily in Germany, with the work of **Caspar David Friedrich,** 1774–1840.

Music

Program music, interpreting the events and moods of a specific story, emerged as a feature of romantic music, using evocative sounds as in Beethoven's *Pastoral Symphony,* 1808.

Science and Technology

Potassium and sodium were discovered, 1806–07, by **Humphry Davy,** 1778–1829, an English chemist.

Jean Fourier, 1768–1830, a French mathematician, discovered that a complex wave is the sum of several simple waves.

The atomic theory, stating that the same elements have the same atoms and that a compound is made up of atoms of elements combined in fixed proportions, was propounded in 1808 by **John Dalton,** 1766–1844.

Principal Events

Napoleon's empire reached its greatest extent, 1812, when with Austria and Prussia he invaded Russia. French forces took Moscow, 1812, but were unable to sustain the Russian winter and were forced to retreat with serious losses.
Paraguay and Venezuela became independent from Spain, 1811, marking the final collapse of Spanish imperial authority.
Napoleon married Marie Louise of Austria in his search for an heir, 1810.

The Americas

From 1810, War Hawks advocated war with Britain, which had been harassing American shipping. In 1812, Congress passed a declaration of war.

Religion and Philosophy

Hegel's Science of Logic was published in 1812–16. In it he developed a dialectical method of reasoning—opposing a thesis with its antithesis to establish a synthesis—with the aim of revealing the nature of the Absolute. Hegel believed history to be a dialectical progression toward the Absolute and considered the Prussian state to be the culmination of this dialectical progression.

Literature

Madame de Staël, 1766–1817, wrote *De L'Allemagne* in 1810, comparing French literature and society unfavorably with that of Germany.
The English middle classes were given perceptive scrutiny by **Jane Austen**, 1775–1817, in *Sense and Sensibility*, 1811, and later *Pride and Prejudice*, 1813.

Art and Architecture

The pastiches of Indian, Chinese, and Egyptian styles seen in the prince regent's Brighton Pavilion, from 1810, by the English architect **John Nash**, 1752–1835, reflected the worldwide process of exploration and colonization by the European powers.
A quasi-religious order, the *Lukasbrüder*, was found in Vienna, 1809, by **Friedrich Overbeck**, 1789–1869, and **Frans Pforr**, 1788–1812. They moved to Rome in 1810 and became known as the Nazarenes.

Music

Orchestral concerts became popular in London, Paris, and Vienna as the middle classes began to support music. The patron and his salon declined in influence.

Science and Technology

Joseph Gay-Lussac, 1778–1850, a French chemist, announced in 1808 that gases combine in certain proportions by volume and suggested that the proportions are linked to the formula of the compound formed. Gay-Lussac's work also led to the correct atomic weights of elements. **Amadeo Avogadro**, 1776–1856, an Italian, argued in 1811 that equal volumes of gases at the same temperature and pressure contain equal numbers of molecules.

Principal Events

The Duke of Wellington, 1769–1852, led the Allied forces into Paris, 1814. Napoleon abdicated and was exiled.
The monarchy was restored in Louis XVIII, r.1814–24.
The Congress of Vienna, 1814–15, restored monarchs to the Austrian and Prussian thrones, and the kingdom of the Netherlands was founded as a buffer against France.
Britain won definitive control of the **Cape of Good Hope,** 1814, on the route to India.

The Americas

In 1814 the British burned Washington. American resistance at Baltimore inspired "The Star-Spangled Banner" by **Francis Scott Key,** 1779–1843.

Religion and Philosophy

The conservative tradition in France found exponents in **Joseph de Maistre,** 1753–1821, and **Louis Bonald,** 1754–1840, who insisted on the supremacy of Christianity and the absolute rule of the Church and pope. De Maistre published his *Essay on Constitutions* in 1814, in which he used his facility for logical argument to oppose the progress of science, liberalism, and the empirical methods of the "philosophes," especially Voltaire.

Literature

The English Romantic poet Percy Bysshe Shelley, 1792–1822, wrote his first major poem, *Queen Mab,* 1811–13.
The first historical novel was the medieval romance *Waverley,* 1814, by **Sir Walter Scott,** 1771–1832. His evocations of the past influenced **James Fenimore Cooper,** 1789–1851.
Brothers Grimm made their collection of folk tales, 1812–15.

Art and Architecture

The work of **Francisco de Goya,** 1746–1828, combined objective reportage and a sense of personal horror at the Napoleonic Wars in "The Disasters of War," 1810–14. He later developed the new medium of lithography. In Russia, **Alexander I** commissioned classical buildings for St Petersburg and encouraged French Neoclassicism in all branches of the arts, particularly portraiture.

Music

A greater variety of orchestral instruments allowed richer tone contrasts. There were few large orchestras, so many orchestral works were published as piano transcriptions.

Science and Technology

Georges Cuvier, 1769–1832, a French anatomist, broadened Linnaeus' classification to include phyla and fossils, thus founding paleontology. The hardness of materials was classified in 1812 by a German, **Friedrich Mohs,** 1773–1839.
Chemical symbols as used today were introduced in 1814 by **Jöns Berzelius,** 1779–1848, a Swede, who later made a correct list of atomic weights.
Dark lines in the Sun's spectrum were identified, 1814, by **Joseph von Fraunhofer,** 1787–1826.

1815-1817

Principal Events

Napoleon returned from Elba and Austria, Britain, Prussia, and Russia formed a new alliance. Louis fled from Paris to return only after Napoleon's defeat at **Waterloo** and exile to St Helena, 1815.

The Holy Alliance aimed to crush the spread of radicalism in Austria, Prussia, and Russia.
Prince Metternich, 1773–1859, crushed similar aspirations in the German states.
Ferdinand I, r.1815–25, regained the Italian throne.

The Americas

Unaware of the Treaty of Ghent, Gen. Andrew Jackson, 1767–1845, won an overwhelming victory at New Orleans in January 1815.

Religion and Philosophy

The rising science of economics was systematized by David Ricardo, 1772–1823, in his *Principles of Political Economy and Taxation,* 1817, which aimed to set out the laws governing the division of the social product among the classes in society. The systematization of this work made him the leading exponent of the classical school in England, and he was influential both among *laissez-faire* economists and their opponents, such as Robert Owen and Karl Marx.

Literature

Grotesque themes were studied by the German composer and author Ernst Hoffmann, 1776–1822, in his tales and in the novel *The Devil's Elixir,* 1813–15.

The psychological analysis of a broken love affair is the subject of *Adolphe,* 1816, by Benjamin Constant, 1767–1830, an ardent liberal and a political journalist, closely aligned with the French Romantics.

Art and Architecture

Neo-Renaissance architecture was developed in Germany by Leo von Klenze, 1784–1864. His Palais Leuchtenberg, Munich, 1816, is the first German example, although the style existed earlier in France.
German Neoclassical architecture first developed after the fall of Napoleon, with the emphasis on purely Grecian forms seen in the Neue Wache, Berlin, 1816, by Karl Friedrich Schinkel, 1781–1841.

Music

Lieder, a German form of lyric song, was raised by Franz Schubert, 1797–1828, to new heights as his piano parts provided a counterpart to the voice echoing the mood of the lyric.

Science and Technology

The safety lamp was invented by Humphry Davy in 1815, to prevent explosions in mines.
The optical experiments of Jean Biot, 1774–1862, after 1815, led to the founding of polarimetry.
The first geological map, of England and Wales, was published, 1815, by William Smith, 1769–1839.
The single wire telegraph was invented in 1816.
Photography was born out of the experiments in 1816 of Nocéphore Niepce, 1765–1833.

Principal Events

The American and Canadian border was fixed in 1818.
Soldiers killed 11 demonstrators in the **Peterloo Massacre** in England, 1819.
A revolt in Naples against the despotism of Ferdinand I was crushed by Austrian forces in 1821. **The British founded Singapore** to rival Dutch Malacca as the center for Far Eastern trade.
Only Nepal, the Sikh and Sind states, and Afghanistan were independent of British rule in India by 1818.

The Americas

In the **Adams-Onis Treaty,** 1819, Spain gave the United States control of both East and West Florida. The Panic of 1819 hurt the US economy.

Religion and Philosophy

Jean Charles Sismondi, an early theorist of economic crisis, warned in his *New Principles of Political Economy,* 1819, against the effects of unregulated industrialism, predicting acute social conflict. In Germany, **Artur Schopenhauer,** 1788–1860, published *The World as Will and Idea* in 1819. His emphasis on man's will and irrational impulses prepared the way for the departure from the 18th-century idea of rational progress.

Literature

The spirit of the Romantic movement was epitomized in the notorious life of **Lord Byron,** 1788–1824, and the tormented, homeless Byronic hero became popular in European fiction. In contrast, his *Don Juan* (first two cantos, 1819), was a biting, un-romanticized social satire.
William Hazlitt, 1778–1830, commented on contemporary English life in astute essays.

Art and Architecture

After 1816, when Dom João VI of Brazil had invited French architects, painters, and sculptors to Rio de Janeiro to "civilize" Creole taste, their neoclassical style dominated the arts for the next hundred years.
In France, **Théodore Géricault,** 1791–1824, took contemporary events as the vehicle for his themes and used large canvases to strengthen their impact in, for example, "The Raft of the Medusa," 1817.

Music

Conductors were required to marshal the expanded orchestra, as it could no longer be led by an instrumentalist. In 1820, **Ludwig Spohr,** 1784–1859, introduced the conductor's baton.

Science and Technology

Electromagnetism was found, 1820, by **Hans Oersted,** 1777–1851, who noticed that a compass needle was deflected by a wire carrying a current. He would later be the first to prepare aluminum, 1825.

1820-1822

Principal Events

Ferdinand VII of Spain, r.1814–33, was captured by liberal rebels in 1820.

The nationalist Greek war for independence from the Ottoman Empire began, 1821. The Great Powers intervened in 1827 and established a Greek kingdom in 1832.

Spain lost Mexico and Peru, 1821, while Brazil became independent from Portugal, 1822.

Opium trade between India and China flourished in the reign of **Hsüang Tung,** 1821–50.

The Americas

The Missouri Compromise of 1820 prohibited slavery north of latitude $36°30'$. The American Colonization Society sent 88 free blacks to settle in Africa.

Religion and Philosophy

Thomas Erskine, 1788–1870, a Scottish theologian, in *Internal Evidence for the Truth of Christian Religion,* 1820, held that the meaning of Christianity lay in its conformity with man's spiritual and ethical needs.

Friedrich Schleiermacher, 1768–1834, a German theologian and founder of modern Protestant theology, in *The Christian Faith,* 1821–22, saw religious feeling as a sense of absolute dependence and sin as a desire for independence.

Literature

Alphonse Lamartine, 1790–1869, moved from the private anguish of *Meditations,* 1820, to the mystical lyricism of *Harmonies Poétiques,* 1830.

A search for eternal perfection is the theme of *Prometheus Unbound,* 1820, by the English poet Shelley. His friend **John Keats,** 1795–1821, wrote rich, ornate narrative poetry, including the *Ode to a Nightingale,* 1819.

Art and Architecture

English Romantic portraiture with its emphasis on drama and psychological investigation was exemplified in the forceful works of **Sir Thomas Lawrence,** 1769–1830, whose portraits of the "Heads of State of Europe" in the Waterloo Chamber, **Windsor Castle,** 1818–20, celebrate the triumph over Napoleon.

Music

Opera centered on Paris. The light lyricism of the *Barber of Seville,* 1816, by **Gioacchino Rossini,** 1792–1868, gave way to the romanticism of **Carl Maria Weber's** *Der Freischutz,* 1821.

Science and Technology

André Ampère, 1775–1836, studied the effects of electric currents in motion, founding and naming the science of electrodynamics by 1822. He also invented the solenoid.

Thomas Seeback, 1770–1831, a Russo-German physicist, invented the thermocouple, an instrument for measuring temperature as electricity, 1821.

Principal Events

A Spanish liberal revolt was crushed with French help, 1823. **The Monroe Doctrine**, 1823, asserted that the American continent could no longer be an arena for European colonial activity. **Britain surpassed other European countries** in her industrial and trading position, but agitation began for more *laissez-faire* trading policies.
The Anglo-Burmese wars began in 1824, following Burmese aggression.

 The Americas

The Monroe Doctrine was enunciated, 1823, by **Pres. James Monroe**, 1758–1831. **The Erie Canal** was completed, 1825.

 Religion and Philosophy

The anti-union Combination Acts were repealed in Britain, 1824, after a campaign led by **Francis Place**, 1771–1854, and **Joseph Hume**, 1777–1855. Place, a follower of Malthus, advocated birth control as a means by which workers could limit their numbers to improve wages.
Leopold Ranke, 1795–1886, a German historian, wrote *History of the Latin and Teutonic Nations, 1494–1514*, in 1824, seeking a history based on scientific methods.

 Literature

The Confessions of an English Opium Eater, 1822, was the autobiography of **Thomas De Quincey**, 1785–1859.
Thomas Peacock, 1785–1866,

skillfully used his satirical novels to attack English views, obsessions, and political dogmas.

 Art and Architecture

Romantic tendencies in art were crystallized in the work of **Eugène Delacroix**, 1798–1863, where truth was no longer merely factual but a glimpse into man's soul. Delacroix set out to achieve this with the use of expressive color and an emphasis on mood and the poetic. His work marked a decisive shift in French painting away from the importance of form and stressed violence and drama, as in his "Massacre at Chios," 1824.

 Music

The symphony found new depths of expression, especially with **Beethoven**, as a personal creation requiring a large orchestra. His *Ninth Symphony*, 1823, is an example.

 Science and Technology

The electromagnet, the first machine to use electricity, was made by **William Sturgeon**, 1783–1850, an English physicist.
Sadi Carnot, 1796–1832, published *On the Motive Power of Fire*, 1824, in which he showed that only a fraction of the heat produced by burning fuel in an engine is converted into motion, which depends only on the temperature difference in the engine. This was the basis of modern thermodynamics.

Liberalism and Nationalism 1825–1850

"View of Mount Fuji," from a series of thirty-six color prints by Hokusai

Simón Bolívar: South American revolutionary leader

Stephenson's *Locomotion* pulled the first public train.

California gold miners sought to strike it rich.

"1830 Revolution" by Delacroix

Charles Dickens: English novelist

Colt revolver, repeating firearm, 1848

Liberalism and Nationalism

★ Principal Events

The spread of industrialism from England to north Europe brought the rise of a solid middle class advocating liberal and nationalist ideas, as well as a new urban radicalism focused by regular economic booms and slumps. In spite of attempts to suppress them, these movements spread throughout Europe, culminating in the nationalist and radical revolts of 1848. At the time this was a failure but the ideals of 1848 would be realized later as Italy and Germany achieved unification and the old empires collapsed.

The United States expanded vigorously westward, her population and industry increasing, while European colonialism was most active in Asia. The impact of British culture was felt in India for the first time and the process of penetration of China began in earnest with the end of the Opium Wars, which forced China to open her ports to foreign trade.

National Events

The United States continued territorial expansion during this period, ultimately extending its boundaries to the Pacific Ocean. There was dispute over the Canadian and Mexican borders. Abolitionist sentiment intensified, and slavery became a heated domestic issue.

♦ Religion and Philosophy

Several European thinkers, principally in France, advocated the application of the observational, or "positive," methods used in the natural sciences to the study of social phenomena.

The growth of the industrial system stimulated much new and radical thought. Saint-Simon and, following him, Comte, argued that industrial society should be governed by a new "priesthood" trained in the positivist method, while the existing forms of social organization were criticized by utopian thinkers who looked forward to ideal societies free from inequality and injustice.

Marx and Engels, who were influenced by French utopianism as well as German idealism and British political economy, argued that in order to end the inequality and injustice of existing society there must be a working-class revolution.

A number of Adventist sects prophesying the return of Christ emerged during these years, especially in the US.

📖 Literature

While Romanticism spread to Russia with Lermontov and Gogol, its brooding introversion began to break down in Western Europe, and the political implications of its rebellion were explored. The Jung Deutschland group insisted on the political role of literature, and in France the realistic depiction of the past or of contemporary society became important new themes. The social and nationalist commitment of these writers found expression in the revolutions of 1848, in

242

which authors such as Hugo and Lamartine played an important role.

In England novelists explored social relationships. Dickens concentrated on the evil consequences of industrialization with a wealth of characterization equaled only by Balzac.

Art and Architecture

Naturalism in painting—the devotion to truth to nature—received a special impetus from work in Britain where scientific advances and the Industrial Revolution affected art.

British landscapists such as John Constable studied natural effects in a scientific manner rather than composing classical panoramas, and the French artists emulated his innovations.

The interest in history and in different historical styles continued throughout Europe and America. A large number of paintings of historical scenes was produced, but it is in architecture that the range of interest in different styles was clearest. Italian models remained a source for the style of secular public buildings but the Gothic revival received a new impetus.

England's new wealthy middle classes were beginning to impose their taste on painting and architecture, while rapid urbanization generated the need for new solutions in town planning.

Music

Romanticism evolved further in Europe, where composers came to consider music a kind of poetry that penetrated to the heart, ennobling the soul and stimulating the imagination. It was at times extravagant and replete with epic works and cult figures, stimulating growth in orchestration techniques and producing such new forms as the symphonic poem.

Science and technology

The rail system that grew up in Britain, providing cheap transport for labor and raw materials, proved a vital precondition for the expansion of any industrial society. The process of industrialization, however, brought more people into the cities and led to a severe worsening of the conditions of working people. In Bristol, England, the death rate doubled between 1831 and 1841, although advances in medicine and public health began to improve matters from 1840 onward. The discovery of asepsis was particularly important in lowering the child mortality rate.

In pure science the discovery of alternative geometries to that of Euclid prompted new inquiries into formerly accepted theories, clearing the way for Mach and Einstein.

The discovery of Brownian motion finally established the existence of unobservable particles, in this case molecules; an important step toward the eventual acceptance of atomic theory.

Principal Events

Following a liberal **Decembrist revolt**, 1825, **Nicholas I**, *r.*1824–55, introduced repressive measures.
Charles X, *r.*1824–30, alienated bourgeois support in France by restoring to nobles land lost in the Revolution.
The British in India ended their titular subservience to Mogul rule, 1827.
The Javanese rebelled against Dutch rule but were put down.

The Americas

After the **1824 presidential election** no candidate had a majority. The House of Representatives chose **John Quincy Adams**, 1767–1848, over **Andrew Jackson**.

Religion and Philosophy

Henri de Saint-Simon, 1760–1825, in *New Christianity*, 1825, sought to combine the ideals of Christianity with science and a belief in industrialism to form a new religion of socialism based on a science of society. He advocated management of society by experts in the new social science, to aid welfare and progress. His theories were further developed by his one-time secretary, **Auguste Comte**, 1798–1857.

Literature

James Fenimore Cooper, 1789–1851, gained international fame with his historical novel *The Last of the Mohicans*, 1826, in which he portrayed the American Indians.
I Promessi Sposi, 1825–27, by the Italian **Alessandro Manzoni**, 1785–1873, is a love story set in 17th-century Italy with delicate Christian idealism.

Art and Architecture

The American ornithologist and painter **John James Audubon**, 1785–1851, published *The Birds of America*, from original drawings in England between 1827 and 1838.
Italian Renaissance architecture inspired the Travellers' Club, London, by **Charles Barry**, 1795–1860, an example of the neo-Renaissance style.
In France oil paints were sold in tubes for the first time *c.*1830–35, which made painting out of doors much easier.

Music

In Philadelphia, the first important music school was founded, 1825, by the Musical Fund Society.
The mouth organ, the Chinese sheng, came to Vienna in 1829.

Science and Technology

The first public steam railroad opened in 1825 between Stockton and Darlington in England. The first train was drawn by *Locomotion No. 1*, built by the British engineer **George Stephenson**, 1781–1848. **Robert Brown**, 1773–1858, a British botanist, observed the random motion of particles, **Brownian motion**, in 1827, thus proving that molecules exist.
Ohm's Law, relating current, voltage, and resistance, was laid down in 1827 by German physicist **Georg Ohm**, 1787–1854.

Principal Events

Lord Bentinck, 1774–1839, built new canals and roads in India and prohibited the customs of suttee and thuggee.
Turkey recognized **Greece's independence** after British and Russian intervention, 1829.
Uruguay was established as an independent buffer state between Argentina and Brazil, 1828.
The Workingmen's party was established in the US, pledged to social reform.

The Americas

The Democratic party was organized 1827. The doctrine of nullification was South Carolina's response to the Tariff of 1828.

Religion and Philosophy

François Guizot, 1787–1874, published his *History of Civilisation in France*, 1829, a study of social institutions using empirical data and a historical approach.
James Mill, 1777–1836, in his *Analysis of the Human Mind*, 1829, developed Bentham's pleasure-pain doctrine in the field of psychology.
John Darby, 1800–82, set up the **Plymouth Brethren** sect in Ireland, 1830, emphasizing the second coming of Jesus Christ.

Literature

The Cenacle group of poets was set up in Paris, 1827, by **Victor Hugo**, 1802–85, and **Sainte-Beuve**, 1804–69.
Hugo's *Odes et Ballades*, 1826, celebrated the theme of liberty.

The romantic poetry of **Alfred de Musset**, 1810–57, and the stoical pessimism of **Alfred de Vigny**, 1797–1863, reflected French disillusionment in the post-Napoleonic era.

Art and Architecture

A craze in France for things English known as *anglomanie* developed in the post-Napoleonic era. Watercolor painting became popular in Paris, where **Richard Parkes Bonington**, 1802–28, worked after 1820. British oil painting techniques were studied by French artists, especially after the exhibition of Constable's work in the Paris Salon of 1824, and **Delacroix** illustrated Byron's poem in his "The Execution of Doge Marino Faliero."

Music

Felix Mendelssohn, 1809–47, revived Bach's music in 1829 after a century of eclipse, giving it the status it enjoys today.

Science and Technology

The polarimeter, which analyzes the passage of polarized light through matter, was developed in 1828 by British physicist **William Nicol**, 1768–1851.
Embryology was founded, 1828, by **Karl Baer**, 1792–1876.
Organic chemistry began with the synthesis of urea by German chemist **Friedrich Wöhler**, 1800–82, in 1828. He showed that organic substances do not always come from living things.
Non-euclidean geometry was developed *c*.1829–30 by **Nikolai Lobachevski**, 1793–1856.

★ Principal Events

The **French liberal opposition** expelled Charles X, replacing him with **Louis-Philippe**, pledged to rule with middle-class support, 1830. This sparked a liberal and nationalist revolt in Belgium, which became independent of the Netherlands.
Nationalist risings in Italy and Germany were unsuccessful.
The French established their authority in Algiers, 1830.
The Young Italy group was launched by Giuseppe Mazzini, 1805– 72; in Italy in 1831.

The Americas

In Virginia, **Nat Turner**, 1800– 31, led a slave uprising (1831) that resulted in 60 white and more than 100 slave deaths. Slave codes became more rigid.

⦿ Religion and Philosophy

Mormonism was founded in New York State by Joseph Smith, 1805– 44, in 1830, based on the *Book of Mormon*. Opposition to their enclosed community life would cause them to settle in Utah, 1847.
Modern Adventism was founded in the US by **William Miller**, 1782– 1849, who began in 1831 to prophesy the imminent end of the world. The failure of his predictions produced many breakaway sects, including the **Seventh Day Adventists**.

📖 Literature

Social realism in the French novel began with the work of **Stendhal (Henri Beyle)**, 1783– 1842. A soldier and critic, he wrote *Le Rouge et Le Noir*, 1830. **George Sand**, 1804– 76, produced idealized novels such as *Indiana*, 1832, and **Prosper Merimée**, 1803– 70, brought archeological exactness to the romantic novel.

🏛 Art and Architecture

The School of Architecture, Berlin, 1832–.35, by Karl Friedrich Schinkel was based on strict units of measurement, and the design used iron frame structures. It had vestiges of classical detail but came close to a "modern," simple, and functional style.
English industrial towns such as Manchester developed the back-to-back house as a solution to the housing needs generated by the Industrial Revolution.

🎵 Music

Hector Berlioz, 1803– 69, made inspired use of the orchestra to express the extra-musical allusions of program music, as in his *Symphonie fantastique*, 1830, with its elaborate story line.

⚛ Science and Technology

Screw threads were standardized, 1830, by the Briton **Sir Joseph Whitworth**, 1803– 87, making mass production viable.
Electromagnetic induction was discovered, 1831, by a British physicist, **Michael Faraday**, 1791– 1867. This discovery led to the electric generator. Faraday also formulated the laws of electrolysis in 1832.

Principal Events

Slavery was abolished throughout the British Empire, 1833.
The German customs union, completed in 1834, became the focus of German nationalism.
Regional opposition to the liberal Spanish regime led to the **Carlist Wars,** 1833–39, in support of Don Carlos.
Louis-Philippe renounced his radical support and introduced strict censorship, 1835.
British trade with China increased after the East India Company's monopoly ended.

The Americas

In 1832, Jackson threatened to enforce the tariff in response to South Carolina's nullification and vetoed the bill to recharter the Bank of the United States.

Religion and Philosophy

The Oxford Movement within Anglicanism began, 1833, under the leadership of **John Keble,** 1792–1866, and Cardinal **John Newman,** 1801–90. They sought to revive the ideals of the medieval Church and reintroduced elaborate rituals.
Félicité Lamennais, 1782–1854, a French Catholic priest, argued in *Thoughts of a Believer,* 1834, for the separation of Church and state and attacked the papacy for its interference in politics.

Literature

The first great modern Russian writer, **Alexander Pushkin,** 1799–1837, broke down the archaic stiffness of the written style, and introduced realistic language. He used peasant folk songs in the poem *The Dead Princess,* 1834, and medieval history as the source for the novel *Eugene Onegin,* 1823–31, and the tragic drama *Boris Godunov.*

Art and Architecture

In England, the taste and buying power of the new, wealthy middle classes resulted in an increasing demand for genre and small-scale historical or romantic scenes with emphasis on narrative, as in "Giving a Bite," 1834, by **William Mulready,** 1786–1863.
Japanese color printing reached its height in "The Thirty-six Views of Mount Fuji," 1834–35, by **Hokusai** and the poetic "Views of Kyoto," 1834, by **Ando Hiroshige,** 1797–1858.

Music

Frédéric Chopin, 1810–49, a Polish exile working mostly in Paris from 1831, wrote dazzling short pieces for piano in such forms as nocturne, mazurka, and polonaise.

Science and Technology

The Principles of Geology, 1833, by **Sir Charles Lyell,** 1797–1875, showed that rocks evolve extremely slowly. **Karl Gauss,** 1777–1855, a German, devised, 1833, a set of units for magnetism.
The Royal William, a Canadian vessel, was the first steamship to cross the Atlantic wholly under its own power, 1833.
With the building of the **Great Western** in 1838 by **I. K. Brunel,** 1806–59, transatlantic services became regular.

★ Principal Events

The Boers of South Africa began the **Great Trek**, 1835, to find new territory free from British rule. British attempts to unite its colonies of **Upper and Lower Canada** led to revolt, 1837. **Victoria**, *r.*1837–1901, succeeded to the British throne. **Britain** attempted to intervene in Persia, 1834–38, to forestall Russian influence, but was repelled by **Muhammed Shah**, *r.*1835–48.

The Americas

The siege of the Alamo in San Antonio, Tex., 1836, by Mexicans under **Santa Anna**, 1794–1876, ended with the massacre of the Texans.

◊ Religion and Philosophy

Probability theory and statistical methods applied to social phenomena by the Belgian **Adolphe Quetelet**, 1796–1874, led to the discovery that the frequency of suicide in a society was constant and therefore predictable. **Ralph Emerson**, 1803–82, an American Unitarian, developed in *Nature*, 1836, a belief called **Transcendentalism**, proposing that spiritual exploration of one's soul in communion with nature led to the highest wisdom.

Literature

Heinrich Heine, 1797–1856, a German poet and a member of the **Jung Deutschland** group, which described romantic idealism and wanted all literature to have a political role, wrote *Die*

Romantische Schule in Paris, 1836.
Giacomo Leopardi, 1798–1837, used the romantic theme of man's helplessness in the face of nature, in *La Ginestra*, 1836.

Art and Architecture

American primitive painting continued in the work of the Quaker painter **Edward Hicks**, 1780–1849, whose naive landscape with animals, "The Peaceable Kingdom," uses simple forms, flat colors, and two dimensions. **French romantic sculpture** stressed dramatic movement and fleeting gestures, poses, and expressions and was epitomized by the "Marseillaise" on the Arc de Triomphe, 1833–36, by **François Rude**, 1784–1855.

♪ Music

Robert Schumann, 1810–56, was an arch-Romantic, especially in his evocative piano music like *Carnaval*, 1834–35. He founded the avant-garde publication *Neue Zeitschrift fur Musik*.

Science and Technology

Robert Brown, 1773–1858, first discovered and named the nucleus of a living cell.
Charles Babbage, 1791–1871, a British mathematician, developed the principles of the mechanical computer in the 1830s.
The electric telegraph was patented in Britain by **Sir Charles Wheatstone**, 1802–75.
The Colt pistol, the first repeating firearm, was patented, 1835–36.

Principal Events

A working-class radical Chartist movement developed in England, stimulated by European economic depression.

China seized opium imports from India, provoking the **Opium Wars** with Britain, 1839.

British industrialists' attempts to introduce free trade led to the foundation of the **Anti-Corn Law League**, 1839.

Ieyoshi, r.1838–53, the Japanese shōgun, opposed mounting pressure for Occidental trade.

The Americas

There was **a major depression,** 1837–43. Conflict over the New Brunswick-Maine border began, 1838, in the Aroostook River area.

Religion and Philosophy

The terms "sociology" and "positivism" were coined by the Frenchman **Auguste Comte,** 1798–1857. His *Course of Positive Philosophy,* 1830–42, argued for the use of positivist methods in social studies. He stated that man's thought had passed through the theological and metaphysical stages and reached the positivist stage. He divided sociology into statics, the study of the interdependence of social institutions, and dynamics, the study of change.

Literature

The prolific French novelist Honoré de Balzac, 1799–1850, wrote over 90 interconnecting novels and stories, 1829–43, set in Paris and the provinces in the 1820s, which he called *La Comédie Humaine.*

Art and Architecture

The Hudson River School of American landscape painters produced picturesque and romantic views of the eastern states, exemplified by **Thomas Cole,** 1801–48, and **Asher Durand,** 1796–1886.

An increased range of oil colors was introduced, including mauves, violets, bright greens, and intense yellows.

Music

Mikhail Glinka, 1804–57, in such works as *A Life for the Tsar,* 1836, heralded the rise of a Russian national school, using folk music and inspired by the Napoleonic Wars.

Science and Technology

The Morse code was invented, 1838, by **Samuel Morse.**

Stellar parallax was detected in 1838 by **Friedrich Bessel,** 1784–1846, encouraging astronomical interest beyond the solar system.

Vulcanization of rubber was discovered, 1839, by the American **Charles Goodyear,** 1800–60.

Theodor Schwann, 1810–82, and **Matthias Schleiden,** 1804–81, both German biologists, in 1839 first described the anatomy of animal and plant cells and cells' role in the organism.

1840-1842

★ Principal Events

Britain annexed **Natal**, 1843.
Upper and Lower Canada were united in 1840 and given responsible government.
The Straits Convention, 1841, among Russia, Britain, France, Austria, and Prussia, closed the Dardanelles and Bosporus to foreign shipping.
Frederick William IV of Prussia, r. 1840–61, encouraged German nationalism.
The Treaty of Nanking, 1842, opened Chinese ports to British trade.

The Americas

The New York Tribune was founded by **Horace Greeley**, 1811–72, in 1840. The Webster-Ashburton Treaty, 1842, settled the US-Canadian border.

Religion and Philosophy

Ludwig Feuerbach, 1804–72, in *The Essence of Christianity*, 1841, advocated a humanistic atheism. His critique of Hegel and his claim that God is nothing other than a projection of human nature influenced Marx.
Alexis de Tocqueville, 1805–59, the first sociologist to examine the impact of democracy on nonpolitical institutions, held that democratic emphasis on equality might suppress individuality and lead to total conformity—a tyranny of the majority.

Literature

Mikhail Lermontov, 1814–41, stands at the beginning of Russia's golden age of prose. Pushkin's successor as poet, playwright, and novelist, he was directly influenced by Western literature, especially the work and the flamboyant romanticism of Lord Byron. His novel, *A Hero of Our Times*, on the tragic theme of a man without a purpose, appeared in 1840.

Art and Architecture

The Gothic Revival in Europe, which had begun *c*.1750 and was based on serious investigation of medieval sources, prompted the decision to build the **Houses of Parliament**, London, 1836–68, in a Gothic style, and the similar exploration of national Gothic styles in the rest of Europe.
Political cartoons reached a high level of sophistication in England in the work of **George Cruikshank**, 1792–1878, and in France with **Honoré Daumier**.

Music

Vienna, in Ferdinand I's reign, 1835–48, was the center of popular dance music, exporting the Viennese waltz and works of the older **Johann Strauss**, 1804–49, to the rest of Europe.

Science and Technology

Jean-Louis Agassiz, 1807–73, a Swiss naturalist, studied glaciers and showed, 1840, that an Ice Age had once occurred, producing glacial action that had helped to shape the land masses.
Anesthesia had its beginnings in 1842, when US surgeon **Crawford Long**, 1815–78, successfully operated on an etherized patient.

Principal Events

The persecution of Christians in Confucianist French Indochina led to French military involvement, 1840–50.

Sanitary reform and slum clearance were introduced in England in the 1840s.

The Anglo-Sikh wars broke out in India, 1845–48.

Texas was annexed by the United States in 1845.

Utopian socialism became popular in France among intellectuals and the working classes.

The Americas

Texas was admitted to the Union, 1845, despite Mexican threats of war. Expansion after 1845 was justified by the doctrine of "Manifest Destiny."

Religion and Philosophy

The Babi movement, which developed into the **Bahai** religion, was founded in Persia, 1844, by **Ali Muhammed**, 1819–50. It drew inspiration from diverse sources and emphasized the unity of mankind.

Sören Kierkegaard, 1813–55, a Danish religious philosopher, published *Either/Or*, 1843. Regarded as the founder of existentialism, he argued against rationalism and emphasized the need to make choices between ethical or aesthetic alternatives.

Literature

The fantastical and tormented aspects of Russian fiction stem from **Nikolai Gogol**, 1809–52. His novel *Dead Souls*, 1842, a moral satire on bureaucracy,

centered on the career of a man who deals in dead serfs.

Adam Mickiewicz, 1798–1855, Poland's national poet, used themes of Lithuanian folklore in his vibrant epic works.

Art and Architecture

Joseph Turner, 1775–1851, in England was one of the first painters to celebrate contemporary technology. His "Rain, Steam, and Speed," 1844, proclaims the power of the machine in a diffuse, misty style suggesting the speed of the train.

The Barbizon School of French landscapists, including **Jean François Millet**, 1814–75, settled near Fontainebleau.

John Ruskin, 1819–1900, emphasized truth to nature in "Modern Painters."

Music

Brass bands, especially in Germany, produced a popular music of their own. The cornet provided a high voice and became a virtuoso solo instrument.

Science and Technology

The mechanical equivalent of heat was first measured and the principle of the conservation of energy put forward by **Julius von Mayer**, 1814–78, a German physicist, in 1842. The British physicist **James Joule**, 1818–89, and the German **Hermann Helmholtz**, 1821–94, established both with more thorough work *c.*1847.

The Great Britain, the first iron-hulled steamer powered by a screw propeller, crossed the Atlantic in 1843.

★ Principal Events

A potato famine in Ireland resulted in mass emigration to the United States, 1846–47.

The US invaded Mexico and occupied the capital in 1847, defeating Mexico after conflict over Texas, 1846–48.

Liberal hopes in Prussia were raised when the **Landtag** was called, 1847, by the king, who asked for funds to build railroads.

The accession of the liberal **Pope Pius IX**, r.1846–78, raised nationalist hopes in Italy.

The Americas

An Anglo-American treaty settled the Oregon border, 1846. In the Mexican War, 1846–48, the United States acquired New Mexico, Texas, and California.

Religion and Philosophy

Pierre Proudhon, 1809–65, a French philosopher, held that "property is theft." His book *The Philosophy of Misery*, 1846, formulated anarchism as a political theory. Together with his fellow Frenchmen **Louis Blanc**, 1811–82, and **Louis Blanqui**, 1805–81, he called for an end to the capitalistic exploitation of labor and for a revolutionary change in the existing social and economic orders. These men participated in the revolt of 1848.

Literature

The English social novelist Charles Dickens, 1812–70, published one of his greatest novels, *Dombey and Son*, 1846–48,

dealing with the Victorian family. **W. M. Thackeray**, 1811–63, wrote his caustic attack on the false face of polite society, *Vanity Fair*, 1847–48, a satirical novel set on the eve of the Napoleonic wars.

Art and Architecture

Photography (daguerreotypes) and the style of early photographic portraits, where the subject had to maintain a still pose during the long exposure period, influenced such painters as **Ingres**, particularly in his portrait of "La Comtesse d'Haussonville," 1845.

Historical architecture spread in the US, as in Europe. The picturesque, Neo-Norman Smithsonian Institute in Washington, 1846, was built by **James Renwick, Jr.**, 1818–85.

Music

Franz Liszt, 1811–86, a great piano virtuoso, toured the capitals of Europe, then retired from the concert stage.

Science and Technology

Nitroglycerine was discovered, 1846, by the Italian chemist **Ascanio Sobrero**.

Neptune was discovered, 1846, by the German astronomer **Johann Galle**, 1812–1910.

Agriculture gained a scientific basis with the publication in the 1840s and 1850s of work by the German **Justus von Liebig**, 1803–73, showing how plants use vital elements in cycles.

The rotary printing press was invented in 1847 by the American **Richard Hoe**, 1812–86.

★ Principal Events

Britain annexed the Punjab and won Sikh loyalty, 1845– 48.
An outburst of urban radicalism brought the expulsion of **Louis-Philippe** in France and the establishment of a republic, 1848.
Metternich resigned in Austria. **Hungary** declared itself independent, and German and Italian nationalist movements emerged. By 1849, Austria had defeated the Italian revolt, and racial disputes split Hungary.
The gold rush in California opened up the West, 1848– 50.

The Americas

Gold, discovered at Sutter's Mill in the Sacramento Valley, 1848, brought *c.*80,000 adventurers to California, 1849. California became a state, 1850.

Religion and Philosophy

The Christadelphians, a pacifistic millennial adventist sect, were founded in 1848 in the US by **John Thomas,** 1805– 71.
Karl Marx, 1818– 83, and **Friedrich Engels,** 1820– 95, wrote the *Communist Manifesto,* 1848, predicting the revolutionary overthrow of capitalism and its replacement by socialism. Marx saw history as a class struggle for ownership of society's material resources.

Literature

Powerful imagination and insight marked the works of the English novelists the **Brontë sisters. Emily,** 1818– 48, wrote *Wuthering Heights,* 1847, an account of ferocious passions set against a raw elemental background. *Jane Eyre* by **Charlotte,** 1816– 55, was published in the same year and *The Tenant of Wildfell Hall* by **Anne,** 1820– 49, in 1848.

Art and Architecture

The Pre-Raphaelite Brotherhood was founded in England, 1848. Its painters sought a return to the purity and moral seriousness of 15th-century Italian art and rejected contemporary academic styles. Their work was characterized by great detail and the use of brilliant colors on a white ground, as in "Awakening Conscience," 1852, by **William Holman Hunt,** 1827– 1910, and "Christ in the House of his Parents," 1849, by **John Everett Millais,** 1829– 96.

Music

At the court of Weimar, 1848– 61, Liszt supported young musicians, and originated the symphonic or tone poem, 1848– 49.

Science and Technology

Asepsis was demanded, 1847, by **Ignaz Semmelweis,** 1818– 65, a Hungarian physician. He showed that childbed fever could be prevented if hospital doctors cleaned their hands regularly.
The St Lawrence Seaway was first opened in 1848.
Reinforced concrete was invented, 1849, by a French engineer, **Joseph Monier,** 1823– 1906.
A telegraphic cable connection across the English Channel was laid in 1850.

Darwin and Marx 1850–1875

Charles Darwin's theory of Natural Selection lampooned

Karl Marx predicted the demise of capitalism.

Henry Bessemer's steel-producing converter

Brutal suppression of Indian uprising at Delhi

William I proclaimed German Emperor.

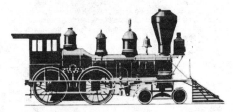

Western and Atlantic Railroad: the *General*, 1855

Darwin and Marx

★ **Principal Events**
The development of ruthlessly pragmatic political planning epitomized by the ministry of Bismarck in Prussia brought about the national unification of Italy and Germany, where the idealism of the 1848 revolutions had failed. Industrial expansion went hand in hand with cynical foreign policies, which with the demise of liberal ideals contributed to the growth of international tensions.

British imperial power was at its peak after the defeat of the Indian mutiny. Britain's economic supremacy, backed up by military strength, made it unchallengeable throughout the world.

The victory of the North in the US Civil War ended slavery and prepared the way for US industrial and political expansion, while the European powers extended their domination in Southeast Asia, and Japan set out to transform herself into modern industrial society.

National Events
The Antebellum period saw deepening differences between the pro- and anti-slavery states. With the election of Abraham Lincoln, 1809-65, the southern states withdrew from the Union. A bitter struggle took place, 1861-65, but following the Civil War the nation moved to achieve real unity.

Religion and Philosophy
The spread of industrialization provoked a major reassessment of moral, social and political thought. Many Christians campaigned to relieve the worst aspects of urban poverty, and sociology developed tools to describe the changes in social relationships, while many political and moral philosophies grew up that rejected urbanization and capitalism, laying stress on personal withdrawal or social revolution. The latter was advocated in particular by Karl Marx, whose work provided a radical attack on capitalist economics and stated that the victory of the proletariat over the bourgeoisie was a historical inevitability.

Darwin's theory of evolution proved as influential as the ideas of Marx, challenging many of the basic tenets of Christian belief and forcing the importance of scientific thought to the fore. Many attempts were made to apply his ideas to the political and cultural fields.

Literature
As the realist novel produced the powerful and candid tragedy of *Madame Bovary* by Flaubert, new literary styles were also emerging in French poetry. Baudelaire's attempt to explore his inner self would lead to the symbolist movement, to which reality beyond the poet's own imagination was irrelevant.

In Russia, Dostoevsky and Tolstoy were writing, and the

moral, psychological, and political issues they explored recurred in the literature of the English Victorian novelists form Charles Dickens to George Eliot.

American literature reached maturity with the poetry of Whitman—a distinct contrast with contemporary European styles—and the strong prose of Melville's epic novel *Moby Dick*.

Art and Architecture

The reaction against academic precepts, which ruled the bulk of official painting in Europe, began in earnest and took the form of the assertion that the subject matter of everyday life was worthy of art.

The Impressionists broke new ground with their revolutionary techniques for representing light and color, best seen in the works of Monet; while Realist painters like Courbet stated that art must have a social and political purpose. In the same period English art saw a distinct reaction against the aesthetics and values of industrial society with the work of the Pre-Raphaelites and the Arts and Crafts movement.

Town planning became a priority in the European capitals, and the use of cast iron revolutionized municipal architecture.

Trading contact with the East and the Meiji restoration in Japan brought an interpenetration of Eastern and Western art.

Music

Romantic ideals were reinforced in 1858 by Darwin's theory of evolution through the survival of the fittest, and confirmed the widely held view that man verges on perfection. The odd conclusion that art, like life, evolves from lower forms to higher led to an increasing distinction between serious and popular music, a distinction still prevalent in the West.

Science and Technology

Science and technology became more closely tied to the needs of industry in this period, especially in Germany where chemists produced dyes and explosives and in the United States where engineers enjoyed a high social status. The abolition of slavery in America and the rise of trade unionism in Europe both raised labor costs and so stimulated mechanization, while the Crimean War provided an incentive for the development of new and better kinds of steel.

While Darwin's theory of evolution, backed by Mendel's researches into genetics, was the most popular scientific breakthrough, chemistry and astronomy both advanced dramatically with the development of spectroscopy in Germany and the application of the Doppler Effect. The former permitted many new elements to be discovered, while the latter, through the measurement of red-shift, produced more accurate estimates of the size of the known universe.

257

1850-1852

★ Principal Events

Napoleon III, *r.*1852–70, restored the French Empire after the upheavals of 1848.

The rights of national minorities were suppressed in the Austro-Hungarian Empire.

California became a free state in 1850, and a compromise was reached on slavery in the United States in 1850.

The vastly destructive T'ai-p'ing Rebellion broke out in China in 1851.

The English in India subdued Burma, 1851–53.

The Americas

California's admission as a free state, upset the balance of slave and free. **Henry Clay's** (1777–1852) Compromise of 1850 postponed the issue.

♦ Religion and Philosophy

The T'ai-p'ing Rebellion in China, 1850, under the leadership of **Hung Hsiu-Chuan**, 1814–64, was a radical religious movement influenced by Protestant Christian teaching, which demanded the communalization of property, equal redistribution of land, and equality between men and women.

T. B. Macaulay, 1800–59, an English historian, published a *History of England* between 1848 and 1861, stressing the victory of liberalism since 1688.

Literature

The American novelist Nathaniel Hawthorne, 1806–64, wrote *The Scarlet Letter*, 1850, and **Herman Melville** produced his allegorical *Moby Dick*, 1851, with an American delight in vigorous prose.

The Victorian Alfred Lord Tennyson, 1809–92, showed in his elegiac poem *In Memoriam*, 1850, verbal grace and awareness of moral dilemmas.

Art and Architecture

Realism reached its height in the works of **Gustave Courbet**, 1819–77, such as "The Stonebreakers," 1850.

Jean François Millet, 1814–75, created an ennobling picture of peasants in his canvas "The Sower," 1850.

The Pre-Raphaelite Brotherhood were defended by **John Ruskin**, 1851.

Prefabricated units of iron and glass were used by **Joseph Paxton**, 1803–65, in the Crystal Palace, London, 1851.

Music

Musical forms still developed themes, much as the classics had done, but the work of composers such as **Liszt** gave music a mystical aura and set it apart from normal experience.

Science and Technology

Entropy, following from the second law of thermodynamics, was conceived, 1850, by the German **Rudolf Clausius**, 1822–88.

The sewing machine was developed, 1851, by **Isaac Singer**, 1811–75, an American.

Physiology advanced with the work, *c.*1851, of the French scientist **Claude Bernard**, 1813–78.

The rotation of the Earth was demonstrated conclusively in 1851 by the French physicist **Jean Foucault**, 1819–68.

Principal Events

Russia's defeat in the Crimean War, 1854–56, checked her ambitions in eastern Europe.
The New York-Chicago rail link was completed, 1853.
The discovery by David Livingstone, 1813–73, of the Victoria Falls, 1855, sparked European exploration of the African interior.
Europe experienced an economic boom, 1852–56.
Camillo Cavour, 1810–61, began the industrialization of Piedmont in northern Italy.

The Americas

The Kansas-Nebraska Act, 1854, allowed popular sovereignty in those territories but did not prevent bloodshed. The Republican party was founded, 1854.

Religion and Philosophy

Frederick Denison Maurice, 1805–72, the major theologian of 19th-century Anglicanism, published his *Theological Essays*, 1853. He helped to found the **Christian Socialist movement** in England, which tried to apply Christian ideals in an industrial society.
Henry Thoreau, 1817–62, an American, described **Transcendentalism** and his simple life in the midst of nature in *Walden*, 1854.

Literature

The fantastic and dream-inspired poems of *Les Chimères*, 1854, by Gerard de Nerval, 1808–55, would influence later symbolists.

The poems of **Matthew Arnold**, 1822–88, were an intellectual expression of Victorian unease as was the poetry of **Robert Browning**, 1812–89, whose dramatic monologues are full of human insight.

Art and Architecture

Honoré Daumier, 1808–79, painted children in "La Ronde," 1855.

Music

Late Romantic composers, such as **Richard Wagner**, 1813–83, and **Anton Bruckner**, 1824–96, aimed for grandeur by using large forces and a rubato (freer) beat to savor the sound.

Science and Technology

Symbolic logic was founded by **George Boole**, 1815–64, a British mathematician, with his *Laws of Thought*, 1854.

259

★ Principal Events

After the Crimean War, the Black Sea was declared neutral and the virtual independence of Serbia recognized by the major European powers, 1856.

The Indian Mutiny, a series of mutinies by Sepoy troops and scattered popular uprisings against British rule, was ruthlessly suppressed, 1857–58.

John Brown, 1800–59, began organizing militant anti-slavery activity in the United States.

The Americas

Dred Scott, c.1795–1858, a slave, took a suit for freedom to the Supreme Court, which declared the Missouri Compromise unconstitutional.

⚘ Religion and Philosophy

Frédéric Le Play, 1806–82, a French sociologist, developed a technique of collating field data that influenced methods of statistical sampling in *European Workers,* 1855. He defined three basic family types, related to general social conditions.

Hippolyte Taine, 1828–93, a French historian, argued in *The French Philosophers* for the use of a scientific (positivist) method in the study of culture, 1857. He had a great influence on later 19th century thought.

Literature

Walt Whitman, 1819–92, published his autobiographical *Leaves of Grass,* 1855.

Gustave Flaubert, 1821–80, published *Madame Bovary,* 1856.

Modern poetry began with *Les Fleurs du Mal,* 1857, by the Frenchman **Charles Baudelaire,** 1821–67.

Theophile Gautier, 1811–72, proclaimed the concept of art for art's sake, 1857.

Art and Architecture

Baron Haussmann, 1809–91, introduced squares, parks, and boulevards into Paris, 1851–68. His wide streets were designed to create impressive views and to ensure easy policing of the city center.

The New Building of the Louvre, 1852–57, and later the Paris Opera, 1861–74, illustrate the powerful Neo-Renaissance and Neo-Baroque forms that were key to the civic architecture of the Second Empire.

Music

Use of rubato tended to slow down performances and to produce rhythmic problems in large ensembles so that performances became dull and turgid.

Science and Technology

The first synthetic plastic material, later named celluloid, was patented in 1855 by the British chemist Alexander Parkes, 1813–90.

Mauve, the first artificial dye, was derived from aniline, 1856, by the British chemist **William Perkin,** 1838–1907. Production of the new synthetic substances stimulated the growth of modern organic chemistry.

Steel was produced cheaply in the converter patented in 1856 by the British metallurgist **Henry Bessemer,** 1813–98.

Principal Events

China was finally opened up by the treaties of Tientsin, 1858.
By the Government of India Act, 1858, British rule in India was transferred to the crown. Administrative reforms and the building of railways followed.
Piedmont drove the Austrians from northern Italy, 1859.
The British raided Peking, 1860.
The Suez Canal construction was begun by de Lesseps, 1805–94.
Russia expanded at China's expense, 1858–60.

The Americas

John Brown, 1800–59, was executed following a raid at Harpers Ferry, Va., 1859. Republican **Abraham Lincoln** was elected president, 1860.

Religion and Philosophy

Charles Darwin, 1809–82, published *Origin of Species*, 1859, arousing opposition from the English Church because he contradicted Genesis and seemed to render the role of God in the Creation superfluous. By implying that man stood at the pinnacle of evolutionary development, Darwin's theory reinforced contemporary ideas of the inevitability of social progress. After defeat in the debate, the Church ceased to intervene in science.

Literature

Adalbert Stifter, 1805–68, wrote of the harmony of man and nature in *Der Nachsommer*.
Ivan Goncharov, 1812–91, wrote

Oblomov, 1859, mocking the bankruptcy of intellectualism.

Art and Architecture

Landscapes by **Jean Baptiste Camille Corot**, 1796–1875, like "The Valley," 1855–60, anticipated the Impressionists with their use of muted colors and soft outlines.
The Arts and Crafts movement in England led by **William Morris**, 1834–96, and **Philip Webb**, 1831–1915, originated in a dissatisfaction with manufactured goods and a respect for the medieval craftsman. It produced wallpapers, furniture, tapestries, and carpets, usually by hand.

Music

Grand opera carried the Romantic ideal to a peak in the works of **Giuseppe Verdi**, 1813–1901, who in *Un Ballo in maschera*, 1859, evoked specific characters and moods.

Science and Technology

Atomic weights and chemical formulae were standardized by the Italian **Stanislao Cannizzaro**, 1826–1910, in 1858.
The principles of molecular structure were discovered by the German chemist **Friedrich von Stradonitz**, 1829–96, in 1858.
The theory of evolution was put forward in 1858–59 by the British naturalists **Charles Darwin**, 1809–82, and **Alfred Wallace**, 1823–1913.
The first oil well was drilled near Titusville, Pennsylvania, in 1858.

1860-1862

Principal Events

Abraham Lincoln, 1809– 65, was elected president of the US on an anti-slavery platform.
The Confederate states took Fort Sumter, 1861.
Giuseppe Garibaldi, 1807– 82, liberated southern Italy from Neapolitan rule and gave it to Piedmont, uniting Italy, 1861.
Alexander II of Russia, *r.*1855– 81, emancipated the serfs in 1861
The French intervened in Mexico, 1861, and installed Maximilian as emperor, 1863.

The Americas

South Carolina seceded from the Union, 1860. In 1861, the Confederate States of America comprised 11 states. Fort Sumter's fall began the Civil War.

Religion and Philosophy

Ferdinand Lassalle, 1825– 64, urged German workers to seek universal suffrage, 1862. His program would form the basis of the German Social Democratic party established in 1869 in opposition to the revolutionary Marxist International, and foreshadowed later social democratic and parliamentary movements.

Literature

An impressionistic realist style based on detailed social observation was developed in France by the brothers **Edmond** and **Jules de Goncourt**, 1822– 96 and 1830– 70, in their *Journals*.

The realist novel in Russia produced a varied account of the conflicts in Russian society.

Art and Architecture

Gustave Doré, 1832– 83, illustrated Dante's *Inferno*, 1861.
Eugène Emmanuel Viollet-le-Duc, 1814– 79, in France, interpreted Gothic architecture in terms of its structural principles and advocated new materials like iron, in his *Dictionary of French Architecture*, 1858– 75.
Japanese draftsmanship, flat expanses of color, and subject matter strongly influenced the Impressionists and later **Van Gogh** and **Gauguin**.

Music

Negro spirituals emerged in the US as blacks took up the singing school tradition of colonial America, but mixed with it a rhythmic work-song style.

Science and Technology

The open hearth process for the production of steel was developed in France, following the invention of the regenerative furnace by **William Siemens**, 1823– 83, and **Frederick Siemens**, 1826– 1904.
Colloids were distinguished in 1861 by the British chemist **Thomas Graham**, 1805– 69. He also discovered osmosis.

Principal Events

An allied Western expedition participated in a violent civil war in Japan, 1864.
Rome remained under papal rule as a virtual protectorate of France.
Slavery was abolished and Lincoln assassinated, 1865.
Karl Marx, 1818–83, presided over the First International in London, 1864.
Christianity was spread in China by missionaries.

The Americas

The Civil War ended at Appomattox Courthouse when Confederate **Gen. Robert E. Lee,** 1807–70, surrendered to Union Gen. **Ulysses S. Grant,** 1822–85.

Religion and Philosophy

John Stuart Mill, 1806–73, an Englishman, attempted to create a political theory uniting the conditions of industrialism with basic tenets of human freedom. He argued in *Utilitarianism,* 1863, that what gives pleasure to man is good, while in *On Liberty,* 1859, he insisted that a man must be free to act as he wishes without disturbing the freedom of others. His political critique of English society brought him close to a socialist position.

Literature

The debate between Slavophiles and Westernizers was described in *Fathers and Sons* by **Ivan Turgenev,** 1818–83, an ardent Westernizer.

Count Leo Tolstoy, 1828–1910, the greatest exponent of the Russian realist novel, dealt in his epic *War and Peace,* 1865–72, with the Napoleonic Wars, combining a panoramic vision with acute analysis of character.

Art and Architecture

A turning point for modern painting was marked by the establishment in Paris in 1863 of the **Salon de Refusés,** which exhibited some of the 4,000 canvases rejected by the official Salon. It included works by **Camille Pissarro,** 1830–1903, **Paul Cézanne,** 1839–1906, **James McNeill Whistler,** 1834–1903, and **Edouard Manet,** 1832–83, whose "Déjeuner sur L'Herbe," of a naked woman enjoying a picnic with friends, created a sensation.

Music

Faust, by **Charles Francis Gounod,** 1818–93, was produced in London, Dublin, and New York in 1863.

Science and Technology

The first underground railway opened in London in 1863.
The Massachusetts Institute of Technology was founded, 1865.
Bacteriology was founded with the work of the French chemist **Louis Pasteur,** 1822–95, in the 1860s. Pasteur discovered that microorganisms cause fermentation and disease, and used sterilization to kill bacteria.
A submarine telegraphic cable was laid across the Atlantic from Ireland to Newfoundland, 1857–66.

1865-1867

★ Principal Events

After the defeat of Austria by Prussia in the war of 1866, the North German Confederation was set up.

American objections and opposition at home led to French withdrawal from Mexico, 1866.

The Dominion of Canada was established by the British North America Act, 1867.

The Dual Monarchy of Austria-Hungary was established, 1867— an unpopular compromise on the nationalist question.

The Americas

The Fourteenth Amendment, 1866, granted blacks full citizenship. The Thirteenth Amendment, 1865, had prohibited slavery.

Religion and Philosophy

Karl Marx, 1818–83, published Vol. I of *Das Kapital,* 1867, providing a theoretical analysis of the workings of capitalism. He argued that industrial profits were made by exploiting the workers, but claimed that capitalism would plunge into chaos through its inner contradictions. **William Booth,** 1829–1912, shocked at the extent of poverty and degradation in London, began his Evangelical ministry in 1865 and later founded the **Salvation Army.**

Literature

The Parnassians, a group of French poets including **Charles Marie Leconte de Lisle,** 1818– 94, and later **Paul Verlaine,** 1844– 96, rejected the emotionalism and loose forms of the Romantics and wrote strictly disciplined, detached verse following **Theophile Gautier.** Their name derived from the journal *Le Parnasse Contemporain,* first published in 1866.

Art and Architecture

Japanese prints were being collected in Paris in the 1860s and were exhibited at the Exposition Universelle, 1867. The influence of Japanese draftsmanship could be seen in Manet's "Portrait of Emile Zola," 1868, and in **Whistler's** "Princess of the Land of Porcelain," 1864.

Music

Light opera centered on Paris and Vienna, with the theatrical humor of **Jacques Offenbach,** 1819– 80, and the lavish settings of the younger **Johann Strauss,** 1825– 99.

Science and Technology

Genetics was founded with the publication, 1865, of the experiments of the Austrian botanist **Gregor Mendel,** 1822– 84.

Dynamite was invented in 1866 by the Swedish inventor **Alfred Nobel,** 1833– 96, who established the Nobel Prize.

Antiseptic surgery was introduced by the British physician **Lord Lister,** 1827– 1912, by 1867. Following Pasteur's research into the nature of disease, he used carbolic acid to disinfect the operating theater.

264

Principal Events

Napoleon III instituted liberal reforms to quell growing opposition, but his empire collapsed in the face of a Prussian invasion, 1870

By 1870 the railway systems of France, England, and Belgium were virtually complete, stimulating heavy industry.

The victory of Mutsuhito, r.1868–1912, in Japan led to a policy of industrialization and an end to the shoguns.

Black suffrage was enforced in the United States, 1870.

The Americas

Pres. Andrew Johnson, 1801–75, was impeached by the House but exonerated in the Senate, 1868. Wyoming territory granted women the vote, 1869.

Religion and Philosophy

Papal infallibility was asserted by the first Vatican Council, 1869–70, which ruled that the pope or an ecumenical council of bishops was immune from error when pronouncing on matters of faith or morals. The pope's increased prestige resulting from this ruling partly compensated for the loss of the Papal States to Italy.

The classic statement of the case for women's suffrage was presented by **J. S. Mill** in *The Subjection of Women*, 1869.

Literature

The great novels of Fyodor Dostoevsky, 1821–81, including *Crime and Punishment*, 1866, *The Brothers Karamazov*, 1879–80, and *The Idiot*, 1868, study totalitarianism, the conflict between atheism and compassionate Christianity, and good and evil in man.

The English novelist Charles Dickens continued his prodigious output of social novels.

Art and Architecture

Mural painting in France was revived by **Pierre Puvis de Chavannes,** 1824–1898, whose monumental style and subdued colors, seen in "Ludus Pro Patria," 1865–69 inspired the Symbolists of the 1880s. The effects of light out of doors on the surface of an object or figure were first captured and faithfully recorded by **Claude Monet,** 1840–1926, in his painting "Women in the Garden," 1866–70.

Music

Wagner revolutionized opera, using a continuously moving harmonic structure over which leitmotif identified dramatic elements. He believed opera should combine all the arts.

Science and Technology

The typewriter was developed commercially after the 1867 invention of American **Christopher Sholes,** 1819–90. He was the first to use today's keyboard. The Periodic Table of the elements was devised by the Russian chemist **Dmitry Mendeleev,** 1834–1907, in 1869. From the table he predicted the properties of three new elements, all of which were found within twenty years.

★ Principal Events

A revolutionary commune set up in Paris, 1871, was ruthlessly suppressed. It rejected the authority of the French government after the surrender to Prussia. **Prussia's seizure of Alsace-Lorraine** completed German unification, and a German Empire was proclaimed under **William I,** r.1861–88.

An American attempt to open up Korea failed, 1871–73, but Britain forced the Treaty of Pangkor on Malaya.

The Americas

Railroad service linked Boston, Mass., to Oakland, Calif., 1870. Scandals rocked President Grant's administration.

Religion and Philosophy

Bakunin 1814–76, a Russian anarchist, stressed the need for violent revolution to overthrow the state and allow the essential goodness of man to develop. His rejection of centralization and subordination to authority in favor of the free spirit of revolt led to his expulsion from the International, 1872, after conflicting with Marx.

Johann von Döllinger, a German theologian, 1799–1890, was excommunicated, 1871, for opposing the idea of infallibility.

Literature

George Eliot, the pseudonym of Mary Anne Evans, 1819–80, described the conflicts within English provincial society in *Middlemarch*, 1871–72.

The early French symbolist poets Arthur Rimbaud, 1859–91, and Paul Verlaine, 1844–96, aimed to devise a truly poetic visionary language; Rimbaud wrote *Une Saison en Enfer*, 1873.

Art and Architecture

Monet's painting, "Impression, Sunrise", 1872, exhibited in 1874 with works by **Pierre Auguste Renoir,** 1841–1919, **Alfred Sisley,** 1839–99, **Edgar Degas,** 1834–1917, **Pissarro,** and **Cézanne,** gave its name to the Impressionist movement with which these painters were associated. **Impressionism** abandoned traditional linear representation, aiming to capture the fleeting effects of light and color by using small dashes and strokes of color.

Music

César Franck, 1822–90, a Belgian working in the classical tradition, attracted little attention in his lifetime but influenced an important group of younger French composers.

Science and Technology

Light was shown to be an electromagnetic radiation by the British physicist **James Clerk Maxwell,** 1831–79. He predicted other such radiations.

Principal Events

The conservative Third Republic was set up in France after the defeat of the Commune, in spite of repeated attempts to restore the monarchy.
Britain bought a decisive share in the **Suez Canal,** 1875, thus acquiring a quick route to India.
French power in Indochina, extended by Napoleon III, was confirmed, 1874.
The revelation of corruption in the Grant administration in the US resulted in financial panic and economic depression.

 **The Americas**

In **1873** a depression struck. Barbed wire influenced the development of the West after 1874, solving fencing problems of prairie settlers.

 Religion and Philosophy

An upsurge of religious revivalism associated with the Temperance Movement, which saw alcohol as the cause of working-class degradation, was started in America and Britain by **D. L. Moody,** 1837–99.
Wilhelm Wundt, 1832–1920, a German who published *Principles of Physiological Psychology,* 1873–74, established experimental psychology. He sought to investigate by introspection the immediate experiences of consciousness.

 Literature

Jules Laforgue, 1860–87, a symbolist, was one of the first French poets to use free verse.

 Art and Architecture

The later Pre-Raphaelite style in England, best represented by the work of **Edward Burne-Jones,** 1833–98, like the "Briar Rose" series, 1871–90, later influenced the Symbolist movement.
London's first garden suburb, Bedford Park at Turnham Green, was designed by the Victorian architect and associate of **William Morris, Richard Norman Shaw,** 1831–1912, in 1875.

 Music

Johannes Brahms, 1833–97, carried on Beethoven's tradition especially in the symphony. Brahms' classical control of the emotional impulses in his music gives it a rich dramatic quality.

 Science and Technology

The Challenger expedition of 1872–76 founded oceanography. Intermolecular forces were calculated by **Johannes van der Walls,** 1837–1923, in 1873. He accurately described the behavior of real gases, using mathematical equations.

The Age of Imperialism 1875–1900

Queen Victoria symbolized the idea of British monarchy.

Alexander Graham Bell invented the telephone.

Sigmund Freud divided the mind and explored the unconscious.

Art Nouveau: interior design by Victor Horta

Paris Exhibition 1889: the
Machine Hall

Maxim machine gun:
quick and efficient

The Benz Velo motor car was invented in 1896.

The Age of Imperialism

⭐ **Principal Events**

Domination of the world outside the Americas lay with a few European states. Among them Britain was still the greatest imperial and industrial power, but Germany now increasingly challenged this position. The US also grew in strength and by 1900 overtook Britain in the production of basic industrial materials.

The emergence of a group of fixed alliances in Europe served to polarize foreign affairs and the Balkans, in particular, presented an inflammatory arena for international conflict.

Improvements in communications, however, and the quest for new bases of economic and political power shifted the focus of rivalries among the states to Africa and Oceania. Britain greatly extended its empire but the other European states, the US, and a newly modernized Japan also joined in the scramble. By 1899 all Asia was in the hands of Europe and China was in thrall to the West.

National Events

The United States began to take its place among the great powers. Domestic issues included labor and Indian unrest. Financial difficulties following the Panic of 1893 continued for nearly five years before prosperity returned. Imperialist interests were manifested in the Spanish-American War.

Religion and Philosophy

Growing interest in the attempt to link social theory to biological evolutionism gave rise to more subtle sociological and anthropological studies in the English-speaking world. Drawing on the experience of colonial administration, such men as Tylor, Spencer, and Frazer developed the notion of a natural progression between "primitive" and "advanced" societies. Meanwhile, in Vienna, Freud began to formulate influential ideas on the subconscious and human nature.

In philosophy the absolute idealism of Hegel found its first supporters in England with Bradley, while in the United States pragmatic thinkers such as William James argued that the truth of an idea depends on its social function.

The ideology of anti-Semitism grew up in the wake of heightened nationalist sentiment, while an evolutionary type of socialism grew more popular than its revolutionary counterpart.

Literature

The pessimistic application of theories of evolution is found in Zola's naturalistic novels, which stressed the limitations on man's actions stemming from his inherited characteristics and the environment and portrayed the most sordid aspects of French lower-class life. In the same period English literature entered a more reflective stage, losing the exuberance of Dickens.

Nationalism still acted as a vital cultural stimulus, creating a school of national regeneration in Spain in reaction to the political weakness highlighted by the war with Cuba, and in Italy celebrating unification. In both, writers turned to their national classics for models. The first self-conscious Latin American school grew up asserting independence from European traditions.

Art and Architecture
A self-conscious and revolutionary avant-garde emerged in European art at the end of the 19th century. In France Van Gogh, Gauguin, and Cézanne, the major innovators of that time, developed their different styles out of their Impressionist origins. The Symbolists rejected the Impressionist vision, turning instead to the past and to the exotic imagery of the later English Pre-Raphaelites in which Art Nouveau, an essentially decorative style and the first non-historical style to win wide acceptance, also had roots. Beginning in Belgium and England, Art Nouveau owed its original character to a semi-abstract use of natural forms and had far-reaching effects in architecture and the applied arts.

Construction in metal became even more popular after the Paris exhibitions of 1878 and 1889, encouraged by the substitution of steel for iron, which also made possible the development of the skyscraper in the US.

Music
Romanticism began to decline as nationalism and impressionism became more important ideals in music. Meanwhile the future of American and European popular music was formed in the United States with the increasing appreciation of the rhythmic genius of black folk musicians and an awareness of the potential of the newly developed phonograph.

Science and Technology
Germany now took the lead in the science-based industries as a result of the emphasis on science and technology in education and a political system that gave power to industry. It possessed a flourishing heavy industry, became the center of early automobile development, and led the field in medicine, now a preventive as well as a curative science, with the discovery of antibodies and of new drugs. Koch's work on tuberculosis was the most important advance. As a result of these technical discoveries combined with the widespread building of new hospitals, mortality rates dropped throughout western Europe. Other technological achievements that would alter society were the inventions of the telephone and phonograph.

Classical physics failed to explain discoveries made in radioactivity and the problem posed by the Michelson-Morley experiment, and entered a time of uncertainty that would only be resolved by Einstein's theory of relativity.

★ Principal Events

Britain bought the khedive's Suez Canal shares, 1875, and annexed South Africa, 1877.
The Slav nationalist forces in the Balkans erupted against Turkey, and the Bulgarian massacres, 1875, aroused a public outcry in Britain. Russia supported the insurgents, hoping to win new authority in the Balkans.
The Satsuma rebellion, 1877, led by conservative forces in Japan, failed to halt the tide of reform and new ideas.

The Americas

Members of the terrorist organization the Molly Maguires were executed, 1876. Indians killed **Gen. George A. Custer,** 1839–76, at the Little Bighorn.

⚱ Religion and Philosophy

Hinduism witnessed the rise of various reform movements under the impact of Western thought. Most important was that led by **Ramakrishna,** 1836–86, an extreme ascetic in the Vedanta tradition, who believed that all religions were essentially identical.
The Theosophical Society, which set out to foster the transmission of Eastern thought to the West, was founded in New York in 1875 by **Helena Blavatsky,** 1831–91.

Literature

English literature after 1875 saw a reaction to the confidence of the high Victorian era, reflected in the Decadent poetry of Alger-

non Charles Swinburne, 1837–1909. His sensual *Poems and Ballads* show traces of symbolist influences.
Gerard Manley Hopkins, 1844–89, described the tensions of his religious vision in lyrical, experimental poetry.

Art and Architecture

A parallel to the Impressionist idea of forms dissolved in light appeared in the work of the greatest 19th-century sculptor, **Auguste Rodin,** 1840–1917, who produced his first free-standing figure, "Age of Bronze," in 1877.

Music

The origins of jazz and blues are found in the work songs that united poor blacks as they toiled in fields, and in gospel songs that united them in church.

Science and Technology

The telephone was patented in 1876 by the American inventor **Alexander Graham Bell,** 1847–1922.
Bacteria were identified by methods of growing and staining cultures, developed from 1876 onward by the German bacteriologist **Robert Koch,** 1843–1910. He found the bacteria that cause tuberculosis, anthrax, and cholera.
The phonograph was invented in 1877 by the American inventor **Thomas Edison,** 1847–1931.

Principal Events

After Russia's defeat of Turkey, 1878, Britain and Austria-Hungary intervened to check Russian ambitions, and the Powers met at the Congress of Berlin, 1878, to decide the future of the Balkans.

Germany and Austria-Hungary formed a Dual Alliance, 1879.

In Afghanistan Britain sought to secure her position in India against Russian expansion 1878–80.

Chile began her successful war against Bolivia and Peru, 1879.

The Americas

In 1878, the Knights of Labor, a secret group formed in 1869, became a national order. Open to both skilled and unskilled, it was the first successful US union.

Religion and Philosophy

The Jehovah's Witnesses, an evangelical movement believing in the second coming of Christ, was founded by **Charles Russell,** 1852–1916, in the United States.

Christian Science was founded in Boston by **Mary Baker Eddy,** 1821–1910, who rejected medicine and saw prayer as the only cure for illness.

Heinrich von Treitscke, 1834–96, fostered German nationalism in his *History of Germany in the 19th Century,* 1879–94.

Literature

Realism in the theater was pioneered by the Norwegian **Henrik Ibsen,** 1828–1906, who dramatized social issues using ordinary conversation, as in *A Doll's House,* 1879. In England **G. B. Shaw,** 1856–1950, also attacked social complacency in plays enlivened by vivid characterization, satire, and wit such as *Mrs. Warren's Profession* and *The Devil's Disciple.*

Art and Architecture

Ballet girls, working girls, and cabaret artists were the subject matter for such works of **Edgar Degas** as "Scènes de Ballet," 1879. He worked in a great variety of media and was influenced by the action photographs of dancers and racing horses taken by **Muybridge.**

A Slavic revival in Russia reached its peak in the 1870s and 80s based on a careful documentation of national cultural history.

Music

Art songs were composed all over Europe, after decades of domination by German lieder writers. The form was finely worked by French composers like **Henri Duparc,** 1848–1933.

Science and Technology

In 1879 **Edison** patented his incandescent light bulb. But in 1878, **Joseph Swan,** a British physicist, had patented the **first successful filament electric lamp.** In 1879–80 both Swan and Edison independently produced a practical light bulb.

Piezoelectricity, electricity produced by the compression of certain types of crystal, was discovered, 1880, by a Frenchman, **Pierre Curie,** 1859–1906.

1880-1882

Principal Events

British imperial expansion in Africa was checked by defeat in the Transvaal, 1881, but British occupation forces were installed in Egypt in 1882.

Under Bismarck, 1815–98, Germany aimed to build a solid European power structure, signing the **Three Emperors' Alliance** with Russia and Austria, 1881, and a similar alliance with Italy, 1882. At home, Bismarck introduced sickness benefits to help weaken the growing appeal of socialism.

The Americas

From 1862–82, there were 200,000 Chinese immigrants to the US. The Chinese Exclusion Act, 1882, banned Chinese workers for 10 years.

Religion and Philosophy

A theory of social evolution was developed by the Englishman **Edward Tylor,** 1832–1917, in his *Anthropology*, 1881. Through studying primitive religion, he concluded that many existing social customs were "survivals" from earlier stages of development. Similar ideas were defended in America by **Lewis Morgan,** 1818–81, who developed the study of kinship systems.

Literature

Native American humor was found in *The Adventures of Huckleberry Finn* by **Mark Twain,** 1835–1910.

The meeting of the New World with the Old was explored by **Henry James,** 1843–1916, in *Portrait of a Lady*, 1881. He probed subtleties of character, temperament, and motive, as in *Washington Square* and the dazzling *The Golden Bowl*.

Art and Architecture

Official painting in England was represented by **Lawrence Alma-Tadema,** 1836–1912, and **Frederick Leighton,** 1830–96, who painted pseudo-classical scenes in a realistic though sentimental manner.

A move away from Impressionism was evident in the works of **Paul Cézanne,** 1839–1906, who achieved an almost abstract quality in such paintings as "L'Estaque," *c.*1882–85, with its emphasis on form, color, planes, and light.

Music

English light opera, notably the deft, tuneful creations of **W. S. Gilbert,** 1836–1911, and **Arthur Sullivan,** 1842–1900, became a craze throughout Europe, the US, and Australia.

Science and Technology

The ether was proved not to exist by the experiments of the American physicists **Albert Michelson,** 1852–1931, and **Edward Morley,** 1838–1923, from 1881. This result led to the theory of relativity.

The electric trolley first ran in Berlin in 1881.

Cell division was described in 1882 by the German anatomist **Walther Flemming,** 1843–1905. Following Koch's work, **Pasteur** used attenuated bacteria to confer immunity to anthrax, 1881, and against rabies, 1885.

Principal Events

Britain consolidated its position on the Afghan border and in Egypt but was defeated by native forces in the Sudan, 1885.
France took Indochina, 1884.
The Treaty of Berlin, 1884, defined the rights of 14 European powers in Africa. This helped stop the scramble for colonies, which could have led to a major war.
Eastern Rumelia's union with Bulgaria, 1885, provoked war with Serbia, and Austria acted to save Serbia from invasion.

The Americas

The Pendleton Act, 1883, required standardized exams for civil service jobs. New York City's Brooklyn Bridge was completed, 1883.

Religion and Philosophy

In Russia, **Peter Kropotkin**, 1842–1921, was the leading theorist of the Anarchist movement. In *Words of a Rebel*, 1884, he emphasized nonviolence and argued that cooperation rather than conflict was the basis of evolutionary progress.
The Fabian Society, founded in Britain, 1883–84, favored a gradual evolution toward socialism.
The Zionist Movement held its first conference in Prussia in 1884 as anti-Semitism grew.

Literature

Naturalism in literature was inaugurated in France by **Emile Zola**, 1840–1902, who explored deterministic notions of the relation between heredity and environment and the casualties of urban society in the novels *Les Rougon Macquart*, 1871–93.
Guy de Maupassant, 1850–93, followed him in his novels and short stories such as *Boule de Suif*.

Art and Architecture

Neo-Impressionism or **Pointillism** was developed by **Georges Seurat**, 1859–91, **Paul Signac** 1863–1935, and **Camille Pissarro**, 1830–1903. A reaction against the spontaneity of Impressionism, it created the optical effect of light by means of dots of color, which were fused by the eye into continuous tones.
The Berlin Reichstag, 1884–94, and the **Victor Emmanuele II** monument in Rome, 1885–1911, used antique forms to create a sense of civic grandeur.

Music

National qualities appeared in serious music both out of patriotism, heard in **Bedřich Smetana's** Czech *Ma Vlast*, 1874–75, and of exoticism, in **Alexis Emmanuel Chabrier's** *España*, 1883.

Science and Technology

H. S. Maxim, 1840–1916, invented the **Maxim machine gun** in England, 1884.
The steam turbine was made in 1884 by the British engineer **Charles Parsons**, 1854–1931.
Motor transport was founded in 1885 with the invention of the automobile by **Karl Benz**, 1844–1929, a German engineer. In the same year another German engineer, **Gottlieb Daimler**, 1834–1900, patented a gasoline engine that he used initially to power a motorcycle.

★ Principal Events

The Canadian Pacific Railway was completed, 1885.
All American Indians were confined to reservations by 1887.
The American Federation of Labor was set up in 1886.
Germany signed a Reinsurance Treaty with Russia, 1887, to minimize the danger of war between them in the Balkans.
Britain, Italy, and Austria-Hungary agreed to maintain the status quo in the Mediterranean and the Near East, 1887.

The Americas

Samuel Gompers, 1850–1924, was the first president of the American Federation of Labor, 1886. The Haymarket Massacre occurred in Chicago, 1886.

Religion and Philosophy

Friedrich Nietzsche, 1844–1900, a German, vehemently rejected Christianity, science, and conformist moralities in *Beyond Good and Evil*, 1886.
Edouard Drumont, 1844–1917, popularized anti-Semitism in *La France Juive*, 1886.
Ferdinand Tönnies, 1855–1936, the German sociologist, published *Community and Association*, 1887, distinguishing "communities," involving moral consensus, from "associations," based on self-interest.

Literature

Symbolist poetry developed in France with the *Poésies*, 1887, of **Stéphane Mallarmé**, 1842–98. He sought an ideal

world, but one of the intellect and not the emotions.
Maurice Maeterlinck, 1862–1949, in Belgium, wrote symbolist plays. In Sweden **August Strindberg**, 1849–1912, wrote plays such as *Miss Julie* in a naturalist vein.

Art and Architecture

Symbolist art, which developed after 1886, appealed to the imagination and the senses. In France its chief exponents were **Gustave Moreau**, 1826–98, whose paintings have a rich, jewellike quality, and **Odilon Redon**, 1840–1916.
Impressionist ideas were taken to England by **Wilson Steer**, 1860–1942, and **Walter Sickert**, 1860–1942, who set up the **New English Art Club**, 1886, in protest against pseudoclassical styles.

Music

Russian music gained its national qualities—lyricism, vitality, and colorful orchestration—in the work of **Peter Tchaikovsky**, 1840–93, and **Nikolai Rimsky-Korsakov**, 1844–1908.

Science and Technology

Aluminum could be produced economically from 1886 by the electrolytic process devised almost at the same time by an American chemist, **Charles Hall**, 1863–1914, and a French chemist, **Paul Héroult**, 1863–1914.
Radio waves were produced about 1887 by **Heinrich Hertz**, 1857–94, a German physicist.
Edison set up a **research laboratory** at West Orange, N.J., 1887, with teams of inventors working together systematically.

Principal Events

The partition of Africa neared completion with Britain dominating the center and south.
In Japan, Emperor Meiji, r.1867-1912, granted a Western style constitution.
In France the war minister **Georges Boulanger,** 1837-91, attempted to seize power.
The US overtook Britain in steel production by 1890.
The Social-Democratic party, the most popular in Germany, was legalized, 1890.

The Americas

The Interstate Commerce Act was passed, 1887. There was a land rush in Oklahoma, 1889. In 1890, Congress passed the Sherman Antitrust Act.

Religion and Philosophy

James Frazer, 1854-1941, a British anthropologist, surveyed a great range of beliefs and customs in *The Golden Bough,* 1890. He claimed that there was a natural progression from magical, through religious, to scientific belief systems.

Literature

Italian nationalist ideas were voiced by **Giosuè Carducci,** 1835-1907. A scholar and anti-romantic, his *Odi Barbare* is a patriotic vision of Italy's glorious past and future destiny. **Verismo,** Italian realism, was developed by **Giovanni Verga,** 1840-1922, whose novels combined a perceptive study of the Sicilian class structure with the personal cares of *Mastro Don Gesualdo.*

Art and Architecture

Vincent van Gogh, 1853-90, a painter obsessed with the problems of expression, painted tormented landscapes and portraits using heightened color and a frenzied and turbulent style seen in "The Sower," 1888.
The Eiffel Tower was constructed in 1889, demonstrating contemporary engineering skills.

Music

Symphonic traditions continued in Europe with vast works by **Anton Bruckner,** 1824-96, and **Gustav Mahler,** 1860-1911, who introduced folk elements.

Science and Technology

The pneumatic tire was invented in 1888 by the British veterinarian **John Dunlop,** 1840-1921. **Photographic film** and paper were developed, 1884-88, by **George Eastman,** 1854-1932, an American inventor. Eastman's work made the moving picture, as well as still photography, a possibility.

1890-1892

★ Principal Events

In Germany, **Kaiser William II**, r.1888–1918, dismissed Bismarck in 1890 and let the treaty with Russia lapse.
The European alliance blocs took shape. **The Triple Alliance** of Germany, Austria-Hungary, and Italy was renewed in 1891. Russia and France made a **Dual Alliance**, 1891.
Brazil adopted a federal republican constitution, 1891.
In the US, the **Populist party** grew out of agrarian protest at currency deflation.

The Americas

In 1890, **Indian** desires to regain land were expressed in the ritual of the Ghost Dance. The Battle of Wounded Knee, 1890, ended the Ghost Dance War.

⚱ Religion and Philosophy

The Neo-classical school of economics was established by the Englishman **Alfred Marshall**, 1842–1924, in his *Principles of Economics*, 1890. He united the "classical" view that prices are determined by costs with the "marginalist" view of **W. S. Jevons**, 1835–82, that prices depend on the interaction of supply and demand.
Kang Yu-wei, 1858–1927, advocated social equality in China and argued that Confucius had supported historical progress.

Literature

In novels of English rural life such as *Tess of the D'Urber-*

villes, 1891, **Thomas Hardy**, 1840–1928, expressed a pessimistic view of life in which man was swamped by cosmic ironies.
The English Decadent movement is epitomized by *The Picture of Dorian Gray*, 1891, by Oscar Wilde, 1854–1900.

Art and Architecture

Synthetism, characterized by strong flat colors in well-defined areas, was developed by **Paul Gauguin**, 1848–1903, in Tahiti. He influenced the **Nabis**, a group of French painters led by **Paul Serusier**, 1865–1927, who rejected Impressionism.
German Expressionism can be seen in the works of the Norwegian painter **Edvard Munch**, 1863–1944, who expressed intense emotion in his "Frieze of Life," c.1890–1900.

Music

National styles developed in the works of composers like **Jean Sibelius**, 1865–1957, in Finland and **Isaac Albéniz**, 1860–1909, in Spain.

Science and Technology

Diphtheria antitoxin was isolated in 1892 by the German biologist **Paul Ehrlich**, 1854–1915.

★ Principal Events

In the victorious war against China, 1894–95, Japan gained Formosa and a free hand in Korea. The Powers' scramble for diplomatic and trading concessions in China began.
Sergei Witte, 1849–1915, reformed Russian finances and stimulated industrialization and eastward expansion, 1890s.
The Dreyfus case, 1894–99, revealed deep splits in French society between the liberal radicals and the Church and army.

The Americas

Wage reductions brought the violent Pullman Strike in Chicago, 1894, led by Socialist Eugene V. Debs, 1855–1926.

Religion and Philosophy

Herbert Spencer, 1820–1903, constructed and popularized a **comprehensive evolutionary theory** that saw all things as progressing from simplicity to complexity. His sociology, based on an analogy between societies and organisms, used the idea of the survival of the fittest.
F. H. Bradley, 1846–1924, was an English proponent of Hegel. He argued that an idea's truth depended on its coherence with the set of ideas comprising the Absolute.

Literature

Knut Hamsun, 1859–1952, a Norwegian, condemned an overemphasis on social issues.
The stories and poems of Rud-yard **Kipling,** 1865–1936, examined the relationship between British and Indian culture.
H. G. Wells pioneered science fiction in *The Time Machine.*

Art and Architecture

Art Nouveau, an international decorative style using flat, flowing, and tendrillike forms. was popularized in England by the graphics of **Aubrey Beardsley,** 1872–98, from 1893, and the buildings of **Victor Horta,** 1861–1947, in Belgium.
Gothic forms and wild extravagant decoration characterized the buildings of the Spanish architect **Antoni Gaudi,** 1856–1926. His church of **Sagrada Familia** in Barcelona, from 1893, is related to Art Nouveau.

Music

Claude-Achille Debussy, 1862–1918, brought Impressionism to music. His intricate tone color and continuous form utilized exquisite harmony and a whole tone scale.

Science and Technology

The cinema was founded with the development of a good cine camera and projector by the French inventors **Auguste Lumière,** 1862–1954, and his brother **Louis,** 1864–1948. The first public showing of their films took place in 1895.
X rays were discovered, 1895, by the German physicist **Wilhelm Roëntgen,** 1845–1923; they were soon used in medicine.

279

★ Principal Events

After the abortive Jameson raid, 1895–96, Britain faced a crisis with the Boer Republics.
On the Nile, Lord Kitchener, 1850–1916, began a campaign to reconquer the Sudan, 1896–98. In **Victoria's** Diamond Jubilee Year, 1897, British imperialism was at its peak. **France** aimed to consolidate the Saharan empire with a sphere of influence in Morocco.
Russia threatened China, where the Powers gained territory and concessions, 1897–98.

The Americas

The ''separate but equal'' doctrine was established by the Supreme Court, 1896, in *Plessy v. Ferguson*. The Yukon Territory had a gold rush, 1897–98.

⚗ Religion and Philosophy

Philosophical pragmatism was expounded by the American psychologist **William James,** 1842–1910, in *The Will to Believe*, 1897. He argued that a belief was true if its acceptance aided the solution of practical problems. **Emile Durkheim,** 1858–1917, stirred French opinion with his sociological study *Suicide*, 1897, which attempted to link positivist social ideas with an interest in morality, which he saw as the basis of society.

Literature

Russian realist drama reached its peak with the work of **Anton Chekhov,** 1860–1904, which had a huge effect on European drama, notably *Uncle Vanya* and *The Seagull*. Chekhov was also a masterly short story writer, able to convey pessimistic themes with a humorous twist.
The Greek poet Cavafy, 1863–1933, wrote about the ironies of man's existence.

Art and Architecture

The Vienna Sezession, set up to promote the Austrian form of Art Nouveau, 1897, was concerned mainly with interior design. **Gustav Klimt,** 1862–1918, was its leading exponent.
The English Vernacular style of domestic architecture pioneered by **C. A. Voysey,** 1857–1941, emphasized natural materials and solid construction and developed many of the designs which became part of a modern (non-historical) European style.

Music

The American John Sousa, 1854–1932, wrote superb **marches** for marine bands, including *The Stars and Stripes Forever*, 1897.

Science and Technology

Radioactivity was discovered, 1896, by the French physicist **Antoine Becquerel,** 1852–1908.
The diesel engine was invented by **Rudolf Diesel,** 1858–1913, and demonstrated in 1896.
The electron was discovered in 1897 by the British physicist **J. J. Thomson,** 1856–1940. Thomson detected electrons in cathode rays and reasoned that all atoms contain electrons.
Malaria was shown to be transmitted by the mosquito by the British physician **Sir Ronald Ross,** 1857–1932, in 1897.

1897-1900

Principal Events

In China, 1898, reactionary forces acted to stop the Westernizing **Hundred Days of Reform**, and an anti-foreign "Boxer" Rebellion, 1900, brought disruption and resulted in foreign intervention.
Britain became entangled in the Boer War (1899–1902).
Faced with depression the US raised its tariff wall, 1897, and joined in expansion overseas, fighting Spain, 1898, over **Cuba** and securing **Puerto Rico** and the **Philippines.**

The Americas

The **Spanish-American War**, 1898, triggered by the *Maine* sinking, brought new territories under US control. The Open Door Policy began in China, 1899.

Religion and Philosophy

Sigmund Freud, 1856–1939, elaborated the main tenets of psychoanalytic theory in *The Interpretation of Dreams*, 1900, developed in the course of clinical experience in Vienna. He divided the mind among the ego, id, and superego, and argued that psychological disorders stemmed from the repression of sexual urges in early life. His emphasis on the subconscious influenced later irrationalism.
H.S. Chamberlain, 1855–1927, spread racist ideas in Germany.

Literature

The height of the **Modernismo** movement in South America was realized in *Prosas Profanas* by the Nicaraguan poet **Rubén Darío**, 1867–1916.
The Generation of '98, a group of Spanish intellectuals, set out to counteract Spanish apathy and revitalize Spanish culture. The group included the poet, philosopher, and novelist **Miguel de Unamuno**, 1864–1936.

Art and Architecture

A large collection of **Benin art**, the first African art well known in Europe, was brought back by a punitive expedition in 1897.
The Chicago school of architecture pioneered a modern American public style, creating the skyscraper. The Schlesinger-Mayer store by **Louis Sullivan**, 1856–1924, begun in 1899, rose to nine floors and had detailing suggestive of Art Nouveau.

Music

Ragtime was played in the US in the 1890s by black pianists, notably by **Scott Joplin**, 1868–1917. The bright syncopation of the style overlaid European dance and march forms.

Science and Technology

The theoretical basis for space travel was provided by **Konstantin Tsiolkovsky**, 1857–1935.
Marie Curie, 1867–1934, working with her husband **Pierre**, discovered polonium and radium in 1898.
Viruses were discovered, 1898, by **Martinus Beijerinck**, 1851–1931.
Radioactivity was found to include alpha rays and beta rays, in 1899 by a British physicist, **Ernest Rutherford**, 1871–1937. In 1913 he would use the rays to penetrate the atom.

281

Europe Plunges into War 1900–1925

Bolshevik revolution: street scene in Petrograd, 1917

Suffragettes demanded the vote and got it.

Wright brothers made the first flight at Kitty Hawk.

Albert Einstein formulated the equivalence of mass and energy.

World War I: German skeleton in the trenches

Model T Ford was first off the assembly line.

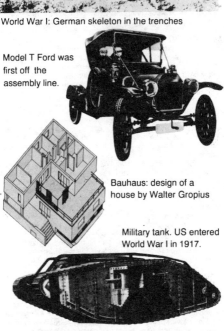

Bauhaus: design of a house by Walter Gropius

Military tank. US entered World War I in 1917.

Europe Plunges into War

Principal Events
World War I, arising from political and economic competition among the European Powers, dominated the period. In it, Europe suffered great losses in manpower and economic strength, while the United States and Japan won new political prestige. The need for organization on an unprecedented scale brought social and political upheaval in many countries. The old empires disappeared, leaving many new nationally based states, an embittered and dismembered Germany, and a communist Russia. Fear of socialism grew stronger and was linked with economic discontent to stimulate fascism in Italy.

The new location of power outside Europe and the rise of nationalism in India and China marked the transition from an international order based firmly on Europe to a world arena of politics, which would lead to widespread decolonization after World War I.

National Events
Technological advances affected labor and industry as well as business practices. The United States was fully recognized as a world power and fought in World War I. Social changes were underway, with temperance advocates, fundamentalist religious groups, and political reformers wielding influence.

Religion and Philosophy
The philosophies of Bergson, Croce, Dilthey, and Husserl, stressing intuition and immediate sympathy as the basic method of understanding, contributed to the development of a concept of the human sciences as distinct from the natural sciences.

Under their influence Max Weber investigated the motives as well as the causes of human action, notably the effect of religion on man's supposedly "rational" economic behavior. Russell and Wittgenstein, however, still took science and mathematics as the paradigm of knowledge in their work on the logical structure of language.

Psychoanalytic theory continued to explore the nature of the unconscious, but two of Freud's colleagues, Adler and Jung, criticized his insistence on the sexual basis of neuroses.

The Russian Revolution accentuated the socialist split between violence and the peaceful battle for working-class rights.

Literature
The need for new forms of self-expression able to encompass a growing awareness of the unconscious gave rise to many strong and individualistic movements in European literature. The surrealists evolved out of the symbolists, and their attempt to "trap" the subconscious in a spontaneous literary form broke down all restrictions of style.

284

In the English-speaking world a more formal school grew up with the modernist poets Pound and Eliot.

The German Expressionists were among the first to voice a lack of faith in society. Their prophecies were realized with World War I, the image of which haunted later writers.

Japan came into contact with Western realist and naturalist schools.

Art and Architecture

Traditional forms and concepts of art were dramatically broken down between 1900 and 1925 as a variety of alternative aesthetic principles developed. In particular Cubism attempted to break away from the conventions of perspective that had ruled European art since the Renaissance, while Dadaism and Russian Contructivism aimed to destroy the distinction between art and life.

In architecture, too, definitive new styles emerged in the US and Europe with the publication of Frank Lloyd Wright's early designs and the establishment of the Bauhaus, both emphasizing asymmetry and plain surfaces. The cinema transformed the whole scope of the visual arts, developing from the early popular experiments of 1900 to the politically motivated films of Eisenstein in Russia (where the Revolution stimulated artistic innovation in many fields), the dramas of Griffith, and the popular comedies of Chaplin.

Music

The Romantic tradition lingered on into the early 20th century. Popular music began to make its mark, and many serious composers sought a radical break with the past while others turned to folk music for their inspiration. The radicalism in the arts that followed World War I produced a variety of new musical techniques as well as altering aesthetic principles.

Science and technology

Einstein's theories of relativity and Planck's quantum theory revealed a new picture of the ultimate workings of nature. Although Newton's theories still proved accurate enough for most predictions, Einstein held that there was no absolute motion, motion in respect of empty space. His relativity principle stated that motion must always appear as the relative motion of one object with respect to another. It related time, mass, and length to velocity and mass to energy, and provided a theoretical basis for the development of nuclear physics.

Although World War I stimulated research and technology in Europe, the impetus for scientific advance shifted to America. The invention of the electronic valve, which allowed the development of the radio transmitter to proceed, and the development of powered flight speeded up intercontinental communications, and the introduction of mass-produced cars revolutionized private transport.

1900-1902

Principal Events

As France and Italy made an entente in 1902, weakening Italy's links with Germany, **Britain** emerged successfully from the **Boer War**, 1899–1902, and formed an alliance with **Japan**. This countered the Russian presence in **Manchuria** and encouraged Japan's expansionist ambitions in Asia.
The US Congress authorized the construction of the Panama Canal, appropriating $40,000,000, 1902.

The Americas

Pres. William McKinley, 1843–1901, was assassinated.
J. P. Morgan, 1837–1913, merged several firms into an industrial combination, US Steel.

Religion and Philosophy

Vilfredo Pareto, 1848–1923, an Italian and a posivitist, wrote *The Socialist Systems,* 1902, a refutation of Marxist economics and sociology. He accepted the existence of class conflict but saw the process Marx described as a series of progressive revolutions as no more than the successive replacement of ruling elites by each other.
The Pentecostal Movement began in America c.1902.

Literature

The Celtic literary Renaissance was a cultural reflection of Irish independence. Ancient legends were revived by **W. B. Yeats,** 1865–1939, **J. M. Synge,** 1871–1909, and Sean O'Casey, 1884–1964.

Revolution and man's capacity to withstand extremities dominate the novels of **Joseph Conrad,** 1857–1924, such as *Lord Jim,* 1900.

Art and Architecture

In Paris **Pablo Picasso,** 1881–1973, began his Blue period, 1901–04, and his Rose period, 1905, producing lyrical, conventionally representational paintings.
The Intimiste painters Edouard Vuillard, 1868–1940, and **Pierre Bonnard,** 1867–1947, used Impressionist techniques in domestic scenes after 1900.

Music

Richard Strauss, 1864–1949, continued the romantic tradition with operas and tone poems in a grand Wagnerian style.

Science and Technology

Blood groups were first distinguished c.1900.
Gamma rays were discovered in radioactivity, 1900, by **Paul Villard,** 1860–1934.
The quantum theory that energy consists of indivisible units was proposed by **Max Planck,** 1858–1947, in 1900.
Guglielmo Marconi, 1874–1937, was the first to transmit radio signals across the Atlantic, in 1901.
The fingerprint system was introduced in Britain, 1901.

Principal Events

The Entente Cordiale, 1904, of France and Britain settled the two powers' outstanding colonial disputes, especially in Egypt.
Japan firmly established her military power, defeating Russia in 1905 in Manchuria.
In defeat Russia was convulsed, 1905–06, with a revolution against tsarist autocracy by the industrial and intellectual classes.
Intervention by William II r.1888–1918, in Morocco, 1905, threatened French supremacy.

The Americas

Wilbur, 1867–1912, and **Orville**, 1871–1948, **Wright** flew the first airplane, 1903. The Industrial Workers of the World was founded by **Eugene V. Debs**, 1905.

Religion and Philosophy

Max Weber, 1864–1920, a German historian and sociologist, was concerned to combat the influential Marxist school of historical materialism. He opposed a simplistic belief in economic determinism and stressed the causal role of ideas in history.
In France, Maurice Barrès, 1862–1923, and **Charles Maurras**, 1868–1952, argued influentially for cultural unity, the supremacy of the state, and the primacy of the national interest.

Literature

Impressionism, a German literary style that set out to describe complex emotional states by using symbolic imagery, is used in *Das Stundenbuch*, 1905, by **Rainer Maria Rilke**, 1875–1926.
James Joyce, 1882–1941, was self-consciously Irish but hostile to the Celtic Renaissance.

Art and Architecture

Cubism, rejecting traditional methods of portraying reality, began in 1907 with **Picasso's** "Demoiselles d'Avignon," 1907. Other Cubists include **Juan Gris**, 1887–1927, **Robert Delaunay**, 1885–1941, **Fernand Léger**, 1881–1955, and **Georges Braque**, 1882–1963.
A reaction in architecture against Art Nouveau produced the simple rectangular forms seen in the **Convalescent Home**, Vienna, 1903, by **Josef Hoffmann**, 1870–1956.

Music

Giacomo Puccini, 1858–1924, brought Italian grand opera to a grand finale with such dramatic and melodic operas as *La Bohème*, 1896, *Tosca*, 1900, and *Madame Butterfly*, 1904.

Science and Technology

The first sustained flight by a power driven aircraft was made by **Wilbur** and **Orville Wright** in the US, 1903. **Detroit** became the center of the automobile industry, 1903.
The first electronic valve was made in 1904.
The special theory of relativity was published in 1905 by **Albert Einstein**, 1879–1955. ·

1905-1907

Principal Events

The Powers met at Algeciras in 1906 to settle the Moroccan question in favor of France.
Tsarist rule in Russia was reimposed with only minor constitutional reforms.
Russia and Japan reached agreement over China in 1907.
Britain, France, and Spain agreed to oppose German naval expansion in the Mediterranean.
An Anglo-Russian Convention covered Persia, Afghanistan, and Tibet and brought Britain into Europe's power blocs.

The Americas

Almost 700 people died in an earthquake and fire in San Francisco, 1906. In 1907, **George W. Goethals**, 1858–1928, directed Panama Canal construction.

Religion and Philosophy

Henri Bergson, 1859–1941, in *Creative Evolution*, 1907, stressed the importance of change through a creative life-force, in opposition to the static scientific view of nature. This view that intuition was superior to scientific or intellectual perception was echoed by **Wilhelm Dilthey**, 1833–1911, in Germany, to support an ethical relativism.
The Modernist Movement in Catholicism was condemned by Pope Pius X in 1907.

Literature

With the publication of *Kormi-chiye*, 1907, **Vyacheslav Ivanovich Ivanov**, 1866–1949, was acclaimed leader of the Russian Symbolist movement, which also included the poet **Alexander Blok**, 1880–1921.
Stefan George, 1868–1933, was influenced by Nietzsche in his desire to ennoble German culture with his esoteric poetry, such as *The Seventh Ring*, 1907.

Art and Architecture

The Fauvist period in painting, 1905–08, was characterized by the use of flat patterns and intense, unnatural colors. "Open Window, Collioure," 1905, by **Henri Matisse**, 1869–1954, is typical, as are the works from this period of **André Derain**, 1880–1954, **Maurice Vlaminck**, 1876–1958, and **Raoul Dufy**, 1877–1953.

Music

Blues grew steadily more popular in the early 20th century in the United States. Their cross rhythms and varying intonation brought great expression to the simple *aab* 12-bar form.

Science and Technology

The cloud chamber, used in detecting the paths of atomic particles, was perfected, 1906, by **Charles Wilson**, 1869–1959.
The third law of thermodynamics, that absolute zero cannot be attained, was put forward in 1906.
Emil Fischer, 1852–1919, showed in 1907 that proteins are composed of amino acids—a vital step in molecular biology.
The first helicopter flew, 1907.

Principal Events

Increasing Anglo-German competition was expressed in a race to build warships.
With Russian agreement, Austria annexed Bosnia-Herzegovina in 1908.
Nationalist unrest in Catalonia disrupted Spain, 1909.
The Powers intervened to prevent a Serbo-Austrian war.
India secured constitutional reforms in 1909.
The former Boer republics helped form a new dominion, the **Union of South Africa,** 1910.

The Americas

The Model T Ford, designed by **Henry Ford,** 1863–1947, was sold in 1908. It was the first automobile made on an assembly line.

Religion and Philosophy

The German historian Friedrich Meinecke, 1862–1954, looked for a meaning within the historical process itself, but sought to avoid cultural relativism. His *Cosmopolitanism and the Nation State,* 1908, acknowledged the significance of the unification of Germany but regretted the death of the culture that preceded it. **Georges Sorel,** 1847–1922, in *Reflections on Violence,* 1908, celebrated the use of violence and rejected all bourgeois values. He influenced Mussolini.

Literature

Modern Japanese fiction began after 1905 with a powerful naturalist school including **Shimazaki** **Toson,** 1872–1943, and **Tayama Katai. Mori Ogai,** 1862–1922, reacted against their obsession with squalor in *Vita Sexualis,* 1909.
The American **Jack London,** 1876–1916, was stirred by social injustices to write popular tales and political tracts.

Art and Architecture

In Germany the Expressionist painting of the **Die Brücke group,** 1905–13, distorted reality to produce a personal view of the world, depicting intense and painful emotions after the style of **Edvard Munch.** They were chiefly represented by **Emil Nolde,** 1867–1956.
The Italian Futurists produced work and manifestos that extolled the technological energy of modern life, from 1909:

Music

New Orleans became the cradle of **jazz** as ragtime bands, using instruments left over from the Civil War, took up improvisation and developed into small traditional jazz bands.

Science and Technology

Ammonia was synthesized in 1908, enabling Germany to produce the first high explosives.
Chromosomes were established as the carriers of heredity, 1909.
Bakelite, a synthetic polymer used for making electric plugs, was invented in 1909. Its success stimulated the development of plastics.
Combine harvesters were common in the US by 1910.
Louis Bleriot made his first flight in 1907 and flew across the English Channel, 1909.

1910-1912

★ Principal Events

In Mexico, Porfirio Díaz, *r.* 1877–80, 1884–1911, was overthrown, and the US intervened by occupying Veracruz. **The Triple Entente powers** of France, Russia, and Britain made military and naval agreements. After the 1911 Agadir incident when the Germans sent a gunboat to frighten the French, they countered German ambitions in Morocco.

A nationalist republic was set up in China in 1911 under **Sun Yat-sen**, 1866–1925.

The Americas

The Progressive party, advocating social reforms, was founded, 1912. The federal government increased its antitrust activities.

⚗ Religion and Philosophy

Sophisticated physics produced scientific theorists such as the Austrian **Ernst Mach**, 1838–1916, and the Frenchman **Henri Poincaré**, 1854–1912, who argued that unobservable entities such as atoms should be regarded only as useful postulates about material nature. **Phenomenology** was founded by the German philosopher **Edmund Husserl**, 1859–1938, who argued that true knowledge stemmed from the imaginative analysis of direct experience.

📖 Literature

The German Expressionists described visions of the collapse of society. **George Heym**, 1887–1912, prophesied a great war in *Umbra Vitae*, 1912, as did **George Trakl**, 1887–1914.

🏛 Art and Architecture

Analytical Cubism, 1910–12, concentrated on pure form, excluding interest in color. **Synthetic Cubism**, 1912–14, involved the construction of an image often by means of collage, such as the "Bottle of Anis del Mono," 1914, by **Juan Gris**. **Der Blaue Reiter** group of Expressionist painters, 1911–14, used color and abstract forms to convey spiritual realities and included **Wassily Kandinsky**, 1866–1944, and **Paul Klee**, 1879–1940.

🎵 Music

The Ballets Russes of **Sergei Diaghilev**, 1872–1929, commissioned major works, such as **Igor Stravinsky's** *Petrushka*, 1911, and **Maurice Ravel's** *Daphnis and Chloe*, 1912.

⚛ Science and Technology

Electrical superconductivity was discovered in 1911. **Nuclear theory**, that the atom contains a central nucleus, was announced by **Lord Rutherford**, 1871–1937, in 1911, in England.

Vitamins were recognized as essential to health in 1906; their classification in 1911 stimulated dietary studies.

Continental drift, the theory that the continents shift, was first proposed in 1912.

Cellophane was first manufactured in 1912.

★ Principal Events

Austria's Archduke Franz Ferdinand, 1863–1914, was assassinated in June 1914 by Serbian nationalists, setting off events leading to world war.
By 1915 Germany and Austria, with Turkey and Bulgaria, were fighting against the Entente allies, with Italy and Japan.
Military operations extended from the main "front" in France and Belgium to the Russian plains, the Balkans, the Middle East, and the German colonies in Africa.

The Americas

The Panama Canal was officially opened in 1914, while World War I began in Europe. A German submarine torpedoed the *Lusitania*, 1915, with 128 US deaths.

♦ Religion and Philosophy

Bertrand Russell, 1872–1970, the English philosopher and mathematician, applied empiricist principles to language, which he claimed to be constructed solely from sensory ideas and logic. In *Principia Mathematica*, 1910–13, he attempted, with **A. N. Whitehead**, 1861–1947, to derive mathematics from the axioms of logic.
Opposition to the war led **Rosa Luxemburg**, 1871–1919, to found the left wing Spartacist party in Germany.

📕 Literature

Guillaume Apollinaire, 1880–1918, dominated the surrealist and avant-garde movements in Paris from 1913 until his death. He used random modes of expression in drama and initiated concrete poetry.
Ezra Pound, 1885–1972, worked on his *Cantos* from 1914 until his death. His allusive, erudite style influenced many English poets.

🏛 Art and Architecture

Russian Constructivism, 1913–mid-20s, was initiated by **Vladimir Tatlin**, 1885–1953, and exploited the concept of Synthetic Cubism. Its emphasis was on abstract structures made of a variety of materials. Tatlin's "Constructions," 1913–14, were made of wood, metal, and glass.
The first long feature films included the Italian *Cabiria*, 1914, and *The Birth of a Nation*, 1915, a drama about the US Civil War, directed by **D. W. Griffith**, 1880–1948.

🎵 Music

The Rite of Spring, 1913, by **Stravinsky**, 1882–1971, gave new emphasis to the role of rhythm in serious music, using irregular meter and highly varied motifs.

⚛ Science and Technology

The proton was recognized as the nucleus of the hydrogen atom by Lord Rutherford, in 1913.
Niels Bohr, 1885–1962, showed, 1913, how changes in the electron orbits of the atom produce energy.
The Geiger counter was used to measure radioactivity, 1913.
Atomic numbers were determined by an X-ray method discovered in 1914.
The life cycle of stars was determined by work done in 1914.
Stainless steel was made in Germany from 1914.

1915-1917

★ Principal Events

Germany started a blockade of British shipping. The main naval battle at Jutland, 1916, was inconclusive. Germany's unrestricted submarine warfare (leading to the sinking of the **Lusitania** in 1915) provoked the US to enter the war, 1917.

The strain of war brought revolution to Russia in 1917. The tsar abdicated, and **Bolshevik** forces led by **Lenin**, 1870–1924, won power and withdrew Russia from the war, after defeating the liberal government.

The Americas

US troops fought in the Mexican Border Campaign, 1916–17. In 1917 the United States entered World War I, and the Selective Service Act was passed.

Religion and Philosophy

V. I. Lenin, 1870–1924, the Russian politician, argued in *The State and Revolution*, 1917, for a party of professional revolutionaries.

Freud's emphasis on the sexual basis of psychiatric disorders led to the defection of two of his followers, **Carl Jung**, 1875–1961, and **Alfred Adler**, 1870–1937. Jung developed a theory of the collective unconscious, while Adler tried to derive a psychology from man's tendency to strive for perfection.

Literature

The "literary revolution" in China in 1917 used the vernacular language in literature.

The English war poets voiced their horror of mass warfare. **Rupert Brooke**, 1887–1915, and **Wilfred Owen**, 1893–1918, died while on duty. **Robert Graves**, 1895–1985, and **Siegfried Sassoon**, 1886–1967, also wrote about the period, both in prose and verse.

Art and Architecture

The Dadaist movement developed in Zurich in 1916 in the work of **Jean (Hans) Arp**, 1887–1966, and **Tristan Tzara**, 1896–1963. It was deliberately "anti-art" and aimed to outrage and scandalize a complacent society. Its chief exponent was **Marcel Duchamp**, 1887–1968, whose "Fountain," 1917, consisted of a urinal.

The films of **Charlie Chaplin**, 1889–1977, including *The Tramp*, 1915, won international acclaim.

Music

Charles Ives, 1874–1954, became the first truly original US composer, working in several keys and rhythms at once, in many works such as his *Concord Sonata*, 1909–15.

Science and Technology

The general theory of relativity was published by Einstein in 1915. The theory explains how gravity affects light and how mass distorts space.

World War I stimulated technological advance on both sides, particularly in weaponry and transport.

Tractors, introduced by Ford in 1915, used the Diesel engine and led to greatly increased agricultural efficiency in the industrialized countries.

Principal Events

Britain, France, and the US defeated Germany in 1918. In the **Versailles Treaty**, 1919, inspired by the democratic ideals of **Woodrow Wilson**, 1856–1924, the US president, new ethnic Balkan states were established, and Turkey was partitioned. **War** guilt and indemnity were assigned to Germany, where an abortive revolution disrupted the new republic, 1919.
Wilson's League of Nations was inaugurated in 1919 but without US participation.

The Americas

Armistice ended World War I, 1918, and the United States, led by **Pres. Woodrow Wilson**, played a prominent role at the Versailles Peace Conference, 1919.

Religion and Philosophy

The British anthropologist Malinowski, 1884–1942, developed **functionalism**, 1914–18, in anthropology, studying social phenomena in terms of their function within an integrated social structure, in opposition to evolutionist anthropology.
Oswald Spengler, 1880–1936, published *The Decline of the West*, 1918–22, claiming that Western civilization had ceased to be "creative" and had become concerned only with materialism.

Literature

The Hindu writer **Rabindranath Tagore**, 1861–1941, translated the mystical *Gitanjali*.

Muhammed Iqbal, 1873–1938, wrote in Urdu and Persian and voiced a growing resentment against the West, in India.
André Gide, 1869–1951, kept his *Journals* from 1889–1949.
Hermann Hesse, 1877–1962, wrote *Demian*, 1919.

Art and Architecture

The de Stijl group founded in Holland by **Theo van Doesburg**, 1883–1931, and **Piet Mondrian**, 1872–1944, developed their art and architecture based on spatial relationships. They used straight lines, right angles, and primary colors.
The Bauhaus school of architecture, design, and craftsmanship was founded in Germany in 1919 by **Walter Gropius**, 1883–1969. It attempted to reconcile art and design with industrial techniques.

Music

Harmony reached a peak of complexity with **Stravinsky**, who worked in several keys simultaneously, and then split asunder in the keyless music of **Arnold Schoenberg** and **Béla Bartók**.

Science and Technology

The first transatlantic flight was made, 1919, by the British aviators **Alcock and Brown**. The flight lasted almost 165 1/2 hours.
The first mass spectrograph was developed in 1919.
The first commercial airplane service, between London and Paris, was set up, 1919.

1920-1922

★ Principal Events

In Russia, reactionary forces with allied aid tried unsuccessfully to defeat the Bolsheviks. **Germany**, struggling against economic chaos after the loss of the major industrial centers, secured Soviet friendship in the **Treaty of Rapallo, 1922**. **Japan**, which had been granted Germany's rights in China by the Versailles Treaty, made peace with China, 1922.
Benito Mussolini, 1883–1945, established fascist power in Italy in 1922.

The Americas

In 1920 the 19th Amendment was ratified, giving women the vote, and the 18th Amendment, ratified in 1919, went into effect, establishing Prohibition.

🕯 Religion and Philosophy

The *Tractatus Logico-Philosophicus* of **Ludwig Wittgenstein**, 1889–1951, an Austrian living in London, was published in 1921; it argued that philosophy was an analytic, not a speculative, subject.
Aimee Semple McPherson, 1890–1944, built the Angelus Temple in Los Angeles in 1922 and preached the religion of the foursquare gospel.

📖 Literature

The stream-of-consciousness technique was used by **Marcel Proust**, 1871–1922, to evoke the past in the long series of novels *À La Recherche du Temps Perdu*, 1913–27, and by

James Joyce, 1882–1941, in *Ulysses*, 1922. This and *Finnegan's Wake*, 1939, are highly experimental, original, and questioning works.

🐝 Art and Architecture

In France **Fernand Léger's** paintings reflected contemporary interest in machinery. His "Three Women," 1921, reduces figures to machinelike forms and uses metallic colors.
Frank Lloyd Wright, 1869–1959, the greatest and most influential of US architects, designed the Imperial Hotel, Tokyo, 1919–22, using an entirely new anti-earthquake construction.

🎵 Music

Bartók, 1881–1945, created a style marked by extreme dissonance and elegant melody, particularly in his six quartets, 1907–39. He collected and studied Hungarian folk music.

⚛ Science and Technology

Diesel locomotives and rail cars came into use *c.*1920. The growing use of internal combustion engines led to a decline in the supremacy of coal as the major industrial fuel after 1910.
Radio broadcasting on a regular basis began in the United States in 1920.
Insulin, a hormone, was isolated in 1922 and first used in the treatment of diabetes.
The teleprinter was developed in 1921, greatly speeding the transmission of long distance information.

294

Principal Events

Germany countered France's occupation of the Ruhr, 1923–25, with passive resistance and suffered massive inflation, which destroyed the economic strength of the middle classes. **The Dawes plan**, 1924, eased the repayment schedule for German war reparations. **Kemal Ataturk**, 1881–1938, president of the new Turkish republic, began modernization of Turkish society, 1923. **The American economy** was booming.

The Americas

Scandals marked the administration of **Pres. Warren G. Harding**, 1865–1923. In Tennessee, **John Scopes**, 1900–70, was convicted of teaching evolution.

Religion and Philosophy

The Hungarian **Gyorgy Lukacs**, 1885–1971, a Marxist influenced by Hegel's idealism, wrote of the role of creative awareness in the development of revolutionary consciousness, in *History and Class-consciousness*, 1923.
Benedetto Croce, 1866–1952, a historian who argued that the past could be understood only when seen in relation to current problems, became the spokesman for the opposition to Fascism in Italy after 1923.

Literature

Luigi Pirandello, 1867–1936, reflected the spiritual confusion of the postwar years in his play *Six Characters in Search of an Author*, 1921.
T. S. Eliot, 1888–1965, wrote *The Waste Land*, 1922, a dense and highly literary meditation on the situation of modern man.
Franz Kafka, 1883–1924, described man's spiritual bereavement in *The Trial*, 1925.

Art and Architecture

Architects in Europe such as **Walter Gropius, Mies van der Rohe**, 1886–1969, and **Le Corbusier**, 1887–1965, convinced of the need for streamlined, functional buildings, used the new media of concrete and glass to achieve a modern style epitomized in Gropius' design for the **Bauhaus**, 1925–26.
The Russian Revolution stimulated experimental cinema, led by **Sergei Eisenstein**, 1898–1948, whose *Battleship Potemkin*, 1925, preached socialism.

Music

Twelve-note or serial music, created in 1924 by **Schoenberg**, 1874–1951, was based on an arbitrarily ordered series or row using the 12 notes of the chromatic (half-tone) scale.

Science and Technology

Radioactive tracers, used for the determination of many biological reactions, were developed in 1923.
Electrons were shown to behave as waves as well as particles, in 1922–24. This discovery made possible the invention of the electron microscope, in 1932.
External spiral galaxies were found by Edwin Hubble, 1923.
Clarence Birdseye, 1886–1956, experimented with quick-frozen foods commercially, 1924.

From Depression to Recovery 1925–1950

Churchill, Roosevelt, and Stalin: The English, American, and Russian leaders met at Yalta.

Messerschmidt-262: Germany waged a fierce air-attack against the Allies.

Victims of Nazi concentration camps

America in depression:
Line outside a soup
kitchen in Chicago, 1930.

Atomic destruction: a test

LA GARRA DEL INVASOR ITALIANO PRETENDE ESCLAVIZARNOS

Spanish Civil War poster
warns against "the claws
of invaders."

Gandhi in Calcutta, 1925.
He emphasized non-
violent revolution.

From Depression to Recovery

Principal Events
The legacy of mistrust and depression following World War I brought a worldwide economic crisis at the end of the 1920s. The stronger industrial powers survived with the aid of new economic and social policies, but in Germany, where the obligation to pay war debts exacerbated the effects of national defeat, the Nazi regime, whose militarist ambitions in Europe would help to precipitate World War II, took power.

In the USSR a policy of forced industrialization was pursued under Stalin, destroying many of the ideals of the Revolution, while the basis for a communist China was laid after a long civil war. India won its independence, but only at the cost of partition.

World War II left Europe shattered and weak and Germany divided, with the capitalist and socialist blocs locked in a continuing, though ostensibly peaceful, struggle for power.

National Events
The Wall Street crash of 1929 had a catastrophic effect on the United States. The economy came to a virtual halt, with unprecedented unemployment. The next decade was then devoted to recovery. US attention then turned to Europe and the Pacific during World War II. Nuclear weapons changed the course of the war.

Religion and Philosophy
Political thought was dominated by the conflict between the democratic ideal and its opponents on the left and right. Marxist political theory developed divergent trends as the Russian and Chinese revolutions took their course, but its influence in the West declined as supporters of liberalism rallied to oppose fascism, with its ideological roots in 19th-century irrationalism. A new democratic philosophy, sustained by Keynes' economic theories of consumer prosperity, became linked with attempts to control political violence on a worldwide scale, marked by the founding of the United Nations.

The Christian Church came face to face with growing secularization in the industrialized countries and the problems of an emergent Third World.

Philosophy remained split between those primarily studying human consciousness and those who used a scientific model to understand reality.

Literature
The insistent excavation of personal experience that had begun with the Romantics and reached a peak with the stream-of-consciousness writings of Proust and Joyce found new exponents in Virginia Woolf and the more consciously Freudian Surrealists. Much European writing of the interwar period, however, reflected a need to grasp the social issues of the time. Some, such as Camus, accepted the fact of social

298

commitment while admitting the ultimate meaninglessness of existence. Others like Brecht developed new artistic forms to embody their political vision with a lesser emphasis on the individual. In the Third World, too, where writers were inspired by the ideal of national independence, a new, more confident literature emerged.

Art and Architecture

In Europe before World War II there was increasing integration among art forms. Furniture design, painting, and architecture were developed by the de Stijl and Bauhaus groups. Formal developments in painting also affected architecture. By 1932 the new International Style had come into existence. The first Surrealist manifesto in 1924, with its emphasis on exploration of the unconscious, represented the culmination of the avant-garde movement which linked radical artistic and political ideas.

Many of the artistic movements of the postwar period found expression in the cinema, but the depression caused the collapse of the film industries of many European countries and introduced a period of Hollywood supremacy based on large studio organizations, which had the effect of suppressing much individual talent, and leading to the development of styles suited to a mass market that had little contact with the traditional arts.

Music

Serious music split into several mutually exclusive schools, most of which attracted few listeners or performers in spite of the spread of the radio and phonograph. However, these devices did help to broaden the audience for popular music, which, in various jazz forms and "musicals," flourished widely.

Science and Technology

Economic depression and war hindered some areas of science while advancing others. In the West, steelmaking, engineering, and agricultural production fell during the thirties, but falling prices stimulated consumer industries, and aviation, radio, the car industry, and artificial fibers continued to develop. The USSR, too, was industrializing fast.

With the rise of Hitler, many nuclear physicists fled to America, where their research insured that Germany's supremacy in physics was lost and that the Nazis would not be the first to possess nuclear weapons.

World War II made great use of science, both to destroy and to save lives. Electronics, radar, nuclear technology, jet aviation, and antibiotics were all products of the war.

In Britain important work was done in astronomy, exploring the implications of Einstein's theories to produce conflicting concepts of the origin of the universe.

Principal Events

Chiang Kai-shek, 1887–1975, gained increasing control of the Kuomintang (nationalist party) in China. He captured Peking and unified the country, 1928, against Japanese expansion.
Germany joined the League of Nations, 1926, which hoped to bring peace by disarmament.
Fascist rule in Italy became increasingly authoritarian.
After Lenin's death, 1924, **Joseph Stalin**, 1879–1953, would begin forcible industrialization in Russia, 1928.

The Americas

Charles Lindbergh, 1902–74, in 1927 landed his monoplane *The Spirit of St Louis* in Paris, completing the first transatlantic solo flight.

Religion and Philosophy

The American J. B. Watson, 1878–1958, developed behaviorist psychology in *Behaviorism*, 1925, seeking to explain behavior wholly in terms of responses to external stimuli.
In **Mein Kampf**, 1925–27, Hitler drew upon the ideas of Gobineau, 1816–82, who argued that the development of a civilization depends on racial superiority and purity, and requires military aggression. Hitler condemned democracy as based on invalid egalitarianism.

Literature

A major writer who met the requirements of socialist realism was **Mikhail Sholokhov**, 1905–84, in his *Tales from the Don*, 1925.

The Bloomsbury Group in London included the novelists **E. M. Forster**, 1879–1970, and **Virginia Woolf**, 1882–1941, who used a personal style of imagery in *To the Lighthouse*, 1927.

Art and Architecture

Expressionist techniques were used by **Chaim Soutine**, 1893–1943, in "Page Boy at Maxim's," 1927, and by **Marc Chagall**, 1889–1985, in "Russian Wedding," 1925.
Expressionist cinema was developed by **Fritz Lang**, 1890–1976, in his vision of the future, *Metropolis*, 1926, while **Dali** explored surrealist cinema in *Le Chien Andalou*, 1928. *The Jazz Singer*, 1927, was the first talking picture.

Music

An English school, including **Frederick Delius**, 1862–1934, **Gustav Holst**, 1874–1934, and **Vaughan Williams**, 1872–1958, produced pastoral music after **Edward Elgar**, 1857–1934.

Science and Technology

Modern sound recording began with electric recording in 1925.
Liquid fuel rockets were first tested in America in 1926.
Wave mechanics, describing the wave motion of electrons, was founded by **Erwin Schrödinger**, 1887–1961, in 1926.
The Heisenberg uncertainty principle, that every observation has a degree of probability, was proposed in 1927.
The big bang theory of the origin of the universe was first put forward in 1927, by **Abbé Lemaitre**, 1894–1966.

Principal Events

The Kellogg-Briand Pact was signed by 23 powers in 1928 to outlaw war.

The last allied forces left the Rhineland, 1929.

Leon Trotsky, 1879–1940, was exiled from Russia, 1929.

The Wall Street Crash, 1929, led to business depression in America, causing economic recession throughout Europe and a rise in left-wing activity.

Gandhi, 1869–1948, began a civil disobedience campaign against British rule in India.

The Americas

A **financial panic** in 1929 resulted in a loss of $30,000,000,000 in stock values. The Wall Street crash led to unemployment and bank failures.

Religion and Philosophy

Existentialism was developed in Germany from Husserl's phenomenological ideas by **Martin Heidegger**, 1889–1976, who was appointed professor of philosophy at Freiburg in 1928. He argued that authentic human existence consists in not being subordinated to the external world.

The word apartheid was first used to describe racial segregation in South Africa in 1929.

Literature

D. H. Lawrence, 1885–1930, challenged the taboos of class and sex in novels such as *Lady Chatterley's Lover*. **John Cowper Powys**, 1872–1963, studied

man in his environment, while **Malcolm Lowry**, 1909–57, wrote of his experiences in Mexico.

A group of left-wing poets in London in the 20s included **W. H. Auden**, 1907–73, and **Stephen Spender**, 1909–

Art and Architecture

Surrealism, founded in Paris, explored the reality of the subconscious. Its leading exponent was **Salvador Dali**, 1904–89, whose "illuminated Pleasures," 1929, shows objects taken out of context and replaced in fantastic juxtapositions. Other important artists were **René Magritte**, 1898–1967, **Giorgio de Chirico**, 1888–1978, **Joan Miró**, 1893–1983, and **Max Ernst**, 1891–1976. **Ernst** and **André Masson**, 1896–1987, practiced automatism, a free-brush style.

Music

Louis Armstrong, 1900–71, created a solo style in jazz with his innovative trumpet improvisations of 1925–30.

Duke Ellington, 1899–1974, began an orchestral style in jazz.

Science and Technology

The anti-bacterial activity of penicillium mold was discovered, 1928, by **Alexander Fleming**, 1881–1955, but it was not made stable enough for medical use until 1943.

John Logie Baird invented a high speed mechanical scanning system, 1928, which led to the development of television.

The distance of galaxies was related to their speed of recession as measured by the red shift, 1929, by **Edwin Hubble** 1889–1953.

Principal Events

The Round Table Conferences on India failed to satisfy nationalist demands, 1930.
The Hoover moratorium on war debts helped Europe to survive the depression, 1931, but the economic slump in Germany brought fighting between left- and right-wing groups.
Japan occupied Manchuria, 1931, after fears that trading with China would be cut.
A republic was set up in Spain, 1931, dominated by liberals and socialists.

The Americas

World War I veterans, numbering 17,000, converged on the capital to demand cash payment of bonuses. The "Bonus Army" was dispersed, 1932.

Religion and Philosophy

J. M. Keynes, 1883–1946, overthrew the neo-classical orthodoxy in economics with two books, *Treatise on Money*, 1930, and *The General Theory*, 1936. He stated that market forces that lowered wage rates would not cure economic depressions; production and investment would only increase if spending by consumers, business, and government went up. His theory influenced the New Deal and economic planning in the West until the 1970s.

Literature

A forerunner of the **Theater of the Absurd,** Luigi Pirandello, 1867–1936, explored the theme of mutual incomprehension. **American writing** was richly varied, ranging from the southern novels of **William Faulkner,** 1897–1962, whose *Light in August* appeared 1932, to *The Grapes of Wrath* by **John Steinbeck,** 1902–68, treating the hardship of the depression.

Art and Architecture

The International Style in architecture, 1932, recognized a new and independent style that had emerged in the twenties. This was typified in the Villa Savoye, 1928–31, by **Le Corbusier,** with its white rectangular exterior and horizontal windows.
The individual history of the French painter **Georges Rouault,** 1871–1958, whose religious works achieve a stained glass quality, can be seen in his "Christ Mocked by Soldiers," 1932.

Music

Musical theater reached a peak of sophistication in the United States, with lavish shows and beautiful songs, notably by **George Gershwin,** 1898–1937, in *Porgy and Bess,* 1935.

Science and Technology

The cyclotron and other circular particle accelerators were developed from a working model made in America, c.1930.
Wallace Carothers, 1896–1937, invented **nylon** in 1931.
Radio astronomy began in 1931 with the detection of radio signals from outer space.
Deuterium, heavy hydrogen, was discovered in 1931.
The first nuclear reaction using an accelerator was activated in 1932.
Neutrons were discovered, 1932.

Principal Events

Japan left the League of Nations, 1933, after condemnation of her action in Manchuria.
Adolf Hitler, 1889–1945, elected German chancellor, set up a Nazi dictatorship, 1933.
Franklin D. Roosevelt, 1882–1945, introduced a New Deal of social and economic reforms in the US to end the slump, 1933.
Stalin began a massive purge of Russian party officials, 1935.
Civil war in China between the left wing and nationalists led to **the Long March**, 1934–35.

The Americas

Pres. Franklin D. Roosevelt, 1882–1945, inaugurated in 1933 his New Deal, legislation designed to bring relief to every phase of the economy.

Religion and Philosophy

Leon Trotsky, 1879–1940, a Russian Marxist, argued for permanent revolution in his *History of the Russian Revolution*, 1932–33. He claimed that socialism in Russia could not survive unless revolutions also took place in more advanced countries, and opposed Stalin's doctrine of socialism in one country.
Gandhi organized *satyagraha* (truth force) campaigns to foster Indian nationalism by nonviolence and emphasized the values of village life.

Literature

"The Lost Generation," a group of Americans in Paris in the 1920s and 1930s, included **F. Scott Fitzgerald**, 1886–1940, whose *Tender is the Night* was an elegy for the American Dream; the masculine **Ernest Hemingway**, 1899–1961; **Gertrude Stein**, 1874–1946, an influential experimentalist; and the less typical **Henry Miller**, 1891–1980.

Art and Architecture

In Germany anti-Nazi artistic expressions by artists such as **Otto Dix**, 1891–1969, **Georg Grosz**, 1893–1959, **Max Beckmann**, 1884–1950, and **Oskar Kokoschka**, 1886–1980, resulted in either suppression or exile for the artists concerned. **Socialist Realism** was officially adopted in the USSR under Stalin in 1934, using an explicit, academic style in order to convey clearly the message of the dignity of the working classes.

Music

Ionisation, 1931, by **Edgard Varèse**, 1885–1965, written solely for percussion instruments, showed that a piece of serious music could be constructed successfully using rhythm only.

Science and Technology

Skyscraper building in the US was interrupted by the depression of the 1930s.
The first radioisotopes were prepared by **Frédéric Joliot-Curie**, 1900–58, and his wife **Irène**, 1897–1956, in 1934.
The meson, a sub-atomic particle, was predicted in 1935.

303

★ Principal Events

The governmental reforms of 1935 in India again fell short of nationalist demands.

Mussolini invaded Abyssinia in 1935 to satisfy fascist imperial ambitions. The League failed to intervene effectively. **Hitler** remilitarized the Rhineland, 1936, and Mussolini proclaimed the **Rome-Berlin axis.** A right-wing coup after the Popular Front won the elections led to civil war in Spain, 1936–39.

The Japanese began their attack on China in 1937.

The Americas

Congress passed the Social Security Act, 1935, to provide retirement benefits. Public works projects were a major part of the New Deal.

Religion and Philosophy

The Vienna Circle, a group of philosophers who met there, 1922–36, including **Moritz Schlick,** 1882–1936, and **Rudolf Carnap,** formulated logical positivism, an empiricist philosophy of language according to which only statements that could be verified were meaningful.

Pope Pius XI, r.1922–39, condemned fascism, 1931, and communism, 1937. He adopted a friendly attitude to Protestant liberalism, although opposing *laissez-faire* social policies.

Literature

Spanish folk traditions and modern cruelty were studied by **Frederico García Lorca,** 1898–1936.

In Germany an aesthetic and idealist style was used by **Thomas Mann,** 1875–1955. His *Joseph and his Brothers,* 1933–43, explores the theme of exile.

A sense of cultural collapse inspired **Robert Musil,** 1880–1942, to write his Viennese novel *The Man Without Qualities.*

Art and Architecture

Ben Nicholson, 1894–1982, one of Britain's leading abstract artists, achieved worldwide recognition in the Cubist and Abstract Art exhibition, New York, 1936. The rectangular, textured "White Relief," 1936, is typical of his style at this time.

Frank Lloyd Wright, the American architect, produced two outstanding buildings—his famous **Falling Water,** Bear Run, Pa., 1936–37, and the **Johnson Wax administrative buildings,** Racine, Wis., 1936–49.

Music

The Neoclassic movement reinterpreted classical form in modern sound. Initiated by **Stravinsky,** the style attracted **Sergei Prokofiev,** 1891–1953, and **Paul Hindemith,** 1895–1963.

Science and Technology

New industries were developed to escape the depression. In Britain and the US, the new interest in consumer expenditure, combined with the completion of the electricity supply, led to the growth of consumer durable industries, while in Germany road building was encouraged.

The citric acid cycle, which occurs in bodily energy production, was found in 1937.

Experiments made by **Robert Watson-Watt,** 1892–1973, after 1935 led to radar's invention.

Principal Events

Germany annexed Austria, 1938.
Europe's powers met at **Munich,**
1938, to discuss German claims
in Czechoslovakia, but failed to
restrain Hitler. **German threats**
to take Danzig in Poland resulted
in Anglo-French intervention. **A
European war** began in Sept.
1939.
Francisco Franco, 1892–1975,
became dictator of Spain after
defeating the Republicans.
Japan had conquered most of
eastern China by 1939.
Germany took France in 1940.

The Americas

President Roosevelt was unsuccessful in an attempt to expand
the number of Supreme Court
justices, 1937.

Religion and Philosophy

Mao Tse-tung, 1893–1976,
adapted Marxism-Leninism to
Chinese conditions, and argued
that the peasantry, as well as the
industrial proletariat, could succeed in making a socialist revolution. Mao later maintained that
socialism could only be reached
by a permanent revolution to
prevent the development of privilege. His studies in guerrilla
warfare were important to his
political success and influenced
later Third World revolutionaries.

Literature

Experimental epic theater was
pioneered by the German Marxist
Bertolt Brecht, 1898–1956.
Many foreign writers fought in
the Spanish Civil War. **George
Orwell,** 1903–50, described it
in *Homage to Catalonia,* 1939.
Important English novelists deal-
ing with traditional themes were
Graham Greene, 1904–
Aldous Huxley, 1894–1963, and
Evelyn Waugh, 1903–66.

Art and Architecture

One of **Picasso's finest paintings,**
"Guernica," 1937, was prompted
by the destruction of the Basque
town by German bombers during
the Spanish Civil War.
Hollywood won international
supremacy in filmmaking during
the Depression, using enormous
casts in lavish productions such
as *Gone with the Wind,* 1939.

Music

Serial music developed further
with the work of **Alban Berg,**
1885–1935, and **Anton von
Webern,** 1883–1945, eventually
submitting all musical elements
to mathematical procedures.

Science and Technology

The Graf Zeppelin (LZ 130) was
built in 1938, the largest airship
to be made. It ran on a regular
transatlantic service.
The Volkswagen "Beetle," designed by **Porsche** to Hitler's
requirements, was built, 1938.
Nuclear fission, developed as a
source of energy in the US, was
first achieved in 1939.
Einstein told the US president of
the possibility of making an
atomic bomb, 1939, to preempt
German research.
Food-dehydration by vacuum-
contact drying was developed.

Principal Events

Germany waged a lightning war in the West, but failed to invade or destroy Britain, which fought at sea and in the air, and opposed Italy in North Africa.

In June 1941, Germany invaded Russia and drove the Red Army back to Moscow.

Japanese aggression in the Pacific, culminating in the attack on **Pearl Harbor**, Hawaii, 1941, brought the US into the war.

Hitler began the systematic genocide of the Jews, 1941.

 **The Americas**

The United States entered the war after Pearl Harbor, Dec. 7, 1941. American-British war aims were defined by the Atlantic Charter, 1941.

 Religion and Philosophy

Phenomenology was developed in France by **Maurice Merleau-Ponty**, 1908–61, in *The Structure of Behavior*, 1942.

Oxfam was founded, 1942, to combat Third World poverty.

Dietrich Bonhoeffer, 1906–45, a German Protestant, argued that God is dead and sought a conception of Christianity relevant to a secular society.

 Literature

The "negritude" movement, calling for black cultural identity, was initiated by **Leopold Senghor**, 1906–

Serious native American drama was created by **Eugene O'Neill**, 1888–1953, and **Tennessee Williams**, 1911–83, who explored the frustrations of urban society. The plays of **Arthur Miller**, 1915–   , deal with individual moral and political responsibility.

 Art and Architecture

American artists turned increasingly to the depiction of provincial life in a realistic style. "Nighthawks," 1942, by **Edward Hopper**, 1882–1967, records with formal precision the isolation of a city at night.

Hollywood cinema escaped the limitations of its genres (westerns, gangster films, and love stories) with *Citizen Kane*, 1941, directed by **Orson Welles**, 1915–85, and *The Grapes of Wrath*, 1940, by **John Ford**, 1895–1973.

 Music

The swing era, 1935–45, dominated the popular music interest in the US, featuring such big bands as **Benny Goodman's**, playing highly arranged jazz with an energetic beat.

 Science and Technology

Plutonium, the first artificial element, was made, 1940.

The first jet-powered aircraft flew in 1941, using an engine made by **Frank Whittle**, 1907–

The first nuclear reactor was built in 1942 in Chicago.

The German development of the **V2 rocket-bomb**, 1942, provided the basis for future rocket development. The war also brought improvements in electronics and medical equipment.

Principal Events

In 1943 Russia stopped the Germans at Stalingrad, and Anglo-American forces took north Africa and invaded Italy.

Guerrilla action, especially in Yugoslavia and France, weakened Nazi control.

The invasion of Normandy by Britain and US in June 1944 opened a "second front," and Allied forces from east and west met on the Elbe in April 1945.

The Allies agreed on Soviet and Western spheres of influence at Yalta in 1945.

The Americas

.n July 1945, an atomic bomb was tested at Alamogordo, N.M. In August, US pilots dropped atomic bombs on Hiroshima and Nagasaki, Japan.

Religion and Philosophy

Jean-Paul Sartre, 1905–1980, in *Being and Nothingness*, 1943, advanced the Existentialist claim that authentic existence requires the individual exercise of free choice.

Karl Popper, 1902–1980, an Austrian living in England, wrote *The Open Society and its Enemies*, 1944. He attacked the belief that there are general laws in history, which he saw as leading to totalitarian politics.

Literature

Salvatore Quasimodo, 1901–68, opposed fascism in Italy in lyrical symbolist poetry.

The Makioka Sisters, 1943–48,

by Tanizaki Junichiro, 1886–1965, owes much to Western realism.

Latin American literature flourished with the "poetry for simple people" of the Chilean Pablo Neruda, 1904–73, and the stories of Jorge Luis Borges.

Art and Architecture

Official war artists in Britain, such as Graham Sutherland, 1903–1980, and John Piper, 1903– , recorded the devastating effects of the bombings.

Mies van der Rohe, in the US from 1938, designed during the war years the campus of the Illinois Institute of Technology, using cubic simplicity and perfect precision in details.

Music

Glenn Miller, 1904–44, leader of the US Air Force Band in Europe, entertained troops with his distinctive "big band" saxophone sound.

Science and Technology

Large diameter pipelines facilitated the distribution of oil, 1943.

Penicillin was produced on a large scale from *Penicillium* mold in 1943.

DNA was shown to carry hereditary characteristics, 1944.

IBM produced a mechanical calculating machine, 1944.

DDT was discovered in 1939 and introduced as an insecticide, 1944, as synthetic fertilizers became available, leading to an increase in agricultural yields.

★ Principal Events

The US dropped two atomic bombs on Japan and ended the war in the Pacific, 1945.

The United Nations was formed in 1945.

The Truman doctrine, 1947, promised aid to non-communist countries, particularly Turkey and Greece.

Britain granted independence to India, 1947, which divided through religious conflict.

The Chinese communists were aided by Japan's defeat, controlling Manchuria by 1947.

The Americas

The UN Charter was drafted and signed in San Francisco, 1945.

The Atomic Energy Commission was established, 1946.

Religion and Philosophy

T. Adorno, 1903–1969, and **M. Horkheimer,** 1895–1973, of the Frankfurt School of Sociology, argued in *Dialectics of Enlightenment,* 1947, that true knowledge could only be achieved by a social revolution, which would liberate man from the idea that nature is independent of, and external to, him.

Literature

In **Deaths and Entrances,** 1946, the exuberant imagery of the Welsh poet **Dylan Thomas,** 1914–53, is at its best.

Russia's history from 1900–30 was the subject of the humanistic novel *Doctor Zhivago,* by Boris Pasternak, 1890–1960.

Italy's leading novelists, **Cesare Pavese,** 1908–50, and **Alberto Moravia,** 1907– , both condemned modern estrangement.

Art and Architecture

Emaciated single figures on wire frames characterized the work of the Swiss sculptor **Alberto Giacometti,** 1901–66, such as "Man Pointing," 1947.

The British sculptor **Henry Moore,** 1898–1986, used his material to express natural forms in terms of stone or wood, as in "Three Standing Figures," 1947–48.

Italian neo-realist cinema relied on simple stories and untrained actors, as in *Open City,* 1946, by Roberto Rossellini, 1906–77.

Music

Bebop, a complex form of jazz featuring virtuoso improvisation, emerged in 1945 as a reaction to the widely popular swing style. Its principal creator was **Charlie Parker,** 1920–55.

Science and Technology

The first nuclear bombs were made in the US in 1945 and tested at Alamogordo, New Mexico, in 1945.

Britain's first atomic power station was built, 1947.

The sound barrier was broken by the Bell XI rocket-propelled American aircraft, 1947.

Radiocarbon dating, a method of accurately finding the ages of archeological discoveries, was perfected in 1947.

Principal Events

The USSR blockaded Berlin, 1948–49, to isolate it from the west.

Zionists declared Israel's independence, 1948.

Mao Tse-tung, 1893–1976, set up the People's Republic of China, 1949.

The North Atlantic Treaty Organization provided for mutual assistance against aggression among the Western powers.

The socialist coup in Czechoslovakia, 1948, extended Soviet control of eastern Europe.

The Americas

The United States participated in a massive airlift to blockaded Berlin. The North Atlantic Treaty Organization was founded, 1949.

Religion and Philosophy

Martin Buber, 1878–1965, a Jewish thinker influenced by the mysticism of the Hasidic tradition in Judaism, advocated a direct, personal relationship of man with God, and praised the new *kibbutzim* in Israel as almost ideal socialist communities, in *Paths to Utopia,* 1947.

The World Council of Churches first met in 1948.

The welfare state, uniting private enterprise with state responsibility, took shape with the British National Health Service, 1948.

Literature

Jean Paul Sartre, 1905–80, gave existential philosophy a literary form in his war trilogy, *Les Chemins de la Liberté,* 1945–

49. The existential dilemma also marks the feminist novels of **Simone de Beauvoir,** 1908–86. **Albert Camus,** 1913–60, formulated his theories of **the absurd** in his novels and essays, notably *The Stranger,* 1942, and *The Plague,* 1947.

Art and Architecture

Abstract Expressionism developed in the US after 1945, expressed in the drip paintings of **Jackson Pollock,** 1912–56, in the "black and white" paintings of **Willem de Kooning,** 1904– , and in the blurred expanses of rich colors in the work of **Mark Rothko,** 1903–70. The Unité d'Habitation, 1946–52, by **Le Corbusier,** a huge block of 337 two-story apartments, was the first building to use rough cast concrete.

Music

Radio and phonograph disseminated music to all developed countries, spreading new forms and styles so widely that national schools could no longer emerge.

Science and Technology

A Jaguar sports car, capable of 120mph (193kph) was put into production in 1948.

The "steady-state" theory of the universe was proposed by **H. Bondi** and **T. Gold,** 1948.

The transistor was invented in 1948. Its invention made possible the miniaturization of electronic equipment and combined with microcircuitry, the computer.

A United States step rocket sent a vehicle to a height of more than 240 miles in 1949.

The Modern World
1950–1975

Riots in Washington after
death of Martin Luther
King, 1968

Vietnamese political
leader Ho Chi Minh

The Beatles were a pop-
culture sensation, 1963.

Fidel Castro, Cuban
Marxist dictator

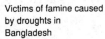
Victims of famine caused by droughts in Bangladesh

The Berlin Wall divided Germany.

Korean War: helicopters used to evacuate wounded

Le Corbusier building design

Apollo 11 astronauts were first on the Moon.

The Modern World

Principal Events

The division of the world into two major power blocs after World War II was confused by a Sino-Soviet ideological split, and after a series of dangerous incidents between Russia and America in the 1950s and early 1960s, the Cold War gave way to a period of official détente.

In spite of continuing imperialism by the major powers, whether militarily or by economic intervention, Third World liberation from European control accelerated, changing the composition of the United Nations as the newly independent African and Asian states have joined to force the industrialized countries to pay a higher price for raw materials.

Economic planning became increasingly worldwide with the rise of development economics and the attempt to control currency exchange rates. In the 1970s serious inflation spread to all the industrialized countries.

National Events

The Cold War, which pitted the free world against the Communist bloc, intensified. The United States became embroiled in the Korean War and later the divisive Vietnam War. Domestic issues involved civil rights, student unrest, and the feminist movement. Political scandals rocked the country.

Religion and Philosophy

American sociology was dominant in the West from World War II, expanding the use of surveys and other observational techniques into a major tool of government policy and developing in the work of Talcott Parsons a complex schema for the understanding of whole societies. Many of the general trends of thought seen in the industrialized countries also originated in the United States, whether in the work of theorists such as Marcuse, in the radical opposition to the Vietnam War, or in the hippie movement, with its complete rejection of political activism and search for increased personal awareness.

In the same period Third World theorists have produced an analysis of the processes and effects of colonialism and the means of eradicating it.

The Christian churches have tried to overcome some of their differences and in the Third World became linked with progressive social policies.

Literature

The rise of a worldwide reading public and the production of cheap and widely distributed books allowed the writer greater freedom of experimentation. Increasingly, confessional novels reflected a sense of the isolation of the individual, and the use of a journalistic approach to deal with contemporary

312

events challenged the very concept of fiction, which traditionally required a distance between the author and his subject. At the same time the beat writers, in seeking to celebrate the spontaneous, questioned artistic form itself.

However, traditional literary forms remained the main vehicle for Third World writers, who set out to portray the conflicts aroused in the individual by the process of colonization.

Art and Architecture

Although America still dominated the visual arts, the increasingly international nature of the market brought a new uniformity of style most clearly seen in architecture, with monumental concrete styles throughout the world.

In painting, attempts to explore the fundamentals of visual language produced an ever-simplified abstract style and the breakdown of traditional distinctions between the disciplines and even between art and life, while Pop art incorporated into art the mass-produced images of consumer society.

The emergence in many parts of the world, including South America, India, and eastern Europe, of the art film, aiming more at expression than at profit, challenged the domination of Hollywood and forced the adoption of new formal styles and greater individual freedom in American commercial cinema, as well as a more critical view of modern society.

Music

New elements appeared in Western music, stemming from new ways of producing sound and of organizing the music. The open texture of Eastern music began to make its mark in the West as Western music, in turn, reached the East. Rock music began simply in the 1950s and soon became highly creative.

Science and Technology

Scientific institutions set up by governments or industries took over from the individual experimenter, as the scale on which scientific research is conducted mushroomed. The growth in prosperity in industrialized countries from 1945 was accompanied by a boom in technologically sophisticated goods available to the general public; in particular, electronic equipment was improved by miniaturization.

Much scientific research was related to the rival arms and space programs of the USSR and the US. But since the completion of the US Apollo Moon program, the emphasis in the US has shifted to the ecological problems that man must solve if he is to have a future on Earth. The hunt for new energy resources was stimulated by a rise in oil prices, and new foods were developed to help cope with expanding population. Small-scale technological innovations benefited Third World economies.

1950-1952

★ Principal Events

War between North and South Korea, which had its roots in the Communist triumph in China, produced UN intervention.
The Arab League powers formed a security pact and began a blockade of Israel, 1950.
No agreement on Germany's future was reached, but peace was made with Japan, 1951.
The US strengthened defense links with Japan and Formosa.
Six European powers joined a single **Coal and Steel Commission**, 1952.

The Americas

Pres. **Harry S. Truman**, 1884–1972, relieved **Gen. Douglas MacArthur**, 1880–1964, of command in the Far East, 1951.

♦ Religion and Philosophy

Frantz Fanon, 1925–61, a West Indian, analyzed the psychological and social repression of the black man in *Black Skin, White Masks*, 1952. He advocated an independent and socialist Third World.
Talcott Parsons, 1902–79, an American, developed structural functional sociology in *The Social System*, setting out to construct a general model for societies, showing the interdependence of their institutions and emphasizing shared values.

📖 Literature

The Theater of the Absurd, which saw man as a helpless creature in a meaningless universe, was explored by **Samuel Beckett**, 1906–89, **Eugene Io-**

nesco, 1912– , and **Jean Genet**, 1910–86.
The "new novel," without form or plot, was developed in the work of **Alain Robbe-Grillet**, 1922– , and **Nathalie Sarraute**, 1902–

🍎 Art and Architecture

Le Corbusier designed **Chandigarh**, the new capital of the Punjab, 1950, in rough cast concrete.
Skyscraper building in the US revived after World War II, with a new reliance on glass and steel, seen in Lever House, New York, 1952.
The growth of film festivals after 1945 led to a less commercial cinema, brought the work of the Japanese **Kurosawa**, 1910– , and the Indian **Satyajit Ray**, 1921– , to the West.

🎵 Music

Traditional methods lived on in the operas of **Benjamin Britten**, 1913–76, and the symphonies of **Dimitri Shostakovitch**, 1906–75, who created personal styles of music by conventional means.

⚛ Science and Technology

Magnetic recording developed during the 1950s. Modern sound and video recording as well as computer operations depend on storing electrical signals in the form of magnetic patterns according to principles discovered by the Danish inventor **Valdemar Poulsen**, 1869–1942, in 1898.
Soya-bean farming increased, *c.*1950, following a growing demand for vegetable oil during World War II.
The first hydrogen bomb was tested by the US in 1952.

Principal Events

Geneva conference, 1955, divided Vietnam into North and South after a Communist victory at **Dien Bien Phu** had forced the French forces to withdraw.
Opposition to British and French imperialism brought terrorist campaigns in Algeria, Kenya, Cyprus, and Malaya.
The USSR opposed the reunification of Germany, 1954, and the **Warsaw Pact** united the Soviet satellites in reaction to West Germany's incorporation in NATO, 1955.

The Americas

In 1954, the Senate censured **Joseph McCarthy**, 1908–57. In *Brown* v. *Board of Education of Topeka*, 1954, the Supreme Court ruled against segregation.

Religion and Philosophy

Joseph McCarthy, 1908–57, led an American campaign against liberals and Marxists as a result of Cold War tension.
The Oxford School of Ordinary Language Philosophy, including **Gilbert Ryle**, 1900–76, and **J. L. Austin**, 1911–60, followed Wittgenstein's later ideas. In *Dilemmas*, 1954, Ryle tried to show that problems in philosophy derive from conceptual confusion and would be resolved if we kept to the normal meaning of words.

Literature

Black American writers gained status with *The Invisible Man*, by **Ralph Ellison**, 1914– , and the writings of **James Baldwin**,

1924–87. The Swiss dramatists **Max Frisch**, 1911– , and **Friedrich Dürrenmatt**, 1921– , and the Frenchman **Jean Anouilh**, 1910–87, share a preoccupation with the tragicomic and grotesque aspects of life.

Art and Architecture

"Brutalism" in architecture was a term coined, 1953, for a functional style which, for example, let electric ducts be seen.
Pier Luigi Nervi, 1891–1979, regarded as the most brilliant concrete designer of his age, helped design the UNESCO building in Paris, 1954–58.
The International Style in architecture can be seen, postwar, at its most elegant in the Rødovre Town Hall, Copenhagen, begun in 1955 by **Arne Jacobsen**, 1902–71.

Music

John Cage, 1912– , pioneered a music in which the score is a set of directions delineating a musical process, giving much freedom to performers. His notorious *4′ 3″*, 1952, is all silence.

Science and Technology

The structure of DNA was found in 1953, leading to closer understanding of protein synthesis in the body and the inheritance of characteristics by the next generation.
Polio vaccine was developed, 1953–55.
Oral contraception followed from the investigations in the 1950s into the role that sex hormones play in reproduction.
The link between smoking and lung cancer was first proposed in 1952.

★ Principal Events

The Soviet leader, Nikita Khrushchev, 1894–1971, denounced Stalinist principles, 1956; a Sino-Soviet split resulted. Soviet troops invaded **Hungary**, to crush a nationalist rising, 1956.
President Nasser, 1918–70, of Egypt, nationalized the Suez Canal Company, 1956, provoking Britain, France, and Israel to military intervention.
The Treaty of Rome, 1957, established the **Common Market** in Western Europe.

The Americas

The American Federation of Labor (AFL) and the Congress of Industrial Organizations (CIO) merged, 1955. Little Rock, Ark., schools desegregated, 1957.

Religion and Philosophy

Paul Tillich, 1886–1965, a Protestant, sought to fuse traditional religious values with a modern emphasis on individual responsibility in the *Dynamics of Faith,* 1956.
Noam Chomsky, 1928– , an American, revolutionized linguistics by analyzing the structure of language. He showed in *Syntactic Structures,* 1957, that grammatical speech depends upon a system of rules too complex to be learned by example.

Literature

English drama was active in the 1950s. Disillusionment with contemporary Britain was vented by **John Osborne,** 1929– , in his play *Look Back in Anger,* 1956. **Harold Pinter,** 1930–

wrote *The Room,* 1957, which he followed with *The Birthday Party,* 1958.
Arnold Wesker, 1932– , wrote socialist plays including *Roots,* 1958.

Art and Architecture

Pop art emerged in London in 1956 in the works of **Richard Hamilton,** 1922– , **Peter Blake,** 1932– , and **Eduardo Paolozzi,** 1924– , using motifs from commercial art.
Hard-edge painting with large, clearly defined areas of bright color, was conceived in New York, 1958, and explored by **Ellsworth Kelly,** 1923–
Kinetic art made use of light and movement for its effects as in *Mobile,* 1958, by **Alexander Calder,** 1898–1976.

Music

Musique concrète widened musical horizons after World War II in France, involving a collage of sounds, both musical and natural, processed into a recording.

Science and Technology

The neutrino, a fundamental particle predicted in 1931, was detected in 1956.
Nuclear power was first generated on a viable industrial scale in Britain from 1956.
Britain introduced a **Clean Air Act,** 1956, after 4,000 died in a London smog, 1952.
International Geophysical Year, an international venture to investigate the Earth, took place, 1957–58, and led to the first space shots.

Principal Events

Discontent in France over the Algerian war brought **Charles de Gaulle,** 1890– 1970, to power in 1958.
China's Great Leap Forward, an economic push in agriculture and industry, 1958, ended in economic chaos after the withdrawal of Soviet aid, 1960.
World opinion was aroused by the Sharpeville massacre, 1960.
Fidel Castro, 1927– , a Marxist, controlled **Cuba,** 1959.
The Belgian Congo's independence, 1960, led to anarchy.

The Americas

The National Aeronautics and Space Administration was established, 1958. The Civil Rights Act, 1960, focused on voting by blacks.

Religion and Philosophy

Structuralism, the attempt to find basic patterns or "structures" for a scientific study of man, was developed by the Frenchman **Claude Lévi-Strauss,** 1908– , in his *Structural Anthropology,* 1958. **Michel Foucault,** 1926–84, applied this method to the history of ideas.
Jean Paul Sartre, 1905–80, tried to link **Existentialism** and **Marxism** in the *Critique of Dialectical Reason,* 1960.

Literature

The work of Jack Kerouac, 1922–69, epitomized the outlook of the American beat generation. Its writers included **William Burroughs,** 1914– , and **Henry Miller,** 1891–1980, and the poets **Allen Ginsberg,** 1926– and **Lawrence Ferlinghetti,** 1919– , all of whom sought "spontaneous living" and the means to express it.

Art and Architecture

Brazilian architecture centered on the building of a new capital, **Brasilia.** Its cathedral, 1959, by **Oscar Niemeyer,** 1907– , used graceful curved concrete structures.
The New Wave of French cinema emerged in 1959 in reaction to the clichés of Hollywood. *The 400 Blows,* 1959, by **François Truffaut,** 1932–84, and *Breathless,* by **Jean-Luc Godard,** 1930– introduced stylistic innovations on a low budget.

Music

Rock music promoted a strong eight-note beat over a static harmony in popular music. At first played on guitars by groups with a lead singer, it later became far more complex.

Science and Technology

Computers entered into commercial use, 1955, and were common by 1960.
The first artificial satellite, Sputnik 1, was launched by the USSR in 1957.
Explorer 1, the first US satellite, was launched, 1958, and detected radiation belts above the Earth.
Stereophonic records first became available in 1958.
The hovercraft was demonstrated in 1959.

1960-1962

⭐ Principal Events

South Africa left the British Commonwealth, 1961, after Britain accepted the trend of decolonization in Africa, 1960.
The Russians built the Berlin Wall, 1961.
After **John F. Kennedy**, 1917–63, the US president, intervened in Cuba, 1961, Soviet missile supplies to Cuba provoked a world crisis, 1962.
Kennedy supported the **Civil Rights Movement**.
Algeria won her independence.

The Americas

The attempted invasion at Bay of Pigs, 1961, involved US-supported Cuban nationals. The Peace Corps was founded, 1961.

✒ Religion and Philosophy

R. D. Laing, 1927–89, studied schizophrenia in a personal rather than clinical way in *The Divided Self*, 1960, and developed a humanistic school of anti-psychology.
The Ecumenical Movement for Christian unity began in 1961–62 when the Eastern Orthodox and Catholic churches met with Protestants at the World Council of Churches, while the Vatican Council, 1962, tried to reconcile differences within Catholicism.

📖 Literature

The damaging effects of Western civilization in African culture were examined in the novels of **Chinua Achebe**, 1930– , and the plays of **Wole Soyinka**, 1934– , both Nigerians. The West Indian novelist **V. S. Naipaul**, 1932– , wrote of poverty in Trinidad with delicate irony in *A House for Mr. Biswas*, 1961.

Art and Architecture

Distorted human forms confined within a claustrophobic space characterized the work of the Briton **Francis Bacon**, 1910– seen in his "Red Figure," 1962.
A move toward formalism was seen in the dramatic use of curved concrete at the TWA buildings, Kennedy Airport, 1961, by **Eero Saarinen**, 1910–61.
Japanese architecture united traditional forms with the new materials of steel and concrete in the work of **Tange**, 1913–

Music

Graphic notation of symbols to portray sound became widespread in the 1960s as composers sought new sounds and effects from electronic and conventional instruments.

Science and Technology

The bathyscape Trieste descended 7 mi(11 km) to the deepest part of the ocean, 1960.
The laser was invented in 1960, and used for precision cutting and optical surgery.
Tiros I, the first weather satellite, was placed in orbit by the United States in 1960.
Manned space flight began in 1961 with a one-orbit mission by the Soviet cosmonaut **Yuri Gagarin** 1934–68.
Telstar, the first communications satellite, was launched by the US in 1962.

318

Principal Events

The Nuclear Test Ban Treaty was signed by the US, USSR, and Britain, 1963, but China exploded her first bomb in 1964.
After Kennedy's assassination, **Lyndon B. Johnson**, 1908–73, signed civil rights bills and built up US forces in Vietnam to oppose the Communist rebels.
Britain granted independence to **Kenya**, 1963, and **Malawi**, 1964, but Rhodesia declared her own independence under white rule.

The Americas

Pres. John F. Kennedy, 1917–63, was assassinated in Dallas, 1963. **Pres. Lyndon B. Johnson**, 1908–73, initiated the War on Poverty, 1964.

Religion and Philosophy

Herbert Marcuse, 1898–1979, associated with the "Frankfurt" School of Sociology, argued in *One Dimensional Man*, 1964, that in modern industrial society there is a process of "repressive tolerance" that diverts the creative impulses in man by satisfying his material needs.
Julius Nyerere, president of Tanzania from 1964, set out to weaken Western influence by nonalignment and to develop socialism and African nationalism.

Literature

Postwar German society was explored in the writings of **Günter Grass**, 1927– , and **Heinrich Böll**, 1917–85.
The American novel flourished in the works of **Saul Bellow**,
1915– , **Philip Roth**, 1933– and **Norman Mailer**, 1923– who also satirized politics in a journalistic style.

Art and Architecture

Two exponents of **Op art**, who studied the effect of optical illusions juxtaposing colors and forms, were the Hungarian **Victor Vasarely**, 1908– , and the Briton **Bridget Riley**, 1931– .
Pop art in America in the 1960s took images from cartoon comics as in *Whaam*, 1963, by **Roy Lichtenstein**, 1923 , and from commercial advertising in the work of **Andy Warhol**, 1930–87.

Music

Simplicity and space marked the experimental music of the 1960s. Composers like **Terry Riley**, 1935– used simple repeated phrases that overlap in ever-changing patterns.

Science and Technology

Syncom, the first communications satellite that is constantly available for use, was put into orbit by the US in 1964.
Radiation at a wavelength of 7 centimeters was first detected from space in 1965, providing support for the big bang theory.
The development of integrated circuits in the 1960s brought new possibilities of miniaturization, stimulating the rise of the electronics industry in the US and making electronic equipment common in the West.

319

1965-1967

★ Principal Events

The Chinese Cultural Revolution aimed to weaken the bureaucracy and stimulate more public participation, 1966–68.
Growing American military activity in Vietnam failed to bring victory.
Biafran secessionist claims led to civil war in Nigeria.
Israel defeated the Arab states in the 1967 **Six-Day War** and extended her frontiers.
France left NATO, 1966, to protest against American strength in Europe.

The Americas

A US military buildup in Vietnam, 1964–68, followed the Gulf of Tonkin Resolution. **Martin Luther King,** 1929–68, led a civil rights march, 1965, in Selma, Ala.

◊ Religion and Philosophy

The American Civil Rights Movement against racial intolerance of Negroes was led by **Martin Luther King,** 1929–68, who believed in the use of moral force. In the mid-60s, however, black leaders such as **Eldridge Cleaver** turned to violence.
The "flower-power" movement, originating with American students in 1967, sought awareness with the aid of mind-expanding drugs. A US counterculture grew up, based on communes and anarchism.

📖 Literature

South American literature reached the West with translations of established writers. The Colombian **Gabriel Garcia Márquez,** 1928– , described the history of a family in a tropical town in *One Hundred Years of Solitude,* 1967.
Mexico's dual heritage of savagery and civilization was the theme of the surrealistic poetry of **Octavio Paz,** 1914–

🏛 Art and Architecture

The "Happening," the creation of an environment simulating the effects of hallucinatory drugs, often with rock music and shifting patterns of color, was pioneered in the US *c.*1965.
Realism in British painting was exemplified in the works of **Lucien Freud,** 1922– , whose portraits and townscapes show detailed draftsmanship, and in the figure paintings of **David Hockney,** 1937– , like "Peter getting out of Nick's pool," 1966.

🎵 Music

The tape recorder, invented in 1942, made all kinds of artificial sound reproduction possible. It was used creatively in popular music, as in the song "Sergeant Pepper," 1967, by the **Beatles.**

⚛ Science and Technology

Plate tectonics developed as a theory to explain continental drift, from 1965.
Mariner 4, US space probe, flew past Mars in 1965 and sent back the first pictures of another planet.
The first heart transplant was performed in 1966.
Research into plant genetics and soil fertility led to the **Green Revolution** in many Third World countries, 1966–70, greatly increasing agricultural yields.

★ Principal Events

Student revolt in France, 1968, was echoed throughout Europe. After referendum defeat, 1969, de Gaulle resigned.
Soviet troops invaded Czechoslovakia to end liberal reforms.
Richard Nixon, 1913–   , resumed bombing North Vietnam, after peace talks and troop withdrawals, 1970.
Tanzania and Zambia secured Chinese support for a railroad linking the copper belt to the sea.

The Americas

The intelligence ship Pueblo was seized by North Korea, 1968.
Astronaut **Neil Armstrong**, 1930–   , walked on the moon's surface, 1969.

◊ Religion and Philosophy

The radical student movement of 1968, originating in America and Europe in opposition to the Vietnam War, stressed individual liberation from the constraints of capitalism, influenced by Third World revolutionaries such as **Ché Guevara**, 1928–67, and the writings of **Marcuse**.
Pope Paul VI, r.1963–78, condemned the use of artificial methods of birth control, 1968, arousing widespread criticism.

Literature

Change of Skin by the Mexican **Carlos Fuentes**, 1928–   , was an "open novel" describing the fluctuations of experience.
Criticism of the Soviet regime in *Gulag Archipelago* led to the exile of **Alexander Solzhenitsyn**, 1918–

The Japanese postwar generation was described in the novels of **Yukio Mishima**, 1925–70.

Art and Architecture

A politically committed documentary style of filmmaking arose in Britain, seen in *Kes*, 1969, by the directors **Tony Garnett**, 1936–   , and **Kenneth Loach**, 1936–
Land Art and "**Arte Povera**," emerged in 1969 as an avant-garde movement that was concerned with art as assemblages of simple elements such as earth and rocks.

Music

Poet musicians became popular in the 1960s, singing their own often highly individual compositions. Most influential was **Bob Dylan**, 1941–

Science and Technology

The Rance estuary power station in France, harnessing tidal energy, was set up, 1967. **DDT** was banned in the US, 1969, following concern about its harmful side effects.
The first Moon landing was made in 1969 by members of the US Apollo 11 space mission. Space research facilitated **invisible light astronomy** and assisted **meteorology**. Spin-offs with industrial or domestic use included aluminum foil and Teflon, convenient for cooking utensils.

★ Principal Events

Massive balance of payments deficits forced a devaluation of the US currency, 1971.
China joined the UN, 1971.
Bangladesh was set up, 1971, after a civil war in Pakistan.
The EEC expanded to include Britain, Ireland, and Denmark.
Nixon visited China, 1972, and secured rapprochement with the Soviet Union.
Salvador Allende, 1908–73, a Marxist, was elected president of Chile, 1970, but was killed after a right-wing coup.

The Americas

During a Vietnam War protest 4 college students were killed at Kent State University, Ohio, 1971. The Equal Rights Amendment was passed, 1972.

Religion and Philosophy

Western religious groups stressing personal awareness included the "**Jesus freaks**" and the **Divine Light Mission**, which had Hindu elements.
The Conservation movement argued that continued industrial growth is incompatible with the preservation of the natural world and its resources.
Environmentalists predicted the imminent disappearance of natural resources.

Literature

Science fiction became increasingly popular, notably in the works of American writers **Kurt Vonnegut, Jr.**, 1922–   , Isaac

Asimov, 1920–   , and **Ray Bradbury**, 1920–
Carlos Castaneda published his *Journey to Ixtlan*, the last of a series of accounts of his meetings with a Mexican shaman.

Art and Architecture

An exhibition in London and Paris of **Chinese art** treasures, including archeological discoveries made during the Cultural Revolution, restored cultural contacts between China and the West.
Conceptual art, practiced by **Barry Flanagan**, 1944–   , and **Keith Arnott**, 1931–   , in England, aimed to communicate through concepts rather than visual images.

Music

The synthesizer became a readily accessible instrument with the development of microelectronics. Its wide range of sounds may well spur future musical advances.

Science and Technology

Earth resource satellites were first launched by the US in 1971 to detect and map the world's resources.
A series of American space probes to look close-up at Mars, Jupiter, and Mercury began in 1971.
Germ warfare was banned by international convention, 1972.

Principal Events

US troops left Vietnam, 1973.
The Arabs fought well in the October War, then forced up world oil prices to put pressure on Israel's western allies.
A coup in Portugal, 1974, led to revolution and the end of Portugal's empire in Africa and Asia.
Communists took control of South Vietnam and Cambodia, 1975.

The Americas

Scandals forced **Pres. Richard M. Nixon** to resign, 1974. He was succeeded by his vice president, **Pres. Gerald R. Ford,** 1913–

Religion and Philosophy

The rapidly growing population of developing countries was the subject of a campaign, 1973–74, organized by **International Planned Parenthood Federation** to introduce birth control programs. The United Nations called 1975 **International Women's Year.** The Korean **Sun Myung Moon** and his Unification Church continued to cause controversy.

Literature

Traditional English drama was represented by **Tom Stoppard,** 1937–   , and **David Storey,** 1933–   , while in America **Edward Albee,** 1928–   , won the Pulitzer Prize for *Seascape,* 1975. **Formal experimentation** in the theater produced the almost silent plays of **Samuel Beckett.**

Art and Architecture

An underground movement of abstract artists in the USSR attempted unsuccessfully to hold an open-air exhibition in Moscow, 1974.
Energy conservation became a major element in architectural design.
The epic disaster film and kung fu and karate films became popular.

Music

American theater saw new musicals *A Chorus Line* and *Chicago,* 1975, and many revivals in the 1970s including *My Fair Lady, Porgy and Bess, Guys and Dolls,* and *Three Penny Opera.*

Science and Technology

The rise in oil prices, 1973, and limited nature of mineral fuel supplies stimulated research into **tidal, solar, and geophysical energy** as alternate sources.
A Soviet space probe took pictures of Venus, while a US probe was sent to Mars. The Soviet *Soyuz* and US *Apollo* spacecraft linked in space in an historic docking experiment, 1975.

Internationalism And Détente 1975–1993

US military force ousted General Noriega in Panama.

The Space Shuttle Challenger exploded, killing all on board.

President Ronald
Reagan with Senator
Howard Baker

Shah of Iran, 1919–1980

President George Bush
was elected in 1988.

Chief Justice William H.
Rehnquist

Internationalism and Détente

★ Principal Events

As Third World countries became a political reality, human rights issues, world hunger, and acts of terrorism came to the fore. The movement to freeze the production of nuclear weapons and then reduce their number was predominant. The "good times" for OPEC slowed as the demand for world oil declined, a sign that the conservation measures of the mid-1970s had taken hold. Reform swept across the Soviet Union and its Eastern European satellites as communist governments faced change and people demanded freedom, equality, and independence. Violent demonstrations and student unrest in China indicated changes to come. Although the Middle East question remained unsettled at the end of the period, apartheid, a way of life in South Africa, was ending. Member countries of the European Community (EC) prepared for unification to be implemented in 1992.

National Events

The inflation of the 1970s slowed in the 1980s, but the trade deficit increased. Corporate takeovers by "raiders" became the norm. The American farmer's income declined; tighter credit led to foreclosures. Increased drug use triggered crackdowns on drug trafficking. Social programs focused on the homeless.

♦ Religion and Philosophy

Ethical questions that characterized this period dealt with such issues as professional ethics, white-collar crime, abortion, aging, euthanasia, genetic engineering, and nuclear warfare.

Pope John Paul II traveled extensively, visiting trouble spots worldwide, promoting peace, restating Roman Catholic doctrine, and working to eliminate differences among religions. Improvement of Christian-Jewish relationships was characterized by a worldwide increased awareness of the Holocaust, as evidenced by the number of former Nazis who were brought to justice and the number of books written and motion pictures and documentaries produced for television and theaters. Television preachers, such as Oral Roberts, Jim Bakker, and Jimmy Swaggart, met their downfall in money and sex scandals. The number of women attending divinity schools increased.

Literature

This period of change was reflected in the literature of the time. Soviet writers made pleas for peace and better understanding among peoples—a foretaste of things to come. The Eastern European writers began to receive recognition in the Western world. Within a period of 5 years, 1980–1984, 3 Eastern-bloc writers won Nobel prizes in literature. African works made the world take notice, and Western ideas filtered

326

into Chinese literature. The feminist movement precipitated a rash of works that dealt with the complexities of the trend, and science fiction and works of fantasy, the American West, and crime continued in popularity. A new force in the United States was regional literature.

Art and Architecture

In general, architectural styles of this period responded to the everyday needs of people and conformed to sites rather than conforming sites to suit the architectural plan. Conservation of energy and resources dictated style. Postmodernism—the use of historic styles in new and exaggerated ways—established itself through most of the period, but it was on the wane by the end of the 1980s. At the other extreme, Romantic hi-tech used austere materials and geometric shapes in imaginative ways. Preservation of old buildings and their styles became very important. When there was new construction, it was often linked to old, restored structures. In art, more and more world-famous collections traveled on loan to museums around the world, and art masterpieces brought record prices at auction. Due to vandalism, pollution, and natural, expected deterioration, the demand for art restorers accelerated.

Music

The revival of jazz, country-western music, gospel music, the big-band sound, reggae, and the sound of the 1950s characterized the period. Popular artists were committed to causes and staged events to benefit world hunger, homelessness, and the American farmer. US-Soviet cultural exchanges abounded. Compact discs (CDs) became popular in the 1980s

Science and Technology

Scientists continued searching for new sources of energy and worked to economize on existing resources. The fact that resource conservation measures had taken hold became evident when an oil glut caused the lowering of prices in the mid-1980s. But by 1990 the threat of another oil shortage prompted warnings against the relaxation of certain conservation measures. Of special concern to scientists was the "greenhouse effect," caused by the growing hole in the Earth's ozone layer that guards against the Sun's harmful rays, that was discovered over Antarctica. Climate changes and increasing cases of skin cancers were some indications of the problem. Air pollution was another concern during this time, and more laws were enacted to clean up the atmosphere. With medical costs escalating and AIDS (Acquired Immune Deficiency Syndrome) spreading, the search for prevention and cures occupied the scientific community. Computer use advanced with the expansion of microchip technology.

1975-1977

★ Principal Events

The Suez Canal, closed since 1967 Israeli-Arab war, opened, 1975.

Shah Mohammed Reza Pahlavi, 1919–80, declared Iran a one-party state, 1975.

The US and USSR signed a dis-armament treaty that limited underground nuclear explosions, 1976.

China lost two leaders, **Mao Tse-Tung,** 1893–1973, and **Chou En-Lai,** 1898–1976, and underwent extensive changes.

The Americas

In 1976, the US celebrated its bi-centennial, and **Jimmy Carter,** 1924– , was elected President. **US-Vietnam** peace talks began, 1977.

Religion and Philosophy

Mother Elizabeth Seton, 1774–1821, canonized, becoming first US Roman Catholic saint, 1975.

The US Episcopal Church agreed to the ordination of women to the priesthood, 1976.

Rev. Sun Myung Moon's, 1920– , Unification Church continued to grow despite the controversy surrounding it, 1976.

Literature

The 1975 Nobel prize for literature went to Italian poet **Eugenio Montale,** 1898–1981, who depicted a bleak world. US writer **Saul Bellow,** 1915– , whose characters were self-examining, captured the 1976 award. In 1977, Spanish poet **Vicente Al-**

eixandre, 1898–1985, who wrote of man as part of the vast cosmos, was the winner.

Art and Architecture

Interest in ancient art was reflected in the successful 2-year US tour of the *Treasures of Tutankhamen,* 1976–78.

Bulgarian-born artist Christo Javacheff created *Running Fence,* 24.5mi (39km) of nylon fabric in California, 1976.

Music

Wagner's opera *The Ring of the Nibelungen* was staged at the 1976 centennial Bayreuth Festival, West Germany; its 19th-century setting caused controversy.

Science and Technology

The conservation movement argued that continued industrial growth is incompatible with the preservation of natural resources.

Supersonic US–Europe transport service began amid controversy, 1976.

An earthquake in Turkey caused the deaths of more than 4,000 people, 1976.

The artificial sweetener saccharin, considered a cancer-causing agent and thus an "unsafe chemical," was withdrawn from the US market, 1977.

★ Principal Events

Spain established constitutional monarchy, 1978, under **King Juan Carlos,** 1938– .

At the **Camp David Summit,** 1978, Middle East peace plan outlined by Egypt and Israel.

Control of the Panama Canal Zone passed to Panama, and the **Soviets invaded Afghanistan,** 1979.

Mother Teresa, 1910– awarded Nobel Peace prize, 1979.

Labor unrest in Poland began, 1980.

The Americas

Cabinet-level Dept. of Energy created, 1977.

Allan Bakke admitted to medical school, 1978, under "reverse discrimination" ruling.

Religion and Philosophy

In **1978, Pope John Paul II,** 1920– , a Pole, became the first non-Italian to be elected pope in 456 years.

Iranian Muslim leader **Ayatollah Khomeini,** 1900–89, rose to power, 1979; 52 Americans were held hostage, 1979–81.

Nearly 900 **People's Temple** cult members died in a mass murder-suicide in Guyana, 1979.

Views of conservative religious organizations such as the **Moral Majority** were reflected in 1980 US elections.

Literature

Isaac Bashevis Singer, 1904– prolific Israeli-born US writer of short stories and novels, re- ceived the Nobel prize for literature in 1978. The prize was awarded to Greek poet **Odysseus Elytis,** 1911– , in 1979, and to **Czeslaw Milosz,** 1911– a Polish poet and novelist, in 1980.

Art and Architecture

An exhibition of **Pompeii '79 AD** toured Europe and the United States, 1977–78.

The **Georges Pompidou National Center for Art and Culture** in Paris opened, 1977. The **East Wing of the US National Gallery of Art,** designed by I.M. Pei, opened in 1978.

Norman Rockwell, 1894–1978, painter of Americana, especially noted for his *Saturday Evening Post* covers, died.

Music

The **Second World Black and African Festival of Arts and Culture** was held in Nigeria, 1977.

Mikhail Baryshnikov, 1948– was named American Ballet Theatre director, 1979.

Science and Technology

The **first test-tube baby** was born in England, 1978.

In **1978,** biochemists at Stanford University, Calif., announced that they had successfully produced **human insulin** using recombinant, self-replicating, DNA (deoxyribonucleic acid).

Spacecraft **Voyager I's** photos of Jupiter in 1979 gave new information about the planet's moons.

Smallpox was eradicated in 1979.

Soviet cosmonauts orbited Earth for a record 180 days, 1980.

Principal Events

US-China diplomatic ties formed, 1980.

US, Canada, Japan, and West Germany boycotted 1980 Summer Olympic Games in Moscow, in protest of Soviet invasion of Afghanistan.

Great Britain's Prince Charles, 1948– , married **Lady Diana Spencer,** 1961– , in 1981.

Egypt's Anwar Sadat, 1919–81, was assassinated.

Britain and Argentina waged war over Falkland Islands, 1982.

 The Americas

President Ronald Reagan, 1911– , appointed first woman US Supreme Court justice, 1981.

Hostages returned from Iran that same year.

 Religion and Philosophy

Robert Runcie, 1921– , became the archbishop of Canterbury, 1980.

The Chinese government relaxed some of its restrictions against the freedom to worship, resulting in the reopening of many Buddhist, Muslim, and Christian churches, 1981.

An assassination attempt on **Pope John Paul II,** blamed on "Muslim fanatics," 1981; the Pope's visit to Great Britain resulted in a pledge for closer Roman Catholic-Anglican relations.

 Literature

Elias Canetti, 1905– , Bulgarian-born writer who wrote in German, received the 1981 Nobel prize in literature. **Gabriel García Márquez,** 1928– , a Colombian novelist and journalist, took the award in 1982 for his ability to portray "a continent's life and conflicts."

 Art and Architecture

A 1980 exhibit of the work of Pablo Picasso, 1881–1973, at New York's Museum of Modern Art featured his painting *Guernica,* which depicted the destruction of the city in 1937. In 1981 the painting was returned to Spain's Prado Museum. Picasso had directed that it not be displayed there until democracy was restored to Spain.

Three distinct architectural styles emerged in 1981—linking the new and the old, neomodernism, and hi-tech.

 Music

In 1980, singer Beverly Sills, 1929– , became director of the New York City Opera.

Beatle John Lennon, 1940–80, was killed by a fanatic fan. His death shocked the world.

Science and Technology

Mount St. Helens, Washington, began its first volcanic eruption in 123 years, 1980, and **El Chichon, Mexico,** erupted for the first time, 1982.

American space probes produced new discoveries about Saturn's moon and rings, Mars' meteorologic features, and Venus' terrain, 1980.

In 1981, *Columbia,* **the US space shuttle,** was reused successfully.

The first successful **surgery on an unborn baby** was performed in San Francisco, 1981.

Principal Events

A world oil glut lowered oil prices, 1982.

International Law of the Sea Treaty ratified by the UN, 1982.

Soviet leader Leonid Brezhnev, 1906–82, was succeeded, in turn, by **Yuri Andropov,** 1914–84, **Konstantin Chernenko,** 1911–85, and **Mikhail Gorbachev,** 1931– .

Drought in Africa triggered famine and starvation, 1983.

South Africa's Bishop Tutu, 1931– , awarded Nobel Peace prize, 1984.

The Americas

1982, Vietnam Veterans Memorial dedicated; **Sally Ride,** 1951– , 1st US woman in space.

US invaded Grenada to protect US citizens, 1983.

Religion and Philosophy

Presbyterian Church (USA) formed 1983 when 2 factions—United Presbyterian Church and the mainly southern Presbyterian Church—split 122 years before, resolved their differences.

In 1984, Indian prime minister Indira Gandhi, 1917–84, was assassinated by her own Sikh bodyguards in retaliation for a previous attack by the Indian army on Sikhism's most holy Golden Temple in Amritsar.

Literature

Great Britain's William Golding, 1911– , author of *Lord of the Flies,* 1954, and *The Paper Man,* 1984, received the Nobel prize in literature in 1983. **Jaroslav**

Seifert, 1901– 86, Czechoslovakian poet and national hero because of his stand against censorship and repression and his championship of social justice, won the 1984 award.

Art and Architecture

Eastman Kodak introduced the disk camera, 1982.

The Vatican Collections: The Papacy and Art toured the United States in 1983.

Buckminster Fuller, 1895–1983, died but left his legacy of the geodesic dome and other futuristic ideas.

The Olympic Arts Festival, in conjunction with the Los Angeles Summer Olympics, drew many viewers in 1984.

Music

A Chorus Line became the longest-runninng Broadway show, 1983.

Singer Michael Jackson, 1958– , reunited with his brothers for a Victory Tour, 1984.

Science and Technology

EPCOT (Environmental Prototype Community of Tomorrow) Center opened at Disney World, Orlando, Fla., 1982.

The first artificial human heart was successfully implanted in a human being, 1982.

The spread of AIDS worldwide concerned scientists, 1982, as did the increasing number of cases of **Alzheimer's disease,** a loss-of-memory disease formerly confused with senility.

1985-1987

Principal Events

Ship *Achille Lauro* hijacked by Palestinian terrorists, 1985.

Ferdinand Marcos, 1917–89, fled Philippines as **Corazon Aquino**, 1933– , elected, 1986.

Accident at Soviet Chernobyl nuclear plant caused world concern, 1986.

US bombed Libya, 1986, in retaliation for terrorist acts.

"Glasnost" and "perestroika" initiated in Soviet Union, 1986.

Swedish prime minister Olof Palme, 1927–86, assassinated.

The Americas

William Rehnquist, 1924–, succeeded Chief Justice Warren Burger, 1907–

On Black Monday, Oct. 19, 1987, stock market plunged.

Religion and Philosophy

In 1986, Pope John Paul II met with non-Christian leaders, including Tibet's exiled Dalai Lama.

Soviet Union released Jewish dissident **Anatoly Shcharansky**, 1948– , in 1986.

Anglican Terry Waite, special emissary of Archbishop Runcie, on a mission to Lebanon to negotiate the release of hostages, disappeared and was believed to have been taken hostage himself, 1987.

Literature

Robert Penn Warren, 1905–89, became the first US poet laureate, 1986.

Recipients of the Nobel prize in literature were French novelist **Claude Simon**, 1913– , in 1985; Nigerian playwright and poet, **Wole Soyinka**, 1934– , in 1986; and US Soviet-born poet **Joseph Brodsky**, 1940– in 1987.

Art and Architecture

Italian treasures from the Basilica of San Marco in Venice were exhibited at New York City's Metropolitan Museum of Art, 1985.

Art owned by Liechtenstein's royalty, *The Princely Collection*, was loaned for exhibition at the Metropolitan Museum in 1986.

Russian-born French artist Marc Chagall's, 1887–1985, death left a gap in the world of modern art.

Music

An American recording, "We Are the World," raised $50,000,000 for famine in Africa and led to the British Band Aid Live Aid concert, which raised $70,000,000.

Science and Technology

An earthquake in Mexico measured 8.1 on the Richter scale, 1985.

During 1986, Halley's Comet passed by the Sun for the first time in 76 years and was visible by telescope from Earth. Flybys by Soviet, European, and Japanese spacecraft informed scientists about comets.

US space shuttle *Challenger* exploded seconds after takeoff, 1986, killing all 7 astronauts aboard, including schoolteacher **Christa McAuliffe**, 1948–86, and jeopardizing the country's immediate future in space.

Principal Events

Gorbachev-Reagan summit, 1987, resulted in elimination of intermediate-range nuclear forces.
In 1988, truce called in Iran-Iraq war, and Soviets withdrew from Afghanistan.
1989, communist governments fell in Eastern-bloc nations; **Berlin Wall** came down.
US troops invaded Panama, December 1989, forcing General Noriega from power.
South Africa's Nelson Mandela, 1918– , freed in 1990.
Iraq invaded and annexed Kuwait in 1990. A US led coalition of forces launched a military campaign in 1991 that forced Iraqi troops from Kuwait.

 The Americas

Pres. George Bush, 1924– , elected, 1988.
Oliver North, 1943– , convicted, 1989, of involvement in 1987 **Iran-Contra** arms affair.
Violeta Burrios de Chamorro took office as president of Nicaragua, 1990.

 Religion and Philosophy

Evangelical Lutheran Church in America formed when the Lutheran Church in America, the American Lutheran Church, and the Association of Evangelical Lutheran Churches merged, 1987.
"Electronic church" television evangelists involved in money and sex scandals, 1987. In 1989, **Jim Bakker,** 1940– , was sentenced to 45 years in prison for fraud and conspiracy.

 Literature

Nobel prizes in literature were awarded to Egypt's **Naguib Mahfouz,** 1911– , in 1988, and to Spain's **Camilo José Cela,** 1916– , in 1989.
Muslims condemned Salman **Rushdie's,** 1947– , *The Satanic Verses,* 1989, as blasphemous.

 Art and Architecture

Van Gogh's *Irises* sold for a record $53,900,000 in 1987; **Edgar Degas'** bronze sculpture *Little Ballerina of 14 Years,* was auctioned for $10,120,000 in 1988.
Deconstructivist style (the look of destruction—loosely constructed walls, floors, ceilings, and roofs) was popular with some architects in 1988.
In 1989, a "glass pyramid" wing was added to the Louvre in Paris in celebration of France's bicentennial of the French Revolution.

 Music

In 1987, "Dancing for Life," a benefit for AIDS research, raised $1,400,000.

 Science and Technology

An earthquake in Soviet Armenia left more than 25,000 dead, 1988.
In 1989, Hurricane Hugo raged through the southeastern United States and the **California San Francisco Bay** area experienced an earthquake measuring 7.1 on the Richter scale.
The **oil tanker** *Exxon Valdez* ran aground, 1989, in Prince Edward Sound, Gulf of Alaska, spilling 1,260,000 barrels of oil, the largest oil spill in US history. Cleanup operations extended into the 1990s.

1990-1993

 Principal Events

The Soviet Union dissolved, 1991. Russian president **Boris Yeltsin,** 1931– , assumed command of the 11-member Commonwealth of Independent States.
Serbia initiated a terror campaign of "ethnic cleansing" against Muslims and Croats in Bosnia-Herzegovina, 1992.
The last Western hostages held by terrorists in Lebanon were released, 1992.
US troops sent to drought-ridden Somalia to safeguard food shipments, 1992.
Czechoslovakia divided into two independent nations, 1993.

 The Americas

Bill Clinton, 1946– , elected 42nd President, 1992.
Riots in South-Central Los Angeles followed the April 1992 acquittal of L.A. police in the beating of a black motorist. Damages totaled $775 million, 52 died, and 600 buildings burned.
Clarence Thomas, 1948– narrowly approved to succeed Supreme Court justice **Thurgood Marshall,** 1908–93, despite charges of sexual harassment.

 Religion and Philosophy

The Roman Catholic Church issued a new "universal catechism" in 1992, the first such document since 1566.
The Church of England (Anglican) narrowly voted to admit women as priests, impairing pending talks to heal 400-year rift with Roman Catholic Church.

 Literature

Nobel Prizes awarded to South African novelist and foe of apartheid **Nadine Gordimer,** 1923– , in 1991, and to West Indian poet **Derek Walcott,** 1930– , in 1992.

 Art and Architecture

A monumental show, including more than 300 paintings, honored **Henri Matisse,** 1869-1954, at New York's Museum of Modern Art, 1992.
The renovated Guggenheim Museum in New York City reopened in 1992.

 Music

Two venerable institutions celebrated anniversaries: **Carnegie Hall** turned 100 in 1991, and the **New York Philharmonic** reached 150 in 1992.
New music directors at American symphony orchestras included **Kurt Masur** at the New York Philharmonic; **Daniel Barenboim** at the Chicago Symphony Orchestra; **Esa-Pekka Salonen** at the Los Angeles Philharmonic Association; and **Wolfgang Sawallisch** at the Philadelphia Orchestra.

 Science and Technology

Hurricanes Andrew and Iniki devastated southern Florida and Kauai, Hawaii, in 1992, with damages reaching $20 billion.
At the world's first Earth Summit in Rio de Janeiro, Brazil, in 1992, 143 attending nations agreed to reduce emissions of greenhouse gases.

Index of Names

Index

336

Index of Names

Index

Index of Names

Index

Index of Names

Index

Index of Names

Index

Index of Names

Index

Index of Names

Index

Index of Names

Index

Index of Names

Index

Index of Names

Index

Index of Names

Index

Index of Names

Index

Index of Names

Index